A HISTORY OF
ACCOUNTING IN AMERICA

A HISTORY OF
ACCOUNTING IN AMERICA

An Historical Interpretation
of the Cultural Significance
of Accounting

GARY JOHN PREVITS

BARBARA DUBIS MERINO

A RONALD PRESS PUBLICATION • JOHN WILEY & SONS

New York • Chichester • Brisbane • Toronto

Library of Congress Cataloging in Publication Data

Previts, Gary John.
   A history of accounting in America.
   "A Ronald Press publication"
   Includes index.
    1. Accounting—United States—History.
I. Merino, Barbara Dubis, joint author. II. Title.
HF5616.U5P72   657'.0973   79-616
ISBN 0-471-05172-1

Printed in the United States of America

10 9 8 7 6 5 4 3 2

To our families

for their patience, encouragement
and understanding

PREFACE

> *. . . accountancy is . . . one of the manifes-*
> *tations of civilization and . . . the laws that*
> *govern the history of accounting are those*
> *which govern the progress of the human*
> *race.*
>
> [Arthur H. Woolf, *A Short History of*
> *Accountants and Accountancy,*
> London, 1912]

This work is written for and dedicated to accounting professionals, be they public practitioners, financial executives, public servants, or educators. It is a *history,* and, like all histories, it must constantly be modified as time passes and more evidence unfolds. Therefore, the work remains by definition unfinished, and by choice focuses upon those persons, institutions, and events most likely to evoke popular as well as scholarly interest.

Each chapter considers the social, political, economic, and personal elements of important eras—from Puritan to modern times. Such an overview as an objective precludes in-depth analysis of any single factor. We attempt, however, to portray the humor, anecdotes, warm friendships, and bitter controversies that underlie the progression of events. We examine the thesis that American accountancy is a unique discipline, which evolved from a complex fabric of influences, and that *The Accounting Establishment,* so termed in a recent Congressional study, has played an increasingly vital role in the American way of life, the *Novus Ordo Seclorum.*

This work synthesizes much extant evidence and provokes a new outlook regarding the practice of accountancy in the American culture. Our work is initially descriptive, but becomes increasingly analytical, particularly in its treatment of accountancy in this century.

Beginning with the formation of a new nation, we draw on

important original accounting writings. The works of such early nineteenth century American writers as Bennett, Turner, Jones, Foster, Folsom, and Packard presage the era of pre-classical, turn-of-the century writings by Charles E. Sprague, Henry Rand Hatfield, John R. Wildman, Roy B. Kester, Robert H. Montgomery, and their contemporaries. A classical period of thought and practice, as delineated by the events surrounding the great depression of the late 1920s and early 1930s, marks a maturity point in American accounting thought and practice. The contributions of W. A. Paton, George O. May, Eric L. Kohler, A. C. Littleton, R. B. Canning, Stephen Gilman, and DR Scott characterize the principal developments of this era.

The coming of a "one-world" or geo-accounting environment following World War II, with expanded international business and investment and persistent inflation, sets apart the present generation of American accounting.

Evidence suggests that the outcome foretold by DR Scott in 1931—that American society would witness the use of accounting as a principal means of political and economic control—seems to have come to pass in the contemporary "bottom-line" culture of the 1970s.

We are mindful of the enormously ambitious scope of our task and anticipate that many opportunities for criticism will be provided as a result. On balance we accept this risk in order to stimulate interest, in the hope that the resultant postive effects will work to the betterment of our discipline.

Our appreciation is extended to Edward L. Lawson for his guidance and support, Felix Pomeranz for his helpful advice, our colleagues, friends who shared our interests and concerns in the preparation of this work, and, especially to our families.

GARY JOHN PREVITS
BARBARA DUBIS MERINO

University, Alabama
New York City
April 1979

CONTENTS

A HISTORY OF
ACCOUNTING IN AMERICA

1492–1775

1 ACCOUNTING FROM PILGRIM TO REVOLUTIONARY TIMES

For emongest althynges nedefull in any nacion, touchying wordly affaires, betwene man and man, it is to be thought that true and perfect reconyng is one of the chief, the lacke whereof often tymes causeth not onely great losse of time and empoverishement of many, who by lawes seke triall of suche thynges as neither partie is well hable to expresse, and that for lacke of perfect instruccion in their accompt, whiche thynge might, if that a perfect ordre in reconyng were frequented of all men, might well be avoided.
[James Peele, "practizer and teacher" of bookkeeping, London, 1553]

Alistair Cooke in his insightful book, *America*, points out that, when Columbus set sail, among the select members of Columbus' crew was an accountant designated by the Spanish monarchs to keep tabs on Columbus' "swindle sheet." On such an auspicious note, our study of *A History of Accounting in America* begins.

The Ideology and Economic Environment of the New World Order *Novus Ordo Seclorum*

The ethics of Puritanism and the religious revolution of the sixteenth century nurtured the economic system that would ultimately discard the condemnation of usury, such that being involved in an undertaking for profit would become not only advantageous but a social duty, that is, "The good Christian was not wholly dissimilar from the economic man" (Tawney 1926: 210).

Pilgrim pioneers who founded the New World Order *(Novus Ordo Seclorum)*, which has evolved into our present system of free enterprise, reflected the tenets of their religion which were consistent with the pursuit of economic gain. Theirs was not an easy task. Their new homeland was a vast wilderness that did not reveal its full wealth. Yet, based on the principles of joint venturing, they commenced their life. It is in the accounting for these joint ventures that we discover some of the early examples of colonial bookkeeping. Accounting, as James Peele observed in the sense of "perfect reconyng," had already become known to be a force in the quest for social order "betwene man and man."

New England's major attraction was its many good harbors, its narrow coastal plain, and its short rivers. The promise of the sea for survival was attractive, and it offered fishing and trade from which the colonial New Englanders developed their settlements and nurtured businesses. The middle colonies became the "bread colonies" because of their wider coastal plains, better soil, and moderate climate. Ultimately, the agricultural surpluses provided a trade basis.

Southern colonies had navigable but sluggish rivers adjoining a broad and very fertile rising coastal plain. These served the developing large agricultural form of the plantation and such crops as tobacco, rice and indigo, as well as ordinary foodstuffs that were produced abundantly in the longer growing season.

Because colonial America was heavily forested along the Eastern coast, settlers cleared the land for acreage with a disregard for conservation. Wood was their essential material, and it was used for everything from building to household and farm implements. Wood as fuel warmed homes and provided cookfires. Ships were built and forest products exported (Dykema 1976).

English settlers provided the major source of population growth in the 1600s. In the eighteenth century, this influx diminished with the expansion of the Industrial Revolution in England. New York had a substantial Dutch population, but during the 1700s, the Scots, Irish, and Palatinate Germans were the most numerous immigrants. To the South, the black slave influx reached close to 500,000 by the time of the Revolution, replacing the need for indentured servants there. The indentured workers system persisted among Germans coming to Pennsylvania, and often resulted in attracting persons with industrial skills. Although the colonial population at the start of the 1700s was not more than 400,000, it was over two and one-half million by 1776.

Pilgrim Capital—The Joint Venture

In 1620, when the Mayflower's contingent of 102 men, women and children embarked upon their journey, which was to end not in Virginia (as may have been hoped) but off the coast of Cape Cod, problems of an accounting nature arose. Williard Stone notes that at least as early as 1620 the Pilgrim fathers were concerned over the matter of finances and suggested that their treasurer, one Mr. Martin, had not fulfilled his duty: "Mr. Martin saith he neither can nor will give any accounts; he crieth out unthankfullness for his paines and care, that we are susspitious of him and flings away, and will end nothing." Less than a year later Governor Bradford received a request from the London financier-merchant, Thomas Weston, to "Give us accounts as perticulerly as you can how our moneys were laid out" (Stone 1975).

Prior to 1692, Massachusetts consisted of two private joint stock companies—the Plymouth Colony and the Company of the Massachusetts Bay. When King William of Orange assumed the British throne he folded Plymouth into Massachusetts, forming a single colony. The first job of the treasurer of the new colony was to take over the asset balances from the separate treasurers of the Plymouth Colony and the Massachusetts Bay Company.

In 1628 the Massachusetts Bay Company had received its charter from King Charles I. The founding "undertakers" then spent two years raising money—the joint stock—recruiting emigrants, buying provisions, and making arrangements for ships. They appointed a governor, a deputy governor, and a treasurer to handle these affairs. The records of the governor and company for 17 June 1629 include the following:

> Auditors appointed for auditing the accompts, vis Mr. Symon Whetcombe, Mr. Nathaniel Wright, Mr. Noell, Mr. Perry, Mr. Crane, Mr.

Clarke, Mr. Eaton, and Mr. Andrewes; these 8, or any 4 or more of them, to meete at a convenient time & place to audite the accompts.

The meeting of the General Court held in London on July 28, 1629 goes on:

> The business treated on at the last meeting was now read; and therupon the accompts of Mr. Gounor, Mr. Deputie, and Mr. Trer, being now psented to this Court, the Auditors, form'ly appointed for auditing the Comp accompts, were now desired to meete & p use & audite these accompts; Weh they have agreed to doe to morrow in th' afternoone.

Plans were then made to establish the company in Massachusetts and to transfer the government to New England, including some of the principal merchants involved in the project. Money continued to be collected and spent as the sailing date approached. At a meeting held on October 16, 1629, the following appears:

> But for that there is a great debt owing by the joynt stock, it was moved that some course might bee taken for cleering thereof, before the gouvmt bee transferred; and to this purpose it was first thought fitt that the accompts should bee audited, to see what the debt is; but the business not admitting any such delay. It was desired that Mr. Gounor & Mr. Trer would meete tomorrow & make an estimate of the debt & p pare the same against a meeting to bee on Monday next, to determine this question.

This businesslike approach to the venture appears to have been retained in the New England settlement. The records for March 3, 1636, include the following: "Mr. Hutchinson & Mr. Willm Spences are deputed to take the accompts of Mr. Simkins & to returne the same into the nexte Court." The procedure of "taking" the treasurer's accounts was followed regularly thereafter.

Regular audits, of course, were not annual audits. Not until over a century later, 1752, was it enacted by Parliament that the first day of January was to be acknowledged as the beginning of the year, and thereby a basis was established for the annualization of accounts.

The financiers of the New England pilgrims were not alone in experiencing difficulties in obtaining an accounting from the colonists. In April 1651 the Dutch directors of the trading companies involved in New Amsterdam engaged Johannes Dyckman as "Bookkeeper in New Netherland." One year later the directors wrote that since they were "not properly informed of prizes captured, ships sold, and so forth," they had sent over another man (Committee on History, 1949A).

There is evidence of accounting not only within colonial joint venture trading companies, but in the records for businesses as well. For example, extant account books of the seventeenth-century Boston merchant John Hull indicate the practice of credit transactions. In 1660 Hull sold eight bushels of wheat on "three months tyme" to John Winthrop, Jr., son of the first governor of Massachusetts.

The earliest evidence of the use of double entry by colonial puritan merchants is found in *The Apologia of Robert Keayne* (1659). In citing the existence of his records, files and accounts, he noted that, of the three books of accounts he kept,

> the third is bound in white vellum, which I keep constantly in my closet at Boston and is called my book of creditor and debitor, in which is the sum of most of my accounts contracted wherein there is (sic) accounts between myself and others with the accounts balanced on either side. . . .   (Bailyn 1964: 68).

By 1667 the Boston *Town Record* reveals the availability of accountkeeping education and the practice of auditing the town accounts.

> 1667: "Mr Will Howard hath liberty to keep a wrighting school, to teach children to write and to keep accounts."

> March 10, 1689/90: "At a publique meeting of the inhabitants of Boston 'Voted that Mr. Peter Sergeant, Mr. Benj Alford and Mr. Samson Sheafe be desired to Audit the Townes Acct with ye Selectmen for the two years past."

Even as noted a historical event as the Salem Witch Trials of the 1690s begat accounting records. Accounts from the Boston and Charlestown jailers evidence payment for locks, chains, irons and wood to nail their jails "witch tight," plus noting the charge of 2s 6d per week per witch in custody (Holmes 1975A). So complete is the series of records that investigation a few years later reveals that in 1697 the Boston jailer had still not been paid for his expenses. He petitioned the General Court to redress his grievance and submitted his accounts, thereby causing the court to decide the following:

Province of the Massachusetts Bay:

At a Session of the Great and General Court or Assembly at Boston, by Prorogation

March 13th 1699/700

in Councill

Resolved,

That the Accompts annexed be referred unto an Auditor Committee to Examin the same; And that Elisha Hutchinson, Peter Sergeant and John Walley Esqr be a Committee of this Board, to joyne with John Leverett Esqr, Capn Andrew Belcher and Mr. Samuel Phips named a Committee by the Assembly to Examin and Audit the sd Accompts: and to make Report thereof unto the General Assembly at their next Session.

Isaac Addington, Secry.

These citations are more than mere curios on the shelves of our history; they are early evidence—earlier than henceforth acknowledged—that companies, joint ventures, political bodies and courts, as well as trading merchants, kept accounts and found them subject to audit as a matter of course, and offered them as evidence for action to recover payment. This all betrays a certain customary role of accounts in early American culture.

Early Education in Accounting

Between 1543 and 1558, at least three works on double-entry bookkeeping are known to have been published in English. The earliest was a translation of Pacioli's 1494 work and the other two were directly or indirectly copies of Pacioli. Luca Pacioli, an Italian friar and mathematician, lived from about 1445 to 1520 and is best known to accountants for publishing *Summa de Arithmetica, Geometria, Proportioni et Proportionalita*, which included a special supplement *De Computis et Scripturis*, on Venetian double-entry merchant accounts. About the time James Peele wrote the opening citation to this chapter, "original" English authorship in double-entry bookkeeping begins to appear, and books on double entry start to be published with frequency in England, the authors being for the most part schoolmasters or teachers.

Records indicate that in 1635 Plymouth Colony engaged a Mr. Morton to teach children to read, write and cast accounts. Casting accounts, as such, did not involve double entry bookkeeping, but "casting up the value of merchandise, tare and tret, interest rule of barter, fellowship, equation of payments, exchange," in short, those subjects which constitute commercial arithmetic (Haynes 1935: 7).

Learning via apprenticeship, namely, working and gaining experience in a "compting" house, was perhaps the singular most practical route to obtain a skill and earn a living for the young settler, or for the, indentured servant, once freed from the provisions of paying for the cost of transport.

American "writing schools" of the 1700s can be traced back to as early as 1709 in New England. George Brownell of New York advertised as a teacher of "Merchants Accounts" in 1731. These schools taught reading, writing, business math, and some form of bookkeeping. By the turn of the century, there were any number of books authored by Americans with titles such as the *Schoolmaster's Assistant* or the like. These usually contained a section relating to business or practical arithmetic. Such commercial textbooks reflected the widespread existence of grammar schools in which arithmetic, handwriting and bookkeeping were taught. In 1774 Byerley and Day of New York advertised to teach "bookkeeping after the Italian method and the practice of the most regular counting houses." Similar references to grammar schools and early commercial education have also been found in Philadelphia and Charleston in the early 1700s.

The Capital Market and Early Public Stock Ventures

The corporation as a common business form ceased to exist in the British colonial empire after 1720. Parliament, in response to the widespread speculation and losses that ensued that year from the collapse of the stock values associated with the South Sea Company, had passed the so-called Bubble Act. It required the personal approval of the monarch of all corporate charters.

The South Sea "bubble" had burst when, over the course of a single month, from August 25 to September 28, 1720 the stock value of South Sea had fallen from £900 to £190; it had once reached a peak of £1050. The company, originally organized to convert the large floating debt of the state into a funded debt, was to take over about ten million pounds sterling of unfunded debt which at the time was worth around 70 percent of par. Holders of the unfunded debt could convert it into South Sea Company stock at par. A secondary objective was to organize a corporation to develop foreign trade.

As the company developed outposts, directors of the company circulated rumors of the great possible profits in the South Sea, and in 1720 they planted a rumor that a 60 percent dividend would be paid at Christmas. As one authority stated, "The nation was so intoxicated with the spirit of adventure, that people became prey to the grossest delusion." It was not only South Sea stock that was purchased in the blind, but that of hundreds of other new ventures that appeared. Poor and rich alike talked of little else; the paper profits they were making were used in turn to purchase other new stock. The market began to tremble when it was recognized that the supply of money was not large enough to meet the installments on the securities purchased on margin as they came due or to absorb the defaulted stock at existing prices if it were thrown on the market. Pressures were applied by the South Sea Company through its purchased influence in Parliament to investigate nonchartered or improperly chartered rivals with a view to having their stock taken off the market. Holders of these "questioned" securities, fearing they would lose all, sold out and prices tumbled. Speculators who had bought on margin were caught and sold their South Sea stock to cover their position. This triggered a run and the failure of the South Sea Company (Hasson 1932).

Trading ventures, formed among joint partners, and even well-established credit risk firms collapsed. The "bubble" caused a financial panic in the British Empire and its colonies that touched almost every investor or consumer, for the actions involved so many stock issues that almost everyone had experienced market losses. Businesses and individual ventures failed at alarming rates.

Accounting Practice and Some Early Public Accountants

In reaction to these events, subsequent business undertakings became more conservative. A role for modern public accounting in the English-speaking world was born out of the chaos and panic of the South Sea bubble. Public agitation demanded an investigation, which got underway in December 1720. One of the directors of the South Sea Company, Jacob Sawbridge, and his partners in the firm of Turner & Co., were the objects of public wrath. Their estates were confiscated and one of the partners, Sir George Caswell, was imprisoned in the Tower of London. Charles Snell, a "Writing Master and Accomptant," was apparently retained to provide information by way of a special investigation of the accounts of Sawbridge & Co.[1] His undated report, probably prepared at the end of the year 1720 or early 1721, is a document which many consider to be more an example of special pleading than independent inquiry. Nevertheless it represents an early example of modern "public" accounting investigation and reporting.

Snell's report was later challenged in an anonymous editorial. If public accounting among our forebears was to set a precedent, one might have guessed it would have been conceived in the midst of controversy and also subjected to criticism.[2]

As noted by William Holmes, we know too that in the American colonies, as early as 1718, Browne Tymms had advertised a public accounting practice in Boston newspapers as follows: "Mr. Browne Tymms Living at Mr. Edward Oakes, Shopkeeper in Newbury Street, at the South End of Boston, Keeps Merchants and Shopkeepers Books." It seems appropriate to acknowledge Holmes' conclusion that Tymms was an early public accountant, the earliest known to have practiced in America.

The evidence that Tymms of Boston had been "advertising" as early as 1718 and that he kept merchant and shopkeepers books, coupled with the activities of Snell in London, suggests that public accounting, in the sense of individuals primarily involved in the specialty occupation of keeping and interpreting others' financial records, performing audits and providing other expert services, existed at the start of the eighteenth century in both England and her American colonies, albeit in a fashion and in an economic environment far different from those of today.

At a later time in this prerevolutionary period there is reference by James Don Edwards to the fact that Benjamin Franklin engaged James Parker to perform functions which were those of one acting as a public accountant, namely, to make an inventory and evaluation of equipment and materials and to present a report on the state of the accounts (Edwards 1960: 44).

In meeting the constantly increasing needs for records being created through trade expansion in the early 1700s, Carl Bridenbaugh observes:

> The increased sums of money and larger number of items handled made it necessary for merchants to maintain staffs of clerks in their counting houses. Bookkeeping by "Double Entry, Dr. and Cr. the Best Method" came into wide use everywhere . . . by 1733 and schools gave instruction in shorthand and the Italian method of keeping books.

Accountants offered their services in all the larger towns . . . (Bridenbaugh 1938: 359).

Merchant Capitalism

The era of merchant capitalism, a period of free enterprise characterized by the market system of the "invisible hand" described in Adam Smith's *The Wealth of Nations* (1776), suggests the economic environment of the British Empire, and to an extent that of her trading and plantation seacoast colonies in North America (Samuelson 1962). The merchants' and planters' accounting systems of the period required few of the sophisticated methods of today. The absence of speed in transport and communication was such that the detailed information about transactions was recorded and transmitted quite differently.

Evidence, in the form of "waste books" or "day books" (a type of financial daily diary from which the journal entry could be originated), journals, and ledgers, has been found and is continually being studied by accounting and business historians to assess the economic state of activities in the early colonies. The financial records of the famous New England Hancock family businesses from 1724 to 1775 have provided a basis for conclusions about some colonial accounting practices (Baxter 1945).

The lack of sound monetary systems required that accounting be not only multidenominational, but multinational; accommodating guineas, doubloons and Portuguese johannes, as well as items of value from flour to salt, that might be bartered in exchange. With this complex of value bases serving as the medium of exchange, it is appropriate to regard this as a period of "barter accounting" which remained until nearly the nineteenth century when cash became sufficiently stable and accepted in daily use to permit the development of a customary basis for "realization" of a transaction.[3]

Eighteenth-century colonial accounting may have been centered in New England, but other studies note that these priorities were typical conduct for account keeping by merchants and planters throughout the colonies. The waste book of Henry Laurens, an early Charleston merchant and landholder, is currently being studied, particularly with regard to the profit calculations recorded during the 1750s. The store records of the colonial merchant William Prentis, which cover the years 1733–1765, have recently been uncovered, as have the memorandum-style account books of Thomas Jefferson, containing entries kept from 1767 to 1826 (Coleman 1974).

The diversity of Jefferson's enterprises, which included his plantation and a small nail factory, and the completeness of the Prentis accounts, provide a newly formed view of the sophistication of colonial commerce that includes forms of management compensation, "dividend" policies, and the familiarity which the account keepers themselves had with the process of maintaining financial records (Shenkir 1972).

North of Virginia several important accounting developments were taking place. On more than one occasion Benjamin Franklin of Philadelphia is noted to have relied on the information of accounts to assist in winding up his business affairs. In Maryland, the Ridgely Account Books, which continue through the eighteenth and nineteenth centuries, were kept in double entry. The records of Robert Oliver, a Baltimore merchant, suggest how profit and loss and certain other impersonal accounting techniques were performed. In Newport, in the early 1700s, the John Stevens Shop kept double entry records through the 1720s. A New York paper in 1729 carried an advertisement noting that, "Any merchant or others that want a bookkeeper or their accounts started after the best methods, either in private trade or company may hear of persons qualified . . . by inquiring at the post office or coffee house." In the 1730s the Brown family of Providence, Rhode Island, noted at least one member, Obadiah, who "taught himself accounting methods using for this purpose *A Guide to Book Keepers According to the Italian Manner*" (London, 1729).[4]

There were, of course, many other texts on the Italian manner (i.e., double entry) available in the prerevolutionary colonies. Scotland's John Mair, a schoolmaster of Perth, thought to be the first popular author of a series of texts, published his first work, *Bookkeeping Methodiz'd*, in 1736. Subsequently, through 1765, many editions were continued and a revised edition, titled *Bookkeeping Moderniz'd* was completed in 1768. Some assert that Mair's book was probably the most widely read on the subject during the era when its editions were available. Mair's *Bookkeeping Methodiz'd or a Methodical Treatise on Merchant-Accompts According to the Italian Form Wherein the Theory of the Art is Fully Explained* was attentive to the mercantilist accountant, in that Chapter VII (seventh edition Edinburgh, 1763), dealt with "The produce and commerce of the Tobacco Colonies (i.e., the American colonies); with a specimen of accompts usually kept by the storekeepers."

BOOK-KEEPING METHODIZ'D:

O R,

A methodical treatife of MERCHANT-AC-COMPTS, according to the *Italian form.*

WHEREIN

The THEORY of the Art is fully explained, and reduced to PRACTICE, by variety of fuitable Examples in all the branches of trade.

To which is added,

A Large APPENDIX,

CONTAINING

I. Defcriptions and fpecimens of the Sub-fidiary Books ufed by merchants.
II. Monies and Exchanges, the nature of Bills of Exchange, Promiffory Notes, and Bills of Parcels.
III. Precedents of Merchants Writings, peculiar to *England, Scotland,* and common to both.
IV. The Commiffion, Duty, and Power of Factors.
V. A fhort Hiftory of the Trading Companies in *Great Britain,* with an account of her exports and imports.

VI. The produce and commerce of the Sugar Colonies; with a fpecimen of the accompts kept by the factors or flore-keepers; and an explication of wharf and plantation accompts.
VII. The produce and commerce of the Tobacco Colonies; with a fpecimen of the accompts ufually kept by the flore-keepers.
VIII. The method of keeping accompts proper for Shopkeepers or Retailers.
IX. A dictionary, explaining abftrufe words and terms that occur in merchandife.

By JOHN MAIR, A. M.

The SEVENTH EDITION.

EDINBURGH:

Printed by W. SANDS, A. MURRAY, and J. COCHRAN, For W. SANDS, A. KINCAID & J. BELL, and A. DONALDSON.

MDCCLXIII.

Title page to the 1763 edition of John Mair's Accounting Text, with a special chapter (VII) on accounting in the American Colonies.

Government Accounts

Perhaps the earliest records of governmental accounts can be traced to the explorers who pioneered the American passage. As noted earlier, Alistair Cooke tells this about the party headed by Christopher Columbus:

> There were forty men . . . aboard the flotilla including a surgeon and the royal controller of accounts, sent along to keep tabs on Columbus' swindle sheet when he started to figure the cost of gold and spices he would accumulate (Cooke 1973: 32–33).

Another early explorer, Henry Hudson, also found it part of his duty to provide a rendering of accounts on the third voyage of his ship, Half Moon, which reached the lower bay of New York on 3 September 1609. The Dutch had come primarily to trade furs rather than to colonize. Hudson spent a month up the river, exploring to a point just below the present city of Albany, but did not find the much sought after northwest passage. Disappointed, he retraced his steps, stopping in England because his crew was a mix of English and Dutch sailors. Hudson dispatched a report of his voyage to the Amsterdam Chamber but was prevented from going himself, because the English claimed he should be considered in their service and not that of the Dutch, betraying the keenness of mercantilist rivalries. Van Meteren, the Dutch historian who was then present in London, remarked: "Many persons thought it strange that captains should thus be prevented from laying their accounts and reports before their employers . . .". (Condon 1968:11)

As early as 1644 New England colonists had been provided with the services of a government official, designated auditor general, whose duties were prescribed on three pages of script. This function was known to have lasted until about 1657. Pilgrim ventures at early stages included self-contained government auditing functions as early as 1620 (the Mayflower group) and thereafter within the Massachusetts Bay Company as referred to earlier.

Linda Kistler's studies of municipal accounting in the Plymouth Colony indicate that annual reports of the audit committee of that colony commenced in 1658. The statements reveal the imposition of fines as a form of governmental restraint on community behavior and a tax system which included an excise tax on real estate and personal property. Public expenditures were used to pay salaries and expenses of officials and to provide military protection. Printed copies of the treasury accounts for the period show payments for a "marshall" and a fine for selling a "pistell to an Indian." Apparently the relationship with Narragansett Indians, following the Pilgrim expedition against the tribe in 1645, had still not stabilized. By the 1680s the colony had developed an effective budget process and a system of levying taxes on each town. The tax rolls suggest that Scituate was the wealthiest community in the colonies in 1686.

An epitaph on a tombstone in the old church graveyard in Jamestown, Virginia, depicts another episode in the early colonial accounting of governments: "Here lies the body of Philip Ludwell who died the 11th of January, 1720 in the 54th year of his age. Sometimes auditor of His Majesty's revenues and 25 years member of the council." (c. 1666–1720).[5]

The Ludwell epitaph suggests that a system of governmental auditing existed in the English colonies. Ludwell's identity as a "sometimes" auditor of revenues is consistent with the fact that prior to the 1760s it was more common for Parliament to consider the colonies as entitled to "home rule" with control of affairs being conducted in town meetings and the influence of the Crown remaining remote. New England towns, for example, maintained their own highways, cared for their poor, supported public schools, regulated business in a minor fashion, and served as the unit of control for the assessment, collection, and audit of government revenues.

The Cultural Significance of Accounts Prior to the Revolution

Several historians have gained attention by proposing or supporting the notion which identifies the period, roughly between 1500 and 1800, as a period of little change from the methods found in Pacioli's treatise, that is, that it was a period of "accounting stagnation"[6] (Wingjum 1970). A study of the state of accounting technique in America and the issue of stagnation need to be separated. This is not to suggest that a knowledge of accounts was prerequisite to survival in the American colonies. But it does seem that by the time of the Revolution double entry had become important if not necessary to the merchant and trader who had experienced the commercial expansion of the 1730s. The general populace, being limited in their ability to write and compute, were not likely to involve themselves with any formal system of accounting. Yet when education was introduced as early as 1635, schools were teaching the fundamentals of "casting accounts." To the educated colonial, therefore, accounts were a useful adjunct to personal record keeping, and provided important information as commerce became more complex.

William Baxter contends in his analysis of colonial accounting that its development was a function of merchant specialization (Baxter 1946). Briefly, the more specialized the culture, the more the need for accounts. Although the bursting of the South Sea "bubble" delayed the popular advent of the medium of the corporate entity to amass capital, colonial businessmen were able to create joint ventures to provide sufficient capital to undertake new, relatively specialized, and often risky ventures. When joint ownership increased, the adoption of early double entry and the requisite proprietary accounts expanded. As specialized colonial trade and commerce increased, Adam Smith's theory of economics, which noted and accommodated the necessity and efficiency of specialization, came to be acknowledged. Within the context of this activity could accounting in America have been "stagnant"?

NOTES

1. Charles Snell, in his folio pamphlet, "Accompts for Landed Men" (London, 1711), makes it very clear, in a full-page advertisement at the end, that "Such Persons as desire, may have their children taught by the *Author*, a most Noble and Generous Way of *Writing all Hands*, and *How to Command their Pen*.

    The *Practical Manner* (of *Arithmetick*) used by Merchants in *Calculating*, and *Examining* their Accompts.
    Foreign Exchanges, their *Calculations, Negotiations*, and *Arbitrations*.
    The True Manner of Keeping *Merchants Accompts* (the *Waste-Book* having been Real Business) stated in the *Italian* Method of *Book-keeping* by *Double Entry*."

    He added, of himself:

    He also Fits Persons for *Publick Offices*; and *Boards* at his House such as desire it.

    Snell was an excellent example of the writing-master/accountant *genre*, which flourished particularly in the 1750–1830 period. Another book of his is a much smaller pamphlet, "A Short and Easy Method; After which Shop-keepers may State, Post, and Balance their Books of Accompts" (London, 1714), in which he styles himself:

    "Writing-Master and Accomptant . . . With whom Young Gentlemen may Board."

    This little book opens with a catechism, the answers to which were presumably to be learned by the heart. *Example:* "*Q.* What is the first Thing I must do, who design to keep my Books of Accompts after this Method? *A.* You must make an Inventory; an Example of which is at the End of these Instructions."

    There are superb examples of the writing-master's art (Dunlop 1968).

2. The speculation over developing new markets during the early 1700s was not confined to England. The financial ruin which occurred in Paris after the bursting of the "Mississippi Bubble," also served as a warning to financial parties in France that speculation, paper money and the market were only compatible to an extent. Controller-General of Finance John Law, who had taken office in the midst of the financial boom, also found himself accountable when the first financial panic in modern French history began to reverberate. Indeed when the shares in Law's Western Company plunged in value after December 1720, the economy of the western world had experienced a double dose of overspeculation.

3. Pure barter was supplemented in the seventeenth century by the use of wampum. Wampum was made of clam and whelk shells and accepted as a form of currency, usually bound in a form of a belt. When wampum factories were set up and counterfeit beads flooded the markets around 1800, the shells were outlawed as legal tender.

4. Some business historians, namely, John Chamberlain, suggest that Obadiah Brown may have been initially responsible for bringing a knowledge of double entry to the colonies. In light of the other evidence and the implications of this chapter, it seems unlikely that Chamberlain's contention is merited.

5. This calls to mind the auditor's epitaph which we have seen cited more frequently, found at St. Mary's Church, Chesham, England:

    Here lyeth part of Richard Bowle, who faithfully served divers great lordes as auditor on earth, but above all he prepared himself to give up his account to the Lord Heaven. He was a lover of God's ministers, a father of God's poor, a help to all God's people. He died on the 16th December, 1626 and of his age 77.

6. "Accounting in 1760 was essentially what it was to Pacioli—a set of arithmetical techniques to assist the businessman to conduct his affairs in an orderly, purposeful, and well-informed fashion. There was no theory, and no deeply-felt need for any; its only immediate use would have been to lighten the labour of mastering double entry in books or in school by substituting knowledge of principles for the hard grind of learning detailed rules by rote, and such consideration for the student was a thing of the future" (Lee 1975).

2 THE BIRTH OF A NATIONAL ECONOMY

> *The greatest moral rectitude necessary for adult persons must proceed from a right knowledge and practice of keeping orderly accounts.*
>
> [Mathew Quin,
> Rudiments of Bookkeeping, 1776.]

Political and Economic Elements of a New Nation

George III ascended to the English throne in 1760. His reign marked the beginning of the end of the American colonies under British governance. Under his rule a series of political decisions, resulting in taxation and regulation deemed intolerable to colonials, would force a conflict of arms, and the birth of an American nation. From these events would flow forth names of remembered revolutionary heroes and traitors—and the places of sacrifice, bitter defeat, and finally victory for the colonies. These outcomes are well known, and the popular understanding of them is such that this reference will suffice as a basis of remarks about the setting of the Revolution. The purpose there is to consider the transformation and accounting consequences of this period as the new nation formed its business customs and developed systems of trade.

Perhaps the most significant development of this era, from the view of long-term impact on the subject of accounting, was to be found in the writings of a moral philosopher thousands of miles removed from the turmoil of the American continent. His book (the shortened title being most popular), *The Wealth of Nations*, predicted the age of industrial specialization, and was the first to analyze and describe free enterprise, the precepts of which America would manifest in its economic system. Adam Smith's work, published in early 1776, was a declaration of independence from mercantilism, an economist's reaction to the heavy-handed influence of the state in setting markets. In Smith's view the market should be set by the collective force of individuals following their own self-interest.

This economic theory of "individual" supremacy and the recognition of the need to accommodate the efficiency of specialization in matters of economic conduct, when linked to the political system and doctrines of personal liberty and responsibilities set forth in the United States Constitution, set the pattern and direction not only of the new nation's government and policies, but of its economic progress (Pemberton 1976).

Individuals were free to pursue their own ends and, even more, they were justified and encouraged to do so in this new, albeit unsettled and hostile, environment that was teeming with resources and potential for trade. The "promises" of individual wealth had already begun to be fulfilled by 1774, for by then Americans already had the greatest wealth per capita of any people in the civilized world. A significant class of wealthy individuals, constituting about 10 percent of the population, did exist, but more importantly, some 40 percent—representing independent small farmers—had also attained a reasonably successful status. A merchant class, with average holdings of about $20,000 in modern value equivalents, also had established itself. Personal wealth per capita in 1776 (again in mid-twentieth-century terms) has been estimated at about $4,000.

The Founding Fathers and Their Accounts

Our Founding Fathers made use of the rudiments of what today is a highly specialized professional pursuit. Washington's expense accounts and his plantation accounts indicate he had a working knowledge of accounting. One writer has observed: "One of the most perused books in his private library was 'Book-Keeping Moderniz'd: Or; Merchant Accounts by Double Entry'. . ."—the very popular and standard work of Scotland's John Mair. We cannot be certain of the extent of Washington's knowledge without a direct reference from Washington's papers that such was the case. However, Mair's book would have been well suited to Washington's needs, for as noted earlier it included chapters on methods and accounts for plantation owners in the colonies (Palmer 1976).

There is reason to believe that recently printed papers and diaries of Washington will reveal much more about his acquisition in assembling the Mount Vernon plantation, his successes and failures in business and land ventures, as well as his acquisition, control, and use of labor. For example Washington's accounts show that from August 3, 1775 to September 1783, he received a total of £80,167, or about $400,000. Washington tried to figure his profits from the above but apparently found the task dismaying. Finally he settled his accounts with his manager in terms of produce instead of money. Additional evidence of his account "rigor" is found on his December 31, 1769 balancing entry which reads: "By cash lost, stolen, or paid away without charging £143.151.2." Washington's business and household accounts, including accounts in the Bank of Alexandria, from 1763 to 1799 were kept at Mount Vernon. Additional records, including his personal expenses "Ledger A" and "Ledger B," maintained during periods of public service are in the collection of the Library of Congress.[1]

John Hancock inherited the business fortune of his uncle, Thomas Hancock, the Boston merchant prince. John might have been less blessed had it not been that "Thomas knew as much about his own affairs from an accounting standpoint as was possible . . ." (Bruchey 1958).

George Taylor, who signed the Declaration of Independence as a representative of Pennsylvania, came to America as an indentured servant bound to the owner of an iron works. He was sent to work as a furnace coaler but it was thought that he was too weak for the job. Because he had a better education than most youth, he was given a job in the business office handling transactions and accounts. Indeed, Taylor had an accountant's flair for opportunity and when the owner of the works died, Taylor married the widow and thereby became the new owner (Previts 1976A).

Perhaps the wealthiest of the signers, Charles Carroll of Carrollton (since at least three other Charles Carrolls were prominent in Maryland at the time, he signed himself "of Carrollton"), is known for both his longevity (he survived until 1832, the last of the signers to succumb) and for his keeping of "meticulous books" (Cadwalader 1975).

Thomas Jefferson also maintained extensive financial records, as was customary for plantation owners, including an entry in his account books for July 4, 1776 noting a purchase of two items and a donation to charity (Shenkir 1972).

DuPont Company wastebook, 1811. The wastebook was the detailed record book from which original journal entries were made. Note the May 29, 1811, details of a transaction with Thomas Jefferson.

Source: Courtesy of Eleutherian Mills Historical Library.

Another signer, Robert Morris, was instrumental in aiding the revolutionary cause by providing the means of financing for the new Congress. Morris, later acting as superintendent of finance, administered the funds for Congress and, with the backing of Haym Salomon, is noted to have "introduced system into financial accounting" related to the new government. Salomon, called the "Good Samaritan of the Revolution," lent over $200,000 to the United States. He died at the age of 45, and the loan was apparently not repaid (Morris 1975).

Henry Laurens, President of the Continental Congress in 1777 and a signer of the Treaty of Paris, used accounts to maintain a record of his personal financial affairs with the state government of South Carolina during the 1770s; and his neatly drawn "Statement of Account with the United States," dated January 20, 1780, provides evidence of the customary importance placed on such records in early government transactions.

Robert Livingston, who along with Franklin, Jefferson, Adams, and Sherman constituted the committee to draft the Declaration of Independence, was absent at its signing due to the need to attend to affairs in New York. Livingston operated many enterprises and used double-entry accounts. The extent and the effectiveness to which Livingston enterprises employed double entry has caused them to be labeled "models" of double entry by business history writers (H. Johnson 1976).

The Commercial and Industrial Setting

In setting out the uses of "bookkeeping methodiz'd" as it was known in this period, one must seek to consider the lifestyle of the times. In 1776 almost all (95 percent) of the estimated 2.5 to 3 million American settlers lived on farms. The population hugged the seacoast and waterways in order to expedite the transportation and trade needed to sustain its relationship with a "Eurocentric" world. Accounting was based as much on barter as on cash, which was in short supply and of unstable value. Payments came in the form of rum, beef, butter, and other forms of commodity money. Merchants kept their records in a series of accounting books beginning with the waste book (a financial diary) from which journal entries were made. Apprenticeship in the accounting house or "compting house" of a merchant was the common form of learning about financial records. Young men, mostly from well-to-do families, were thus apprenticed before being sent into business (Previts 1977). Annual reporting was only beginning to achieve acceptance and was not of the statement type we know today. Through the 1790s and 1800s several hundred business incorporations took place. As the turmoil of the American Revolution and the War of 1812 were replaced by a stable political environment, Americans set out to restore their trade and expand their holdings of new lands west of the Allegheny Mountains. Technical inventions and their labor saving efficiency tended to reduce costs, and as turnpikes, canals and then railroads appeared, new markets were opened for goods which, in turn, induced specialized manufacture and early forms of mass production. Industry and commerce had become rooted in the midst of a predominantly rural society.

By the close of the era companies that were predecessors to the giant railroads, which would spin a web of steel over the country, were being formed and beginning operations (Chamberlain 1974: 58–72).

The Capital Markets

One of the most important events in the economic development of the new nation occurred in New York on May 17, 1792. A group of merchants and auctioneers gathered on Wall Street to fix a daily meeting time to carry on the trading of a heretofore scattered market for government securities, as well as the shares of banks and insurance companies. They had recognized that the unorganized and irregular fashion of the coffeehouse auction impeded the trading of securities and decided to meet daily at regular hours to buy and sell securities under an old buttonwood tree on Wall Street only a few blocks from the present site of the New York Stock Exchange.

These first brokers handled the public's buy and sell orders in new government securities, as well as in shares of insurance companies, Alexander Hamilton's First United States Bank, the Bank of North America and the Bank of New York. This step toward an auction based capital market, regularly scheduled and located in a principal trading and commercial center, evidenced not only the logistical benefit of a convenient capital marketplace, but also the realization of businessmen that the raising of capital for ventures had reached substantial and public proportions, although a "national" capital market as such was not established since regionalism more clearly identified the character of investment interest. In addition, effective, timely and reliable communication systems were lacking and no systematic financial reports were likely to be provided. Traders therefore depended on their knowledge of the situation, their local sources of information, and their expertise and command of local business prospects—all of which would tend to govern the scope of their capital investments. Nevertheless, the seeds of modern capital markets and a future source of demand for the services of financial accountants can be traced in the deeds of the twenty-four founding members of this exchange when they commenced regular trading.

By 1793 the brokers moved indoors locating in the newly completed Tontine Coffee House at the northwest corner of Wall and William Streets. By this time shares in larger banks, as well as state and federal debt issues, were regularly traded. During the remainder of the decade, 295 chartered companies were formed, most of them banks, insurance companies, dock construction ventures, road companies and mining firms. Although the public was not trading in all of these firms, the pattern for trading and the regular and ready recourse to the market enhanced the value of shares. Private financial activity was checked for a time by the War of 1812, but peace brought the formation of new enterprises and New York State bonds, issued to pay for the Erie Canal, joined the issues traded on the exchange. Private businesses also expanded. The cotton textile industry, able to boast of only a few mills in 1804, was operating half a million spindles by 1815. The tempo of business quickened as the country headed into a postwar boom. By 1827 the stocks of twelve banks and nineteen marine and fire insurance companies, the Delaware & Hudson Canal Co., the Merchants' Exchange, and the New York Gas Light Company—the nation's first public utility—also were traded on the exchange.

New York was not alone, of course, in providing a capital market for ventures. Regional capital markets were a key attribute of early enterprise in the United States because they afforded the added assurance of being convenient to both investors and sources of information. It is important to recognize that in Boston, Philadelphia, Baltimore and Charleston, local capital markets were operating. Indeed there was a rivalry of some degree between the Chestnut Street brokers of Philadelphia and the traders on Wall Street. This competition was accented when the Bank of the United States was formed in 1791 and headquartered in Philadelphia. The Philadelphia Bank's stock market price influenced brokers in other cities, particularly in their trading of bank stocks. But New York remained the home of risk capital, where the speculators and equity holders were to be found, and it was in New York that many early stock ventures (which included the right to assess shareholders on a pro-rata basis for new equity needs) were used to underwrite high risk "industrial" undertakings.

Accountants in the New Nation

There are few similarities between the routines of today's financial accounting systems in modern multi-level international enterprise and the accounting records of the colonial citizens, aside from their foundation in the system of double entry. Business historians note that by the time of the Revolution the use of double entry accounting was widespread. Harrington reports that "most" wholesale houses in New York appear to have used double entry by the eve of the Revolution. Of course, this does not mean that double entry information was used in the same fashion as it is today. In this era, an era of the merchant capitalist, one made use of accounting primarily as an internal administrative device, and statements of accounts as such were not widely circulated or published as they are today.[2]

William Weston, an English author of bookkeeping texts, was among the first to be in a position to influence American accounting practice as to "annual" taking of balances. In 1754 Weston wrote a book for young Englishmen who were going to America to become plantation managers or factors. In his text of 260 pages, he prescribed that books were to be balanced once per year and were to be proved by adding all the debit entries and all the credit entries in the ledger (Sampson 1960).

Many of the bookkeeping texts of the period began to reflect this trend toward annual "reckoning" as noted in the observation of the author William Gordon in 1765:

> Merchants generally, at some fixed period, once in the year, balance or close the Ledger not only because the space allotted for account may be for the most part full, but likewise to show the true state of affairs and to determine what increases or diminutions his capital has suffered by last year's transactions (Brief 1964: 18).

This emphasis on determining changes in personal capital was a significant development and perhaps the major informational "output" of books kept for business during the period of merchant capitalism. It was common for texts written after the revolution up to the turn of the century to note this information. For instance, in 1796,

E. T. Jones, an accounting text writer from Bristol, wrote: "Once a year, most persons in trade have a statement of affairs made out, by taking off the balance of every account in the ledger."

The Counting House

Bookkeeping in this era has been identified as "barter bookkeeping" because of the lack of specie and stable paper money as well as the absence of a banking system, which led to exchanges of commodities for other commodities. Not until the early 19th century was currency sufficiently stable that "cash accounts" began to appear as a matter of routine in records (Baxter 1946).

How widespread and how well developed was the practice of keeping accounts during this era? What institution represented the locus of its practice? How significant was accounting information to those who developed it?

Perhaps more than any other element of its age, the development of the merchant counting house was both a force and an effect in the maturation process of account keeping in this country. From the prerevolutionary period through the first legal recognition of public accountancy in 1896, the counting house supplied a central environment for early accounting functions. The colonial counting house was the "records center" of the merchant; it was also the established center for educating aspiring young businessmen and merchants. Training of this type was common throughout the colonies. John Hancock and Henry Laurens, two signers of the Declaration of Independence, were both schooled in counting houses. They went on to be successful merchants, the former in New England, the latter in South Carolina.

Account keeping per se, as it was practiced in the counting house, reflected increasingly ingenious steps to simplify and routinize "processes." The columnar arrangement, the order and form of entering the information in double-entry style, and the techniques of learning suggested by the books of the period all claimed to advance and to simplify the method. The principles of economic measurement and consistent reporting which underlie our third-party oriented accounting methods of today do not appear to be matters of concern then, perhaps because the merchant kept accounts primarily to suit his own, and not third party, needs. Nineteenth century merchants had elevated their account books to a place of special prominence, physically keeping them separate in what has been described as a "throne room."

In that throne room lay the bookkeeping records which made it possible for all the strings of diverse enterprise to be controlled by the hand of the resident merchant (Bruchey 1958).

Thus, from the early eighteenth century to a later, more advanced stage in the mid-nineteenth century, we can presume that a significant popular knowledge about the benefits of accounts for purposes of controlling business came about through the apprenticeship system of the counting house. That is to say, based on apprenticeship training in rendering accounts, merchants became aware of and dependent upon financial records. As trade and business expanded, following the War of 1812, a stable currency medium was provided, and thus a monetary basis to underlie transactions was established which enabled efficiently summarized and comparable accounts to be prepared so that rapid evaluations could be made. This development was to make it more necessary for the many, not just the few, to become knowledgeable in accounts. As account keeping became a requisite skill, and counting houses handled larger volumes of transactions, they became less well suited as a learning place and source of apprenticeship. Instead, textbooks and teachers of accounts began to make their presence felt in the larger towns.

Education of Accountants

At the start of the nineteenth century, private institutions of accounting education, operated in many instances by textbook writers, had begun to offer specialized courses, first in the home of the authors and then gradually at locations in the commercial district.

James Bennett, noted for his textbooks, the first published in 1814, was listed as a "teacher of bookkeeping" in the New York City *Directories* through 1835. The twelfth edition of his text provides a testimony that Bennett had instructed thousands "many of whom, prior to their attendance in the Author's lecture, possessed no knowledge whatever of accounts. . . ." Bennett further noted that he had "instructed persons from thirteen different nations of the earth" (Holmes 1974).

Another American identified as an early educator and author was Thomas Turner, of Portland, Maine. Turner's 1804 text shows a set of

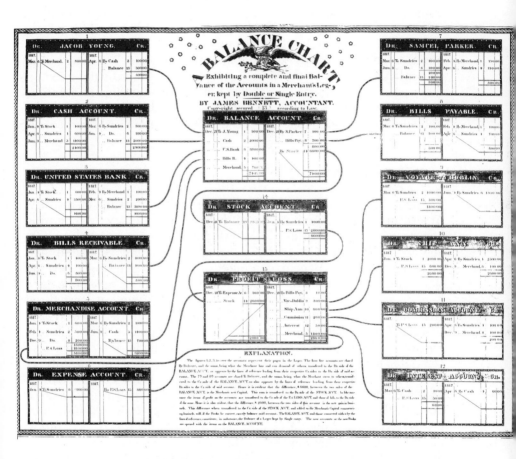

Bennett's balance chart. The details of the chart depict transactions of 1817. Other versions of the chart were used as late as 1845 without changing the basic transaction date of 1817.

Source: Hans Johnson, "Merchant Accountants," *Management Accounting,* October, 1976.

books for an individual proprietorship and for a partnership, and states that a "senior school boy can within a few months obtain a foundation of the principles and a perfect knowledge of the method. . . ."

The techniques of Bennett and Turner contrast the varieties of accounting instruction emerging at the start of the 1800s.[3] Turner emphasized the need to teach the "school boy" as it had become common to teach the methods of accounts in New England from early times whereas Bennett's lectures were a type of forerunner of the business colleges which would emerge to educate "working" class students. In each case there was a response to the growing need on the part of business people to have an understanding of accounts because of "(t)he increase of commerce in this country and the unbounded field open to it for specialties and commercial prospects."

Early Textbooks

There is little agreement on the origin and authorship of the first American text on account keeping by double entry. Accounting historians in this century acknowledge William Mitchell's 1796 volume, *A New and Complete System of Bookkeeping* (Philadelphia), as being the first. Recent evidence, however, indicates a text by Benjamin Workman, *The American Accountant; or Schoolmaster's New Assistant*, to be the earliest known.[4] It survived at least three editions. The first appeared in 1789, and the third, revised and corrected by R. Patterson, appeared in Philadelphia in 1796. Thomas Dilworth's *Young Book-keeper's Assistant* (Philadelphia, 1789) also competes for the honor of being one of the early texts on the subject printed in the newly united colonies (Haynes 1935: 11–13). Others credit Benjamin Booth as having been the first American to write a book on this subject (*A Complete Service*, etc.,). His work, however, was published in London in 1789 and may not have had recognition for this reason. Chauncy Lee's *American Accomptant*, which contained 297 pages and was printed in Lansingburgh, New York in 1797, was the first "serious" work on the subject by an American, for it reflected an innovation of "The Italian Mode of Bookkeeping agreeable to Gordon's system of accomptantship." Gordon's works were written in Great Britain and survived several editions. They were in widespread use in the three decades before the end of the eighteenth century.

In his 1789 text, Booth's introduction related the effects of the Revolutionary War on his own life, noting on the title page that he was "Late of New York, and now of London, Merchant," he laments further "Being cut off, by the late War, from the friendships formed in my youth; and prevented by the Peace that succeeded it, from pursuing the line of business to which I had long been habituated. . . ."

This disconsolate remark by the expatriate author suggests that merchant account keepers were as vulnerable then as now as to the process of politics and the pains of war. It may have been that Booth had had Tory sympathies and was thenceforth banished from the colonies when the new nation took form. Yet in his efforts to make himself "useful to society," he responded to the creative task of writing a complete system of bookkeeping from the viewpoint of an American now functioning in England. Booth's contribution may be all the more significant because it flows "against the grain," in that the major texts had been coming to the colonies by way of Britain before the Revolution, and now shortly thereafter, an American writer was introducing his system to the English as noted in his remark:

> It is surprising, that, in a commercial country like this, there should not be one treatise on this subject, which when applied to a large scale of business, can be reduced to practice. Those I have seen, appear to have been written, either by persons who have not the ability sufficient for the undertaking, or by such as never had the opportunity of bringing their theories to the test of experience. . . .

Booth emphasized the need to present effectively summarized transactional data, noting that several firms had failed because they could not cope with the extensive business of the house, which reflected the expanded scale of business in general. Whether or not we should recognize the uniqueness of Booth's "summary" approach remains to be determined. But his comments testify to the state of commercial expansion and the increased scale and complexity of business, wherein business failure could be traced to the lack of adequate accounts and summaries.

Public Practice and Disclosure of Accounts

The linking together of sources of capital via regular markets and an auction price setting mechanism was a major step in the emergence of an American economy that was slowly divesting itself of regional prejudice and supplying capital to enterprises located beyond the realm of customary travel and influence.

It is perhaps difficult to perceive the significance of this development in light of our multi-national, modern capital markets. But it should be apparent that the movement toward a national capital market required increasing use of reliable financial summaries in evaluating the prospects of a distant company. At the same time, it is worthwhile to recognize that the information needs of these early markets were not met by what we would identify as financial statements. Formal account summarizing was not much beyond a mere debit-credit total, and balancing probably was not far advanced from the "balance chart" technique taught by Bennett (see Figure 2-2). Financial information of the sort deemed useful for investment decisions of this age was based upon whatever information was "eked out" of counting house employees or learned from associates or the owner of the business or the promoter of the venture.

The ledgers of Robert Oliver, a merchant of Baltimore (1796–1806), indicate that periodic trial balances were used, not for the purposes of disclosure but solely for compiling the balances of all open accounts in order to determine bookkeeping accuracy. These early trial balances condensed into 3 or 4 pages the financial information from as many as 500 pages and grouped debtors and creditors as well. A modern trial balance could have been constructed from Oliver's trial balances, but no evidence of a more advanced form was found. Although it is quite likely that proprietors were learning the value of a systematic and effectively summarized set of books, there is no clear evidence that investors expected, demanded or relied upon financial information set forth in such a conventional and convenient fashion[5] (Bruchey 1946: 117).

References to British auditors' visits to the colonies and to the investments that likely would have caused such visits are commonly referred to in the history of accounting.[6] But public accounting listings in directories are few and public newspaper announcements by accountants such as one found in the *New Jersey Journal* of July 8, 1705 were probably rare. An apt conclusion for this time is that the public practice of accounting seems to have been combined with teaching and writing on the subject of bookkeeping.

Managerial Accounting

Since the retailer and merchant were prime users of account records at this time, one might also wonder about the early industrialists' uses of account data in ventures and barter. If the books aided the memory of the trading merchant, were they not as necessary in the complex transactions of manufacturers in cotton mills, iron foundries and construction firms? Information about early American industrial cost-accounting practices is sparse. The major industries of the western world were located in and effectively protected by the trade patterns and policies of Great Britain. U.S. manufacturers, though on the rise, were clearly in their infancy (Bruchey 1965: 86). It was not until 1820 that manufacturers' associations came into being under the leadership of the National Institution for the Promotion of Industry. A newspaper, *Patron of Industry,* was also introduced to inform and influence public and political opinion in favor of a protective tariff to aid developing industry (Cochran and Miller 1942: 17). It is perhaps necessary then to distinguish that although *cost* accounting came into evidence only after 1800 and developed during the American industrial revolution, industrial bookkeeping practice and techniques were of earlier origin.

Among firms in the shipbuilding industry, excerpts from account books around the time of the revolution indicate a very rough and ready type of receipts and expenditures system, with no clear view of accounting for overhead allocations or the loss of fixed asset value via depreciation.

Reports of accounting for iron manufacturers of the period indicate that double-entry records were modified to accommodate inventory information. These records were sufficient, if employed by a person with knowledge of accounts, to afford the basis for estimating costs of production, although information such as cost of production was not clearly set out or summarized as part of the record-keeping procedure (Gambino 1976: 18–19).

Federalist Policies

Having only recently acknowledged their *interdependence* the thirteen "United States" ratified a Constitution, which took effect in March 1789. The general weakness of the Constitution in establishing provisions for monetary unity became a serious impediment to trade and the movement toward an economy unified by a national market. The value of paper money, in particular that of the Continental Congress, was suspect. Each state jealously guarded its state's right to include the issuance of its own coin and currency.

The need for a unified monetary system became apparent to George Washington when he became President. Washington appointed Alexander Hamilton as Secretary of the Treasury. The act creating the Treasury Department in 1789 charged the treasurer with the responsibilities of: (1) preparing plans for the improvement and management of the revenue and support of the public credit; (2) preparing and reporting estimates of the public revenues and public expenditures; (3) superintending the collection of the revenues; (4) deciding on the forms of keeping and stating accounts and making return; and (5) granting under prescribed limitations, warrants for drawing money from the treasury. Hamilton's brilliance can be credited for three significant events that took the colonial economy from a barter system to sound financial exchange with a unified and stable monetary unit. Hamilton's accomplishments included:

1. Establishment of the Bank of the United States. From its headquarters in Philadelphia and through its eight branches the bank provided monetary stability and established a precedent for advancing federal notes as currency in place of money.
2. Development of the Coinage Act of 1792. Two precious metals, gold and silver, underwrote the new monetary unit of the United States, the dollar. The act provided that all public offices and all proceedings in the court of the United States "had to be kept in conformity with the new coinage regulations thereby insuring that the new coins and the dollar-decimal monetary system would take precedence over competing state units."
3. Federal funding of foreign and domestic war debt. This strengthened the fiscal and credit posture of the new republic. All features of this were included in a single act passed in August 1790.

Hamilton and the Federalists hoped that notes of the United States Bank would circulate as currency and thereby serve as a substitute for the paper money which the public had come to mistrust. Meanwhile, state banks, which had been actively multiplying, set forth hundreds of issues of paper currency, creating confusion and ultimately a panic when, by 1837, over 8000 issues were outstanding. Of course a much more involved political story lies behind the Federalist movement and the history of banking in the new Republic. This period marks the initiation of a monetary system based on federal note issues of sufficient stability and general acceptance to warrant the use of "cash" accounts in ledgers, thereby noting the beginning of the end of the "barter" economy prevalent up to this time.[7]

One of the most valuable sources of information about the financing of the early Federal government is Albert Gallatin's *A*

Sketch of the Finances of the United States (1796). Gallatin's work provides narratives on the revenues, expenses and debt of the Federal government and a set of nineteen statements (for example, see Figure 2-1) which detail financial sources from the start of the Constitutional government in 1789 through January 1, 1796.

Gallatin (1761–1849) came to America from Switzerland and served in the House of Representatives where he led the fight for congressional control over the "purse strings" of government. In part due to his efforts, the forerunner of the House Ways and Means Committee was established. In 1801 he became Secretary of the Treasury under Jefferson and served for twelve years.

Gallatin's *Sketch* is important in the way it classifies and sequences government accounts. Earlier tabulations of Federal government receipts and expenditures, which were not much more than lists of single entry transactions, had been publicly available. However, Gallatin "consolidated" the entire period of operations from 1789 to 1796 in his statements and thereby developed a single source of information as to comparative amounts of revenues and costs. The detail for each line in Statement A is further explained in Statement X printed elsewhere in the book.

State and Municipal Government

Business historians observe that state aid for the construction of canals and turnpikes during this period are examples of government involvement in public works and commercial activities and that states indirectly subsidized agriculture in much the same way. Before 1830 corporations had difficulty raising large amounts of capital without government assistance. This was in part because of the high degree of risk of some ventures or, in the case of manufacturers, due to the fact that domestic investors sought the assurance of a strong government to protect infant industries.

Overseas investors wanted additional evidence to judge those situations far removed from their own environment and sought a promise of the faith and credit of a governmental agency to further insure the potential of a proposed enterprise. For this reason very few American corporate securities were well known or traded in Europe before 1830, except those related to the United States Bank itself.

Considering the many problems encountered in constructing a new national fiscal system to include the Federal assumption of state debt, the levying of taxes, and the establishment of a central government bank, there were major innovative developments in what

A general View of the Receipts and Expenditures of the United States, from the eftablifhment of the prefent Government in 1789, to the 1ft of January 1796.

RECEIPTS.

Years	1789 to 1791		1792		1793		1794		1795					
	Dols.	Cts.	Dols.	Cts.	Dols.	Cts.	Dols.	Cts.	Dols.	Cts.	Dols.	Cts.	Dols.	Cts.
Balances of Accounts which originated under the late Government, viz.														
Cash in hands of Commiffioner in Holland,	132,475	31									132,475	31		
Other balances paid at different periods,	11,001	11	4,702	82	8,448	58	693	50	5,317	97	30,163	98	162,639	29
Revenues, viz.														
Duties on imports and tonnage,	4,399,472	99	3,579,499	06½	4,344,358	26	4,843,707	25	5,588,961	26	22,755,998	82½		
Internal duties,			72,514	59½	248,654	00	231,447	65	337,255	36	889,871	60½		
Postage of letters,					11,021	51	29,478	49	22,400	00	62,899	00		
Excefs of dividends on bank bank flock, over interest payable on bank flock loan,			8,028	00	38,500	00	55,500	00	66,233	34	168,261	34	23,877,030	77
Incidental, viz.														
Fines and forfeitures for crimes,	311	00	118	00							429	00		
Fees on patents,					660	00	570	00	600	00	1,830	00		
Sales of arms,	8,962	00	4,240	00							13,202	00		
Profits on remittans, &c.	238,661	7	134,210	90	67,701	14½	28,670	91			469,244	02½		
Miftake in treafurer's accounts,				10								10	484,705	12½

Receipts

Loans, viz.

	1789 to 1791 Dols.	Cts.	1792 Dols.	Cts.	1793 Dols.	Cts.	1794 Dols.	Cts.	1795 Dols.	Cts.	Total Dols.	Cts.
Foreign loans in Amsterdam and Antwerp,	5,420,000	00	2,380,000	00	400,000	00	1,200,000	00			9,400,000	00
Domestic do. obtained in anticipation of revenues,	246,608	81	556,595	56	600,000	00	3,200,000	00	2,500,000	00	7,103,204	37
Other domestic loans,			2,000,000	00			200,000	00	800,000	00	3,000,000	
											19,503,204	37
Total of Receipts for each Year,	10,457,492	29	8,739,909	4	5,719,342	49½	9,761,396	89	9,349,438	84	44,027,579	55½

EXPENDITURES.

Years	1789 to 1791 Dols.	Cts.	1792 Dols.	Cts.	1793 Dols.	Cts.	1794 Dols.	Cts.	1795 Dols.	Cts.	Dols.	Cts.
Civil List, *	706,720	29	368,319	86	334,263	29	431,999	47	352,233	36	2,193,536	27
Pensions, Annuities, and Grants, viz.												
Pensions to military invalids,	175,813	88	109,243	15	80,087	81	81,399	24	68,673	22	515,217	30
Annuities and grants,	13,102	96	5,597	72	5,329	51	33,921	87	2,970	20	60,922	26
											576,139	56
Military Establishment, viz.												
Army and militia, magazines, &c.	630,499	65	1,092,920	96	1,130,249	08	2,597,047	93	2,422,612	31	7,941,361	30
Indian department,	127,000	00	13,648	85	14,340	06	13,042	46	81,773	50	123,823	16
Fortifications,							42,049	66	410,562	03	471,971	00
Naval armament,							61,408	97				
											8,537,155	46
Intercourse with Foreign Nations, viz.												
Diplomatic department,	1,733	33	78,766	67	89,500	00	74,995	00	15,005	00	260,000	00
Extraordinary expenses,	13,000	00					56,408	51	897,680	12	967,088	63
											1,227,088	63

Years	1789 to 1791	1792	1793	1794	1795	
	Dols.　Cts.	Dols.　Cts.	Dols.　Cts.	Dols.　Cts.	Dols.　Cts.	Dols.　Cts.
Sundries, viz.						
Light-houfes and navigation, ...	22,591 94	38,976 68	12,061 68	37,496 36	29,861 30	140,987 64
Mint eftablifhment, ...		7,000 00	17,366 49	23,153 12	22,400 00	69,919 61
Contingent and mifcellaneous,	28,343 15	28,856 65	5,527 49	34,174 99	46,825 41	143,727 69
						354,634 94
Charges on Public Debt, viz.						
Intereft on foreign debt, ...	947,862 12	669,359 08	719,252 88	746,564 37	769,523, 38	3,852,561 83
Do.　on domeftic debt, ...	1,140,177 20	2,313,049 82	2,005,199 67	2,383,015 84	2,193,031 16	10,034,473 69
Do.　on debt due to foreign officers, ...		33,657 87				33,657 87
Do.　on domeftic loans, ...	2,598 12		18,753 41	48,694 44	149,333 33	219,379 30
Commiffions and brokerage in Holland, ...	222,800 00	125,000 00	17,948 28	54,062 20	4,480 00	424,290 48
Premiums paid on the old Dutch loan, ...	36,000 00		40,000 00		48,000 00	124,000 00
						14,688,363 17
Principal of the Public Debt, including Arrears of Intereft to 31ft Dec. 1789, viz.						
Payments on the French debt, ...	2,238,527 83	1,777,554 42	1,172,265 09	380,700 31	301,352 66	5,870,400 31
Do.　on the debt due in Holland, ...			400,000 00	400,000 00	400,000 00	1,200,000 00
Do.　on the Spanifh debt, ...			241,681 95			241,681 95
Applied to purchafes of the domeftic debt, ...	699,984 23	318,347 88	408,807 98	172,840 76	18,955 19	1,618,936 4
Payment of two per cent on fix per cent flock, ...					515,972 72	515,972 72
Payments on debt due to foreign officers, ...		30,696 92	39,000 47	44,752 35	11,883 68	126,333 42
Reimburfement of anticipations.	246,608 81		556,595 56	1,100,000 00	1,400,000 00	3,303,204 37
Do.　of other domeftic loans,			200,000 00	200,000 00	200,000 00	600,000 00
Unfunded debts paid in fpecie,	298,479 94	136,877 84	7,120 29	3,855 86	61 59	446,395 52
						13,922,924 33

Subscription to the Bank-Stock of the
 United States, ... 2,000,000 00
Lotfes on remittances, ...

	Dols.	Cts.
	2,000,000	00
	13,779	03½
	43,513,621	39½
	513,958	15½
	44,027,579	55

Total of Expenditures for each Year, . 7,451,843 45   9,147,874 05   7,515,350 99   9,035,862 74½   10,363,190 16
Balance in cafh on 1ft January, 1796,

13,779 03½

Balances of accounts which originated under the late

	Dols.	Cts.
Government, as per Receipts, ...	162,639	29
Loans effected during the above period, ...	19,503,204	37
	19,665,843	66

	Dols.	Cts.
Principal of Public Debt paid during the above period	13,922,924	33
Subfcription to the Bank Stock of the United States, ...	2,000,000	00
Balance in cafh on 1ft January, 1796, ...	513,958	15
Excefs of Expenditures beyond the Revenues received, ...	3,228,961	18
	19,665,843	66

Figure 2-1

Schedule A, U.S. Government Receipts and Disbursements, 1789–1793.

* Compensation for: President 85,827.83; Vice-President 14,000; Judiciary 79,491.48; Legislature 364,559.08; Public Offices (e.g. Treasury; State; War; others) 146,611.33; Government of Territories 16,230.57; Total: 706,720.29. See Schedule X, Gallatin for detail.

Source: From Gallatin's *Sketch of the Finances of the United States*, published in 1796. Typeset in the original archaic style.

would now be recognized as a pioneer era of national (macro) accounting.

The problems of financial record keeping at the local level were probably less complicated, since incorporated municipalities were not common or especially large. At the time of the Revolution only about fifteen cities had been chartered, ranging from hamlets to urban centers such as New York and Philadelphia. Since states tended to maintain control over a city's fiscal destiny, the system of financial accountability responded to whatever system prevailed in state government, which had evolved from either the monarch–colonial responsibility system or the town meeting–peer accountability system.

Accounting in a New Nation

During the period of the Revolution and the establishment of the new Republic, American lifestyles changed in response to the politics and economics of self-interest and modern capitalism found in the writings of Adam Smith. An 1819 Supreme Court decision heralded the advent of the corporate era in American enterprise when Chief Justice Marshall's *Dartmouth College* opinion provided a legal foundation for modern corporate capitalism, recognizing the distinct quasi-personal legal attributes of the corporate form.

Individualism and opportunity were accented during these years by a surge of expanded trade, commerce and manufacture. Industrial technology made an impact in the Northeast in the form of labor saving mechanically powered devices. A national economy came a step closer to realization, although the influence of state banks and regional capital markets was not to be replaced for several years.

The initial development of a transport network is noted from the fact that 55 turnpike companies were chartered in Pennsylvania between 1793 and 1812, along with 57 in New York and 105 in Massachusetts. Canal construction, from South Carolina through Maryland and Virginia and up through New York required nearly $3,000,000 in capital by 1807. That amount it should be remembered would be many times greater in terms of today's prices (Callender 1902).

The economy and its populace were still rural in form and agrarian in substance. The industrialization of the economy and urban concentration were yet to be experienced. To have attained a formal education was the exception reserved for the well-to-do. Account keeping was performed customarily in the merchant's counting house, where it was learned as an essential management skill—and where it would continue to be relied upon in ever increasing subtlety as the system was streamlined for purposes of managerial use.

As the need for financial data began to expand, in response to the growing commerce of the new era, instruction in accounting became a separate activity and American teachers, often using the title of "professor," offered public lectures and courses to those seeking a future in the business world.

There was marked competition among American authors to provide "the" complete system that was most fitted to the commerce of the United States and most useful to management. In the main, instruction was geared to accounting in a rote form. Abstract discussion of value, in the economic sense, was not emphasized, since it was not deemed the province of the bookkeeper to be concerned with the *nature* of value, only the *quantity* of value, be it the cash or commodity at hand. The merchant or proprietary party was the individual who was believed to be sufficiently skilled in the notions of the values of his trade and competent in the skill of numbers produced by his account books to fuse their meanings into successful business decisions.

The era of the corporation was destined to change much of this. The previous proprietor's managerial function would soon have to be discharged at a higher level: the engine of corporate capitalism would begin to generate demand for expert financial and accounting advice as owners and managers governed the multiple activities of these enterprises.

The close of this era marked the end of the age of colonial merchant accounts and the dawn of the era of corporate accounting. No scene could be more fitting to depict this transition than what occurred in 1826, when Charles Carroll who, at 92, was the only surviving signer of the Declaration of Independence, came to lay the cornerstone of the first station house of the Baltimore and Ohio Railroad, a line he had helped to finance. As the nation passed out of the hands of Carroll and the revolutionary Founding Fathers, it clearly passed into the era of the railroad, a corporate venture that would spawn many supporting industries and develop the role of the capital markets to the extent that a professional class of accountants would emerge to service the needs of business, investors and society.

NOTES

1. For a light hearted, but thorough "investigation" into the "padding" of expenses by Washington, read *George Washington's Expense Account*, by Marvin Kitman, 1970 (Simon & Schuster), or consult the review which appears in *Management Accounting*, December 1970: 60.

2. Statements on an annual basis would have been rare before 1752, for it was not until then that an Act of Parliament promulgated that the first day of January would be considered the beginning of the year for all purposes.

3. Bennett's twelfth edition appeared in 1829, but the illustrations of his later editions remained largely unchanged. Note that in the balance chart illustration in this chapter, the accounts are dated 1817. Forty-one editions of his work are known to have been printed through 1862.

4. Workman's citizenship is not known, and thus the assertion that he was the first American author is tenuous. Textbooks by writers alleged to be British, which were printed in American cities before 1776, are also being investigated to determine whether or not they were in fact of American authorship but disguised with pen names to appeal to a market that favored British authorship and expertise. Evidence is now being gathered that will likely support the premise that accounting texts were printed in the colonies several decades before those now being cited.

5. The rare book room at the Washington Square School of Business of New York University contains several bound volumes of very early railroad reports. The existence of these reports suggests that some distribution, formal or informal, of basic financial information was taking place before 1850.

6. The debate over identifying the era of the origins of professional public practice in America is not likely to be resolved by the materials provided in this work. However, it seems warranted to propose as unfounded the position previously held by James Anyon and Richard Brown that it was not until 1880 that America witnessed the birth of a public accounting profession. Neither Anyon nor Brown were native Americans, the former having come to the United States from England in 1886 and the latter having written in Edinburgh.

7. Accountants of the early nineteenth century learned to "reduce Federal money to Old Lawful" and "Old Lawful to Federal Money." Daniel Adams' book, *Scholars' Arithmetic or the Federal Accountant*, which supplied countless examples of these conversions, was widely used throughout the first three decades of the 1800s.

3 FROM FIELDS TO FACTORIES: THE BEGINNING OF AN INDUSTRIAL AGE

It is true that the man who is experienced in the mechanical operation of an art may be more generally useful at any particular moment than one who is merely acquainted with its scientific principles but this facility of manipulation does not prove the superiority of an art over science; because the mere practician must have been indebted for his power to exercise the act to rules deduced by others from the truths of the science. . . .
[B. F. Foster,
Double Entry Elucidated, 1849.]

The Political Economics of Antebellum America

From the start of the second quarter of the nineteenth century through the period bounded by the events giving rise to the start and end of the Civil War, the people of America experienced the flush of expansion, technological change, massive immigration and political hostility.

A blaze of democratic nationalism, kindled during the era of Andrew Jackson's popular prominence, consolidated the voting strength of the small farmers of the new West and the laboring classes in the growing urban centers of the East. The precious belief in an idyllic Republic, fostered by Jefferson—a land to be kept for the husbandman and kept from industrialism—was not to be.

Alexander Hamilton had cast the political philosophy of our nation's new industrialism during the turbulent period that followed the War of Independence. By tying the Bank of the United States through offerings of debt to the business and the propertied class, he created a "national debt" from which the political wisdom of business and wealth was afforded a permanent basis of influence. Talleyrand, the brilliant yet cynical European statesman and cleric, was a friend of Hamilton, having spent several years in America. He is reported to have said, "I consider Napoleon, Pitt and Hamilton as the three greatest men of our age, and if I had to choose between the three, I would unhesitatingly give the first place to Hamilton" (Fuller 1977).

The cornerstone of Federalist political philosophy required that the propertyless masses be kept from obtaining countervailing power through popular suffrage. With property and political power joined, extending the vote to those without property could damage that linkage, a relationship that was predicated on developing an alliance of business and government into the industrial America envisioned in Hamilton's celebrated *Report on Manufactures*.

Although political scientists may argue about the particulars of Federalist and neo-Federalist policies, in fact the alliance of property and politics at this stage of the economy's formation was essential in order to gain exposure from the press, the pulpit and the courts. Such exposure was necessary for this version of the "American system" which acknowledged, protected and rewarded those who were successful in accumulating property. Such a socio-economic philosophy would underwrite the aspiration of ambitious young Americans—both native born and immigrants—as they sought to transform an agrarian land rich with industrial resources into a cornucopia of the goods produced by men and machines in urban factories. For in the 1830s it was not clear that the technology, capital and talented labor required to achieve such a marked transition from Jefferson's landowner's state was to be found.

The political competition and separation between the voting but unpropertied segment of the population and those who had money power and controlled the physical means of production, initially and ultimately provides an explanation of the need for financial accounting and reports. This need is made more obvious when voting power, resource control and resource ownership themselves are separated in a society.

Personal traits and the ideals of thrift and hard work, noted as the

Puritan work ethic, became blended with the curious American propensity for mechanical tinkering (Yankee ingenuity) and the pursuit of property wealth. This was to become the "American way" and it was to be achieved through an industrial system.

There were less than 20 million Americans in 1830, but by 1865 that number would grow to approach 30 million including over 1.5 million immigrants from the United Kingdom alone who represented nearly one third of the total immigration for the period 1840–1860. As settlers pushed into Ohio, Missouri and the Dakotas, more and more urban centers formed as transmission points for goods once imported but now being manufactured along the sea coast city complex of the North and East.

Only the South persisted in a landed gentry lifestyle, reflecting a commitment to the way of life Jefferson had foreseen. The economic power of agriculture however was linked to its cotton crop, and for the most part to foreign markets. In the final test, the power of industrialism and corporate manufactures would subdue the plantation agrarian system, end the use of blacks as slaves, and generate an even more interdependent life style.

During the decades before the resolution of these social philosophies and throughout the Civil War, American industrialism was becoming centered on the economics of railroad development. Traditional commerce remained dependent upon sea trade, but as the new West was settled, internal East-West trade became significant. The political policies of Jackson, who opposed the rechartering of the U.S. Bank and identified himself with the small farmer and urban worker, awakened the hopes for popular suffrage, and kindled the ambition of those who saw opportunity in the farm lands of the new West.

More than any other sole phenomenon, the "iron horse" presaged the birth of American industrialism. The railroads' capability to provide relatively cheap and rapid transport across a seemingly vast land, to stitch together commerce by linking suppliers and users of commodities at places where waterways were unknown and other transport was impractical, was a technological and economic feat of unprecedented importance. The corporate form of business served as the essential vehicle for railroad capital formation. It established a demand for legions of other corporate entities and a multitude of supporting industries and skills including coal mining, steel milling, and civil engineering, such that huge sums of capital would be needed to finance each new venture. Capital markets, money men, and accounting information were to become important in the planning and production of the hard goods and services that railroading would bring forth.

In the midst of this blooming of the iron flower of the railroad came occasional panics in the capital market, for not until the 1840s, with the magic of electrical telegraphy, was it possible to provide immediate communication among the financial centers of the eastern seaboard—Baltimore, Philadelphia, New York, and Boston.

One should not be too quick to conclude, however, that the railroad, although a central economic agent of this period, was the sole significant industrial activity. The economy of the antebellum era was also blessed with at least one other essential industrial technology, the production of textiles in New England. The clipper ship also added an important ocean transportation element, extending the arm of trade and adding the factor of speed by which it could be conducted. Speed in transport and communication, in any form of action for that matter, became a symbol of the new American way.

The masses of new immigrants, combined with corporate railroads and textile producers supplying a country spreading westward, and a growing popular belief that each could fulfill a personal goal in an American system that associated acquiring property with success provide the political and economic setting for this chapter of *A History of Accounting in America.*

Profile of the Capital Markets

By 1840 dozens of railroad securities were being traded in the New York stock market. Although the center of international finance remained in London, the New York Stock Exchange had been located permanently by 1863, denoting the establishment of a logistical pattern and a headquarters for American capital market activity.

The capital requirements of the railroad versus the textile corporation were different and reflected changing attitudes regarding the manner of financing various forms of enterprise. Textile capitalism was regional—centered in the financial district of Boston and throughout the relatively close environs of New England. It relayed capital among families of established generations of New Englanders, bound in a common trust based on regional and personal acquaintance. The closely held, family ties of textile capitalism sharply contrasted with the sprawling and ever westward moving demand of railroad capitalism, which was linked with the coal, steel and lumber suppliers across their routes and involved shippers and passengers, whose patronage would ultimately decide the outcome of their venture.

The origin of the financial reporting requirements of this era is based upon the assumption that creditors as well as investors and institutional sources of capital wanted to know financial information relating to their holdings. Furthermore, when equity and debt holders were both foreign (chiefly British) as well as domestic parties, the form and content of disclosure tended to respond to the needs and expectations of those parties. The British investor, having experienced the disclosures of the Companies Acts, would expect comparable disclosures and, in the absence of some, would perhaps exercise caution in investment. Widespread domestic ownership interest also spurred intrastate regulation of railway companies creating, as never before, a need for internal auditing, annual reporting and capital accounting.

For a multiplicity of reasons railroading also created a demand for new business and management skills, including the services of an emerging class of accountants and auditors. As the joint-stock railroad company became an accepted institution for economic progress, the government poured 150 million acres of public domain into its pathway to augment development. Telegraphy and railroads provided a "one-two" communication-transportation punch that rocked the agrarian base of the nation and finally tumbled it firmly into the arms of merchants and manufacturers who now had access to a national market being swelled by immigration and led westward by the forty-niners in their quest for gold.

The financing of railroads required not only federal grants of land and investor equity but also loans and bank credit. Railroad bonds were sold by the millions, often without any promise that financial accountabilities would be provided. The capital markets, such as they were, whipped themselves in a railroading frenzy which was only outdone by state legislatures and local politicians who lent their influence in exchange for a part of the shareholdings. Lobbyists dispensed railroad securities to smooth the way over judges, legislators, mayors, governors, aldermen, or whoever may have represented opposition (Jenks 1944). Popular speculation in and uncontrolled distribution of these securities, together with the failure of many of these poorly conceived rail ventures, ultimately cast a pall over the markets causing a panic in 1857 which, in the absence of a United States bank, was unprecedented in severity. New York banks had acted to provide reserves in the absence of the national bank, but as the western inflow dried up and western depositors began to call their reserves, New York speculators found that their money and margins had gone, and they were forced to liquidate securities to repay called loans. Stocks were sold at any price. In a week thirteen leading issues dropped 40 percent; the best bonds were down 10 percent. In six weeks four major railroads had failed and the market was in collapse, as were the banks, for they had depended upon rail securities for their own collateral.

Southern agriculture and the cotton crop survived the disaster; in fact they had provided the economic stability to overcome the crisis. Yet even after the market recovered, suspicion as to the motives and strategies of northern industrialists remained among southern capitalists. Southerners felt unrequited in terms of their dwindling political influence, if not scorned because of the slavery issue which was linked to the plantation system. Popular suffrage was carrying the political power away from the South to the urban Northeast. The wealth of cotton was being dissipated in terms of control over the economic destiny of the country. The seeds of suspicion and dissension were being sown (Schmidt 1939).

Antebellum Educators, Writers, and Publications

Some writers would be satisfied with assigning this period of accounting the title "Accounting in the Railroad Age" and in that context, preparing an explanation of accounting. Such as it is this title would not consider accounting as a discipline itself. Therefore it is more to the point to discuss the intrinsic elements of accounting during this period, namely, the methods of instruction, the state of theory and the types of practice, with railroad accounting as a consideration among the latter.

Schools and Texts

In the East teachers and writers on the subject of accounts already had been active for several years. Among the most notable were John Caldwell Colt, brother of Samuel Colt, namesake of the Colt revolver; Thomas Jones of New York, an important author and teacher; Benjamin Franklin Foster of New York, and later London, a colorful and controversial competitor and imitator of Jones; George Comer of Boston; S. S. Packard of New York and E. K. Losier of Baltimore.[1]

By the 1840s Colt, Jones, and Foster had brought forth several editions of their works on double entry as part of the wave of texts being used by the masses of students enrolled in business and commercial colleges.

The decade of the 1850s represents an important initial point of commercial education in the "new West": on May 9, 1851, E. G. Folsom, professor of the science of accounts, incorporated his Mercantile College to be opened in Cleveland. Among Folsom's first students were H. B. Bryant and H. D. Stratton who later acquired the Folsom College and developed an international chain of more than fifty commercial colleges, leading the growth movement in business education from 1853 to 1866 (Corfias 1973).

Practical Models

Correspondence among the newly developed community of commercially trained accountants was beginning to surface in the form of articles and reviews appearing in business magazines. *Hunt's Merchants Magazine and Commercial Review,* founded in 1839, contained many commentaries and problems related to bookkeeping and accounts. An 1840 issue included the following:

THE POETRY OF BOOKKEEPING

Attentive be, and I'll impart
What constitutes the accountant's art.
This rule is clear: what I receive
I debtor make to what I give.
I debit Stock with all my debts,
And credit it for my effects.
The goods I buy I debtor make
To him from whom those goods I take;
Unless in ready cash I pay,
Then credit what I paid away.
For what I lose or make, 'tis plain,
I debit Loss and credit Gain.
The debtor's place is my left hand,
Creditor on my right must stand,
If to these axioms you'll attend,
Bookkeeping you'll soon comprehend,
And double-entry you will find
Elucidated to your mind.

An early problem printed in *Hunt's* was submitted by Thomas Jones and represented an attempt to test the skill level of accounting readers. *Hunt's* also contained reviews of new accounting texts. In an 1839 number, for example, a detailed, laudatory review of the fourth edition of J. C. Colt's *The Science of Double-Entry Bookkeeping*. . . . , was included, a portion of which stated:

> In a commercial community like ours, the scientific mode of keeping accounts is a study of surpassing interest. For many years it has attracted attention commensurate with its importance. At the present moment, when our mercantile concernments are so widely extended, and when consequently the qualifications for success must so far exceed those formerly demanded, the mysteries of Bookkeeping have excited such increased notice, that the press swarms with commentators.

This anonymous review of Colt's book notes that the work provided a number of "practical models" for keeping books which had never been given by any writer before Colt.

Hunt's was also a forum for the early views of nineteenth century American accounting theorists. Thomas Jones, for example, who is acknowledged by Henry Rand Hatfield and others as having the distinction of being perhaps the first American to clearly distinguish between real and nominal accounts, wrote a series of articles in *Hunt's* on bookkeeping education, instructing on the general principles of the discipline that was becoming fundamental to the emerging industrial style of life. Jones pointed out:

> The object is not to make every man a bookkeeper, but to make him competent to understand whatever accounts may come under his notice, and to detect and expose erroneous results, however ingeniously they may have been drawn (Jones 1842).

Another instructive episode relating to the state of practice is reflected in the outcome to a challenge problem prepared by J. W. Wright for the July 1844 issue of *Hunt's*. The problem involved a partnership dissolution and the remaining partner's inability to close the books. In September 1844, Wright wrote the editor stating:

> Sir—the receipt of forty-three communications, ineffectually attempting to solve my "Question for Accountants," in your last number, has placed me in possession of the absolute existence of facts, with which I have long since been but partially impressed, namely, that the generality of our public teachers of bookkeeping, and, as a legitimate consequence, our private accountants, are lamentably deficient in a thorough knowledge of the theoretical laws and practical adjustments of complex

accounts, . . . How strange that no two of your correspondents agree, either in details or aggregate results!

The public instruction of accounting and the commercial college movement criticized by J. W. Wright received a major impetus from the efforts of Bryant and Stratton, the young men who studied under Folsom in Cleveland. Through their chain of schools, numbering close to fifty by 1865, and texts they supplied the mechanism for a uniform manner of instructing the "uneducated" about accounting.

The task of writing the premier text for the chain was undertaken by Silas S. Packard, a proprietor of one of the franchise schools. Packard lived to become acknowledged and celebrated as one of the most influential business educators of the nineteenth century. His *Counting-House Bookkeeping* became a standard work abroad as well as in America. It was an ambitious and highly practical undertaking, not unlike the intermediate textbook of our contemporary programs, but of course, designed to function in the discipline of a nineteenth-century environment. Packard's *Counting-House* covered a breadth of topics, describing the principal books of account and discussing dividend policy for joint stock companies within the 350-page content. There was also material related to "specialized" accounts including farms, banks, commission houses as well as proprietor, partnership and agency accounts.

Thomas Jones and Benjamin Franklin Foster

The teaching and writing careers of Thomas Jones and Benjamin Franklin Foster coincide over nearly four decades beginning in the 1830s. Foster was at one time a teacher in a New York commercial school of which Jones was the director. Historians note that Jones is considered to be the father of the first modern American accounting text, because he sought to abandon the "rote and rule" approach to education, insisting that financial statements, rather than ledger balances, were the purpose of the account-keeping process.[2]

Jones' attention to statements is evident in the examples shown below in his 1859 work, *Bookkeeping and Accountantship*.[3]

Jones' system of focusing on the financial statements plus his emphasis on the "merchant's position" affords him the unique position of being a leading, if not the first, expositor of proprietary accounting in the first half of the nineteenth century.

Benjamin Franklin Foster, who can be credited with "borrowing" the best of Jones' ideas and marketing them to the far corners of the

PART I.

SECTION I.

EXEMPLIFICATION.

BOOK-KEEPING implies a systematic arrangement of mercantile transactions, the purpose of which is to afford at all times ready access to the Resources and Liabilities of the party whose operations are recorded, thus:

RESOURCES.		LIABILITIES.		
Cash	5,850	*Bills Payable*, outstanding		3,000
Bills Receivab'e	3,800	*I owe James Blackwell*		1,000
George Irving owes	1,000	Total *Resources*,	11,150	
Ira Perego "	500	" *Liabilities*,	4,000	
		My present worth is		7,150
	$11,150			$11,150

Each particular item of the above forms the subject of an "*account*" (see definitions), thus there is one account of Cash, another account of Bills Receivable, another of Bills Payable, another for James Blackwell; so that the statement of Resources and Liabilities can at any time be drawn up by reference to the book of accounts called the Ledger, and the whole art of Book-keeping is merged in the peculiar arrangement of this book.

There are but two methods of Book-keeping in use, the one called Single, and the other Double Entry.

Single Entry affords only the above statement; but when accounts have been arranged by Double Entry, they enable us, by additional accounts, to draw up another statement, viz. of the Profits and Losses resulting from the same operations, for example :—

LOSSES.			PROFITS.	
On Railroad Stock		850	*On Merchandise*	1,950
Business Expenses		579	" *Bank Stock*	500
Total Gain	2,579		" *Exchange*	129
Total Loss	1,429			
Net Profit		1,150		
		$2,579		$2,579

Capital at commencement	6,000
Net Profit	1,150
Present worth . . .	$7,150

Figure 3–1

Initial text page from nineteenth-century bookkeeping text by Thomas Jones of New York.

50

North Atlantic community, was a prolific writer, and an accounting historian of sorts. Although he "confessed" to having copied the principal feature of his own system from Jones (in a letter to the latter dated 1 August 1838 and published in the back page of Jones' 1859 edition of *Bookkeeping & Accountantship*), Foster probably carried the Jones technique to more people than would have otherwise been done and thereby advanced the state of the art, albeit with dubious credit to his own originality.

Foster did, however, make a timely contribution in his 1852 volume entitled *The Origin and Progress of Bookkeeping*. As are most inveterate accounting writers, Foster was a bibliophile, and his pride in having amassed an impressive collection of early works probably caused him to write this slim 54-page work which was in the form of an annotated bibliography and a listing of the books in his personal collection plus several he had not collected but had reviewed. The work is of value and interest because it provides an important historical reference point, listing over thirty texts written in the first half of the 19th century by American authors, and providing a total list of 156 books.[4]

J. C. Colt's text on the science of double entry, the subject of a *Hunt's* book review mentioned above, is also related to the melodrama and tragedy that befell Colt when a disagreement arose relative to a later work on the subject. The story warrants retelling.

John Caldwell Colt was born in Connecticut in 1810, the oldest son of eight children. He left home at seventeen, having had to abandon his education and aspiration for military school. He roamed about the country holding various positions. By 1834, at age twenty-four, he had drifted South first to New Orleans and then seeking cooler weather to Louisville, teaching the craft of bookkeeping in order to defray expenses. He wrote his first text which was ultimately published through eight editions in three years. Moving back East to New York in 1839, Colt sought to sell (along the seaboard) the copies of another ill-starred publication venture. It was during this period that his work, *The Science of Double Entry Book-keeping* . . . appeared. The fourth edition, published by the New York firm of William Jackson, Robinson & Franklin, was the subject of the review in *Hunt's*.

Colt's new authorship success notwithstanding, he found, by the summer of 1841, that there would be need for a new version of his materials. A printer, Samuel Adams, and Colt were, however, having a disagreement about failure of the printer to deliver on schedule and the fees to be paid for printing.

Adams called at Colt's office in midafternoon Friday, September 17, 1841, apparently to settle the dispute. He was not seen alive afterward. Howard Ross relates the tale as follows:

The disagreements between the two men resulted in a bitter argument, blows were struck and a violent struggle ensued. Colt stated that he was being choked when he grabbed a hatchet from the table and struck Adams twice on the head. Adams fell to the floor and died immediately. Colt washed up the blood that was spattered about and remained in the office until evening, trying to decide what to do, then he went out and walked the streets and made one attempt to communicate with his brother Samuel. Finally, he resolved to conceal the killing and returned to his office. His plan was to force the body into the large packing box and dispatch it by ship, via New Orleans, to an address in St. Louis. Part of this plan was carried out that evening, then he went home very late and returned to the office early the next morning. He then accompanied a drayman to the steamer Kalamazoo, saw the box placed in the hold, and obtained a bill of lading which he promptly destroyed.

THE ARREST OF COLT

A public notice, reporting Adams' disappearance, was published on Tuesday the twenty-first, and the authorities began an investigation. Adams' employees told of his intention of going to Colt's office, suspicious noises in Colt's office were reported by other tenants, and the janitor told of the box being taken down the stairs on the following morning. On the strength of these and other affidavits, the Mayor, Robert H. Morris and other officials went to Colt's office on September 24th and arrested him. He was charged with suspicion of murder and confined in the City Prison known as The Egyptian Tombs or simply The Tombs. On the following day the box with Adams' body was located in the ship which was still in the harbor. (Reprinted from *Dividend*, the magazine of the Graduate School of Business Administration, University of Michigan)

The result of the murder of Adams was not only a sensational trial but a touch of scandal as well, for shortly after Colt's incarceration, a son was born to Colt and Caroline Henshaw, a young woman he had met in Philadelphia, and who had moved to New York to live with Colt. Marriage was considered, but Colt's lawyers suggested delay, for her appearance as a defense witness was not deemed advisable if she were his wife. Colt was found guilty of willful murder by the jury even though there was no evidence of premeditation and the Judge had instructed the jury on that point, namely, that premeditation had not been shown in the evidence.

On the day scheduled for his execution Colt and Caroline Henshaw were married in the presence of friends and his brother Samuel. Caroline left early and later was followed by the others, his brother Samuel being the last to leave.

Shortly before four o'clock the sheriff's party arrived to conduct Colt to the gallows. They found him dead, having been stabbed in the heart, an apparent self-inflicted act. No one was able to say how he had obtained the knife (Ross 1974). This somewhat chilling mystery elicited widespread news coverage in papers and even resulted in a book about Colt's life, *Authentic Life of John C. Colt* (S. N. Dickinson 1842).

One can speculate if it is important that a well known American accounting writer of the first half of the nineteenth century earned that distinction not solely because of his contributions to accounting but because he was convicted of murdering his publisher and then himself met a mysterious death!

Steamboats and Stagecoaches

Americans have seemed, at least for the last century or so, to be fascinated with the means of transport and the speed with which distance, any distance, can be covered. Perhaps because such a vast continent lay before them, it was not unusual to have such a preoccupation with distance and speed. But for whatever reason transportation intrigues Americans, in the nineteenth century, as today, transportation businesses required a specialized accounting process.

The steamboat was the premier means of transport for Americans until it was eclipsed by the flexible and speedy service of the railroad. One early publication of note, *The Western Steamboat Accountant*, written by Peter Duff, appeared in 1846. The book included ". . . a new and complete system of bookkeeping; arranged and practically adapted for the use of steamboats navigating the great western rivers and lakes, exemplified in one set of books kept by double entry . . . designed for the use of schools, bookkeepers, steamboat masters and owners." An ambitious undertaking it would seem! This edition, of 63 pages, was followed by another written by Duff of approximately the same dimensions under the title "*The Steamboat Accountant . . .*" Duff, perhaps sensing the changing transportation environment, also wrote other books, giving particular attention to railroads. These appeared until near the end of the century.

Of even more interest, and much more revealing, were the facts disclosed in the information about the 1864 operations of Wells Fargo, the famous western stagecoach and express company. The frequent mention of holdups and recovered loot from bandits, along with rewards and arrests, paint a vivid picture of the "Old West" by means of a peculiar "brush," the company's 1864 income statement.

Wells Fargo—1864 Income Statement

The profit and loss statement for 1864 . . . shows considerable attention to robberies. Apparently the bookkeepers could find no account in which they could enter the cost of robberies.

Other Credits

Overland Mail Co., rent and commission		$ 900.00
Special contract, Virginia City		1,777.77
Revenue taxes		12,000.00
Washoe robbery, bullion recovered		3,430.79
Claim against insurance company for genl. avge. St. Oregon remitted to Treasurer for credit of California		4,042.82
Express earnings for year		188,255.10
Total Credits		$210,406.48

Charges

Robbery, express box. A. Austin		$ 1,522.34
Genl. Avge. Str. Oregon [?]		4,042.82
Reward for arrest and conviction of Fiddletown robbers		1,000.00
Coulterville robbery:		
Willowman Bros. Company	$ 306.00	
Sullivan & Cashman	1,100.00	
D. N. Field	248.00	
Expenses—July	44.00	
Reward to sheriff	500.00	
Expenses—August	565.00	
Expenses—September	175.00	2,938.00
Washoe Road robbery:		
Donahoe & Ralston Co.	534.85	
Levy & Company	700.00	
J. C. Dagley	50.00	

No. Kee & Company	236.00	
H. Kohn & Company	500.00	
F. Garasche	2,240.00	
Reward for post [age?]		
recovered	2,179.30	
D. B. Sullivan	70.00	
Owens M. Co.	140.00	
Rewards—July	1,790.73	
Expenses—August	702.50	
Reward for robbers killed		
at San Jose	1,500.00	
Sheriff, expenses	263.08	
I. C. Goods—Lawyer	645.00	
Attorneys in cash Washoe	1,175.00	$ 12,726.46
Old packages sold for charges		$ 783.35
Silver Bar lost, Washoe stage		1,944.08
Robbery, Aurora express		645.00
Hanford arrest—escaped convict		105.00
Total Charges		$ 25,707.05
Balance Profit and Loss Account		$184,699.43

One thing seems obvious from this statement: Wells, Fargo & Company did not hesitate to spend money to track down robbers or to recover stolen treasure. Also, it is interesting to note that, with silver at roughly $1 an ounce, that particular bar of silver weighed about 125 pounds. One wonders what happened. It should be hard to lose a 125-pound bar of silver.

Source: Taken from *Wells Fargo* by Noel M. Loomis. Copyright © 1968 by Noel M. Loomis. Used by permission of Crown Publishers, Inc.

Figure 3–2

Railroad Accounts and Reports

Early railroad accounts such as the Utica & Schenectady report of 1841 (Figure 3-3), were cash basis summaries with an overtone of statistical operating information. Previous historical research in the matter of early railroad reports suggests that, in part because of this emphasis on reporting and analyzing cash from operations, eventually the "funds" statement or the statement of balance sheet changes developed (Rosen 1969).

By 1842 the Utica's report (Illustration 3-4) is reflective of the "where got—where gone" cash analysis format (Boockholdt 1977).

The 1842 report covered the entire period of the company's operation, and follows an arrangement believed to be fairly standard for the next several decades.

Utica and Schenectady Railroad
Report of the Treasurer (1841)

THE CAPITAL OF THE COMPANY IS 20,000 SHARES		$2,000,000
THE TOTAL COST OF THE ROAD, FROM ITS COMMENCEMENT		
TO THE 1ST JAN. 1841, INCLUDING THE RIGHT OF WAY,		
$322,470, AND THE PURCHASE OF THE MOHAWK TURN-		
PIKE, $62,500, WAS		1,901,785
THE CALLS ON STOCKHOLDERS HAVE BEEN	$1,500,000	
DITTO, DERIVED FROM DIVIDENDS	300,000	
		1,800,000
THE AMOUNT RECEIVED FROM PASSENGERS, THE MAIL		
AND ALL SOURCES IN 4 YEARS AND 5 MONTHS, FROM		
COMMENCEMENT OF ROAD TO 1ST JAN., 1841		1,618,517
THE TOTAL EXPENSES DURING THE SAME PERIOD		552,598
NETT EARNINGS, 71 PER CENT ON 4½ YEARS		1,065,918
THE DIVIDENDS DECLARED TO 1ST JAN. 1841,		
BEING EQUAL TO 13½ PER CENT PER ANNUM		
ON THE CAPITAL OF $1,500,000, DURING		
4½ YEARS		917,000
THE TOTAL COST PER MILE OF THE 78 MILES		
INCLUDING MOTIVE POWER, RIGHT OF WAY AND		
TURNPIKE, IS	$23,580	
OFF RIGHT OF WAY AND TURNPIKE	4,934	
		18,446

Source: *Hunt's Merchants Magazine,* May 1841.

Figure 3–3

Another example of the general receipts and expenditures format, as commonly found before the middle of the century, is supplied in the 1846 report of the South Carolina Railroad. This report, as the others, was published in a financial periodical, and employs a single receipts and expenses aggregate format for each semiannual period of operations.

Evidence of the development of accrual accounting is also found in the accompanying property statement for the South Carolina Railroad. Note the final item in the credit portion of the statement before the totals.

Utica and Schenectady Railroad
Report of the Treasurer (1842)

AMOUNT RECEIVED FOR	INSTALLMENTS ON STOCK	$1,800,000.00
''	TRANSPORTATION OF PASSENGERS	1,864,691.53
''	'' U. S. MAIL	83,047.10
''	TOLLS OF MOHAWK TURNPIKE	22,834.78
''	INTEREST ON MONEY DEPOSITED	10,226.87
''	FROM MISCELLANEOUS SOURCES	49,134.71

TOTAL RECEIPTS FROM ALL SOURCES TO DEC. 31, 1841 $3,829,934.99

DEDUCT EXPENDITURES FOR ALL ACCOUNTS UP TO DEC. 31, 1841, VIZ:

ON CONSTRUCTION ACCOUNT	$1,968,022.17
ON TRANSPORTATION ACCOUNT	709,230.12
ON DIVIDEND ACCOUNT	1,017,000.00
TOTAL EXPENDITURES	3,694,252.29

BALANCE, BEING EXCESS OF RECEIPTS OVER
EXPENDITURES UP TO DEC. 31, 1841 $ 135,682.70

Source: *Hunt's Merchants Magazine,* November 1843.

Figure 3-4

South Carolina Railroad
General Statement of Receipts and Expenditures
For the Year 1846

GROSS RECEIPTS FROM ALL SOURCES IN FIRST HALF YEAR	$251,741.36
ORDINARY CURRENT EXPENSES FOR SAME TIME	193,592.21
NETT PROFITS FOR THE FIRST HALF YEAR	$ 58,149.15
GROSS RECEIPTS FROM ALL SOURCES SECOND HALF YEAR	$337,340.16
ORDINARY CURRENT EXPENSES FOR SAME TIME	224,578.96
NETT PROFITS FOR SECOND HALF YEAR	112,761.20
NETT PROFITS FOR THE YEAR 1846	$170,910.35

Source: *Hunt's Merchants Magazine,* January 1848.

Figure 3-5

South Carolina Railroad
Property Statement, December 31, 1846

DR.	
TO STOCK—FOR $35 PER SHARE ON 34,800 SHARES	$2,610,000.00
" INSTALLMENTS FORFEITED	312,417.65
TO SURPLUS INCOME	40,708.52
TO BALANCE OF INDEBTEDNESS	2,765,090.74
TOTAL	$5,728,216.91

CR.		
BY PURCHASE OF CHARLESTON AND HAMBURG RAILROAD,		
EMBRACING ROAD, MACHINERY, & C.	$2,714,377.50	
BY PURCHASE OF LAND ATTACHED THERETO	59,741.30	
'' NEGROES	11,963.19	
		$2,736,081.99
BY CONSTRUCTION OF COLUMBIA BRANCH		2,863,654.49
BY LANDS PURCHASED SINCE JAN, 1844	5,083.83	
BY LESS TO CREDIT AIKEN LANDS	35.35	
		5,048.48
BY NEGROES PURCHASED SINCE JAN, 1844		800.00
BY SUSPENSE ACCOUNT		8,490.00
BY RAIL IRON PURCHASED		15,773.97
BY IMPROVEMENT OF DEPOTS		8,680.29
" PROPERTY		30,437.49
BY SHARES IN THE RAILROAD		40.00
BY AMOUNT DUE ON PAY-ROLLS AND BILLS NOT CHARGED,		
BUT FORMING PART OF BALANCE OF INDEBTEDNESS		9,210.60
TOTAL		$5,728,216.91

Source: *Hunt's Merchants Magazine,* January 1848.

Figure 3-6

An Audit Role and Early Annual Reports

The geographic dispersion of railroad operations made it desirable to have traveling auditors conduct purely financial audits for the principal purpose of verification of the mathematical accuracy of accounts at branch locations. Methods of basic auditing included recalculation, comparison with standard railroad rate cards, ticking and checking of totals and cross totals. During the antebellum years railroads performed many novel accounting tasks within the financial framework of the modern industrial corporate form of business (Boockholdt 1977). They dealt with the problems of expensive, widely dispersed rolling stock, "round house" plant and maintenance costs, stock subscriptions, capital costs during construction, obsolescence from technology and problems of long-term construction contracts. In their attempts to solve the complexities of these issues, accountants (or consulting accountants, as the more successful practitioners chose to call themselves) attained status as important advisors and experts on reports.

Cash basis reporting was commonplace in these early corporate systems as evidenced in the prominence of cash statements, with reference to financial transactions of railroads being stated in terms of January 1 beginning cash balances and column details of cash receipts and disbursements leading to the December 31 cash balance.

The New England Railroads Reports

William Holmes has located among the records of mid-nineteenth century New England railroad records, several examples of railroad auditor reports and relates that it took time to develop the new ideas, new systems and new techniques to meet these new circumstances. However by the 1850s obvious signs of progress are found.

In part to overcome the problem of control, railroads created divisional sections with superintendents in charge of each. A division had its own "accountants" who reported to a central treasurer's office. An auditing function existed for purposes of reviewing the treasurer's activities and reporting to the directors. It was common to find audit reports included in the annual report to shareholders in the years before 1860. In fact using the Massachusetts Western Railroad Corporation's annual report as a base, one finds an abundance of apparently well-designed and meaningful detail on the operations of the corporation.

Auditor's Report

**To the President and Directors
of The Western Rail Road.**

GENTLEMEN:

In discharge of my duties as Auditor, I have once each month during the past year, thoroughly examined the Books of the Treasurer, ascertained that the amount of moneys received and paid out, were correctly entered upon his books from the proper vouchers in his possession, and that the balance represented to be on hand by his cash book, was actually on deposit in various Banks, as shown on the first day of each month by their accounts current and books of deposit.

A statement of transfers made and a balance sheet of the Stock Ledger has been handed in to you monthly by the Treasurer, examined and certified by me as correct. Having been engaged in making up the Dividends for the past three years, I can with confidence assert that the whole number of Shares issued by the Western Rail Road Corporation on which Dividends have been paid is 51,500.

The accounts of the Treasurer have been compared with those of the Cashier at Springfield and found to agree.

The books of the different Departments at Springfield and at the Stations on the Road are well kept, and written up to the end of the year.

Annexed you have a list of the uncollected freight at Stations for the year ending November 30, 1855, showing the amount unpaid on the 15th day of December to be $448,92.

Yours, Very Respectfully,

WILLIAM RITCHIE, Auditor.

Boston, Dec. 27, 1855

Source: William Holmes, "Accounting and Accountants in Massachusetts", (Part Three), *Massachusetts CPA Review*, May-June, 1975, p. 17.

Figure 3–7

An even more interesting example is that included in the Annual Report of the Boston & Worcester Railroad for 1857. The entire auditor's report is spread over four full pages but the following excerpts will give the flavor of it.

An Example of an Audit Comment Letter

Boston & Worcester Railroad,
Auditor's Office, Jan. 14, 1857

To the President and Directors:

Most prominent among the duties of this office, is that of examining and approving all the bills, pay rolls, or other claims against the Corporation, prior to their payment by the Treasurer.

In order to perform this duty satisfactorily, the Auditor ought to know personally the value of all articles purchased, or services rendered. . . .

As an additional protection against error, and to insure the means for immediate reference to the original account which has in any case been allowed, I have adopted a plan by which all the bills are retained in this office, and in their place a certificate sent to the Treasurer, which describes each one in a few words, and upon being receipted, serves every purpose as proof of payment.

These certificates, as well as all other vouchers in the Treasurer's hands for charges on his books, have been examined both by the Auditor and Committee on Accounts, and found uniformly correct and satisfactory. . . .

Another and important portion of an Auditor's duty should be to inform himself as to all the courses of revenue, and see that each produces its proper amount.

Passengers

The amount to be received from Passengers and Freight constitutes the great bulk of income on all roads, and is affected primarily by the schedule of prices charged, that being determined by the Directors through the Superintendent.

Each of the departments is in charge of an efficient head, and in their respective offices it is ascertained whether the several agents on the road account for all the tickets or the freight bills with which they stand charged.

So far as the sale of tickets is concerned, there is no difficulty in imposing a sufficient check. But all passengers do not purchase tickets, and I believe their number increases year by year, and that the rule which has been made in regard to such is either of no use or not enforced.

In this respect I think there should be a change.

Freight

The quantity and price of freight to each station having been properly billed, and the agent is charged therefor, and then as the several sums due are collected and returned, they are checked off and the charge cancelled. . . .

It is very clear that a short road, at the terminus of a long line, cannot afford to incur large risks in the collection of monies of which so small a portion comes for its own service.

Such risk should either be avoided altogether, or shared by other parties to the same business.

Mail, Rents, etc.

The amount received for mail service is determined by contracts with the government, and requires but little notice.

The income from rents is becoming more and more important, and requires constant care.

A schedule of all property under rent is kept in this office, with which the collections are from time to time compared.

Sales of Old Materials

These sales are made only by the Superintendent, or under his direction.

The amount is returned through this office to the Treasurer, and by him credited to the proper accounts.

Transfers of Stock

All stock certificates signed by the President, are recorded in the Auditor's office, and copies kept of all transfers of stock by the Treasurer.

The stock ledger and dividend books have been carefully compared and found correct.

I annex the Treasurer's trial balance at the close of the month of November last, and a condensed statement of the financial condition of the Corporation on that day. . . .

All which is respectfully submitted.

David Wilder, Jr., Auditor

Source: William Holmes, "Accounting and Accountants in Massachusetts" (Part III) *Massachusetts CPA Review,* May-June, 1975, pp. 17–18.

Figure 3–8

As can be seen, this is not only an "auditor's report" on the treasurer's accounts but an early form of an auditor's letter to management on weaknesses in control with recommendations for improvement, and indicative of a sophistication not known to exist in accounting texts of the times. The auditor of today can point to this traditional involvement in an advisory role to identify important precedents for contemporary advisory services.

Integrating Cost Accounts: A Signal Event

Paul Garner's *Evolution of Cost Accounting to 1925* remains an important standard of reference for considerations about developments in cost accounting during the nineteenth century. In the time since the conclusion of Garner's research, however, the findings of Williard Stone and H. Thomas Johnson have assisted in developing a better understanding of the evolution of standard cost processes as found in the early textile plants. These writers have also found important evidence of early systems that pioneered integration of the cost and financial records in these mills. The impact of this accomplishment is held to be nearly as significant as the origin of the system of double entry itself, for it signals the development of an essential capacity to the accounting system in the era of industrialism.

When the enormous economic significance of the cotton industry to the American economy is contemplated, we begin to appreciate that cost accounting practice in the mechanized ginning, spinning, and looming of cotton textiles represents an important part of this first high technology, mass production, capital intensive industry as America moved from a chiefly rural-agrarian society to one of an urban and industrial nature.

When the first industrial securities gained popular acceptance for trading on stock markets, it was incumbent that the procedures for effective internal cost keeping would be forthcoming. The pioneering management controls in the DuPont Powder Company, founded in 1804, suggest that there were many important uses of accounting data for operational control throughout this vertically integrated company during the era ending before the Civil War (Johnson 1975).

Further research points to new materials contained in the manuscripts of the eighteenth century British pottery and china producer, Josiah Wedgewood, wherein there is convincing evidence of the influence of scientific albeit rudimentary cost accounting in the business dealings of Wedgewood (McKendrick 1970).

Stone's research, based on the use of the 1810 cost accounting system records of Charlton Mills of Manchester, England, has discovered "prime cost" collection points at fourteen cost-centers, and cost-center gain or loss calculation in bimonthly trial balances (Stone 1973). The Wedgewood and Charlton Mills evidence from England increases probability that similar types of profit calculations and cost systems were used in New England operations at about the same time. Johnson has noted that the Boston based Lyman Mills operations used a double-entry cost accounting system, integrating a work-in-process account, as early as 1856. While evidence linking the influence of English textile accounting on American practice has not been developed to a conclusion, there is little risk in affirming that by the close of the period studied in this chapter, manufacturers' cost accounting practices had matured into effective information systems for management for purpose of inventory cost, profit measurement and prime cost collection.

If cost accounting of the antebellum period lacked any single evidence of maturity, it was perhaps in the fact that insufficient materials were available in textbook form to share and expand the level of knowledge and experience gained in developing early cost systems. Parts of F. W. Cronhelm's text, *Double Entry by Single* (1818), published in London, discuss inventory records for a production operation and important uses of early scientific management techniques are expressed by Babbage (1832); but overall this is a relatively "silent" era as to the exposition of cost accounting progress. If there was a traditional view of keeping such internal matters "secret" to avoid providing techniques that would assist rival firms, the lack of published works is to be expected. The silence should not be taken to mean that cost accounts were not being kept in a progressively improving fashion. But the silence suggests that, in the antebellum era, industrialism was second in significance to mercantile interests, and accounting attention was still focused on the latter. A comment in the first issue (January 3, 1857) of *Harper's Weekly* supports this view:

> We are a nation of shopkeepers, and none the worse for that. . . . It is very important, then, for us to sustain a good commercial name; and to do this, we must take care that the debit does not overbalance the credit account in our ledgers. If we allow too large a margin for our expenses, we shall be sure, whatever may be the profits of dry goods and hardware, to fall short in the final account with our creditors. . . .

Federal and Municipal Accounting

With the advent of Federalist policies and national government control over a public debt, the role of accounting in the public sector continued to expand—particularly with the passage of a personal income tax to fund the cost of the Union effort during the Civil War. Financing the war through taxes and controlling public expenditures were problems creating unique demands upon those who were trusted with public accounts. States and their growing municipal sub-areas faced the problems of providing regulatory controls over public utilities, including railroads, and other transport operations. As the need for government activities grew so did the need for tax bases from which to draw revenue. Although there was a traditional dislike among people and politicians toward "internal" taxation, sole reliance on tariff duties for revenue was proven to be inadequate.

Under the Federalist leadership of Alexander Hamilton, an early internal tax was levied on whisky, but was repealed by the opposing party when they came to power in the political aftermath of the Whisky Rebellion. Nevertheless an important precedent had been thus set and the Federal government had made clear its power to levy internal duties in case of need. The rising trade and its positive effect on custom collections, supplemented by public land sales and ultimately the sale of public debt via treasury notes—as originally devised by Hamilton—afforded the central government the funds to survive the periods of need during the War of 1812, the panic of 1837, and the Mexican War. When the Civil War commenced with the firing on Fort Sumter on April 12, 1861, the Union forces met several early setbacks, and a need for internal taxes became inevitable in view of the changed expectations regarding the duration of the hostilities, i.e., from "short" to long.

The program by Lincoln's treasury secretary, S. P. Chase, was to finance the war through some direct taxes on income. The tax bill passed by Congress was intended to bring $20 million and was assessed on free and slave states alike, to the amount of 3 percent on all income over $800 (Langenderfer 1954: 106). This established a precedent for keeping personal records and signaled the birth of tax accounting.

The financing and fiscal administration of the growing cities and towns during this period is less than well documented. Political "bosses" in many of the eastern cities were in control of the ballot mechanisms necessary to insure their power. Municipal governments were ill prepared to construct administrative safeguards to insure a proper measure of public safety and welfare. For the most part industrial cities in America were an entirely new phenomenon. In the four decades spanning the pre-Civil War era, the new Midwest's urban population increased from only about 50,000 to over 1,000,000 persons (Dodd 1976). The previous methods of government and taxation seemed inadequate and corrupt under the spoils system and "machine" politics. In part city governments failed because they lacked a "doctrine" that could serve as the basis of appeal for recognition from the legislature and the courts. Lacking the vehicle of widespread municipal incorporation and a budgetary process, municipal executives were unable to act effectively, for they had no basis to coordinate planning, control, and execution. But although municipal governments were unsound, it would be nearly a generation before their situation would become so chaotic as to render reform essential.

The Significance of Antebellum Accounting

It is most challenging for relatively well educated twentieth century accountants to consider the functions and uses of accounting information in the United States during the turbulent period of its adolescence over a century ago.

Entrepreneurs such as Cyrus Field, the man who linked England and America with the Atlantic cable, had found in the meaning of accounts a message of fulfillment. By his use of an accounting expression perhaps we can begin to understand how poignantly "accounts" had begun to affect the American lifestyle. As the story is told:

> Field traveled tirelessly in the British Isles, selling his idea to financiers. Lord Clarendon, the British Foreign Secretary, was among many skeptics. "Suppose you make the attempt but lose your cable on the ocean bottom? What will you do?"
>
> "Charge it to profit and loss and go to work to lay another," Field replied (Fleming 1974).

Early nineteenth century mercantile businessmen also found guidance in their counting house records, and they took pains so that their journals and ledgers were kept secret and apart from the other business records.

Young people and immigrants aspiring to become businessmen and accountants flocked to the metropolitan proprietary business colleges to learn the ways of commerce. One such young man, later called "a bloodless . . . bookkeeper" by a wildcat oilman he had visited, was trained in the points of scientific accounting at Folsom's Business College in Cleveland in 1855. When a group of money men from Cleveland sent this prim twenty-one-year-old bookkeeper, John D. Rockefeller, off to assess the prospects for the commercial future of oil in Pennsylvania, a chapter of American history was begun.[5] (Cooke 1973: 259)

Businessmen were not alone in their interest and exposure to accounts. Inventors and philosophers too felt the touch of accounting on their lives. George Eastman, the genius of modern photography, was born in Rochester in 1854, and began working as an insurance office clerk and ultimately became a junior bookkeeper in the Rochester Savings Bank.

Thoreau, the philosopher of *Walden*, demonstrated the necessity of "accounting" during his hermitage from 1845 to 1847 when he sought to prove the advantage of living the simple life in the midst of the ever expanding urban and industrial civilization. Thoreau portrayed, through these accounts of this primitive life, that there is an essential need for the economic order supplied by the accounts regardless of the lifestyle. In the midst of the modern and advancing systems and records being ever more widely taught, Thoreau's "accounts" suggest that a form of (primitive) preconceived rationale exists as a man considers the incomes and outgoes of human value based ventures. His careful record keeping of the Walden experience is summed up in the following statement about his process: "Nothing was given me of which I have not rendered some account" (Kaysan 1975).

Accountants of this era had begun to develop an appreciation for "practical models" such as those introduced by J. C. Colt and for disclosure through accounting statements and methods as were being shown in reports of the railroad companies. Books and ledgers of account were also becoming standardized in manufacture in part because of the increasing availability of inexpensive paper account books and perhaps because of the influence of standardized instruction through widely marketed texts and chain type proprietary business colleges.

Progress was also made in reducing the routine work load of the bookkeeper by improving the systematic approaches to recording journal entries in preprinted columnar books and by teaching various series of "recording rules" via textbook cases.

With the advent of railroads and corporate stewardship, annual financial reports were becoming used for public summary reporting. Evidence of accrual accounting concepts in financial statements of railroads and in the texts of popular authors was also beginning to appear. Peter Hain reports that of some fifty texts published between 1788 and 1899 about one in ten mentions accrual or other balance sheet type adjustments. Bryant and Stratton (*National Bookkeeping,* 1861) show an item "Interest payable on mortgage" and call it "a somewhat novel feature" (Hain 1972). This attention to the principle of accrual suggests that practicing accountants were starting to step away from memorized and rote techniques when faced with complex transactions and unique economic consequences. Holmes supplies a light-hearted example of such early "conceptualizing."

> Interest and rents have been accrued for a long time, but other prepaid and deferred debits and credits are of comparitively recent origin. The earliest example I have been able to find in an American textbook is in Mayhew's *Practical Bookkeeping,* first published in 1851 out of Michigan. Many of Ira Mayhew's examples in his book are naturally related to farming. In one of his examples he charges the current year with only ½ the expense of manuring, . . . because the land was permanently enriched, and the benefit will probably be realized in the next three crops to as great an extent as in this. It is hence apparent that but one-fourth of the expense of enriching should be debited to this crop.

> I find it entirely appropos that perhaps the first account to be thus deferred in America and spread from year to year should be Manure (Holmes 1976).

BALANCE SHEET, LEGER, SET II.

Philadelphia, February 28th, 1852.	L. Fol.	Face of Leger. Dr.	Cr.	Profit & Loss. Dr.	Cr.	Stock. Dr.	Cr.	Balance. Dr.	Cr.
Stock	1	. . .	1,190 00	. . .	. . .	. . .	1,190 00		
Cash	1	6,561 92	. . .	. . .	. . .	. . .	. . .	6,561 92	
Merchandise	1	1,855 38	. . .	1,855 38	. . .	. . .	. . .		
Reading Rail-Road Stock . .	1	1,250 00	. . .	150 00	. . .	. . .	. . .	1,100 00	
Bills Receivable	1	3,340 64	1,100 00	. . .	. . .	. . .	. . .	3,340 64	
V. C. Burrell & Co. . . .	2	596 50	. . .	. . .	. . .	. . .	. . .	596 50	
Bills Payable	2	. . .	7,680 00	. . .	. . .	. . .	. . .		7 680 00
Charles T. Mayland . . .	2	. . .	2,300 00	. . .	. . .	. . .	. . .		2 300 00
Burgess & Pinkerton . . .	2	. . .	565 56	. . .	. . .	. . .	. . .		565 56
Levi Williams & Co. . . .	2	. . .	960 44	. . .	. . .	. . .	. . .		960 44
Evans, Peters & Co. . . .	3	. . .	1,150 50	. . .	. . .	. . .	. . .		1,150 50
Profit & Loss	3	225 11	. . .	225 11	. . .	. . .	. . .		
Allen Thompson	3	18 75	. . .	. . .	. . .	. . .	. . .	18 75	
Discount	3	. . .	1 80	. . .	1 80	. . .	. . .		
		13,848 30	13,848 30						

By Stock, for Net Loss . . . 2,228 69   2,228 69

2,230 49   2,230 49

Net Insolvency . . . 1,038 69

2,228 69   2,228 69

Total Resources and Liabilities   11,617 81   12,656 50
Net Insolvency, as pr. Stock   1,038 69

12,656 50   12,656 50

Figure 3–9

1852 worksheet for a corporation.

Source: S. W. Crittenden, *An Elementary Treatise on Book-Keeping by Single and Double Entry* (Philadelphia, 1877).

Harry Clark Bentley, an early twentieth century New England accounting educator and author, contends that the developments and contributions by accounting writers during the first half of the nineteenth century surpassed those of the second. Of course, this second era is another story—one which we set out to consider in the next chapter.

NOTES

1. Texts during this period were not as scarce as some historical writers would have us believe. For an interesting analysis of an accounting primer published in Boston in 1831, refer to the article by Kistler and Jennings listed in the bibliography. The article examines the 116-page book *The Young Accountants Guide: . . .* , and its approach to accounting instruction.

2. Jones referred to the balance sheet and income statement result as follows: "A merchants position is defined by reference to his accounts, each of which shows by its result some item of his Resources, Liabilities, Gains or Losses."

3. The single-entry ledger, according to this treatise, consisted entirely of personal (individual) accounts. No impersonal accounts were kept, not even for cash. At the end of the year an inventory of assets would be taken, which included "Cost and other effects." This, together with personal accounts receivable, minus accounts payable, constituted the proprietor's "net worth."

4. In considering, from the view of the development of accounting instruction, the importance of Jones and Foster, it is not difficult to regard Jones as deserving credit for distinguishing between "real" and "nominal" accounts and for a path-breaking effort among American writers. His regard for the "merchants position" and the role of financial statements is significant. Foster too had the shrewdness to recognize an important idea when he saw it, and notwithstanding his copycat ways, deserves just credit for his missionary efforts in behalf of the concept as well as for his important efforts to provide a brief history of accounting in the midst of an active career.

5. Although it is not clear that financial statements were widely used as they are today for purposes of evaluating prospective acquisitions or obtaining credit, the "ledger focus" of mercantile account systems seems to suggest that merchants preferred to limit the "account books" information and its contents to being a means of controlling an enterprise. Chamberlain tells us also that when Rockefeller was sent on business in the 1850s, "He came as the agent for Cleveland businessmen who had been impressed with . . . his ability to judge a balance sheet" (Chamberlain 1974: 149).

4 PRELUDE TO THE MODERN AGE

> As more details are learned about the 1880's and the 1890's it becomes ever clearer that a great many occurrences in the last double decade of the nineteenth century played an important part in making it possible for accounting in the twentieth century to be what it is. [A. C. Littleton, 1946]

Political and Social Environment in the Gilded Age

Many consider the post World War II period as a time of unprecedented growth and change in American life. A study of the changing economic, social, political, and technological environment of the post–Civil War era indicates that these years were also ones of high opportunity, intense activity, and national achievement. It was the era of manifest destiny in the West beyond Missouri and unity among farmers of the Great Plains with the birth of the grange movement. In the East it was a time of capital intensive industrialization and urbanization as steam power and machinery brought about important changes in the demand for labor. The South, staggered by the consequences of the Civil War, submitted to a period of "reconstruction."

World power was on the horizon as the American nation moved away from a century-long tradition of isolation in global affairs. Inventions such as the incandescent light, patented by Thomas Edison in the 1880s, and the telephone, first used in Boston in 1876, foretold important changes. It was also an era of Scott Joplin's ragtime, Victorian morality, and the birth of the American golf, with the first club forming in New York City in 1888.

Youth found inspiration in "Horatio Alger" success stories about young people who turned pennies into fortunes through hard work and unceasing application of their talents in the marketplace. It was all at once the age of P. T. Barnum's showmanship, the industrial "robber barons," and unbridled competition among vast enterprises that were to form the first business trusts.

Cities swelled with the waves of Ellis Island immigrants who had viewed the Statue of Liberty as they entered New York harbor. The statue had been dedicated in 1886 as a gift of the people of France. In the thirty years spanning 1860 to 1890 America's population doubled from 31 million to 62 million (Schlesinger 1939: 132). By 1880 some business historians suggest, American had become a metropolitan economy although the population had not shifted to a predominantly urban pattern and would not for another thirty years.

Social Philosophy

During these decades before the turn of the century, businessmen were relatively unencumbered by government involvement in the carrying out of their pursuits. Americans held to the traditional belief of laissez-faire, the right of citizens to be left alone in their economic activities. This posture, combined with the rapid industrialization and growth of businesses, seemed justified in the hope of the benefits anticipated from economies of scale. Before the century ended, the misdeeds of laissez faire, cut throat competition, and the creation of trusts and monopolies would popularize the movement for a countering system of government regulatory controls over utilities and other major businesses that affected the interstate domain. Yet, these early government powers, once attained, would not be widely applied to check the abuses of corporate power until the early years of the twentieth century.

The model for the modern integrated industrial concern developed from the post–Civil War railroad merger movement, one of the most notable amalgamations being the creation of the New York Central System in 1867. Such combinations, it was demonstrated, made it possible for the public to receive better service at apparently lower prices. With the opening of the West, keynoted by the completion of the transcontinental railroad in 1869, it became possible for Americans to benefit from the superior efficiency of large scale rail operations. Travel from New York to Chicago had been cut to twenty-four hours from fifty hours as a result of Cornelius Vanderbilt's consolidation of the New York Central. Americans could travel coast to coast in a week versus months by ship. But an indirect price for this speed and efficiency included abuses such as corruption of public officials, watering of corporate stock, and manipulation of securities in unregulated stock markets, effectively transferring business control from the owners to the managers of corporations. Americans, however, still eschewed direct government involvement in the conduct of business. The potential for growth and the prospects of unlimited business opportunity supported the popular sentiment for unrestricted individual freedom in business (Cochran 1942: 122-123).

In January 1882, the Standard Oil Trust was formed and a new vehicle for consolidating corporate operations was initiated. The trust device was the brainchild of Samuel C. T. Dodd. After considering and discarding several forms wherein the Standard Oil Corporation could devise a legal structure to incorporate all its operations, Dodd recommended to Standard officials that they create a corporation in each state in which Standard had a major investment. Superimposed on these state corporations would be a "corporation of corporations,"—a trust, which would be, in terms of control, the only important vehicle. The trust would hold the voting stock of the subsidiary companies; trust certificates would be issued to the companies on a percentage basis according to the amount of stock contributed, and the management of the entire organization would reside in the trustees of the trust. The trust afforded Standard the opportunity to develop complete vertical integration of operations, including barrel making, pipelines, selling agencies, storage facilities and byproducts merchandising.[1] (Gressley 1971: 5).

Railroads, followed by more oil and then steel companies, were organized along the lines of the trust. Trusts also were formed in tobacco, sugar and coal. The money trust, banks, was the financial soul of the gilded age just as the railroads were the economic heart. Even as late as 1898, approximately 60 percent of the listings on the New York Stock Exchange were railroad securities. Federal legislation ultimately banned the trust vehicle, but large integrated corporations were then consolidated in other ways via modified legal frameworks, such that by 1901 the first billion dollar "super consolidation," the United States Steel Corporation, came into existence.

The Constitution and Case Law

In 1888 the Supreme Court affirmed that the protection under the due process clause of the Constitution was not, like that of the privileges and immunities clause, confined to citizens, but extended to all persons, including corporations. This decision reflected an earlier court ruling which recognized the corporate entity as an "artificial person," thereby extending the civil rights of the corporation to a point of practical advantage. Even smaller business operations began to adopt the corporate form. Prior to this, the corporate form had been of benefit mostly to financial institutions, insurance companies, railroads, and a few major industrials, with a major segment of American enterprise conducted in the partnership or proprietary form.

The Fourteenth Amendment, enacted in 1868 primarily to establish the Civil Rights of the recently freed slaves, also afforded the means for expanded federal involvement in the area of regulation of corporations. Corporations were "legal persons" and the Fourteenth Amendment restricted states from discriminatory regulation against such corporate persons. In substance, states were preempted from regulating interstate corporations. The passage of the Fourteenth Amendment and the subsequent enactment of the Sherman Antitrust Law brought into effect the federal movement to regulate interstate corporations.

Urban workers and labor organizations grew in number and strength during this period. The long span of the post–Civil War period (1865–1890) saw hourly wages rise by nearly two-thirds. In the face of the continuing drop in the price level (deflation), "real" wages therefore increased even more. Labor groups combined to form the American Federation of Labor (AFL). At first numbering approximately 150,000, the AFL would increase to over 500,000 by the turn of the century and represent 90 percent of the skilled labor population. This increased strength of organized labor via unions sparked popular concern about shifts in power just as did the rise of the corporate trust structure. The 1890s were marked by violent strikes, including the Homestead Steel Strike in Pennsylvania and the bloody Pullman strikes in Chicago where workers seeking redress on wage reductions confronted government troops in the streets.

The Politics of the Gilded Age

A panic originating in the European money markets spread to the United States in 1873 causing corporate credit to crumble. This, when combined with the rumors of corruption in the federal government, brought about major economic disturbances (Fels 1951).

More than 5,000 concerns failed, and losses mounted to $220 million, a significant amount in those days. Three million workers were unemployed and farmers found that their grain could not be sold on the wheat markets. Conditions were aggravated by the revelation that several members of President Grant's administration held stock, for which they had never paid, in the Credit Mobilier, a holding company which had constructed the Union Pacific Railroad. The shares had been distributed by a congressman and an officer of the company, with the intention of receiving protection from government inquiry into company affairs.

The cloud of popular mistrust created by this scandal within the federal bureaucracy was to linger until the election of 1896. The 1896 election was one of the most intensely fought in American history. The East saw William Jennings Bryan as a threat to society as they knew it. His platform championed the free coinage of silver and opposed the gold standard. The election of 1896 resulted in a significant political realignment. Two years earlier, in 1894, the Republicans had secured control of the House with the largest gain in a congressional election in the nation's modern history. In that year the Democrats failed to return a single member to Congress in twenty-four states. The presidential race of 1896 revealed equally strong shifts in sentiment which favored the Republicans. An analysis of this change, although complex, revealed that it was caused largely by workers and immigrants who had blamed the Democrats for the severe depression sparked by the panic of 1893. Workers were suspicious of the economic interests of the farmers and organized western political elements (Hoffman 1956).

The panic of 1893, an intense contraction, was one of the most severe depressions in the history of the United States. Unemployment in manufacturing and transportation mounted to over 9 percent of the work force.

Although there may be dispute as to whether the 1880s or the 1890s was the period during which the economic momentum switched from agrarian to industrial, it is important to recognize that these decades together provide the formative influence for our culture in industrialized America.[2] For example, this era witnessed the birth of the modern city. Census data reveal that the number of cities with 8,000 or more inhabitants increased from just 280 in 1880 to over 500 by 1896. Many cities doubled in size and some, such as Chicago, showed spectacular rates of growth.

In the West, under the sponsorship of the Homestead Act, the population was drawn to farming and ranching. The "Go West Young Man" fever created the western version of a corporate buccaneer, namely, the cattle baron. Ambitious ranchers underwrote a series of Indian wars, and fought to free the land from native influence. Investors were attracted to the cattle industry in large numbers by the late 1870s. Subscribers to the stock in cattle companies were of varied ages and backgrounds: Boston dry goods merchants, land speculators, and southern land owners (Gressley 1971: 71). Mining speculation also attracted eastern investors, including stock brokers and other merchants from the midwest (Brewer 1976).

The Birth of the Modern Capital Market

After the 1870s, the failure of the gold supply to keep pace with money growth demands generated by industrial expansion enhanced the position of the investment banker who was skilled in managing and providing both cash and capital. Bankers controlled important power to determine and direct major economic decisions affecting capital structure, scope, and existence of developing businesses. Investment banking during the period between 1873 and 1884 in particular was characterized by the actions of J. P. Morgan. Initially in partnership as Drexel and Morgan, the operation was renamed J. P. Morgan and Co. in 1895. Morgan's first successful major venture was in 1879 when he became involved in marketing overseas stock for the Vanderbilt family to provide capital for the expansion of the New York Central, yet preserving control for the family. In exchange for his services he came to be appointed a member of the New York Central Board of Directors. Morgan's influence over this period through the year 1900 provides a guiding thread to the elements that affected the capital markets.

Railroads and their financing were the center of attention in the capital markets. The funds for railway construction came from bank credit and foreign exchange supplied by European investors. Every new burst of railway construction was met by a corresponding burst of investment from abroad, including England, Holland, and Germany. A boom that lasted from 1866 to 1873 was fueled by such investment; and when the depression of 1873 struck it took a heavy toll of foreign investors. By 1887 another depression had hit. English investors sold off to American investors at greatly reduced prices, the result being that Americans had gained ownership in the railroads at a small portion of the original investment. It was established that foreign investors had lost heavily, perhaps over $250 million on railroad bonds alone.

The House of Morgan survived the economic panics of the 1880s and 1890s. This survival itself enhanced its reputation and prestige. During the failures and panic of 1893, Morgan's money, expertise and organizational abilities aided many shaky railroad capital structures. Morgan put into effect reorganizational plans that permitted many of the railroads to survive. The essence of his reorganizational plan was to scale down fixed liabilities and exchange them for stock. If bondholders were unwilling to exchange their bonds for stock, they were persuaded to take bonds of lesser yield (Chamberlain 1974: 173).

It is impossible to consider this period of American industrialization without being drawn into a controversy that has engaged historians for the past half century. The names Morgan, Vanderbilt, Durant, Stanford and Fisk evoke a certain popular resentment because some industry leaders of the late nineteenth century were characterized as "robber barons." Were they robber barons or captains of industry? Josephson, who coined the robber barons term in a book of that name, electrified and outraged readers with what appeared to be indisputable data about the shameless buccaneers of capitalism. Yet historians note that the alleged predatory acts were accomplished only through collusion with and assistance from government officials.

The most important case in point is revealed in the story of the Credit Mobilier, the financial holding company that built the Union Pacific Railroad. The Mobilier scandal was brought to light by members of the House of Representatives and was a type of nineteenth century "Watergate." One of the House investigators summarized the situation by saying, "With absolute fairness we have striven to obtain the truth and in the sentence I declare in all the history, I never saw a scheme of villainy so profoundly arranged, so cunningly carried forward, so disastrously executed as this one disclosed in the report now submitted to the House." The corruption reached into all branches of President Grant's administration and into the offices of various members of Congress (Green 1959).

Not only through the Mobilier but in other ways during this era, railroad companies had received substantial subsidies from federal and state agencies. The Erie Railroad combine including Gould, Fisk and Drew made their fortunes through secret stock manipulations only because the New York legislature was dominated by public representatives whom the Erie group was known to control. Central Pacific Railroad's control over the legislature in Sacramento, California, ultimately led to that state's government granting monopolies over certain prize routes.

Yet not all of the railroads or their entrepreneur promoters were embroiled in this type of government sponsored chicanery. Unprotected and competitive railroads, such as those owned and controlled by Vanderbilt and Hill, grew without government-aided monopolies and were also known to be as profitable to their stockholders and probably less costly to their shippers. Although the eastern roads did not depend on illicit subsidies financed by taxpayers, they were characterized by sharp and often vicious competition for routes, in turn affording these roads the benefits of a legal monopoly without having to obtain the sanction of the government.

To assess the developments in this period, marked by the birth of many rail and industrial empires, it is important to consider that it may have been impossible to raise the large quantities of scarce capital required by such operations had it not been for the intense promotion of early entrepreneurs. The economy's appetite was almost boundlessly growth oriented. The success of investment bankers in early corporate promotion is suggested by statistics that by 1893 there were 1,250,000 shareholders out of a population of 62 million people in the United States. (This can be contrasted with the ownership for the post–World War II information in Figure 8-2.) The strong will and tactics of this early group of "captains of industry" in large part accounted for the establishment of an efficient corporate form of enterprise in a period when any other form of organization, given the nature of the market, might not have similarly provided for growth.

In 1889 the daily *Wall Street Journal* began publication, assuring a comprehensive source of investment news to supplement other weekly published sources. By 1890 tickers and telephones were commonplace and it was possible to instantaneously transmit stock trading data to points far beyond Wall Street. By the turn of the century New York's Wall Street was about to emerge as the leading location of international finance surpassing London's Lombard Street. This rise in the influence of American capital markets came quickly and at the hands of but a few men, with little or no governmental regulation. These men virtually controlled America's business life: Morgan in banking and finance, Rockefeller in oil, Vanderbilt in railroads, Carnegie in steel. These were the titans amidst the tycoons, men whose annual incomes were in the millions, who paid no income taxes, and whose control over organizations and battles with one another for the whole industrial empire are legend (Sobel 1965: 158).

A colorful insight into this group is found in a early biography of the Vanderbilt family. Commodore Vanderbilt had a personality about which no single statement could be more revealing than the following found in the text of a letter the old commodore sent to a competitor. "'You have undertaken to cheat me,' he wrote, 'I won't sue you for the law is too slow. I'll ruin you.' And he did" (Campbell 1941). The commodore's fortune, as did Carnegie's and Rockefeller's, ultimately provided the funding for a major private university.

Although one cannot condone their swashbuckling techniques, it is difficult to readily condemn them either. The force of the work ethic and the pace of change and opportunity nearly a century ago are not clearly perceived today. These forces were likely more complex and competitive than one can appreciate today and were an influence that shaped outcomes of countless entities beyond the enterprises of the "robber barons" themselves.

The economic environment of this era was also influenced by the fact that throughout the post–Civil War period there was a gradual but steady increase in purchasing power of the dollar brought about by general price deflation. Furthermore, the economy was beginning to change character. By 1880 the United States had entered into a metropolitan style economy characterized by the growth and significance of industrial urban areas as key points of demand, distribution, and political influence.

In addition to the East's industrial cities and capital markets, it is also important to recognize that in this era of manifest destiny, crops, land, mining, and cattle also played an important role in the functioning of the American capitalistic system. Both eastern and European investors were attracted to western mines, ranches, and cattle as investments. Furthermore, the abundant American wheat harvest of 1879 offset the disastrous European crop failures which had resulted from poor weather. This led to the export of millions of bushels of wheat per day and served as the source of an agricultural boom that finally led the American economy out of the serious depression which had lingered since 1873. Without these western investments and the strength of American agriculture, it is difficult to expect that our economy would have had a balanced attractiveness to investors at home or overseas.

The history of eastern investments in western mortgage companies, land, and cattle is interesting and involved. The conservative lending policies of major eastern capital sources led them to protect their customers from sustaining substantial losses in western investments. But, because they did not venture into high risk-return situations, the involvement of the conservative New York money sources did not in itself account for the entire capital of western ventures.

As the westward movement gained momentum after the Civil War, the demand for mortgage credit grew rapidly; at the same time, credit funds also grew rapidly in the East and in Europe. Important amounts of these funds were attracted by the temperament and potential of the West. Perhaps it was in part that the eastern investors were enchanted by the potential of the cattle industry, although researchers suggest that investments in cattle arose because the eastern investors had originally made investments in other areas of the West, usually mining, railroads or real estate. As such, investment in cattle was a part of an "associative spirit." Investors in the cattle industry included merchants, bankers, financiers, and industrialists, although there was also a small group of professional men. Names commonly found include those such as Marshall Field, the Chicago merchant; Teddy Roosevelt; August Busch; and David Goodrich.

By the end of the 1800s both the western manager and the eastern investor had learned a modicum about the economics of the cattle business. Expenses were closely scrutinized and curtailed, dividends were postponed as necessary, and improved procedures of operation were being adopted. Only when these business procedures were followed did cattle companies show an accounting ledger based profit. Intensive investment in the cattle industry from 1882 to 1885 represented the high point of activity. The low point came from 1886 to 1888 followed by a short period of recovery and a much larger resurgence from 1898 to 1900.[3] Thereafter, the cattle industry in the plains underwent a radical change wherein ranching became increasingly locally controlled.[4]

In 1884 following a panic in the economy, a Democrat was returned to the White House for the first time since the end of the Civil War. Whether this reflected public disenchantment with an administration tied to the Credit Mobilier or whether it indicated a new populism is not clear. Nearly simultaneous with the changing mood which brought the Democrats into power, there was a decline in the use of the trust as a device to direct the growth and expansion of corporations. Although trusts continued in existence through the turn of the century it was in the mid-1880s, perhaps in response to the panic of 1884, that the consolidated holding corporation began to emerge as an alternative to the trust as an operating and control mechanism.

With the creation of the Interstate Commerce Commission (1887) and the passage shortly thereafter of the Sherman Act (1890), the days of laissez-faire were coming to a close. These actions communicated a message that the federal government would respond to popular political pressures to curb the abuses of unrestrained competition and corporate monopoly. It would not be, however, until the early years of the twentieth century that the provisions of these laws would be enforced to the extent that there would be a curb on widespread trust abuses and monopolistic practices.

Accounting Reports, Financial Disclosure and Regulation

Financial reports before the turn of the century reflected the influence of the railroad corporation, the trust form of business, and the large manufacturing corporation. This section considers the format, content and influence of financial reports of the period including regulatory and legal aspects, the role that accounting systems played in internal administration of large organizations, and attempts by the private and public sectors to establish uniform accounts.

To consider this era without focusing on railroads would be inappropriate and ineffective, for railroad securities were the dominant factor in the capital markets. Increasing public interest in understanding railroad reports gave birth to financial analysis before the turn of the century. Among the early pioneers of financial analysis were Thomas F. Woodlock, John Moody, and a proponent of need for publicity of corporate accounts, Henry Clews. It was Clews, a noted author in financial circles, who suggested that expert accountants in the private sector could provide the requisite service needed for appropriate publicity of the corporate accounts. He stated that publicity could be accomplished by the employment of skilled accountants because certified results of their examinations would be accepted as conclusive. Thomas Woodlock's book, *The Anatomy of a Railroad Report*, was published in 1895 and acknowledged by others, including Moody, as a popular and authoritative presentation on the subject matter of railroad operations and financial reports.

Analysis of financial statements by banks, credit establishments and other institutions was an activity that affected the entire economy as evidenced by the fact that by 1900 there were more than a million individual stock owning investors.

Moody, a pioneer financial analyst, noted concern over matters of secrecy. In *How to Analyze Railroad Reports*, Moody observed that until the early 1890s balance sheet secrecy was a distressing characteristic of financial statement disclosure by railroads. For example, during the 1870s and 1880s the New York Central Railroad rendered no annual reports to its stockholders. Also, in responding to an inquiry from the New York Stock Exchange for financial information, the Delaware, Lackawana and Western Railroad, whose stock was also traded on the Exchange responded ". . . the Delaware, Lackawana and Western Railroad makes no report, publishes no statements, and . . . (has) not done anything of the kind for the last five years." (Sobel 1965: 85)

The secrecy surrounding financial affairs was cited in a 1900 government report on the subject. The report noted that "while the chief evil of large corporations is a lack of responsibility of the directors to the stockholders . . . the directors . . . practically never make reports to the individual shareholders for periods." The public's concern over disclosure was evidenced in a passage which appeared in the *Railroad Gazette* (January 6, 1893): "The annual report of a railroad is often a very blind document and the average shareholder taking one of these reports generally gives up before he begins."

Another common feature of accounting systems of this age was the use of the "private ledger" which was an account book equipped with a lock and key wherein were kept the capital expense accounts, the record of officers' salaries, controlling accounts of sales and purchases, and any other cumulative accounting information the firm desired to keep confidential. A partner or trusted employee posted the essential figures from the usual accounting records and only this person saw the trial balance and knew the condition of the important accounts (Roberts 1975).

British trained accountants in America had a convenient and authoritative set of examples, which could be modified and applied to the American scene from such sources as the British Companies Acts. A replacement method became widely adopted, under which the asset cost remained as book value, without regard for depreciation. An expense account was used to even out the differential in charges resulting from costs of renewal and maintenance. The Remington Arms Company, for example, showed no depreciation on their financial statements until after the turn of the century (Williamson 1952: 120, 402). Another factor affecting the development of an appropriate method for valuation of fixed assets in quasi-public corporations was the occurrence of a general price level decline in America. During the period of 1875 to 1900 there was an increase in purchasing power such that the historical cost values assigned to fixed assets, if not adjusted in book value for "wear and tear" or other loss in value, were in effect being *written* up by deflation. In addition to matters of technical accounting, political considerations significant to

Let us add all these equations together into one, grouping those of the same letter.

$$
\begin{aligned}
(17.)\quad
&\begin{aligned}
&(I + i_2 + i_3)\\
+\ &(K + k)\\
+\ &L\\
+\ &U\\
+\ &(V + v)\\
+\ &W\\
+\ &P\\[4pt]
+\ &x_2
\end{aligned}
\qquad = \qquad
&\begin{aligned}
&(i + i_4 + i_5)\\
+\ &k\\
+\ &L\\
+\ &U\\[14pt]
+\ &P\\
+\ &Q\\
+\ &x\\
+\ &R\\
+\ &Y\\
+\ &Z
\end{aligned}
\end{aligned}
$$

80. Chronicles Transformed to History.—Examination will show that this grouping process has given us the materials for a history of each department of the business.

All the increase and decrease of cash, for example, is denoted by the terms $i_2 + i_3$ on one side, and $i + i_4 + i_5$ on the other.

31. Posting.—The grouping process is called in book-keeping "posting." The matter of the journal is re-written in a form known as the **"Ledger."**

32. The Ledger.—This form of the equation differs from the journal in this: it allots a page or space, called an **account,** to each department of the business, just as in the above equation we alloted a line to each letter. The account must have two sides (just as the equation has,) one for the "debits" and one for the "credits." The journal is gone through line by line and dissected; each amount in the Dr. column is transferred to the Dr. side of the account named on the same line of the journal; each amount in the Cr. column is transferred to the Cr. side.

(*Continued.*)

THE READING RAILROAD COMPANY'S BOOKS.

(*Concluded.*)

The following is a copy of the last report made by the President and Managers for the information of stockholders, which was submitted January 12th, last past:

Dr.   GENERAL BALANCE-SHEET OF THE PHILADELPHIA AND READING RAILROAD COMPANY, NOVEMBER 30, 1879.   *Cr.*

CAPITAL ACCOUNTS:		CAPITAL ACCOUNTS:		
Railroad..........	96,818,977.68	Total mortgage loans *		
Depots...........	4,194,711.89	6 pr. c. $ debent'e loan, 1866-88, coupon	1,198,500.00	57,303,877.94
Locomotive engines and cars	9,855,449.04	... debt now " , 1870-90		

ASSETS

...Mahanoy Railroad Co. stock			
Mine Hill & Schuyl. Haven Railroad Co. stock		24,225.01	
Phila. and Reading Coal and Iron Co. stock		175,297.75	
Phila. and Reading Coal and Iron Co., bond		8,000,000.00	
Phila. and Reading Coal and Iron Co., bond and mortgage, July 1, 1874	29,737,965.53		
Phila. and Reading Coal and Iron Co. bond and mortgage, December 28th, 1876	10,000,000.00		
Steam-colliers		89,737,965.53	
Susquehanna Canal coal-barges		2,561,245.24	
Schuylkill Canal coal-barges		25,872.80	
Schuyl. Navigation Co. works and franchises		437,640.70	
		1,000,000.00	
			101,265,544.16
Add:			
Schuylkill Canal new barges	22,410.44		
Less:			
Balance of installments Susquehanna Canal new barges	4,494.35	17,966.09	
			101,288,530.25
ASSETS:			
Cash on hand	228,029.94		
Bills receivable	24,861.00		
Freight and toll bills receivable in December, 1879	778,561.36		
Stocks and bonds held by the Company	1,082,402.89		
Materials on hand	7,088,811.43		
Debts due to the Company:			
Sundry branch roads	735,599.99		
Philadelphia and Reading Coal and Iron Co.	1,780,298.05		
Sundry accounts	5,177,919.78		
	1,653,207.19	8,561,425.02	
Funded coupons not yet matured:			
Phila. & Reading Railroad Co. coupons	2,248,889.00		
Schuylkill Navigation Company "	123,000.00		
Susquehanna Canal Company "	230,195.00	17,862,738.88	
Discount, commission and expenses of general mortgage loan, 1874–1908, issue of $10,000,000 in January, 1876		2,602,084.00	
		500,000.00	
INCOME ACCOUNTS:			
Loss, per report November 30th, 1878	1,041,440.99		
Add loss year ending November 30th, 1879	1,063,421.73	2,104,862.72	
			128,853,215.80

LIABILITIES

Loan of Schuyl. Nav. Co., matur'g 1895	1,200,000.00		
" " " 1913	756,650.00		
" " " 1915	631,600.00	2,578,250.00	
Loan of E. Penna. R. R. Co. mt'g 1888	495,900.00	8,074,150.00	
			77,924,761.04
Common stock		82,726,375.28	
Preferred stock		1,551,800.00	84,278,175.28
LIABILITIES:			
Floating debt		7,550,079.54	
Debts due by the Company, including rentals, and principally for current business		1,572,665.48	
Wages, materials, drawbacks, and connecting roads for November business		870,911.18	
Coupons and interest on registered loans to December 1st, 1879, inclusive		805,240.95	
State tax on capital stock and gross receipts		98,165.71	
Sinking fund loan, 1886-88		156,070.45	
Sinking fund Schuylkill Navigation Company improvement bonds		298,000.00	
Credit balance of insurance funds		347,296.65	
Credit balance of renewal fund		11,847.57	11,650,277.48
			128,853,215.80

* We have omitted the items which make up this amount, deeming it necessary only to give the aggregate of mortgage indebtedness.

Figure 4-1

A balance sheet of the Philadelphia and Reading Railroad Co., November 30, 1879.

Source: *The Book-Keeper*, 17 August 1880, p. 37.

the relationship between a regulated industries' rate for services and the capital asset rate base caused the issue of fixed asset ac-counting to be prominent.[5]   A view of the railroad as a quasi-public corporation, and a concern over the result of government influence on rate setting and return on railroad investments, focused attention on the value of capital assets and appropriate methods of accounting for the same. At first, the courts had not recognized the rights of regulated corporations or public service corporations to deduct depreciation in the determination of their rate base. By 1876 the Supreme Court did acknowledge the right of railroads to take depreciation yet it was not perceived to be an expense, in the sense of an expenditure, for railroad accounts were kept primarily on a cash basis. Later courts, in a fashion reflecting the 1898 Supreme Court decision, *Smyth* v. *Ames,* indicated that a "fair return to regulated industry could be based on the 'present value of the property,' " as opposed to historical cost as often used in early uniform systems.[6]

Without a depreciation expense concept, companies incurred costs for wear and maintenance and charged the amount to surplus accounts and avoided income statement disclosure. This practice was popular in those years when companies suffered falling profit margins. Moody described the practice as follows:

> In the past, especially, many railroads followed the policy of keeping down their current operating costs including maintenance but at the same time spending the necessary money on their properties and then at the close of the year deducting from the surplus shown above charges the amounts currently spent but not currently charged up. So in the final result they would have no surplus at all, and the item 'surplus above charges' or 'surplus above dividends' would simply be a book-keeping entry (Moody 1916: 170).

Moody goes on to say ". . . it is one of the strong arguments in favor of uniform accounting requirements that railroads coming under the jurisdiction of the interstate commerce commission cannot do this any longer. They are now required to charge to maintenance the items which properly belong there and can only put in improvement or betterment accounts the actual expenditures of such nature."

As early as 1880 business periodicals reviewed the subject of compulsory regulatory accounts. In 1889 an issue of *Office* magazine reported the speech of George Ramsdell, president of the Western Gas Association, regarding the lack of uniformity of gas company accounts and announcing the appointment of an association commit-tee to investigate the lack of systematic accounting. These references suggest an awareness on the part of the practitioners and businessmen for self-regulation of accounting practice.

Concern over the fairness of reporting as indicated by Moody in part explains the justification for the creation of the Interstate Commerce Commission in 1887. In 1894 the commission established a system of accounts entitled, "The Classification of Operating Expenses."[7]

This act evidenced the birth of regulatory agencies, the fourth branch of modern federal government. With this focus on the classification of operating expenses at this point in time, it is evident in the literature of the period that earning capacity was becoming, in the words of John Moody, the factor that should be studied *"in advance of everything else"* (Moody 1916: 18).

How were the accountants to provide leadership in this complex of regulation and legal precedent? Would they be relegated to the status of "busy examiners of detail"? As these early pressures manifested themselves the emerging accounting profession was poorly organized in terms of institutions and literature to cope with public demands for financial reporting. Yet interesting and important precedents were being established. The first consolidated accounts were prepared for the American Cotton Oil Trust in 1886 and Maurice Peloubet suggests that consolidation accounting developed in the United States before it did in Great Britain. In Great Britain the appropriate disclosure for holding companies involved adjusting and amplifying the holding company investment account per se whereas in America there was a growing custom to take a consolidations approach to present a picture of the enterprise as if it were a whole. (Peloubet 1955: 31) This is an example of the ability of American accountants to benefit from the expertise of the British professional and at the same time to innovate, adapt, and progressively determine new and different schemes of disclosure in light of the different environment of the American capital market.

As the trust and holding corporations gained headway (Figure 4-2) popular writers and prominent authorities predicted that such businesses would fail. Their belief was founded upon the view that no one person or board of directors could successfully master such large organizations in a competitive environment. But accounting administrative control systems being developed during this period provided the information and means of direction to place at the disposal of management data factors relevant to operations. Steel companies, rubber companies, munitions works, and transportation, sugar, and refining companies provide examples of the success of such internal management accounting system operations during this period for such large scale enterprises (Wildman 1914). In 1900, Collier surveyed the evolution of the business trust. A summary of his findings suggests the substantial financial structure and the diverse nature of this industrial device:

The Structure of Pre-1900 American Business Trusts

			Capitalization in Millions		
Product Process	Number of Trusts	Year(s) Established	Common Stock	Preferred Stock	Bonded Debt
Food	14	1887–1899	252	105	84
Distilling and Brewing	10	1894–1899	123	49	29
Tobacco	5	1890–1899	106	79	4
Paper	6	1898–1899	123	53	26
Textiles	6	1896–1899	160	56	16
Leather and Rubber	5	1892–1899	154	143	10
Wood	3	1892–1896	100	—	1
Glass and Clay	5	1890–1899	84	17	—
Chemicals, Oils and Paints	11	1882–1899	274	96	5
Iron and Steel	18	1887–1899	408	287	55
Machinery and Hardware	8	1893–1899	122	105	—
Electrical Manufacturers	11	1891–1899	140	40	10
Minerals, Metals, and Coal	6	1891–1899	121	47	4
Printing	1	1892	3	3	—
Warehousing	2	1895–1897	20	8	18
Cement, Munitions, and Other	7	1889–1899	119	43	—
			2,309	1,131	352

Source: W. M. Collier, *The Trusts, What Can We Do With Them? What Can They Do For Us?* (New York: Baker and Taylor, 1900), pp. 8–13.

Figure 4–2

Sophisticated techniques such as an estimated bad debts treatment of uncollectible accounts were described as early as 1880 in the periodical literature of accounting. Other examples of internal innovations include the development of loose-leaf and columnar books. These types of records, when compared to bound inflexible style book sets, made it possible to sequence, amend and control information. The voucher system also came into use as a system of controlling cash payments and for determining liability and working capital requirements.

Disclosure

With the settling of the West, the Winchester rifle had become a symbol of the times as a weapon in both hunting and war. The role of accounting information in the mass manufacture of arms at the Winchester Repeating Arms Company is in part portrayed in the rudimentary balance sheets reconstructed by Harold Williamson. The activities sketched by these statements portray some of the important financial events of the company over the period of its early development and growth. The content and structure of the statements suggest the fundamental role of balance sheets in communicating financial information and reveal a step in the evolution of financial reporting and disclosure in America.

As noted in a previous chapter, the writings of Thomas Jones of New York mark the beginnings of the modern period of financial reporting. Jones' instruction emphasized the financial statements as the end result of the system of accounts. In the post–Civil War period the ledger had begun to lose its preeminent position in the system of financial accounting. External capital interests required statements which periodically synthesized the results of changes in the asset position of the firm. This betrayed the increasingly important role played by external capital sources in the financing of large enterprises. As businesses became more widely held and financed, statement extracts of the journals and ledgers were being required in concise, uniform, and understandable form.

Another observation regarding the widespread use and importance of financial information in records of this time can be found in Gressley's *Bankers and Cattlemen*. Gressley points to the fact that his ability to compute the dividends paid by successful land and cattle companies was based on the information on the ledger sheets available from the companies for the periods during the 1870s and

1880s. He determined the average declared dividend as just over 8 percent and thus concluded that few eastern investors found a pot of gold in the West. It is appropriate to observe that since a century later it was possible for Gressley to determine this information it is likely that such information was used immediately for similar evaluations.

Gressley's research additionally reveals that a small percentage of early land and cattle companies did show excellent returns. For example, Marshall Field and Levi Leiter reaped dividends averaging 11 percent on their stock investments over a ten year period in the Pratt-Ferris Cattle Company. Financial records provided a means for the eastern financier to determine the profitability of investment. While more research is needed as to the implications and the significance of such records in these early companies they serve as examples of the likely influence of accounts on investment in non-manufacturing enterprises.

Beginning with the post–Civil War period the analytically prudent investor became acquainted with statements of financial information as the object of financial reporting and disclosure systems. Before the turn of the century Peter Earling of Chicago, a pioneer writer in the field of credit analysis, had developed practices useful in bank credit departments and had written a book entitled, *Whom to Trust: A Practical Treatise on Mercantile Credits.* Earling's system was based on the methods and experience of his mercantile credit practice. "Prior to and concurrent with Earling's ideas the amounts of credit to be granted had been estimated from statements submitted by the borrower, but the analysis of the statement appears to have gone no further than a careful reading of the figures and investigation of their accuracy" (Brown 1955: 11). Earling's work illustrated an approach and gave birth to a much more analytical method. He investigated asset valuation and recognized the variation of financial data among industries and also expressed relationships or proportions between assets and liabilities and net worth. This was the dawn of the era of scientific credit granting.

Across a wide spectrum of companies, from arms manufacturers to cattle companies and railroads, examples of increasingly sophisticated accounting disclosures and information are found. Railroad statements provide landmark examples because of the dominant position of railroad securities on trading markets. Railroad reports of this period contain the forerunners of the concept of working capital and funds flow disclosures. Statements based on this type of information can be found beginning as early as the 1870s. Thus by 1893 it is common to find statements entitled, "Statements showing resources and their application during the Year"; the purpose of which was to show changes in the solvency position and the effects of some inter-entity transactions. To the extent that corporations were unresponsive to demands for financial data, regulatory agencies began specifying classifications of accounts relative to legal decisions which affected the basis for the evaluation of assets and the determination of a fair return.

It was not until 1899 that the New York exchange took definite steps to require financial statement reports on a regular basis from listed companies. (Sobel 1965: 177)

Emerging Public Accounting Practice

The accountants of the post–Civil War period were prototypes of the modern professionals. Who were they? What were the elements of their practice? What was the nature of their education? How did they contribute to the overall formation of professional associations and to the legal recognition of accounting? The process of seeking answers to these questions provides the basis for a better understanding of the birth of modern public accounting.

A University of Illinois study on early public accountants published in 1942, conducted by A. C. Littleton, reveals that in 1850, nineteen accountants' names are listed in the city directories of New York, Chicago, and Philadelphia. Considering this low number it would be difficult to support the view that public accounting practice or accounting practice per se was widespread at this time. Consider also that even as late as the 1870s it was common practice for teams of stockholders to make periodic visits to corporate offices as a means of attempting to verify reported information. Stockholder verification of this type was perhaps practical because of the limited size and convenient locale of corporations. As late as 1875 it was still difficult to find a manufacturing company with $10 million in assets whereas over 100 companies had assets exceeding $150 million by the close of the second decade of the twentieth century (Newman 1967: 40). The rapid growth in the size of corporations indicated by these statistics suggests that the demand for public accounting services was only beginning to mount at the start of this era.

Accountants were called on to assist in a wide variety of matters. They became involved in the preparation of disputed cases for arbitration or suit. They were hired to detect improper entries and fraud as well as to discover errors in the books and records of the companies.

Defalcations, breaches of trust, irregularities, and swindling schemes were matters of daily occurrence in this environment. As one practitioner of this era stated:

> The professional accountant is an investigator, a looker for leaks, a dissector and a detective in the highest acceptation of the term; he must have a good knowledge of real estate, machinery, buildings and other property. His business is to verify that which is right and to detect and expose that which is wrong; to discover and report facts as they exist, whether they be plainly expressed by clear and distinct records or whether they be concealed by the cunning naive or hidden under plausibly arranged figures or as is frequently the case omitted from the records entirely. He is a reader of hieroglyphics, however written, for every erasure, altercation, (sic) interlining, dot, dash or character may have a meaning. He must interpret, rearrange and produce in simple but distinct from self explanatory and free from mysteries of bookkeeping, the narrative of facts, the relation to each other in results. He is the foe of deceit and the champion of honesty (Keister 1896).

Accounting practice was almost exclusively the province of men. Although records reveal that, after the turn of the century, several women were admitted to practice as certified public accountants, these were exceptions to the rule.[8]

Since expert consulting accountants provided skills and had the experience needed to insure results, the investment community and general public would begin to recognize the need for special talent and training, and the demand for accountants' services would grow. Yet there were too few statutory disclosure laws,professional associations, or publications to assist in the exchange of ideas or development of techniques to meet this new demand.

By 1885 cities and their directories began to reflect an increasing number of persons offering services as expert accountants. The city of Louisville, Kentucky, located at a distance from the financial and commercial centers of the East, listed the services of five practicing accountants. The city directories of New York, Chicago and Philadelphia indicated a rapid growth in the numbers of public accountants, from 81 in 1884, to 322 in 1889. As Ernest Reckitt, an early Chicago practitioner, observed, there was some turnover within these numbers, that is, persons who started and then withdrew from practice. Therefore the total number of individuals who had undertaken to practice publicly would be even greater than indicated. Littleton's study revealed that for the three major cities noted, during the period from 1850 to 1899, some 1,370 different individuals appeared in listings as accountants and 662 of these appeared only once. Despite the high number of nonrepeaters in the listings the number of those that did repeat, in relation to the total population, suggests that this period can be identified as having witnessed the birth of modern public accounting practice. This period also witnessed an unprecedented wave of corporate mergers which peaked in the 1890s. These mergers fueled the demand for accounting services which involved more than the review of clerical accuracy or the detection of fraud. The breadth of accounting services now expanded from the testing of values, financial advising, and various audit services to include report writing, even though statutory disclosure requirements did not exist. In the 1890s the forerunners of at least three of the national public accounting firms were established, and in April 1896, the first state legislation recognizing and establishing the title of certified public accountant was passed in the state of New York.

Prior to the merger wave of the 1890s, accountants and auditors, particularly those who had come from Great Britain, benefited from the brewers boom of the 1880s. During this period British capital was attracted to America especially for the purposes of investing in breweries. In such far-flung locations as St. Louis, Chicago, San Francisco, Baltimore, Milwaukee, Denver, Springfield, Indianapolis, and other locations, brewing companies were formed and as a consequence accounting investigations and subsequent audits of considerable length were required.

James T. Anyon, an English bred early CPA leader, suggests that the "back parlor" (moonlighting) nature of many American accounting practices raised doubts among the public about the quality, ability and character of early native accountants. He noted that accountants were viewed as "men of figures"—those who dealt in and loved figures for themselves, who calculated balances in accounts, prepared elaborate statements, and looked for errors. Accountants were viewed as the type of persons who thought figures, sometimes juggled them, and always wrote and talked them.

If this image betrays a lack of popular appeal perhaps it is well to explore the reasons for this perception. During this period accounting work was identified with musty drudgery. The bulky old bound ledgers in which records were kept were complicated affairs. It was quite impossible when starting a new ledger to determine with any accuracy the number of pages that an account might require before another ledger was opened. It was common to forward accounts as they filled up pages such that an account starting on page 10 might be forwarded to page 99, then to page 150, then to page 209, and so on. Unless the account was indexed by page, an outside auditor found it quite difficult to follow. Not until the loose-leaf ledger became practical to employ around the 1880s, was the cumbersome bound ledger replaced. About the same time special journals and voucher journals were achieving wide attention and use. Thus they provided an additional reduction in the repetitive and needless duplication of entry information. Accounting reports rendered during this period were prepared and submitted in longhand, since the popular acceptance of the typewriter did not occur until the mid–1890s. One of the requisite skills of the accountant was to have "an accomplished hand" in penmanship and a modicum of patience. For when multiple copies were required they had to be produced in the same tedious and exacting longhand.

Accountants as might be expected were skeptical as to the advantages of the typewriter when it first appeared. "Why should I pay $125 for a machine when I can buy a pen for two cents?" some asked. Other accountants thought it offensive to be the object of impersonal typewritten correspondence, likening it to receiving a printed public handbill (Reckitt 1953: 9).

Auditing techniques of the period included the following: vouching all cash disbursements, checking all footings and postings, and checking the ledger to the trial balance and the trial balance to the financial statements. As much as three-fourths of the audit time was spent on footings and postings. Experience showed however that about three quarters of the defalcations were hidden by failures to account for income or cash receipts. Frequently books would have been out of balance for months or years and locating errors was a terrible task.

In 1869 *Auditor's Guide*, by H. J. Mettenheim, appeared (Moyer: 1951). Only sixteen pages, it was hardly adequate for the times but it suggested techniques for preventing fraud, including that all entries be clear, full and explicit, that money columns be ruled to prevent slovenly work, and that the cashier be required to use a voucher for every payment. In 1881 Selden R. Hopkins' book, *Manual of Exhibit Bookkeeping*, dealt in part with auditing matters. In 1882 G. P. Greer's *Science of Accounts* contained some significant sections on auditing, including that proof should be sought outside the books in attempting to verify statements of debtors and creditors. Greer went on to specify certain internal control requirements which should be established in corporations, for example, that obligations of the corporation should be authorized by the vote of the directors and that all payments of large amounts should be made by check or draft on a bank of deposit. Greer also noted that when receipts or disbursements passed through the hands of a treasurer, a cashier and a different collecting or disbursing clerk should check and prove each other.

Considering the techniques and the auditing theory of the period, it becomes clear that such early audits were effectively audits of the bookkeepers. The primary targets were error and fraud. Two out of three new audit engagements during the 1890s were likely to reveal defalcations. Such statistics do not come as a surprise in light of the fact that there had been no prior audit, fidelity bonds were not in existence, and few if any internal controls, including the division of duties, existed (Moyer 1951).

All of this suggests that the type of services and the qualifications of the individuals practicing public accounting during this period probably varied widely. There was little to prevent someone from advertising as follows in public directories or newspapers:

Complicated, disputed and confused accounts; also accounts with executors, trustees and estates in assignments investigated and stated. Books opened and closed. Suspected accounts confidentially examined. Partnership settlements made.

Such touting pronouncements were not restricted to public directories and newspapers. Expert account cards were also circulated referring to similar services being offered to include expert work with joint stock companies, banks, and other corporation accounts.

The Institute of Accountants and Bookkeepers formed in New York on July 28, 1882 was the first professional accounting organization in the United States. Its aims during its first decade were almost wholly devoted to education for accounting and providing accounting literature. At institute meetings technical and professional subjects were discussed. Subsequently the institute changed its name to the Institute of Accounts and at the turn of the century published the monthly periodical *Accountics*. The Institute of Accounts required a full test of qualifications before admission. Unfortunately, little is known of the operations of the institute after the turn of the century since its records have not been located and only a few of its examiners are known. Yet for a quarter century, from 1882 until about 1908, the Institute of Accounts provided a professional association which admitted members from public as well as commercial practice. Its membership in 1884 numbered eighty persons, and over the years included such notable members as Charles E. Sprague, Selden Hopkins, Charles Waldo Haskins, Farquhar MacRae, and Henry Harney.

Topics of meeting speeches for the period from 1883 to 1887 included the following: "Costs Accounts in Metal Factories," by A. O. Kittredge; "The Unlearned Profession," by Silas S. Packard;" "Documents as Related to Accounts," by Charles E. Sprague; "Account Keeping of Telephone Companies," by Charles Dothan; "Prices and Profits," by Joseph Hardcastle; and "Mechanical Consolidation Items," by Captain Henry Metcalfe. At the meeting of December 15, 1886 Charles Taller, a member of the institute, gave an address entitled "French and American Account Keeping Contrasted". This is the first known professional address on international accounting matters in America. Later during this meeting a catalytic event leading to the formation of an association exclusively serving public accountants occurred. As an interesting sequel to Taller's speech on French and American accounting, Edwin Guthrie, FCA, guest of the evening, gave by request a description of the Institute of Chartered Accountants in England. Guthrie had come to the United States at the invitation of James T. Anyon who had arrived in October of the same year (Webster 1954).

British auditors had begun to reside in America as London firms found it less expensive to provide services on an extended basis by establishing resident offices in major U.S. cities. As business increased, the English firms were slowly Americanized by taking on staff of either British born naturalized Americans or native born Americans. Prior to 1888 such British firms serviced primarily British capital investments in fire insurance, railroad, and mortgage companies via monthly audits. With the subsequent "brewers boom" mentioned above, British firms became involved in the audits of American breweries in several distant points in the United States.

The British contingent served as a nucleus to influence the founding of the American Association of Public Accountants (AAPA). In addition to having known many British practitioners, Anyon had become acquainted with several American accountants of prominent stature, including William Veysey, John Heins, and others. The history of the AAPA, which after several reorganizations and mergers through the twentieth century ultimately became the American

Institute of Certified Public Accountants (AICPA), is well known. The writings of John L. Carey in *The Rise of the Accounting Profession* (vol. I) detail many of the particulars of the early formative matters that were addressed by the AAPA.[9]

At this point only the Institute of Accountants and the American Association of Public Accountants have been cited, but it is also important to note the existence of similar associations across the country during the 1880s. Between November 1874 and January 1886 six bookkeeping and accounting societies were organized in as many cities. Five others were organized in 1887, two in 1888, and three in 1889. These associations were not restricted to public accountants and were located in principal cities, including St. Louis, Chicago, Cleveland, Boston, Dayton, Kansas City, Pittsburgh, Detroit, Chicago, San Francisco, Buffalo and Memphis.

Among the most active of these groups was the Bookkeepers Beneficial Association of Philadelphia which was organized in 1874 with thirty-five members and grew to a membership of nearly 300 by 1888. This association celebrated its fiftieth anniversary in 1924 but was dissolved sometime thereafter. It is not clear that this association acted as did the Institute of Accounts to screen membership by a set of rigorous examinations.

Several accounting periodicals serving these organizations also appeared during this period. *The Bookkeeper*, edited and published by Selden R. Hopkins and Charles E. Sprague, appeared in July 1880 and continued until 1883. Other publications included *The American Accounting Room* and *The Treasury*. These were succeeded by *The Office* published by A. O. Kittredge. Each of these reported a circulation of 3,000 or more and extra editions of 10,000 issued as samples were sent out widely to accountants and others.

The certificate of incorporation of the American Association of Public Accountants was filed on September 20, 1887. The first president was James Yalden, an Englishman. The vice-president was John Heins, an American born accountant. The secretary was James T. Anyon and the treasurer was William Veysey. The most formidable obstacle facing public practitioners at this time was a lack of formal legal recognition of their public practice. It is noted by Carey that the existence of the AAPA did little to change things immediately. Both the Institute of Accounts and the AAPA began via separate routes to investigate securing legislation to achieve such legal recognition. Norman Webster and George Wilkinson have provided us with a legacy of details and information regarding the pre–1900 CPA movement. Although some historical essays on the subject of these early years suggest that a noble "onward and upward" spirit existed between British and American accountants, other interpretations do not support this view. The early AAPA was a hybrid of the English Club-Medieval Guild patterned after the Institute of Chartered Accountants. It did not become an "American" organization for several years. Part of the evidence of its lack of acceptance by native Americans before 1900 is found in the fact that it had fewer than 100 members at the turn of the century and these were predominantly English born residents of New York. Accountants from other states were noted in Association records as "non residents." Early professional activities were marked by the existence of these two camps, the British and the American. Although harmony would be forthcoming it is important to note that, in addition to the problem of lack of legal recognition, the professionals themselves had not yet achieved a sense of unity and self-identity. As long as practitioners were thus divided it would be difficult to achieve legal recognition (Wilkinson 1928).

A dozen years before the CPA Law of New York was passed, the Institute of Accounts issued certificates to Fellows who had passed the strict practical and technical entrance examinations. The prerequisite of technical competence as a basis of self regulation therefore had been established prior to the existence of a law.

But the professional associations lacked the power and complete authority to control the growing ranks of all practitioners. Therefore in 1895 an initial attempt to obtain CPA legislation was made by both organizations. During the winter of 1894-1895 a rough draft of a bill providing for a professional examination and a distinctive title was prepared by Henry Harney, president of the Institute of Accounts. Many years before Harney had committed to paper some ideas along this line. He appointed Charles E. Sprague to convey the draft to Albany and see what could be done toward having it enacted into legislation. Sprague was a friend of Melville Dewey, secretary of the regents of the University of New York. Dewey advised that the enforcement of the law be put under the jurisdiction of the regents of the University of the State of New York which was the body that had the capability to conduct such examinations. Furthermore, he pointed out that this would give the measure something of an educational character. The legal designation, Certified Public Accountant, was agreed upon at this time.

In the meantime, acting independently in every respect, several members of the AAPA prepared a draft for a bill providing that no person shall practice as a public accountant after the passage of the act unless he be licensed by the regents of the University of the State of New York. No distinctive title was sought under the AAPA bill. This bill was introduced in February 1895, before the senate of the state of New York.

Two weeks later the institute's bill was introduced in the assembly of the state of New York. The institute's bill contained two features which were clearly disadvantageous to the large British born membership of the AAPA. First, it required that CPAs be citizens of the United States and second it provided that only Certified Public Accountants of the state of New York should be appointed or employed to act as examiners of accounts, expert accountants or paid auditors by court administrators, receivers, state, and county or municipal officers.

A meeting was called in March 1895 to attempt to negotiate differences between the two bills and the rival organizations by means of delegating a special committee to resolve the differences between the bills. This "Committee of 14" was to determine the proper action to be taken with regard to the bills before the legislature. Two of the members of the committee representing the AAPA were Anyon and Yalden. Among those representing the institute were Harney and Charles Dutton. There were also nonmember representatives including Silas S. Packard and John E. Hourigan. The committee lost little time in determining that the association's bill proposing a license should be dropped and the institute's bill proposing a title should be pushed. The committee also determined that an attorney should be retained to watch the progress of the bill before the legislature. A subcommittee of the "Committee of 14" retained E. G. Whittaker to represent the committee at the assembly and the subcommittee met with the assembly's committee on general laws to advocate passage of the bill. The subcommittee was unable to influence the legislation. Assemblyman Wylds who had introduced the bill could not be persuaded to report it favorably to the House. Meanwhile, in the senate, the bill which had been substituted for the institute's version failed to receive a majority vote.

The AAPA quickly followed up to reintroduce the provisions of the bill in the following year's meeting of the legislature. Perhaps because the AAPA represented the practicing *public* accountants and not a mixed group of accountants it was deemed most appropriate for them to pursue the passage of the bill in the next session. Frank Broaker became the chairman of the association's subcommittee. He turned the bill over to Senator Albert Ray of Brooklyn, who introduced the bill in the Senate in January 1896. It was referred to the Committee on Judiciary. During the same period a bill under the same title was introduced in the House by Assemblyman Marshall. The bill passed the Assembly on April 3 by almost unanimous vote, passed the Senate on April 7, and was approved by the governor on April 17, 1896.

A significant single amendment to the bill, made as a result of apparent cooperation between the rival professional groups, assured its passage in 1896. The amendment provided that the Certified Public Accounting designation was available to any citizen of the United States or *person who had duly declared his intention to become such a citizen.* The success of the 1896 legislation may have hinged importantly upon that provision which opened the way for many British chartered accountants and other non-Americans who had not as yet secured their papers as U.S. citizens. Without the amendment a split in the support for the bill between American and British professionals might have developed because of the restrictive provisions in the act regarding state directed accounting engagements. When the bill did take effect many British chartered accountants who chose to retain their British citizenship moved to other states to set up their practice.

In the years 1896 and 1897, 112 certificates were awarded, 108 under the waiver which had been established by the Board of Regents to grant the CPA certificate to those who could prove they had been in reputable practice as public accountants since January 1, 1890. The waiver certificates were awarded in alphabetical order. Frank Broaker received the first CPA certificate. The first examination under the new law was held in December 1896. Only three of the four who passed this examination are known; they include Edward C. Charles, Joseph Hardcastle, and William H. Jasper (Wilkinson 1903: 9).

The First CPAs	
New York Certificate Number	Names
1	Frank Broaker
2	Richard Chapman
3	Leonard Conant
4	William Sanders Davies
5	Rodney S. Dennis
6	Charles Waldo Haskins
7	Brownell McGibbon
8	Frederick Manuel
9	Charles J. Mercer
10	E. W. Sells
11	C. E. Sprague

   A typical profile of American born CPA candidates who sat for the exam at the turn of the century would include being thirty years old, attending public schools for grammar education and working as a commercial or government clerk or bookkeeper, before engaging in the public practice of another accountant and/or returning to teaching at a commercial college. Thereafter upon setting up practice in one's own name the CPA exam would be taken and professional activities commenced.

Figure 4–3

A lighthearted sketch of Frank Broaker, CPA No. 1.

Source: Souvenir program of the 1906 Annual Meeting of the American Association of Public Accountants, Columbus, Ohio.

In response to the initial passage of CPA legislation, other states soon followed in obtaining similar legislation. A Pennsylvania CPA law was enacted in 1899. Maryland passed a CPA law in 1900, California in 1901, Washington and Illinois in 1903. Thus by 1921 all states in the Union had CPA legislation. As expected CPAs now began to form separate professional associations. John Hourigan of Albany appears to have been an important catalyst in the formation of the New York State Society of CPAs, whose initial meeting was held at the Hotel Waldorf on March 30, 1897. Earlier Hourigan had solicited via a letter the interest of accountants in the state, to form a society similar to those of physicians, architects and civil engineers. Hourigan served as an incorporator of the New York Society and its first vice-president. (Committee on History 1953a)

Although the New Jersey law was not enacted until April 1904, public accountants in the state organized their society in January 1898. This society, through one of its members, Richard Stevenson, a New York CPA practicing in Newark, was instrumental in eventually overcoming the opposition of the New Jersey legislature to achieve passage of the CPA bill.

Leading Figures

The many early CPA movement leaders, including Hopkins, Sprague, Harney, Broaker and MacRae, reflected a diversity of backgrounds. Hopkins for example, had contributed a section to a book entitled, *Dollars and Sense*, written by the famous showman Phineas T. Barnum. Hopkins' section, "Money, Banks and Banking," focused on "where money came from and where it went." In addition, Hopkins was editor of *The Book-Keeper*, a magazine published in the 1880s, and wrote books on the subject of bookkeeping practice. In 1888 he had written a "Horatio Alger" type novel, *A Young Prince of Commerce*.

Charles E. Sprague should be assigned much credit for gaining the instrumental support and advice of Melville Dewey to secure passage of the CPA law. He was a man of many talents. By vocation a banker, he had an interest in foreign languages and also had been involved with Hopkins in the publication of the *Book-Keeper*. Long active in affairs of his alma mater, Union College of Schenectady, he was also the author of the "The Algebra of Accounts," a lengthy series which first appeared in the issues of the *Book-Keeper* in the early

1880s. Sprague achieved fame after the turn of the century as having made a major contribution to the theory of accounts through his algebraic demonstration of the systematic concept of "Assets equal Liabilities plus Proprietorship" (A = L + P) (Sprague 1908: 20). A veteran of the Civil War, he had been wounded at the battle of Gettysburg.

Frank Broaker, the first CPA, was born in Millerstown, Pennsylvania in 1863. He was the son of John Strawbridge but took his stepfather's name. He worked for John Roundy, a Scot accountant, from 1883 to 1887 and then worked in his own name before entering partnership with Richard M. Chapman (the second CPA under the provisions of the 1896 Act). He was active in the American Association of Public Accountants having been vice-president from 1892 to 1896 and president and ramrod of the legislative efforts in 1896.

Broaker was involved in a minor scandal relating to the publication of *The American Accountants Manual,* a book which he had prepared in 1897 based on the first CPA examination questions. The manual contained recommended solutions to the examination and sold for three dollars with the proceeds going to his private account. In addition to the matter of revenue, Broaker had been charged with forming a society of accountants with himself as president. It was alleged that he had urged accountants to join the society, and that they were led to expect that if they did so, the regents might be induced to waive the examination as was provided in the law for a person possessing the necessary experience qualifications. In response to complaints about Broaker's actions with regard to the manual, the State Board of Regents effected a reorganization of the State Board of Examiners of Certified Public Accountants by appointing James T. Anyon to replace Broaker and by appointing Charles Waldo Haskins and Charles E. Sprague, who had served on the first board of examiners for the Certified Public Accountant certificate. A published comment in an 1897 issue of *Accountics* notes that the summary dismissal of Broaker for allegedly violating the precedent for treatment of revenues from such a manual was severe and perhaps unwarranted.

Henry Harney, born in Baltimore in 1835, had been the chief accountant of the Bank of Richmond from 1856–1861 and had served in the Civil War on the side of the Confederacy. He became a member of the Institute of Accounts in 1886 and served five successive terms as President. It is interesting and colorful to note that two adversaries in the Civil War, Sprague and Harney, served effectively together to bring the CPA profession into existence.

Farquhar J. MacRae, a native of Brooklyn born in 1862, worked for Selden Hopkins and Henry Harney and was listed as a public accountant in the New York Directory of 1892. MacRae became a member of the Institute of Accounts in 1890, secretary in 1892, and a member of the executive committee in 1897. He served four terms as vice-president. He later became active in the State Society and the Federation of State Societies of Public Accountants after the turn of the century. In 1894 an advertisement by MacRae and Cowan, expert accountants, read as follows:

> Forty dollars per week; five years experience; and Members of Institute of Accounts; $20 per week English chartered accountant who has sufficient experience in this country to render them familiar with modern methods of bookkeeping.

As part of his research on the American Association of Public Accountants, Norman Webster lists the backgrounds and important data known about early members of the professional association. One of the most interesting profiles is that of Ferdinand W. Lafrentz. Lafrentz migrated to the United States, living in Chicago, in 1873. Subsequently, he moved West, working in Ogden, Utah, and serving as a member of the Wyoming legislature in 1888. In response to the request of a friend who was traveling to the West Coast, Lafrentz became familiar with the activities of the American Surety Company and was employed as an accountant in 1893. He subsequently became president and chairman of that organization. At the same time he had established a practice in his own name, F. W. Lafrentz and Company. Later Lafrentz's organization was formalized into the American Audit Company with offices located in the Waldorf Astoria. The American Audit Company became F. W. Lafrentz & Company in 1923. Lafrentz continued his service to the American Surety Company past his ninetieth year. He was a poet, having authored a book of poems called *Cowboy Stuff* and a book in German about his boyhood days in Fehmarn, an island in the Baltic Sea just north of the German mainland. Lafrentz received some of his accounting training at a Bryant and Stratton Business College. He was a member of the American Association of Public Accountants and held certificate number 20 in New York State. He also lectured at the New York University School of Commerce, Accounts and Finance.

As the business world moved into the twentieth century, economic theory, the legal system, and society all were shifting their attention toward growth of large enterprises under the system of capitalism. The need for a trained corps of public accountants was becoming recognized and addressed through the passage of CPA legislation and the formation of professional accounting associations. The problems and the challenges were many. For one, the associations of practitioners were not growing as rapidly as key members believed they should. In part this may be attributed to the fact that the rules of admission were rigorous and restrictive. Although some early writers have stated that American public accounting was not in existence before the 1880s, it would be more appropriate to say that public accounting was viable before 1880 but not visible until after 1880. Evidence supplied by Littleton and Webster indicates that accounting activity prior to the 1880s was importantly preparatory for the establishment of a widespread qualified, competent and professional discipline which began to emerge in the 1880s and the 1890s.

During these years before the turn of the century the full energies of this small group were devoted to:

1. Organizing at the state, local and national levels.
2. Securing passage of laws and initiating appropriate administration of such laws.
3. Initiating attempts to establish university programs of accounting.

In light of these tasks this young professional group was not sufficiently large to be extensively engaged in matters of developing uniform technical standards, and it would not seem to be a valid criticism of these pioneering CPAs that they did not make headway in the area.

Accounting Education and Textbooks

Business was beginning to require a type of training that existing schools, both high schools and universities, did not supply. In some ways the attitude of businessmen discouraged universities from undertaking business education on a widespread scale. For example, Andrew Carnegie stirred up a controversy which lasted well into the 1890s commenting that "college graduates are not successful businessmen." The old ironmaster thought that young men destined for business ought to be mingling with men who did business.

Prior to 1875 bookkeeping was perhaps the only subject that could be classified as a business topic regularly taught in high schools. Even after 1875 formal business education was still unknown in universities. In the face of the growing demand for individuals trained in business procedure to assist large corporations and other developing business enterprises in the conduct of their affairs, business colleges sprang up throughout the country during the post–Civil War period to provide trained personnel. Chain schools such as the Bryant and Stratton Business Colleges and pioneering business educators including Silas S. Packard, an accountant and later president of the Institute of Accounts, were among the important names in the business college movement of the pre-1900 period.

Figure 4–4

A classroom scene typical of the post–Civil War era.

Source: *The Countinghouse Arithmetic* (Baltimore, 1889).

In 1883 the first course in accounting to be sustained at the collegiate level was offered at the Wharton School of the University of Pennsylvania, which had started only two years earlier. The contents of the course, which included two terms of instruction, involved several technical requirements, as well as a series of lectures on "The Theory and Practice of Accounting." According to the recollections of one of the first students there were 12 pupils in this first collegiate accounting class. The next offering of the course found two textbooks being used, including Selden Hopkins' *Manual of Exhibit Bookkeeping* and C. C. Marsh's *Theory of Bank Bookkeeping and Joint Stock Accounts*. While the Wharton School initiated sustained university level accounting courses, it should be noted that several other attempts to form schools of commerce had been undertaken at other locations (Lockwood 1938).

Just before the turn of the century the University of Chicago authorized the establishment of a College of Commerce and Politics which was renamed the College of Commerce and Administration. In its initial academic year, 1898–1899, ten students were registered and within three years there were 89 students in total. Henry Rand Hatfield recalled that accounting at the University of Chicago, which he taught, relied upon the early writing of Professor J. F. Schar of Germany, who had written on the matter of single and double entry during the 1890s. The lack of suitable textbooks no doubt hampered the effectiveness of accounting at the university level. The pioneering efforts of the Wharton School, the University of Chicago and, after the turn of the century, the School of Commerce, Accounts and Finance at New York University and the Amos Tuck School at Dartmouth in 1899, provided important first steps in collegiate education in accounting.[10]

Business Colleges

University business programs developed toward the end of the era; the bulk of the training and education of businessmen and accountants *during* the era came by way of the proprietary business colleges. At a banquet for Silas S. Packard, on the occasion of his seventieth birthday in 1896, toasts and testimonials acknowledged his important role in the business college movement. Packard had organized and conducted a general exhibit of the American Commercial and Business Schools at the Chicago World's Fair. For over fifty years Packard had taken upon himself the work of commercial teaching and the promotion of business education. His schools included training the so-called "Packard boys" and young women as well who had an interest in business education. Packard, born in an Ohio log cabin in 1826, was a type of Horatio Alger success story. As one put it, ". . . inspired by poverty in youth he had learned the necessity for labor and for struggle." (Complimentary Banquet: 1896)

Packard wrote texts on accounting and bookkeeping for the chain of business colleges that he established. These books in revised form were still in use through the 1900s. Packard's books are recognized to have had an influence beyond the United States, to include Canada and Japan. Before 1876 William C. Whitney, an American business school proprietor, had journeyed to Japan and established a commercial school at the invitation of the Japanese minister to Washington. Whitney had operated a Bryant and Stratton business college in Newark. He took with him to Japan texts that dealt with the science of accounts. Two such texts which were prominent in the revolution of Japanese accounting during the period include Packard's *Manual of Theoretical Training in the Science of Accounts*, New York 1868, and Folsom's *Logic of Accounts*, New York 1873.

Packard had taught at various places before opening his own commercial college as a part of the Bryant and Stratton chain. In 1867 he bought out the interests of his partners, abolished the Bryant and Stratton affiliation, and founded the Packard Business College. This was a step toward terminating chain system influence in business education and laid the foundation for solely owned schools. The chain movement of business schools faltered after the initial success of the Bryant and Stratton system partly because of internal weaknesses involving changes in policies as well as the lack of uniformity with regard to the practices of individual schools under local leadership.

Just as Packard was the patriarch of business education in the East, George Soulé was a patriarch of education for business in the South. New Orleans, which had flourished in the post–Civil War years, also experienced an acute need for persons trained in business subjects. Soulé authored successful and widely used accounting texts as did Packard. Soulé's book was introduced in 1881 with subsequent editions through the early 1900s.

As business colleges began operating on a proprietary and profit basis, they grew rapidly. In 1889 Packard described business colleges as "strong in number and financially prosperous." Response to the success of these colleges included some public school competition to meet the demands heretofore served by the private business colleges. Cities recognized that business college subjects would pay their own way. But the point remains that private business colleges filled the educational void for a significant period.[11]

Textbooks of the Times

An examination of the textbooks that were used to teach account keeping during this period reveals the standardization of the worksheet step of the accounting cycle. In this step, the pro forma work sheet, based upon the unadjusted trial balance through to adjusted profit and loss and balance sheet columns was used much the same way as we find it in the accounting cycle of today.[12]

A common weakness of the general financial accounting texts of this period seems to have been the lack of technique for dealing with corporation accounts. Even late editions of Soulé's *Science and Practice of Accounts* were oriented to proprietary ownership rather than to capital stock companies. However, some editions did treat opening entries and techniques for capital stock companies.

It would seem that the experience of the practicing accountant in the handling of corporate accounts was not yet flowing into the classroom. Practical experience, not academic research, provided the source of technical innovation which was then disseminated through popular textbooks. Most of the native born accountants in the United States who had reached middle life before the turn of the century had graduated from the ranks of the bookkeeper. By the turn of the century the CPA examination emphasizing the theory of accounts, practical accounting, auditing, and commercial law began to assume a leading and conditioning influence as to the educational training pattern suitable for aspiring professionals. High school education followed by "university training in accountancy and its allied branches" was to become the recommended route as early as 1905.

The Birth of Preclassical Theory

The study of theory development during this period leads to the conclusion that several important beginnings in the attempt to conceptualize accounting practice were initiated. Most notable was the appearance of Charles E. Sprague's "Algebra of Accounts" series. This was the forerunner of the theory which was ultimately presented in his important work, *The Philosophy of Accounts*, published shortly after the turn of the century. Sprague's writing in the "Algebra of Accounts" evidences a capability for abstract and axiomatic approaches in accounting thought well before such ideas were popularly recognized. His early works provided a classificatory and deductive framework for notions being widely discussed in the publications of

Carlton & Fowler's Balance Sheet. Set V.

New York, May 31st, 1876.

L. Follo.		Ledger Balances Dr.	Ledger Balances Cr.	Profit and Loss Losses	Profit and Loss Gains	H. L. Carlton Dr.	H. L. Carlton Cr.	Geo. R. Fowler Dr.	Geo. R. Fowler Cr.	State of Affairs Assets	State of Affairs Liabilities
1	H. L. Carlton,		20,100 00				20,100 00				
1	George R. Fowler,	1,164 99						1,164 99			
1	Cash,	2,432 90								2,432 90	
1	Bills Receivable,	1,852 13								1,852 13	
1	Bills Payable,		2,917 50								2,917 50
1	Merchandise,	14,847 01	17,241 88		2,394 87					17,241 88	
2	Interest and Discount,	152 33		152 33							
2	Fixtures and Expenses,	284 50		284 50							
✓	Personal Debtors,	2,896 08								2,896 08	
✓	Personal Creditors,		612 44						652 68		612 44
		23,629 94	23,629 94	436 83	2,394 87		1,305 36				3,529 94
				1,305 36					512 31		20,893 05
				652 68					1,164 99	24,422 99	24,422 99
				2,394 87	2,394 87	21,405 36	21,405 36	1,164 99			

Total Losses and Gains,
{ H. L. Carlton's, ½ gain,
Geo. R. Fowler's, ½ " }

Firm's Net Gain $1,958.04.

Net Capital, $21,405 36

Net Insolvency,

Total Assets and Liabilities,
{ H. L. Carlton's Net Capital, $1,405.36.
Geo. R. Fowler's " Insolvency, 512.31. }

Firm's Net Capital, $21,405.36.

Figure 4–5

Textbook examples of financial reports, 1876.

the time and linked early accounting notions to mathematics and economics.

Sprague began his exposition by noting that accounting "is a history of values." His basic accounting equation, *assets = liabilities + proprietorship*, appeared in the 1880 series of articles as, "what I have plus what I trust equals what I owe plus what I am worth," which was written symbolically as $H + T = O + X$ (Sprague 1880). Through sets of symbolic equations he provided the reader of accounts a logical and systematic approach to gaining a command over the accounting cycle. Rather than requiring that one memorize an endless series of rules, Sprague emphasized that the keeping of accounts involved certain equations in which addition and cancellation are the central techniques employed. He also noted the importance of uniform value in determining net wealth as follows:

> Annals or chronicles merely relate facts which have occurred; but true history groups together facts of the same tendency in order to discover if possible the cause of happiness and misery, prosperity and ruin; so true bookkeeping, being a history, should group together similar values in its equations to discover the causes and effects of Loss and Gain. (Sprague 1880)

He concluded, "In the equation of accounts the answer sought or 'unknown quantity' is what am I worth? This we will represent by the letter X."

Although Sprague's exposition did not go beyond the proprietary model, the forty-two paragraphs of this early treatise included notational operations for balancing and measurement which were suitable for more than proprietary operations.

Sprague's accounting equation $(A = L + P)$ was destined to become the starting point of today's approach to accounting education as well as the focal point of subsequent modifications. In this way Sprague axioms have become recognized as the essence of a preclassical school of American accounting theory. His writings were evidence of the unique and essentially complete theory wherefrom modern American accounting developed. It was within this framework that conceptual concerns over issues such as costs and value, income and outlay, inventory and depreciation, would be argued.

As has been noted earlier this is also a crucial time in the debate over the appropriate treatment of what is now recognized as the depreciation of fixed and wasting assets. A comment in the May 1897 issue of *Accountics* betrays the importance and state of the issue at that time. A speech given at a regular meeting of the Institute of

Accounts in New York on Thursday evening January 14, 1897, given by Frederick W. Child, a member of the institute, and attended by a large audience, was the subject of a feature in the magazine. The main point of Child's address was with respect to depreciation of plant, tools, fixtures, and so on, and the plan he recommended for managing the accounts respecting the same. He proposed that such accounts as machinery and tools, buildings and similar items should show the total cost of those items or the amount of the capital invested therein and that the amount written off for wear and tear, depreciation of value, and so forth should be credited to special reserve accounts. "Thus," he noted, "if tools and machinery which cost $27,000 were in the estimation of the managers of the enterprise, depreciated in value by reason of use and other causes to an amount at a certain time equal to 10 percent, then the amount of depreciation ($2700) instead of being credited to tools and machinery account, should be passed to a credit for reserve on tools and machinery." This is one of the earliest publicly discussed examples of reserves for accumulated depreciation in America.

Under Child's approach, successive percentages, the results of which were entered during a term of years, would be credited to the reserve account. The allowance for depreciation, he urged, should be regarded as an expense in the factory account and should be spread over the goods produced. He did not believe that satisfactory results from the accounting point of view were ever obtained by carrying the amount of depreciation of machinery and plant into the loss and gain account directly, for he held that depreciation of plant was part of the cost of the product.

The pages of *Accountics* also reveal another discussion in the same year on the subject of goodwill. Although the article focused upon court cases, particularly those in England, it did, after thorough discussion, indicate that the accountants of the period were involved in debating the issue. Other conceptual concerns are also evidenced. Several years earlier at a meeting of the Institute of Accounts in October, 1889, Sprague delivered a lecture on the subject of "income and outlay." He clearly suggests that the appropriate treatment was tied to the principle of *periodicity:*

> The artificiality of profit and loss and its tributaries results partly from their relation to time. The reciprocal action and reaction of outlay and income are continuous, but for convenience we treat them as periodical. We are compelled to cut them into even lengths for purposes of comparison. (Sprague 1889)

In this lecture Sprague distinguished between losses and expenses indicating that if the bookkeeping is that of a business concern then expenditures made under such headings as insurance and so forth are in no sense losses as the title profit and loss suggests. They are, he concluded, business outlays, deliberately made for the purpose of producing income which is hoped will exceed outlay.

As early as 1880, the literature contained subjects of modern interest to include a discussion of a treatment of extraordinary items of expense versus expense items incurred in ordinary operations.

In the writings of Soulé we find descriptions of the use of suspense accounts, in particular a type of allowance for doubtful accounts as a device for treating accounts receivable values. It is also interesting to note that the term "principles" was employed in the description of the methods applicable to accounts as early as 1890.[13]

Two notable expositions on the theoretical and valuational aspects of accounting during the post–Civil War period were published before Sprague wrote his important series. The 1868 work of Silas S. Packard entitled, *Manual of Theoretical Training in the Science of Accounts*, and *The Logic of Accounts* written by E. G. Folsom and published in 1873 were forerunners in this preclassical era. Folsom's name is not well known in the history of accounting. What is known about his past begins with his activity as the founder of a business college in Cleveland, Ohio, where he trained two enterprising individuals, Bryant and Stratton, who, as mentioned earlier, later formed their own chain of commercial colleges. In 1875, while proprietor of a different business college in Albany, New York, he published *The Logic Of Accounts*, which had been written in 1873. The book focused on "valuation" problems in accounting. He classified value initially under two headings, commercial value and idea value. As he observed:

> With the view of reducing double entry accounts to an exact science we begin with value as a generic or universal term applicable alike to all things and divided, first into two distinct classes; then each class into species of its own, until ultimate simple values are reached, as shown by the analysis.

It may have become apparent that his notions were not useful or operational in practice, for his message appears to have had no great following. It was not until Sprague's writing that a clear point was made about the value of an asset and that such value could be measured in services given or the cost incurred. Sprague saw both

TOPICAL ANALYSIS OF VALUE.

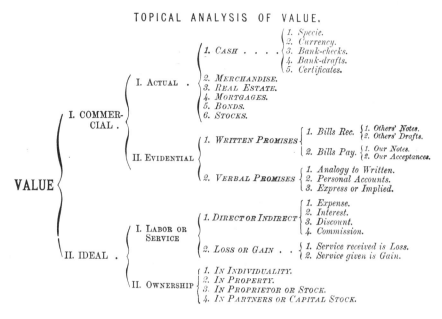

Figure 4-6

Folsom's "value theory chart."

Source: E. G. Folsom, *The Logic of Accounts* (New York, 1873).

the supply and demand aspect of value. Folsom probably saw the distinction between value in use and value in exchange much earlier but only from the supply side. He valiantly tried to incorporate it as the core of his accounting system but, again, his method failed to gain the distinction it merited.

This quarter century of American professional accounting was marked by attempts to establish the role and function of the practicing accountant. Accountants devoted considerable editorial and manuscript attention to what the public accountant *was* and what the public accountant *did*, or to respond to such rhetorical questions as, "What is an accountant, as distinguished from a bookkeeper?" or "What is an auditor?"

The passage of the New York CPA law and the exposition and influence of Sprague's theory of accounts provided the basis upon which to solidify a self view of accounting and its theory.

In this period, in part due to the notions identified with Sprague, it became possible to represent the activities of accounts in a notational and axiomatic fashion which facilitated abstraction and modeling of accounting transactions. Without these achievements it would seem unlikely that the developments of the first thirty years of the next century would have come to pass, particularly in terms of the accounting techniques needed to communicate the financial data and statements that characterized the growth and complexity of the corporation. The influence of Sprague on the writings of later and equally eminent account thinkers may be inferred from the following remarks made by W. A. Paton in referring to Sprague:[14]

> It was these writings that aroused my interest in accounting, and without this spur I am quite certain that I would never have shifted from teaching economic theory to a career primarily in the accounting field. . . .
>
> Above all, he pushed the door ajar to a realization that accounting constitutes the outstanding approach to a pervasive understanding of business enterprises . . . . (Paton 1972: iii, v).

Cost and Managerial Accounting

During the 1850s, Paul Garner has noted, industrialism was beginning to have an impact on the character of account keeping. The post–Civil War steel industry boom was a response to the demands of the westward drive of the railroads. For the first time many text writers began to consider accounts related to factory and production costs. John Fleming's *Bookkeeping by Double Entry,* published in Pittsburgh in 1854, included several changes to reflect cost accounting considerations. Fleming changed the name of the merchandise trading account to "factory account" and also attempted to determine the appropriate treatment for factory buildings. Whether these adjustments truly reflected a general need for cost system information because of the many iron and steel mills near Pittsburgh can only be speculated. But at about that time Andrew Carnegie was pioneering the introduction of cost accounting in his mills, and maintaining a considerable staff in his cost department. He was noted to have indicated that his financial success was in part due to his ability to know his costs in the steel industry. (Reckitt 1953: 18)

Up until the 1880s, text writers appeared to neglect industrial accounts at the very time that industry was being revolutionized by the factory system, widespread use of mechanical equipment, and devices for rapid communication and transportation. Perhaps a lack of experience and expertise in this first generation of management accounting explains the lack of writing. One can speculate that prior to 1885 the lack of detailed writings about the methods used by management and factory accountants was assignable to incomplete knowledge or at another extreme, to a desire to retain the advantage of their knowledge by keeping it a secret. Several small societies of accountants and bookkeepers existed even prior to 1880, therefore, there were professional circles through which this information could have circulated. However, there were few professional accounting magazines prior to 1880, and the lack of an effective means of such communication may also have impeded the transfer of knowledge. There is also the possibility that while developments were being achieved in the area of cost controls at this point there was still not a sufficient basis of practice to lend credibility to generalizations about the value of a given approach or system.

Recent historical research by H. T. Johnson and W. E. Stone which focuses upon the pre 1880 period and earlier, considers factory records themselves as a device for determining the true state of the management accounting art prior to 1880. Their research indicates that the systems in existence were much more sophisticated than could be determined from the literature and textbooks of the time. Johnson has observed that as the vertical integration of large complex businesses occurred (such that from source supply to consumer, a single organization was involved in transforming the raw material to the final product), it was necessary that an organization structure and an accounting system be developed to integrate the entire effort under a unitary form of managerial accounting that featured independent departments as well as central office communication and control features.

A Bitter View

Not all business writers were content with accounting or the persons who practiced it (Wells 1970). Kirkman, for example, writing in *Railway Expenditures* in 1880, slashed out the following personal attack:

> When I was very young I remember to have been much cast down at the evident want of interest which railway managers manifested in statistical lore. I can recall, now, that my ideal officer was a man of delicate physical structure, of towering intellectual front, with pale, weak eyes and sickly complexion withal, his shoulders bowed with study and the contemplation of the subtle phases of railway polity. My ideal

was, in fact, not a manager at all, but a statistician, a clerk, an accountant. I had not then learned that the class of men I had in mind were never leaders in the affairs of life, but the followers only—the pack-mules, so to speak. The managers of our railways are never of an active statistical turn of mind, and as I said before, it is perhaps fortunate for the owners that this is so (pp. 22–23).

He then notes with alarm

The rapid growth of the railroad interest has developed everywhere embryo accountants in more or less profusion, whose greatest delight seems to have been to introduce in connection with the property with which they were identified all the new and strange forms and observances that occurred to them. In the progress of their work what was before luminous such men make wholly incomprehensible; with them the dawn is ever succeeded by eternal darkness. In this gloom it is their happiness to live; it does not, however, retard their development or decrease their numbers. They multiply indefinitely like bats in a cave. Everywhere they will pursue their theme with industry and enthusiasm, but it will be the enthusiasm of the bigot, born of ignorance and fostered and perpetuated by ignorance.

It is the happy privilege of such a class to believe that they possess the divine power to create. Having no capacity or room for additional knowledge they are consequently insensible to their manifold deficiencies; disregarding that which is, they exercise their circumscribed minds in producing something that does not exist and that ought not to exist. (p. 31).

Kirkman's bitterness toward the inflexible mode of "statistical" accounting which typified railroad financial reports, is an uncharacteristic view, but not unique, particularly among harried railroad managers who found themselves bound by a chain of ledgers and a rote litany of debit and credit passages that seemed to have little to do with the "cash basis success" of the business. Again, quoting Kirkman:

The balance of cash that remains in the treasury after collecting the earnings and paying the operating expenses of a railway company, constitute its net income.

Herein lies the essence of accounting; this is the goal; every thing else is collateral to it. Bookkeeping was an after-thought, a device adopted for the purpose of recording and classifying affairs and preventing roguery. (p. 2)

A Point of Progress

In 1885 there was a turning point in the maturity of American literature in the field of cost accounting. That year Henry Metcalfe, an American army ordinance officer, published a book entitled, *Cost of Manufactures.* Metcalfe's work and his position as an authority were probably recognized in professional circles. For example, during the 1880s he spoke at a meeting of the Institute of Accounts in New York.

In the period 1883–1887 other lecturers at institute meetings often dealt with topics on the subject of management accounting, including accounting for branch stores, account keeping for telephone companies, and cost accounts in metal factories. The institute was not restricted to public practitioners, but included among its members company and managerial accountants.

An overview of the practice of cost and managerial accounts as indicated by the records of businesses and by the contents explained in the leading textbooks of the period reveals the following types of cost accounting systems and terminology:

1. *Burden:* The term burden, or overhead, as we know it today, was noted as early as 1862 in the writings of Nassau Senior, an English economist who had developed a theory to distinguish between fixed and variable overhead cost. Overhead was called various names—including "on cost." "On costs" were manufacturing costs which were to be added "on to" the total of labor and material in arriving at total cost.

2. *Depreciation:* Williamson's study of the Winchester Company indicates that its internal accounting practices did not consider depreciation. He also indicates that the first cost controls appear to have been installed in the late 1880's in reaction to competition in the industry so as to determine where costs could be reduced.

3. *Interest:* Certain writers of the period argued for the inclusion of interest on capital employed as a burden cost or cost of manufacturing. Economic theory had not clearly defined whether or not such was appropriately treated as a division of profits or a payment for a factor of production.

4. *Cost Flow:* Studies of the Shelby Iron Works records for the periods from before the Civil War through the 1880s indicate that the management of the firm was able to determine a broad cost of production via aggregative summaries of costs. (The management of Shelby was able to determine cost per ton of pig iron as early as 1847.) There did not appear, however, to be any recognition of cost flow. Their aggregative method of determining cost per ton was essentially an averaging approach and was still used as late as 1887 (Cauley 1949).

By the turn of the century several American writers were contributing to the literature of cost accounting. Even the all-purpose accounting textbooks widely used in business colleges began to refer to cost accounts. This marked the birth of teaching the first specialty subject within the field.

Cost accounting, however, would not begin to mature for several years, subsequent to the wave of corporate mergers and of a unitary form of organization. The typical pre–1900 manufacturing firm was still operating with an accounting system geared to provide information about short run operations. In railroading and textiles it could be observed however that by the 1890s cost systems had become more sophisticated. These industries represented forerunners of the form of future manufacturing and corporate organizations. An 1874 report of the Atchison, Topeka and Santa Fe railroad serves as an example in that it included as an exhibit a table of distribution of

---

WINCHESTER REPEATING ARMS COMPANY*
Estimated Balance Sheet, April 1, 1867

CURRENT ASSETS		
Cash	$ 1,374.65	
Accounts Receivable from New Haven Arms Company	182,234.20	
Inventory	72,447.74	
Chilean-Peruvian Assets	57,000.00	
Stock Subscription Receivable (payable April 1–December 1, 1867)	82,936.99	$395,993.58
LESS: CURRENT LIABILITIES		
Accounts Payable from New Haven Arms Company	188,493.58	
Due Stockholders of New Haven Arms Company	136,500.00	324,993.58
NET WORKING CAPITAL		71,000.00
FIXED ASSETS		
Value of New Haven Arms Company Plant	150,000.00	
Other Assets		
Burnside Rifle Claim[1]	21,000.00	
Mexican Matter[2]	58,000.00	
Patent Rights	150,000.00	379,000.00
NET WORTH (represented by Capital Stock)		$450,000.00

[1] The nature of this claim is not revealed in the Company records.
[2] Amount due from sale of arms and ammunition to Mexico.

Reproduced with permission from Williamson, *Winchester: The Gun That Won the West*, 1952, p. 464, A. S. Barnes.

Figure 4–7

A textbook illustration of a worksheet, 1876.

WINCHESTER REPEATING ARMS COMPANY*
Balance Sheet at December 31, 1889

CURRENT ASSETS		
Cash	$ 575,676.09	
Bills Receivable	83,768.81	
Sundry Receivables	145,706.14	
Inventories	915,963.69	
Investments	630,998.45	$2,352,113.48
LESS: CURRENT LIABILITIES		90,555.48
NET WORKING CAPITAL		2,261,558.07
FIXED ASSETS		
Real Estate, Plant and Machinery, 4/1/67	150,000.00	
Estimated total expenditure from 4/1/67 to		
12/31/89	2,483,444.00	
Patents		
Acquired from O. F. Winchester	150,000.00	
Expenditures from 4/1/67 to 12/31/89	340,176.00	
Investment		
Remington Arms Co.	178,075.00	
TOTAL FIXED CAPITAL		3,301,695.00
ESTIMATED NET WORTH AT DECEMBER 31, 1889		$5,563,255.07

(*Note:* As in previous balance sheets the figures above include *total* expenditures on capital assets without allowance for depreciation.)

Reproduced with permission from Williamson, 1952, p. 467, A. S. Barnes.

Figure 4–7–cont.

operating accounts, that is, overhead expense in proportion to revenue from freight service and passenger service.

Still there was a general skepticism about the amount of accuracy that could be obtained from cost accounts. Were they as reliable as commercial accounts? If not, should not integration of cost and financial accounts be avoided? If so, how did one integrate these two systems of accounts? Although instances of integrating commercial and cost records could be found, there was still controversy over whether or not to integrate cost accounts and financial records. In a speech given in 1897, Frank Broaker suggested the use of a double entry technique of integration based on a consumption journal. Such attempts to describe the basis of integration indicate that a generally accepted technique was not yet in existence.

Another important influence on cost accounting during this period was the appearance of "scientific management" techniques. From

1860 to the 1890s factory systems developed increasingly from "systematic" to "scientific" using sophisticated forms of organization for production. In 1890 J. Slatter Lewis's text, *The Commercial Organization of Facilities*, indicated the use of staff-and-line techniques which had become formalized as part of overall management systems. In 1895, Frederick W. Taylor, the father of scientific management, suggested a revolutionary approach to labor costing with the introduction of the piece rate system. This was the start of what was to be scientific labor time and motion efficiency in manufacturing.

Under this theory of systematic management, the "system" maintained the operation with the aid of the accounting and production records. The logic of processing and supply at each work station therefore dictated the process of the factory's system. Scientific management added the study of efficiency of effort at each station and at each motion of operation, thereby affording the ability to establish standards of performance. The existence of the systematic and scientific management of industrial operations created a need for cost accountants who could develop "price tags" for operations in order to make monetary comparisons within this system of standards.

State and Local Accounting

By the mid 1890s, American cities were growing at a rate about three times as fast as rural areas. By 1920 the census would show that the urban population of America exceeded the rural population. With this unprecedented expansion of cities, the demands for services such as water supply, property protection and public health became apparent. Certificates such as the one shown here for the City of Baltimore, were issued in the larger municipalities. This certificate is evidence of the debt used to fund expansion of a water supply system. Issued in 1874, it was scheduled to mature in 1894.

In the face of this growth and the need for cities to begin to finance their increasing system of services on a larger and more complex scale, there was a need for uniform accounting and supervised reporting for state and local entities. As early as 1878 and 1879, the states of Minnesota and Massachusetts enacted legislation that affected county administrations, specifying activities that would enhance the efficiency with which county officials fulfilled their duties.

The Minnesota act provided for the appointment of a state examiner to be named by the governor and required that the examiner should be a skilled accountant. The examiner's duties included the inspection of state accounts and the accounts of county officials. He was also charged with enforcing a correct and uniform system of bookkeeping. The Massachusetts act also focused on the financial administration of county officers such that by 1887 the scope of this supervision included the establishment of the Office of Controller of County Accounts (Potts 1976: 50).

The influence of these early precedents trickled down to the municipal level and served to define the duties of appropriate officials. Although it was uncommon for cities to issue financial reports prior to the twentieth century, certain examples, notably in the cities of Boston and Milwaukee, do exist for years prior to the turn of the century.

Figure 4–8

City of Baltimore Security, 1894.

Source: *The Countinghouse Arithmetic* (Baltimore, 1889).

Concern over the adequacy of financial disclosure of municipalities served as one cause for the formation of citizen groups
that initiated reform movements to change the poor quality of
administration in city government. The era of "Boss Tweed" and
excessive political patronage that followed the Civil War, impacting
most sharply on the large eastern cities, had now reached a point
where the public had become restive and was dissatisfied with city
administrations. In 1891 James Bryce wrote, "There is no denying
that the government of cities is one of the conspicuous failures of the
United States." New Yorkers took it upon themselves to slay the
Tammany tiger. In 1894 the National Municipal League was formed.
The Citizens Union was formed in 1897, representing leading citizens
who acted together to bring about better government. By the time of
the National Conference on Good City Government in 1896, 245
organizations were functioning. The concern of city dwellers about
municipal government served to influence the type of financial and
accounting systems that would be forthcoming after the turn of the
century. (Dahlberg 1966)

An initial audit of one major city's financial accounts which took
place before the turn of the century seems to convey an example of
the state of affairs. Ernest Reckitt was invited by R. A. Waller, the
controller of the City of Chicago, to make a "spot" audit of the books
of the city of Chicago in 1898. For a fee of $2500, an amount not
anywhere near sufficient for the size of the operation to be undertaken, Reckitt agreed to start the audit. He immediately employed
twelve men for the assignment, which took a period of approximately
three months. Among the irregularities Reckitt found was a deficiency of about half a million dollars in the special assessments funds
as well as the overall chaotic condition with respect to the payments of
city bonds and coupons.

Reckitt recalls that when he requested to examine the actual
bonds and interest coupons for one of the periods, he was taken to a
vault where all the bonds and coupons paid during a number of years
were lying in a disordered array. He observed that it would have been
virtually impossible to put the bonds in numerical order so as to
commence any audit, and it was therefore impossible to verify the
control over the bonded debt and the interest payments of the city.

The reported deficiency in the special assessments funds raised
considerable public interest particularly since the investigation had
only touched the "high spots" and was specific only with respect to
the listing of the balances of all assessments from 1871, the date of the
Chicago fire. All prior records had been destroyed in that fire.

As a result of Reckitt's audit the city government commissioned the detailed investigation of all assessment records in both the controller's office and the city clerk's office. The firm of Haskins & Sells was selected, having submitted the lowest bid. Sells later informed Reckitt that the audit had resulted in a considerable financial loss to the firm. However, on an overall basis, in part due to the fact that there was a fee generated from detailed investigations of other city departments, the firm was given an opportunity to recover some of the large loss that it had suffered on the original contract. Such service by public accounting firms within city government resulted in the inauguration of improved systems of accounting so that future audits could be more intelligently and inexpensively conducted.

An early American treatise on the subject of governmental accounting, a booklet entitled *Public Accounts*, dealt with the keeping of state and municipal accounts and was written in 1878 by E. S. Mills (Potts 1976: 47). This brief twenty-seven-page work described a double entry system for county treasurers, whom Mills viewed as acting as general business managers for the people. The Mills system was designed to report the following by way of a proposed comprehensive financial system:

1. Cash on hand at the beginning of the period
2. Delinquent taxes due at the beginning of the period
3. Total collections of the past year
4. Receipts from state funds, fines, licenses and other receipts
5. Expenditures for the past year
6. Abated taxes of the last year
7. Delinquent taxes due at the close of the year
8. The cash balance at the end of the period

There is no evidence that Mills' scheme was widely used or regarded. Nevertheless, it presented an early systematic attempt to deal with the perceived problems of municipal accounting. Not until after the turn of the century was a comprehensive municipal accounting system developed, including budgetary accounts. Frederick Cleveland's dual system is recognized as the first of this type.[15]

The Importance of "Gilded Age" Accounting

The year 1877 officially marked the end of the period of reconstruction following the Civil War. It also effectively marked the start of the era of big cities and big business. It is probably useful to our view of accounting's progress since then to consider that it was only a century ago.

Among the important accomplishments which occurred during the "Gilded Age" was the profession's ability to achieve important gains in public identification and legal recognition. Formal education, standardized textbooks and a system of accounting principles were nascent or nonexistent. Municipal accounting was being shaped by the demands of citizen groups and initial audit engagements in large cities were beginning to provide information which would lead to the passage of legislation to require a more uniform system of accountability.

By the turn of the century the economy was recovering from the severe depression of 1893, and had turned to a policy of "sound money" in the election of 1896. The important role of accounting was being recognized in the financial and business community as corporations began to hire expert auditors to replace the annual audit visit of shareholders.

The practices of quasi-public enterprises, including transportation and utility companies, were profoundly influenced by the legal arrangements based upon cash receipts less cash disbursements notions of reporting and profit. The precedent of this regulation would serve to underlie the formulation of accounting measurement and policy for years to come. This was true particularly with regard to a view that all accounting information could be rigorously and perfectly prescribed in the form of a cash-like "operating statistic."

Since the early promulgations of the Interstate Commerce Commission (ICC), accountants and businessmen have become increasingly sophisticated as to their notions of value and techniques of measurement in attempting to determine the proper basis for establishing an adequate and fair system of measuring and reporting return on investment. To this day the century old concept of an accounting information system with an objective of providing a "cash statistic" lingers and has led to confusion and contradiction. Is the notion that accounting information should be contained in a cash-like statistic if it is to be useful for measuring return on investment, relevant in light of advances in popular economic knowledge? This cash statistic procedure, a relic of America's early industrial age, does continue to influence our regulatory practice and thinking. Similarly the basic accounting equation developed by Sprague (Assets = Liabilities + Proprietorship) continues to appear in textbooks as a means of explaining the relationship of accounts. Perhaps no two other notions so fully dictate our current practice as the early cash paradigm of regulation and the Sprague equation.

Before long, uniform listing requirements of stock markets would emphasize the need for filing of financial statements by corporations trading their securities. The need to attract capital, along with the increasing attention given by businessmen and legislators to the problem of providing sufficient financial information, would provide dual justification for the unprecedented growth of public accounting practice and periodic financial disclosure.

A popular history of the profession may suggest that 1896, the year in which the first CPA law was passed in New York, represents the birth of the accounting profession in America. Closer examination suggests, however, that the post–Civil War era—the Gilded Age— witnessed the birth of the modern professional societies, all of which have served in part or in whole to establish today's practice.

NOTES

1. By 1880 Standard Oil of Ohio noted that approximately 90% of the oil refining business was under its control.

2. It is important to consider the gilded age as distinct from the years of the Civil War. Too often there is a tendency to equate the origins of the gilded age solely as an aftermath of the Civil War. In fact, the industrial propensity of America was established before the Civil War and even may have been retarded by the Civil War.

3. There is no convincing evidence that the cattle business responded any differently to the peaks and depression of market conditions, investment enthusiasm and overall national economic conditions, than did any other phase of the economy. What has been largely overlooked in economic, business and accounting history is the existence per se of mine, railroad and cattle investment and the part it played in the development of a central capital market.

4. For the last two decades of the nineteenth century the total number of incorporated cattle companies in the west numbered as follows: Montana, 181; Wyoming, 188; Colorado, 324; and New Mexico, 186. The aggregate capitalization for these respective states came to $27 million for Montana, $94 million for Wyoming, $102 million for Colorado and $61 million for New Mexico (Gressley 1971: 105).

5. Several studies by Professor Brief and other sources describe the aspects of the controversy over fixed asset accounting in this period.

6. The prevalent method of rate setting during the 1890s provided for a fixed return for the railroad investment, predominantly in capital assets. It is significant that the increased use of this criterion approximately coincides with the increased use of the retirement method for asset valuation, the demise of the use of appreciation reserves among railroads and a trend toward capitalizing rather than expensing new assets. One concludes therefore, that railroads found it expedient

to use accounting practices for asset valuation which maximized their base for rate setting calculations regardless of the validity of underlying valuation. Some historians suggest that the Interstate Commerce Commission Act and the potential implications for regulation of the railroads may have been a significant factor in creating financial uncertainties and panics in 1893. Others argue that the classification of operating expenses requirements of the ICC went into effect in 1894, in response to the financial panics of 1893, so as to begin to supply some vestige of uniformity to financial reports of railroads.

7. Deficiencies in railroad reports also pointed to the value basis of assets, as another writer in the *Railroad Gazette* noted: "It's not what a railroad has cost that the stock and bond holders want to know; it is the value in gold, and this will not be given except by legal compulsion." These sentiments were perhaps fanned by the panic of 1893 and may have influenced the Interstate Commerce Commission's first excursion into regulation with its July 1, 1894, implementation of the classification of operating expense format. This action established a precedent for what was to become a system of uniform accounts and standardized reports for railroads under its jurisdiction (Boockholdt 1977).

8. One of the difficulties of research about women arises from the fact that names are not always a suitable clue. Florence, for example, though predominantly a feminine name, is occasionally bestowed upon male offspring as well. So when we find Florence Crowley listed as an accountant in the New York Directory in 1797 at 237 Water Street, in 1798 at 59 Cherry Street, and in 1802 at 16 Banker Street, and Florence Crowdy similarly listed in 1801 at 9 Frankford Street, we cannot be sure whether Florence Crowley, or Florence Crowdy, was a man or a woman.

9. Joseph Sterret of Pennsylvania, writing in 1898, is somewhat "cool" about the importance of AAPA: "The association has done some excellent work as a pioneer, but as each state has charge of its own internal affairs (The AAPA was incorporated in New York) it has been found that better results can be accomplished by separate state organizations, and these have been effected in several states."

10. Ohio University established a commercial college coincident with the University of California in 1898.

11. High schools in the post–Civil War period were few in number in relationship to the total population (there were as few as 108 high schools in 1859 and that number had increased to only 536 by 1873, with a total estimated student enrollment of only 40,000). Their curriculum was directed largely at college preparation, not commercial education. The high school had usurped the character of the academies. During the early years of the development of the high school, very little was accomplished toward placing commercial courses in the curriculum. After 1875 however, a gradual increase in commercial course offerings ensued, but these were not deemed sufficiently rigorous, and the training and the status of such a curriculum was deemed inferior by other high school faculty.

12. S. W. Crittenden's 1877 text on bookkeeping and accounting however was not substantially changed from earlier editions which date back to the pre–Civil War period.

13. In 1890 E. D. Moore's *Principles of the Science of Accounts* was published.

14. Paton also considers the works of Hatfield to have been as influential as those of Sprague in determining his career choice.

15. It should be remembered that, prior to the turn of the century, for the most part cash basis public agency systems were in use. There was only a stirring of interest in uniform accounting in the large cities as a form of reaction to public concern over the lack of effective accountability on the part of politicians. Within twenty years of passage of the county administration practices act in Minnesota and Massachusetts, the effects of such legislation were leading to applications of fiscal controls over duties involving public funds at the municipal level. States also began to take an interest in the supervision of municipal accounts in that they were providing examiners with review guidelines.

5 THE FORMATION OF AN ACCOUNTING PROFESSION

An excellent monument might be erected to the Unknown Stockholder. It might take the form of a solid stone ark of faith apparently floating in a pool of water. [Felix Riesenberg]

Henry Steel Commager has called the 1890s the watershed of American history. By the turn of the century, the United States had made the change from agrarian simplicity to industrial complexity. The corporate form dominated American industry. Over 70 percent of those working in manufacturing were employed by corporations, and they produced 74 percent of the value added by manufacturing. Technological advances had expanded production possibilities, a nearly complete railroad network permitted mass marketing, and communication improvements facilitated centralization. A large percentage of the country's economic resources were being controlled by a relatively small number of men who managed the industrial trusts. The consolidation of industry led to a reexamination of existing social and economic philosophies and their relevance in a corporate society (Commager, 1950: 406–411).

For many decades Americans had accepted the idea that "commerce had been the world civilizer" and that the interests of both society and the private entrepreneur could be simultaneously promoted by permitting the maximum amount of freedom to the individual.[1] Classical economics provided the English-speaking world with its fundamental economic model. The individual was at center stage. The capitalist, by striving to further his own interests, automatically promoted the public good. In an autonomous competitive market, an automatic mechanism, "the invisible hand", was assumed to result in the most efficient allocation of society's scarce resources. Government's role was passive; competition ensured protection for the public. But, in the 1890's, the effectiveness of competition, given the domination of many industries by a few industrial giants, was open to question.

Social Darwinism exalted individual freedom and was used by some to justify the unequal socio-economic conditions that existed in the United States during the last quarter of the nineteenth century. Industrialist Andrew Carnegie believed that society must accommodate "great inequality in the environment, the concentration of business industrial and commercial enterprises in the hands of a few, and the law of competition between these as being not only beneficial but essential to the future progress of the race." Carnegie modified the harshness of this doctrine by emphasizing the concept of stewardship. "The fundamental idea of the gospel of wealth" he wrote, "is that surplus wealth should be considered a sacred trust to be administered by those into whose hands it falls, during their lives, for the good of the community." But stewardship was purely voluntary, and he did not advocate public accountability.[2]

Similarly, legal theory, prior to the third decade of the twentieth century, reflected concern for individual rights. Agrarian and democratic values combined with a deep respect for the freedom of the individual in the market place to lend credence to the tenets of "individualistic law." Legal theories evolved "to deal with physical harm to ownership or possession of tangible property" but "were totally inadequate to protect the intangible values represented by security interests in the modern corporation" (Green, L., 1937, vol.3: 62ff).

As long as social, economic, and legal theories emphasized the rights of the individual and ignored the community, little demand for the services of independent public accountants was generated. Most businessmen heeded the advice found in [Lowell's] *Bigelow Papers,* which cautioned "no never say nothin' without you're compelled and then don't say nothin' you can be held to" (quoted in Haskins, 1901B). But in the 1890's serious questions were being asked about the validity of the "traditional American creed." It was with the inception of doubt about the ability of such a philosophy to promote the social welfare that public accountants began to have a major role in the United States. An examination of the conditioning environment of this period shows that accountants were in the mainstream of social reform and were given a social obligation necessary for attainment of professional status.

The Rise Of Financial Capitalism

Perhaps the most important development, in retrospect, for the emergence of the public accounting profession, was the rise of financial capitalism. For it became clear that management would become divorced from ownership and that a financier, such as J. P. Morgan, would yield enormous power. Before the panic of 1893, business consolidations were normally effected through vertical integration and internally financed. Among the more important consequences of the panic in that year was the increasing involvement of bankers and outside promoters in the operations of American corporations. Before 1893 it had been rare for a banker or financier to sit on a board of directors. By the eve of World War I, it had become almost common for representatives of investment banking houses or financiers to occupy directors' chairs and sometimes to be in positions of control. By 1913 the "money trust" held 341 directorships in 112 corporations, controlling resources and assets capitalized at around $22 billion (Hacker 1961: 26f).

Classical economics emphasized that the amount of capital wealth was fixed and determined the amount of industrial development possible in any given place (Johnson, 1902). This was obviously not the case in the United States where credit markets had evolved which expanded the productivity of industry. The need was apparent for methods to rationally channel capital funds into the nation's credit stream; this need became the genesis for demands that a viable, independent accounting profession be established. Slowly the conviction grew that corporate financial publicity was required to mitigate speculative pressures arising in a situation that encouraged the attitude that finance gimmickry rather than production was the easiest way to make money.

Henry Clews, President of the New York Stock Exchange at the turn of the century, had written that

> The financiers, of course, were still interested in producing goods for sale, but they were likely to be equally if not more interested in profits to be made from issuing securities and powers to be gained in arranging mergers and acquisitions (Clews 1900: 28).

Securities became the vehicles for accumulating wealth. Even those who conceded the need for industrial combinations to extract maximum benefits from economies of scale denounced the "vile demon avarice," which often motivated promoters to realize large profits from nonproductive finance transactions while ignoring manufacturing operations. Contemporary thought became increasingly hostile to those who defended corporate secrecy. Following the failure of one trust after another—tobacco, leather, whiskey, ice, sugar—demands for publicity to enable investors to make informed decisions came from both public and private sources, including progressive leaders within the business community itself. The spectre of "unsocial individualism" mandated regulation of some kind.[3]

Demands for Protection of Investors

As early as 1890, Clews had been an avid proponent of publicity of corporate accounts. He believed that this could be accomplished best "by the employment of skilled accountants because the certified results of their examination would be accepted as conclusive." Such examinations would result in verified statements of earnings, profits, expenses, capitalization, indebtedness, dividends, property valuation, liabilities, and assets (Clews 1906). Clews's position that expert accountants in the private sector could provide the requisite services was unique. Most contemporary advocates of reform who did support the publicity of accounts as a viable means of control did not share his confidence in the nascent accounting profession.

Economists, who at that time were the only generally accepted business oriented academicians, also demanded publicity to protect investors' interests. J.B. Clark and Frederick Cleveland declared that publicity provided the best remedy for abuses. The investor was the "most conspicuous of the trusts' victims." Publicity was the "most effective means" of control of the trusts (Cleveland 1905, Clark 1900).

Demands for corporate accountability to stockholders were being echoed in the political sector as progressive reformers advocated and sought public oversight of the activities of coporations. This development worked directly to the benefit of accountants because the vast majority of contemporary reformers did not advocate, and most of them specifically opposed, a direct federal intervention in or regulation of the financial affairs of corporations.[4] The progressive movement was central in identifying a social role and obligation for accountancy.

The Political Climate

Pragmatism has been called the operative philosophy of the progressive impulse. Formulated in a dynamic environment, pragmatism attempted to utilize empirical, investigative techniques of physical science to arrive at philosophical and social "truth." Charles Pierce, William James, and John Dewey defined truth in relation to its practical consequence. Emphasis was on "action rather than logic, immediate practicality rather than theory . . . new solutions rather than holding fast to old standards" (Dewey 1939: 396). Dewey refined earlier pragmatic theories by adding that truth must result in desirable social consequences. Thus truth was relative, but it was not Machiavellian.

Experience and education became key factors in enabling a person to determine truth. Since any data was valid only if it met the needs of practical life, a person must have sufficient experience to be able to recognize those changing conditions which might invalidate what formerly has been considered a normative truth (Dewey 1900: passim). Today pragmatic and expedient are often used interchangeably, but that usage tends to obscure pragmatism's central point: for a theory, conception, policy or idea to meet the test of truth it had to have desirable social consequences. Pragmatism gave philosophic justification to political reformers' demands for government planning within the private sector.

The Progressive Movement

Progressivism is best understood as an eclectic term for an attitude that incorporated such elements as pragmatism, moralism, fundamentalism, socialism, and prohibitionism. Progressive thought embraced "a faith in democracy, a concern for morality and social justice" and expressed an "exuberant belief in progress . . . and the efficacy of education" (Thelan 1969). Fond of speaking in abstractions, the progressives drew support from a broad spectrum of the public including businessmen.[5]

Progressivism, as used here, is not meant to connote "liberalism." The movement did not articulate a single, unified philosophy nor did all progressives embrace a single common cause. There were in fact several progressive movements which are often combined and described as "the quest for social justice." There were few true radicals among the ranks of progressives. Socialism, which gained adherents in Europe, never became a strong political alternative in the United States (McNaught 1966:504).

Progressives and pragmatists both called for government to take an active role in defining social goals in an industrial society. But they never suggested that government assume operational control of business. One of the important themes of progressivism was the "gospel of efficiency." Reformers had a tendency to "turn to the expert as a disinterested person who could divest himself of narrow class or parochial" interests (Grantham 1964). Progressive demands for efficiency in government, regulation of business, and tax reform all had positive effects with respect to the development of the profession of accountancy in the United States. For it was the independent public accountant, the disinterested expert, who could provide the necessary services to implement progressive reforms.

Demands for Government Efficiency

Political progressives' conviction that corruption and inefficiency lay at the root of social ills in the United States was reflected in their demands that public officials be held accountable for their actions. Muckrakers like Lincoln Steffens skillfully used popular journalism to stimulate public awareness of the issues. New governmental accounting systems became mandatory under state laws and resulted in significant improvements in the conduct of public business. This kind of activity, which required and obtained the cooperation and participation of accountants, was a major factor in bringing accountancy to public attention.

As early as 1895, when Charles Waldo Haskins and Elijah Watt Sells received Senate commendation for their work on the Dockery Commission, accounting practitioners became a vital force in the reform movement. The National Civic Federation and the National Municipal League received the patronage, interest and participation of accountants. Demands for greater efficiency in federal government brought accountants to national attention. The Keep Commission (1905) had called upon the American Association of Public Accountants for expert advice in plans to reorganize the federal bureaucracy. Official recognition of the association as the national voice of the profession was a milestone in those early days.[6]

The President's Committee on Economy and Efficiency, which Taft proposed in 1911 to facilitate the introduction of business techniques into the federal bureaucracy, immediately called upon leading practitioners to serve on a Board of Consulting Accountants. J.E. Sterret, E.W. Sells, F.F. White, and W.B. Richards were appointed to this board. The President's Secretary, Charles Norton, wrote that "the subject of administration lies largely in your hands," and suggested that accountants allow the commission the "added privilege of submitting written reports for your criticism while we are formulating and starting our constructive program" (U.S., Executive, 1912–1914).

The commission was composed of three political and three expert appointees. Frederick A. Cleveland, the chairman, and Harvey S. Chase, the municipal accounting expert, were primarily responsible for the papers issued on auditing and reporting problems. Conferences were held and opinions submitted on such topics as "constructive recommendations with respect to the principles which should govern expenditure accounting and reporting," issued as Treasury Circular No. 34, 20 May 1911. Many similar questions were discussed and resulted in either Treasury circulars or commission reports (U.S., Congress, 1913, H. Doc. 104).

Chase's work solidified his position as an expert on municipal reform and, like many other early practitioners, he traveled extensively within the United States to act as a consultant to municipalities installing new accounting systems. The American Association of Public Accountants, recognizing the opportunity inherent in administrative reform, established numerous standing committees to provide advice and accounting services for political reform agencies.

The Regulation of Business

Perhaps more important to the development of public accountancy were the political reformers' demands for corporate responsibility. The most universally suggested and accepted remedy for the overt abuses which accompanied the rise of financial capitalism was the publicity of corporate accounts. Both businessmen and government officials preferred that control be left in the private sector. In 1898, with the establishment of the Industrial Commission, it became apparent that accountants had a golden opportunity to join the mainstream of the business reform movement.[7]

The Industrial Commission was established to investigate and to report on questions relating to immigration, labor, agriculture, manufacturing and business. Experts were employed in each field, and it probably was a reflection of the status of accountants in 1898 that none were engaged. But one of the conclusions reached in the commission's preliminary report, which appeared in 1900, was that an independent public accounting profession ought to be established if corporate abuses such as stockwatering and overcapitalization were to be curtailed effectively.

Many of the persons who testified before the Industrial Commission, including most of the businessmen, felt that corporate publicity was the best alternative available for reducing various corporate abuses. Certainly there were a few men who objected vigorously to any form of corporate control and maintained that the doctrine of *caveat emptor* must apply to the investor as well as the consumer. The best known of those who opposed publicity was Henry O. Havemeyer who, however, did little to promote the continuation of government laissez faire.

The exchange between Havemeyer and John North, lawyer for the commission, seemed to reinforce rather than mitigate the demand for published financial statements. Havemeyer, president of the American Sugar Refining Company, was asked, "How do you carry on business at a loss and still declare dividends?" Havemeyer responded: "You can carry on business and lose money, you can meet and declare dividends. One is an executive decision and the other is a business matter." Somewhat bewildered, North asked: "Where do you get the money?" "We may borrow it," said Havemeyer. Puzzled, North continued. "How many years can the American Sugar Refining Company keep up the practice?" "That is a problem to everyone," conceded Havemeyer, and explained that "we should either buy or sell (our) stock if we knew that." (U.S. Congress 1900 132f)

Some witnesses had opposed publication of financial reports contending that the information signaled by the payment of dividends was sufficient to permit investors to make informed decisions. Havemeyer's testimony negated that argument and most businessmen conceded that some form of corporate publicity was needed.[8]

Recommendations of the Commission

In its preliminary report, which appeared in 1900, the commission stated that its prime objective would be "to prevent the organizers of corporations or industrial combinations from deceiving investors and the public, either through suppression of material facts or by making misleading statements." The final report, issued in 1902, concluded that:

> The larger corporations—the so-called trusts—should be required to publish annually a properly audited report, showing in reasonable detail their assets and liabilities, with profit and loss; such a report and audit under oath to be subject to government regulation (U.S., Congress 1902:650).

A minority report, rejected by the Commission, advocated that a bureau be established in the Treasury Department to register all state corporations engaged in interstate commerce and to secure from each an adequate financial report, to make inspections and examinations of corporate account, and to collate and to publish information regarding such combinations. (U.S. Congress 1902: 649ff)

The only argument presented in opposition to the reporting of financial data, which the commissioners conceded was a convincing one, was that no independent group of technically qualified professionals was available to perform the necessary audits. The lack of an organized accounting profession appeared to preclude reliance on the private sector for adequate, accurate, and reliable information. The conclusions of the Industrial Commission established the need for independent public accountants. After 1902, accountants could also count on the support of businessmen. Although they may have preferred corporate secrecy, the real threat of direct government intervention in corporate affairs rendered the alternative—independent audits by established professional accountants—more attractive.

Tax Reform

One of the few permanent progressive reforms was the graduated income tax. For accountants, the 1909 corporate excise tax had become a highly profitable nightmare. The law as passed clearly stated that revenues and expenditures must be calculated on a cash, not an accrual, basis. Accountants objected vigorously and eventually the Treasury issued a regulation that permitted the use of the accrual method of determining net income.

With the ratification of the sixteenth amendment to the constitution, the income tax became a permanent fixture of American life. Accountants, through the American Association, worked closely with the federal government throughout the period to assure no more debacles like the 1909 corporate excise tax.[9] In 1913, Robert H. Montgomery, as president of the association, reminded the Ways and Means Committee of the House of Representatives that "the American Association of Public Accountants . . . shall always be ready and glad to render every assistance in our power to further the preparation of efficient legislation." ("Corporation Tax Returns" *Journal of Accountancy*, Feb. 1913:139).

But the impact of the income tax law on the accounting profession was not as evidently salutary as were calls for reform in the government and corporate sectors. Accountants, who had enhanced their image as being in the mainstream of the social reform movement through municipal and corporate audits, may have lost a little of their perceived independence through the tax reform. There is nevertheless little doubt that tax reform created a very definite need for accounting services and had a dramatic impact on the development of the profession.

The Role of the Accountant in the Reform Movement

The progressive movement conferred upon the public accountant a specific social obligation. But this should not be interpreted to mean that all accountants were reformers or progressives. Within accountancy there were divergent opinions as to the value and desirability of progressive reforms. There were few more scathing denunciations of the "money trust" than those found in the editorials of *The Bookkeeper* (May 1899: 11–13). Edward L. Suffern, president of the American Association of Public Accountants, recognized the new "social consciousness" in the nation and advised his colleagues that if accountants were to gain professional status, they must be aware of their social responsibility (Suffern 1912). But although public accountants benefited from the reform movement, the profession remained closely allied to the business community.

Most practitioners readily agreed with the contention that politicians were corruptible and that therefore systems must be installed to insure greater accountability in the public sector; they were less willing to accept any indictment of business morality. They certainly never agreed that government intervention in the private sector was either called for or wise.

This is not surprising since economic theory still did not advocate any form of government planning in the free market. Although the neoclassical economics refined by Alfred Marshall and John Bates Clark added equilibrium analysis, it remained essentially a static theory focusing upon competition to insure the best possible allocation of society's resources. Despite the obvious increase in monopolistic and oligopolistic industries, most economists continued to stress the efficacy of competition. The more radical economic doctrines such as the "economy of abundance" posited by Simon Patten (1907) or institutional theory delineated by Thorstein Veblen and John R. Commons never gained widespread acceptance.[10]

Most accountants empathized with the opinion expressed by the famed jurist Oliver Wendell Holmes, who is purported to have said that the "Sherman Anti-Trust Act is based on pure economic ignorance and the Interstate Commerce Commission isn't fit to have rate making powers" when asked his opinion of government efforts to regulate business (Persons 1958: 273).

Holmes commended Elijah Watt Sells's widely distributed pamphlet, *Corporate Management Compared with Government Control*, which denounced government intervention in the free enterprise system. Sells contended that "it is an unassailable truth that almost anyone of the men who stand at the heart of our great business institutions is far more competent to run the government, and would run it more economically, more wisely, and more honestly than any of those who are in the business of running government"[11] (Sells 1908).

Despite the fact that accounting practitioners often expressed a personal belief in the concepts of the "traditional American creed" rather than in the newer social philosophies, they did accept certain assumptions of the reform movement. Three general tenets of progressivism which accountants could accept were (1) a fundamental faith in democracy, a concern for morality and justice and a broad acceptance of the efficacy of education as a major tool in social amelioration; (2) an increased awareness of the social obligation of all segments of society and introduction of the idea of accountability to the public of business and political leaders; and (3) an acceptance of pragmatism as the most relevant operative philosophy of the day (Hofstadter 1944: 318f).

The British Influence

Thus far little has been said about the influence of the English chartered accountants in gaining recognition for accountancy in the United States. Undoubtedly, increased British investments, which required close scrutiny given the wild, free-wheeling business environment in the United States in the 1880s, brought English professional accountants to the United States. But until there was some call for control of business, chartered accountants were not very successful in promoting accounting services. One has only to look at the blatant techniques used by Jay Gould who, when called to account for defrauding English investors of $60,000, simply asked for the return of the stock certificates to verify the amount of investment. When the certificates were returned to him, he promptly shredded them, destroying any evidence against him. There was no strenuous objection voiced in the United States, and it was several years before British investors recovered their losses. Initial demands for reform did not evolve to protect British investors but rather because social conditions in the United States became intolerable to many. Undoubtedly, the arrival of chartered accountants added to the prestige of the profession, but it seems that the domestic reform movement was more important in gaining recognition for accountancy in the United States. Despite the obvious rhetoric concerning corporate control, no federal corporation law was enacted nor were any statutes similar to the English Companies Acts promulgated.[12]

The progressive movement, accompanied by demands for municipal and corporate accountability and the income tax reform all had salutary effects on the development of accountancy. Pragmatism gave philosophic justification to political demands and had a decided impact on the evolution of accounting theory, educational standards, and ethics. Accountants had to provide an institutional framework if the profession was to respond effectively to contemporary demands. Initial efforts here concentrated on securing legislation, which gave statutory recognition to the profession. The first CPA law was passed in New York in 1896 and for the next twenty years efforts to secure similar legislation in the remaining states preoccupied accountants.

The Institutional Framework

In the United States, under our federal system, both professional licensing and education are deemed state prerogatives. Accountants' early organizational efforts, therefore, were oriented to forming viable separate state professional organizations. Thus, after 1896, the American Association of Public Accountants had ceased to be an effective institutional instrument and quickly became moribund even in New York as state societies addressed the major issues confronting the profession. Hostility surfaced between native-born practitioners and the chartered accountants who had gained effective control of the association, and that rift severely hampered its operations. Rivalries developed among different state organizations, and that, too, delayed steps towards professional unity. Three major state societies—New York, Pennsylvania, and Illinois—assumed preeminence in the profession until 1905.

The Emergence of State Societies

There can be little doubt that the existence of these powerful rival societies tended to divisiveness, deterring effective national organization of the profession. A brief examination of the major societies demonstrates that until 1904 (when the International Congress of Accountants convened at St. Louis) efforts at unity were hampered by divergent goals. A pattern did begin to emerge as each state sought, after securing CPA laws, to address the issues of education, university affiliation, and professional publications.

New York State Society of Certified Public Accountants (NYSSCPA)

New York's CPA law limited the granting of certificates to "citizens or those who intended to become citizens," which effectively barred many resident British chartered accountants from certification in New York. The waiver privilege was of very short duration and decisions to seek U.S. citizenship had to be made quickly. (See Chapter 4, pp. 100 ff., in this book.)

The NYSSCPA revealed the direction it would take when fifteen men met to incorporate the society in 1897. The American Association (dominated by the British) was virtually unrepresented. Eleven of the fifteen charter members had never joined the association; three of the remaining four who were Association members had joined only for the duration of the effort to secure a CPA law, and all but one were native born. Conspicuous by their absence were men like W. Sanders Davies and Frank Broaker. Davies was a naturalized citizen; Broaker was native born but he studied in Scotland and was closely allied with the British element in the Association (Webster 1954: 336, 343).

New York State practitioners pioneered efforts for cooperation between universities and accountants. Many of the NYSSCPA members had been associated with the abortive New York School of Accounts; most were convinced that a major factor in its failure was its isolation from any established institution.[13] Leaders of the New York state society had approached several universities, often to be met with condescension and ultimately rejection, for accounting was not deemed an appropriate element of a higher education curriculum.

Success, as so often the case during those formative years, was primarily due to the efforts of a single man. In this case, the man was Charles E. Sprague. He rented a faculty house at Washington Square for the summer, near the home of Henry M. McCracken,

Charles E. Sprague.

president of New York University. Each night, Sprague managed to accompany McCracken on his habitual walk, and never failed to mention the value that a school of commerce would afford citizens of New York (Jones 1933: 357–357). In October 1900, New York University agreed to the proposal advanced by the New York society for a new school of commerce. Accounting practitioners served as guarantors against any and all financial loss and agreed to furnish a large part of the necessary faculty. This pattern was to be emulated by practitioners in other states who held the strong American faith in the efficacy of formal education.

The Pennsylvania Institute of Public Accountants

Pennsylvania practitioners' experiences roughly paralleled those in New York. There, however, the bitterness and hostility toward chartered accountants evident in New York did not arise, for from the beginning the profession in Pennsylvania was in the control of native-born accountants (Ross 1940A: 8–12). The Pennsylvania Institute was incorporated in 1897; a CPA law was enacted in 1898. Inspired by the New York society's example, in 1902 the Pennsylvania institute inaugurated evening courses in accountancy. The institute continued efforts to affiliate with a university, an effort made more imperative when members who taught the courses began to feel the pressures of practicing and teaching, too. Finally, in 1904, the University of Pennsylvania's Wharton School of Finance agreed to take over the institute's program (Bennett 1922: 60–64).

Pennsylvania accountants added another dimension to the role of state societies when the institute inaugurated *The Public Accountant.* Although shortlived, the publication was recognition of a real need and foreshadowed early leaders' emphasis on the importance of appropriate professional literature for American practitioners.

The New York and Pennsylvania experiences are somewhat reflective of all early efforts in industrialized states along the east coast, with the exception of Massachusetts. The comparative advantage eastern states enjoyed in securing legal recognition meant that after 1902, practitioners there could focus their energies on a national organization. In other sections of the nation, practitioners' efforts necessarily were concentrated on local issues.[14]

The Illinois Society of Public Accountants

To reply to an obvious question—where did the chartered accountants go after New York State passed its carefully drafted CPA laws?—one has only to look west to Illinois to find a powerful British presence. The Illinois legislature, under strong populist influence, resisted early efforts to enact a CPA law. One state senator, whose notion of equality meant free entry of all into any profession, lack of training or ability notwithstanding, distrusted accountants' motives in seeking a CPA law. The senator was alleged to have announced to George Wilkinson: "I would like to know what youse fellows want; if youse want a lead pipe cinch, I am agin you" (Ross 1940A: 16). Given such attitudes, Illinois practitioners had to demonstrate that they meant to exclude no one. The Illinois state society had earlier opposed incorporated audit companies. In 1903 the society admitted Edward Gore, of the Audit Company of Chicago, and Maurice Kuhns, of the Safeguard Account Company; their influence was needed to lobby for a CPA law. Another result of the political necessity of excluding no one was that chartered accountants, citizens or not, were eligible for membership. In 1903, twenty-one of the society's fifty-three members were from the firm of Price Waterhouse, practitioners who could not be certified in New York State because they were British subjects, but who could be certified in Illinois under broad waiver provisions (Wilkinson 1904). Even after Illinois accountants finally extracted a CPA law from a hostile legislature, practitioners there had to be constantly alert to petitions to undercut certification standards in the interests of persons who complained of discrimination (Reckitt 1953: 73–74).

The Illinois society followed the pattern of other states in convincing Northwestern University to inaugurate a school of business and commerce. Practitioners from New York and Pennsylvania joined their Illinois colleagues as guarantors against financial loss to the university. Among the most lasting contribution of the Illinois society was the publication of *The Auditor*, a professional journal later taken over by the American association and renamed *The Journal of Accountancy*.

The Illinois experience reflected the hostility accountants faced in many midwestern and southern states. Efforts in 1902 to bring about a national unity to the profession appeared to have failed largely because regional differences had not been properly appreciated by the national leadership.

The Federation of Societies of Public Accountants in the United States

Practitioners met in 1902 ostensibly to discuss means of forming a national group to promote CPA laws in every state. The fruit of their efforts was the organization of the Federation of Societies of Public Accountants in the United States with the announced intention of promoting uniform CPA laws. But the three major state societies of New York, Pennsylvania, and Illinois were engaged in heated competition. Available evidence suggests that an unnamed objective of the federation had been to mitigate the effects of this legacy of rivalry and bickering which many concerned practitioners feared threatened to undercut professional goals (Suffern 1922). George Wilkinson worked diligently to gain the cooperation of those three powerful states, and is granted the major credit for the federation's organization. The New

York State society, never enthusiastic about the federation and reluctant to surrender any of its prerogatives, made two demands at the organizational meeting which created dissension and almost at once precluded the federation from ever becoming an effective national body. The New York delegates demanded that federation membership be based exclusively upon affiliation with a state society and closed to individuals and also insisted upon an invidious distinction between CPA and non–CPA societies. The first demand was accepted, the second defeated, and it was only after extraordinary efforts by Federation supporters among the New York society members that that state agreed to join the federation (NYSSCPA, *Minutes*, 1902: 17).[15]

The reluctance of the New York state society to participate fully and completely in the federation centered on a fundamental disagreement as to goals. The federation's announced goal was to seek CPA legislation in those states that lacked CPA laws. New York accountants perceived that goal as considerably less important than the development and enforcement of professional standards. In 1904 New York state society members voted 28 to 18 to withdraw from the federation and suggested the unification of existing organizations (NYSSCPA *Minutes*, 1904: 89). This position formed a principal element of the agenda of the 1904 International Congress of Accountants.

Meeting in St. Louis

The St. Louis meeting in 1904 was a milestone in the development of accountancy in the United States. It marks the coming of political maturity within the profession's leadership. The most difficult task facing the delegates was to convince practitioners that their professional interests could be best promoted by a national organization. The ability to bring together in a cooperative enterprise men who, by the nature of the profession, were strong-willed and independent, and accustomed to defending personal positions, was critical during those first organizational efforts. Compromise, moderation, discussion, accommodation—perhaps the true politics of any profession— were mandatory. Subsequent to the negotiations at the congress, the federation agreed to merge with the AAPA in 1905. Once again accountants had a single national voice, but fundamental divisions as to goals and priorities remained unresolved.

The American Association of Public Accountants, 1905-1916

Many of those participating in the International Congress viewed the merger of the two national organizations as the first step in obtaining uniform national standards for the accounting profession. But it soon became apparent that the AAPA simply did not have the authority to enforce meaningful standards. The merger had treated but failed to heal bitter regional and ethnic divisions among practitioners.

The association's presidential election of 1906 confirmed that chartered accountants were viewed with hostility in most states and would soon be systematically excluded from positions of leadership. The nominees for president that year were Arthur Lowes Dickinson and Elijah Watt Sells. Meeting just before the annual convention of the AAPA, the New York State society threatened to withdraw from the association if Dickinson were elected. A motion was offered stating that the New York society's interests would be best served only if the president of the AAPA was "a distinctly representative American professional accountant . . . familiar with American institutions and customs" (NYSSCPA, *Minutes*, 1906: 160–162). Sells himself was horrified, and moved that the society simply resolve to support whomever was elected. Although Sells's motion was overwhelmingly defeated, he managed to have the original resolution tabled. Webster recalled that this election was especially vitriolic and observed that "those who spoke for or against particular candidates seemed not to have thought of professional ethics" (Webster 1954: 141). One goal of the New Yorkers was achieved in that before 1916 no chartered accountant ever became president of the association. The 1906 election exacerbated anti-British sentiment. It narrowed effective control of the AAPA to a small group of practitioners from New York and Pennsylvania and the national authority the association sought was never realized. Accountants faced severe criticism from outside the profession and the AAPA was powerless to respond adequately and effectively.

Inadequate CPA Legislation

One of the major goals of the association was the standardization of CPA laws. The association had adopted the federation's "model bill for CPA legislation," which John A. Cooper had drafted, and endeavored to use it as a yardstick to determine the effectiveness and acceptability of new state legislation.[16] But the Association could do little to upgrade inadequate legislation or to gain passage of new CPA

Lighthearted sketches of Arthur Lowes Dickinson and Elijah Watt Sells.

(Source: program of the 1906 Annual Meeting of the American Association of Public Accountants, Columbus, Ohio.

laws which conformed to Cooper's ideal. The hardworking Committee on State Legislation conducted voluminous correspondence but to no avail. In 1911, Ohio, Georgia and Louisiana enacted CPA laws totally unacceptable to the national leadership. (AAPA, *Yearbook*, 1911: 834) The Association refused to recognize CPA certificates from those states and practitioners in them were not eligible for Association membership. By 1915 the situation had deteriorated to the point that the AAPA would not accept the CPA certificates issued by nine of the forty-two states which had CPA laws.

Criticism, especially from federal authorities, that a CPA certificate often was worthless and afforded little protection to the public began to appear in the press. The Association certainly could not argue convincingly that existing legislation could ensure professional competence. The call for more stringent laws became a major factor in reinforcing beliefs that an "eastern establishment" allegedly in control of the association did not care about promoting accountancy nationwide. Southerners and midwesterners argued that, given the strong antipathy among legislators in their states to any CPA law at all, even a bad law was better than none. Insistence upon legislation that conformed to the Cooper model, they argued, meant no CPA law at all.

Disillusioned with the experience of dealing with state legislators, the association attempted to solve the problem by appealing to the federal government. As early as 1889, John A. Cooper had formulated a scheme of federal registration of accountants who met certain qualifications, to be known as Registered Public Accountants.[17] The association's committee on Federal Legislation, under the leadership of Robert Montgomery and Edward L. Suffern, explored that possibility over several years. Practitioners, with few exceptions (among them Cooper), continued to believe that the federal authorities would permit the association to define and control admission standards. Cooper himself had declared it to be an unrealistic assumption and believed that any federal registration plan would probably have to be administered by the Civil Service Commission or a similar body (Cooper 1913). Nothing appeared to move Washington; suddenly, in 1914, Federal Trade Commission Chairman Edwin Hurley announced a plan for the commission to recognize a limited number of accountants as "zone experts." The proposal was a shock, and the association quickly backed off from its earlier enthusiasm for federal recognition (AAPA, *Yearbook*, 1915: 199–200). Hurley's plan for "audits according to rigidly prescribed procedures . . . under a predetermined fee schedule" made accountants wary of the notion that outside authorities could put the profession's house in order without exacting a price.[18]

By 1916 the national organization and its leadership found itself in a critical situation. Legislation proved inadequate in some states; efforts to seek federal recognition almost resulted in government administration of the profession itself. This dilemma alone probably would have been enough to lead to the association's demise. Nevertheless, another issue arose which had serious repercussions throughout the profession: critics outside the profession contended that established practitioners were seeking to secure a monopoly.

Professional Exclusion

The charge that in certain states, especially New York and Illinois, established CPAs had restricted entrance into accountancy through unreasonable admission standards, was devastating. When James G. Cannon, president of the Fourth National Bank of New York, publicly charged that CPAs were conspiring to create a monopoly, knowledgeable practitioners were dismayed (AAPA, *Yearbook*, 1908: 120–124). During the 1890s Cannon had been among the first advocates of independent audits for credit purposes, and subsequently had been considered a strong ally of the profession. Many accountants, including most of the officers of the association, were especially sensitive to the allegation that the qualifying examination was a tool for monopoly because they had received their certificates through waiver.

Newspapers in New York and Chicago were especially critical of the profession's alleged policy of deliberate exclusion. The *Chicago Herald* revealed that in Illinois, between 1903 and 1908, 111 persons sat for the CPA examination and only six had passed. Moreover, no less than ninety-eight certificates had been granted by waiver. The situation in New York was, if anything, "worse." The New York State annual failure rate had always been above 90 percent; in 1916, even that record was broken when 3 of 156 candidates were issued CPA certificates. W. Sanders Davies, who rejected the monopoly charge publicly, privately considered the situation intolerable. He contended, ". . . a man in my office . . . doesn't dot his I's or cross his T's just where the examiners require them to be dotted or crossed. This may be alright for schoolboys but not for accountants" (AAPA, *Minutes*, 1916A: 54–55). Had that been Davies's perception alone, reform might not have been necessary. But a New York State examiner corroborated the allegation for picayune grading when he remarked that he allowed "one-fifth for the correctness of an answer and four-fifths for the arrangement" (Suffern 1909).

The American Institute of Accountants

By 1916 a decade of bitter frustration convinced association leaders that the national body must be reorganized to still criticism of the profession. The charges of professional exclusion and meaningless CPA certificates had to be answered if federal intervention was to be averted.

A critical element of the reorganization scheme of 1916 was to permit the national organization (hereafter called the institute) to admit new members on an individual basis. Among the requirements for membership was five years of practical experience and passage of the institute's examination. One of the reasons for individual memberships was to give residents of such states as New York and Illinois, notorious for apparently arbitrary CPA examination grading, an opportunity to enter the profession. The same reasoning applied to residents of those states whose CPA qualifying procedures were unacceptable; good men could enter the profession free of the taint of poor standards. A major purpose, overriding others, appeared to be to bring under the control of the institute, all practitioners who for one reason or another had formerly belonged to no professional group at all.[19]

The plan for direct, individual admission to the institute of persons who met its qualifications and passed its examination appeared to many to be an abandonment of nearly a quarter century's effort to gain legislative recognition for the profession.[20] Ironically, the very men who inaugurated the reform of 1916 had also been in the vanguard of the CPA movement in New York, Illinois, and Pennsylvania. They now faced charges of selling out. The 1916 reorganization achieved two major objectives: criticism of a CPA monopoly abated and, for a time, federal intervention was forestalled. But the abandonment of the CPA certificate left the institute open to challenge as the "national" body and a rival organization, the American Society of CPAs, would soon emerge. Therefore, although the reorganization of the national body was politically effective, control over the profession remained illusory. The institute, like the association, had no recognized, legitimate power by which to enforce professional standards.

The Evolution of Professional Standards[21]

"Legislation for a profession only grants opportunity," observed Joseph Sterrett in 1904. He continued, "Education must be underneath and around all our legislation and organization" (Sterrett 1904). His advice reflected native-born practitioners' faith in the efficacy of education, a belief which had a unique influence upon the development of accountancy in the United States.

Early practitioners' view of education's role was influenced by contemporary ideas of the nature of a profession. The most widely accepted definition of a profession at the end of the nineteenth century was " . . . an occupation that involves a liberal education or its equivalent and mental rather than physical labor" (Joplin 1914A). The concept of "liberal education" incorporated the Aristotelean concept of "spiritual condition," and was in its essence ethical. Education imparted not only academic skills but imbued the young person with such values as righteousness, wisdom, and a sense of justice. Experience in the broadest sense completed the educated man. One must keep that background in mind when discussing and evaluating early practitioners' actions and recommendations on education.

Accountants at the turn of the century lived during a time of endemic change induced by the economic and social adjustments that rapid industrialization had introduced in the United States. Rapid change can precipitate political and social instability; but it may also promote intellectual flexibility and receptiveness to new ideas. American pragmatism advocated the injection of practical skills into education and provided the necessary philosophical justification for the introduction of accounting into university curricula; the progressive movement advocated the kinds of reforms that created a social need for accountancy.

The major constraint to the fulfillment of practitioners' ideal of placing the profession firmly upon an educational base was the hostility of state legislators. Reluctant even to incorporate rudimentary technical prerequisites in CPA laws they were finally induced to enact, state legislators could not be expected to accept formal educational requirements which lawmakers often interpreted as attempts to restrict free entry into the profession. Before World War I, it was rare for most people to complete high school. In 1900, the median number of school years for the general population was between seven and eight years; the practitioners' ideal of at least a high school diploma for accountants faced insurmountable opposition

American Association of Public Accountants 1910 *Muir Woods*

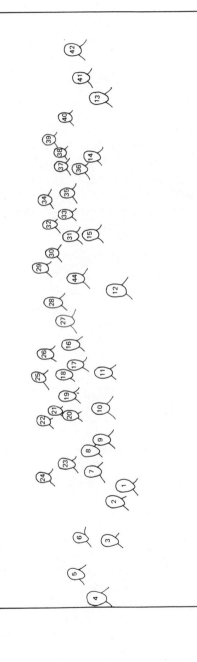

1. Jno. F. Forbes
2. Herbert Brace
3. W. Sanders Davies
4. J. W. Barber
5. Geo. R. Webster
(6. Unidentified)
(7. Unidentified)
8. T. Cullen Roberts
9. Norman McLaren
10. Public Stenographer
11. Edward L. Suffern
12. J. P. Joplin

(13. Unidentified)
14. Wm. A. Smith
15. Harry J. Cooper
16. Geo. T. Klink
(17. Unidentified)
18. John A. Cooper
19. Alphonse Sutter
20. J. E. Sterrett
21. Robert H. Montgomery
22. R. E. Brotherton
23. Ernest Seatree
(24. Unidentified)

25. John R. Ruckstell
26. David Levi
(27. Unidentified)
28. Chas. Lewar
29. Ralph D. Webb
(30. Unidentified)
31. F. W. Dedshimer
(32, 33, 34 Unidentified)
35. Ed. Gore
36. Page Lawrence
(37, 38, 39, 40, 41, 42, 43, 44 Unidentified)

(Counts 1922). Practitioners concluded that under those circumstances no single criterion—formal education, relevant experience, passing the CPA examination—could be sufficient. Some combination of criteria therefore was believed necessary to assure the competence of aspiring accountants.

Educational Qualifications

Practitioners recognized that at the turn of the century they could not realistically demand a high school diploma; the term most commonly incorporated into CPA legislation was "high school degree or its equivalent." Enforcement and interpretation were left to individual states' examining boards, and consequently applicable standards varied. At that time, the completion of high school appears to have signified a level of sophistication significantly higher than present day expectations.

Most early practitioners held as a model the preliminary examination then administered in Scotland. (It is important to note that the preliminary examination was designed to test general background; it was *not* the CPA qualifying examination). In Scotland, the candidate was required to write from dictation: compose an essay; display competence in arithmetic and algebra to include quadratic equations and the first four books of Euclid; have knowledge of geography, Latin, and English history; and demonstrate mastery in two fields chosen from Latin, Greek, French, German, Italian, Spanism, higher mathematics, physics, chemistry, physiology, zoology, botany, electricity, light and heat, geology, and stenography. Under Sterrett's influence, Pennsylvania implemented an examination based upon the Scot model, but in most states the high school equivalency procedure was a sham (Sterrett 1905).

The CPA Qualifying Examination

Early practitioners revealed a decided reluctance to rely upon a single examination to support entry into the profession. They believed that CPA legislation was justified only if it provided some protection for the public. Standards among the states varied widely, and the comprehensiveness of early examinations often left much to be desired. What concerned practitioners most about the situation was that the public risked relying upon certificates that were meaningless.

Edward Suffern spoke for the most thoughtful practitioners when he wrote that accountants must seek to safeguard "the interests of the public . . . which should not be misled through supposing . . . protection where none exists" (AAPA, *Yearbook*, 1911: 99).

The most common criticism of early CPA examinations was their tendency to be narrowly technical; practitioners were naturally reluctant to place reliance upon such a single prerequisite for entry. John Cooper wrote that

> Not one with any practical knowledge of affairs can argue that a mere passing of an examination is proof of intellectual superiority, and still less that it is a guarantee of judicial temperament, common sense, logical faculty, and professional instincts (Cooper 1970C).

To understand this attitude one must recall that these practitioners tended to view the awarding of the CPA certificate as a sign of professional competence. Therefore the candidates' preliminary education and experience became vital elements of the certification process. But the ultimate goal was to combine education and experience, and practitioners looked to universities to provide the requisite educational programs.

University Affiliation

State societies from their inception promoted accounting courses in universities. Practitioners faced the task of convincing university administrators, who shared a common view that only the arts and sciences were proper subjects for higher education, that schools of commerce and business had a legitimate place among more traditional faculties. The business world exhibited a similar skepticism about the value of a college education.[22] Some accountants found it difficult to convince businessmen of the value of education. If anti-intellectualism was not common, there was a definite attitude that long formal educational preparation was neither necessary nor desirable for business careers.

American practitioners had no precedents and no models when it came to outlining the kinds of courses of study the new business schools might offer. As Charles Waldo Haskins pointed out:

> The question could not be answered in Great Britain, because of the absence there of any system of commercial education in which to place it; it could not be answered on the Continent, from which has come the

present wave of activity in economic education, because bureaucratic bookkeeping is still the continental idea of accuracy (Haskins 1901A: 10).

The Role of University Education

The original purpose of the first higher educational programs in accounting was to train practitioners' assistants. After securing acceptance for accounting curricula in universities, accountants began to advocate an expansion of university education to realize the goals of broader, more conceptual programs. Most practitioners considered mastery of the technical procedures of auditing and accounting to be most effectively learned through practical experience; education's role was to develop analytical ability. Accounting, they believed, required a wide range of knowledge and minds trained to think analytically and constructively. They supported a broad program emphasizing theory and philosophy and were disappointed when the evidence accumulated that accounting educators tended to emphasize narrow, technical training.

It was the university accounting educators who moved from the theoretical approach and turned to procedural orientation. As early as 1907 the association's Committee on Education received repeated requests for practitioner-teachers. Practitioners did respond, and most of the faculties in schools of business were composed of practicing CPAs. Academicians supported their requests for practitioner-teachers on the grounds that "professional subjects must be practically applied (and) theoretically oriented professors could not handle accountancy in a satisfactory manner."[23] It is possible, though not certain, that those first academic accountants might have been influenced by contemporary developments in major university law schools. The law schools were restructuring curricula to accommodate the so-called case method of legal instruction, which was designed as a deliberate departure from traditional emphasis on legal theory and philosophy.

After 1910, one specific issue, the ever increasing orientation of academic programs toward the CPA examination, aroused the wrath of most of the national leadership (AAPA, *Yearbook*, 1912: 138f). Some academicians joined with the institute in voicing criticism. Duncan noted that whenever a question on a specific industry— railroads, utilities, breweries—appeared on a CPA examination, accounting departments went searching for an expert to add one more narrowly specialized course to the program (Duncan 1914: 145). In

1918 W. Sanders Davies, president of the institute, chided educators for proceeding on the "erroneous assumption (that) preparing men for the CPA examination was what was most needed," and said that as a result academicians "placed too little emphasis on accounting theory" (AIA, *Minutes*, 1917: 46). The debate continued into the 1920s; but the introduction of practice sets and their growing use in accounting courses was clear evidence that Davies's position had lost ground and that accounting curricula had repudiated conceptual approaches in favor of technique and procedure.[24]

Perhaps this change in emphasis in accounting curricula reflected what one might have called a "generation gap." The "first" accountants, who reached maturity and position by 1900, believed in the concept of broad, general and liberal education. The accounting educators of the next generation were influenced by John Dewey and his followers, who stressed practicality and relevance. Unfortunately, "progressive" education became interpreted to mean a kind of vocationalism with little sympathy or use for so-called "classical" subjects. Deeply disappointed with the trends in the university business schools they had done so much to foster, some practitioners advocated yet another reform similar to the present-day movement for professional accounting schools. Interviewed for the *New York Post* in 1921, a disillusioned Joseph Sterrett recommended that "every young man who wishes to take up accounting (ought to) take up, if possible, a full college course in general subjects, followed by post graduate work in accounting" (Watson January 18, 1921).

What may now appear to be the inadequacy of the evolution of accounting curricula notwithstanding, early practitioners made a significant and major contribution to American culture. Accountants, in many states, were responsible for introducing business subjects into universities. They had convinced educators of the legitimacy of business subjects; they had either financed directly or guaranteed against loss of the first university business schools; and they provided faculty. Nevertheless, they did not believe that education alone was sufficient, and retained a deep conviction of the need for practical experience to assure true competence.

The Experience Requirement

A significant development prior to World War I was that, despite the expansion of accounting and applied business courses in institutions of higher education, the recommended practical experience requirement for CPAs was consistently lengthened by both state and national organizations.[25] It is possible that this development was a function of practitioners' efforts to adapt the British apprenticeship system to the American environment.

American practitioners presented what they believed were sound philosophical apologies for the experience requirement. Both the classical tradition of liberal education and the progressive reforms advocated by the Deweyites supported practitioners' advocacy of experience. John Dewey, in "Education and Experience," declared that experience, not formalized education, was the vital factor in developing an educated person. Experience enabled a person to interpret "truth" in different circumstances (Dewey 1939).

Among accounting practitioners the principal justification for experience was the need to develop "professional judgment." An actual, functioning accounting practitioner's office was perceived as an ideal environment within which to inculcate in the aspirant a "proper . . . attitude." Also, although no formal programs may have existed, the necessity to sensitize the young accountant to the ethical norms of the profession was another key element in defense of the experience requirement.

Ira Schur remembered his early years with S.D. Leidesdorf, and recalled that developing an appreciation of ethical standards was a fundamental element of a "young man's practical experience." Schur could not explain specifically how it occurred. The attitude "was just there, it was just there." He added that "S.D. told me to watch him closely, if he ever did anything I thought was wrong, to tell him because we all wanted to sleep at night" (Schur 1976).

Practical experience had a second purpose, important to practitioners at a time of varied and uncertain entrance standards, which was to enable established, reputable CPAs to screen aspirants and prevent incompetent or unethical persons from entering the profession. Experience completed the process of professional preparation. (Merino 1977)

Early accountants found no lasting solution to the problem of assuring that all licensed CPAs were competent professionals, but they developed an initial conception of professional "attitude." They accepted the idea that accountants had an obligation to protect the public from unqualified practitioners and concluded that no single instrument could function as a reliable admission standard. They formulated a combination of education, experience, and the CPA qualifying examination as the best of possible compromises. They conceived professional attitude as proceeding from recognition of moral responsibility, which required appreciation of professional ethics.

Ethics

Edward Ross wrote: " . . . the patron of (a) calling which involves the use of highly technical knowledge, since he is not qualified to judge the worth of the services he receives, is in a position of extreme dependence (and requires assurance) of the trustworthiness of the practitioners he engages" (Ross 1918). The stress that practitioners placed upon the need to protect the public's interest was an identifiable theme throughout the progressive era. A clear manifestation of that concern was the reliance early practitioners placed upon ethics to insure acceptable technical standards were maintained. Among the commonest criticism of the profession by outsiders was that accountants considered their discipline to be essentially ethical rather than "scientific" (Smith 1912: 169f).

Finding the means to introduce and impress new members with the ethical norms of the profession was not an easy task. There was little agreement over whether it was more effective to rely on informal systems of internalization through monitored experience in a practitioner's office, or to attempt to enforce compliance by adopting a written code of conduct that provided strict sanctions against improper conduct.

Two practitioners, Joseph Sterrett and John Alexander Cooper, became acknowledged spokesmen for the American association on the subject of professional ethics. Although in basic agreement that professional standards must be maintained, they differed in their approach to the problem. Sterrett, in his classic 1907 paper, "Professional Ethics," suggested that a written code of conduct was necessary but expressed some serious reservations.[26] First, he warned his colleagues,

> Let us first divest ourselves of the thought that any system of professional ethics for accountancy . . . can or should supercede or even modify those fundamental principles of right and wrong . . . which from the beginning of time were formulated and given expression in the decalogue (Sterrett 1907).

Secondly, he noted that ethical standards were not absolute, they were evolutionary, and, therefore, rules incorporated into any formal code of ethics must change over time. His position may be called "pragmatic" because he recognized that what was "fair" or "true" or "just" was dependent upon social norms; what one generation considered ethical might not be appropriate for future generations. Sterrett firmly believed that there were absolute fundamental principles that superceded any written rules. At the same time, he maintained that any standards that were set would be viable only so long as they met the social needs of the day, and therefore he supported limited written rules (Sterrett 1907).

The idea that written rules must inevitably be the result of compromise and therefore would only be minimum standards was accepted by many early accountants. John Forbes perhaps expressed the sentiment against written rules best when he said, "I have an abiding impatience with written rules of conduct . . . I have a deep contempt for him whose obedience to a natural principle of right must be regulated by a few poorly constructed lines over the meaning of which he would probably quibble." (AIA Minutes)

Cooper, in his 1907 response to Sterrett, insisted that the association should promulgate an ethical code immediately. He felt that every possible rule of conduct that could be codified, should be. Inflexible, sardonic, and totally unwilling to compromise, Cooper often aroused hostility among his colleagues.[27] He continuously introduced rules proscribing contingent fees, advertising, and audit companies which not only were opposed by many accountants but also would have provoked external criticism from those who thought CPAs were trying to create a monopoly by stifling competition.

Historical Foundations

Henry Rand Hatfield perhaps best summed up the prevalent view within the profession when he reviewed Montgomery's *Auditing Theory and Practice* (1912). He mentioned the special section on professional ethics but maintained that the importance placed on professional integrity and personal conduct throughout the book was far more significant (Hatfield 1913). Fundamental and pervasive concepts, such as confidentiality and independence, were not codified. For many believed that to do so meant inevitable dilution of intent. Accountants sought, rather, through the national organization and within the practitioners' offices, to internalize those values so that they were completely accepted and respected by everyone who entered the profession of public accountancy. They believed that independence and confidentiality were absolutes that must apply in all circumstances.[28]

It was assumed that any person permitted into the ranks of accountancy had been conditioned to accept both independence and confidentiality as fundamental norms during his period of practical experience. If that were not the case, then the practitioner-mentor had an ethical and moral responsibility to see that the person who did not measure up was prevented from admission into the profession. Practitioners rejected the idea that by promulgating rules, which by their nature could have dealt only with peripheral matters, either confidentiality or independence could be assured.

To imply that accountants were independent because they observed certain minor prohibitions was considered dangerous. For the public might be misled by assuming that this guaranteed independence, which was not true. The most telling argument appeared to be that if a practitioner was going to be influenced by a relatively minor interest (ownership of stock or a seat on the board of directors of a client company) then he certainly might be equally swayed by the threat of losing the audit fee. (Montgomery 1907)

One could also suggest that since the association had no power to enforce compliance with its rules (its strictest sanction was expulsion of the offending member and to forbid his use of the phrase "member of the American Association of Public Accountants " on business correspondence), any rule was subject to constant violation.[29] In an area such as independence, the benefits of rules that could deal with form only and not substance were considered minimal.

Confidentiality

Confidentiality was the second fundamental concept of the profession. Although there had been at least some discussion of rules to deal with independence, there was no such debate concerning confidentiality. Most practitioners sympathized with this norm and agreed that it was pervasive. Without confidentiality there could be no profession. Practitioners large and small, from all regions, were united in this belief.

In several states, accountants sought statutory recognition of their responsibility to remain silent concerning clients' affairs. Recollections of young men entering the profession are clear on this point. Established practitioners, whether in small or large firms, told their assistants "to keep their mouths shut" about any client's business. There seemed little need for any rule, for any assistant violating a client's confidence faced the prospect of losing his job and thereby expulsion from the profession.

Rules of Conduct

As might be expected, since formal rules of conduct were necessarily the result of compromise, they really did not deal with substantive issues. Only eight written rules were promulgated and they dealt primarily with issues classified today as "other responsibilities and practices." The only agreement which the group was able to reach was that a code of ethics that dealt with overt abuses (which were admittedly not infrequent in this time period) might be beneficial. Minimal standards in some areas were perceived as better than none. But even those rules enacted that dealt with obvious violations of professional conduct were often ignored by state societies.

The most effective means that the national organization had to control practitioners (given its limited power) was not by enforcement of its code of ethics but through a provision incorporated in its bylaws, known as "acts discreditable to the profession," which was a concept broadly interpreted to deter professional misconduct.

Acts Discreditable

The observation that early practitioners treated accounting as an "ethical" system and resisted demands for the establishment of uniform technical standards is well founded. In the absence of technical standards, the notion of "acts discreditable" became the primary means of ensuring technical proficiency among practitioners.

The concept of acts discreditable was common to most professions but its application within accounting was unique. The medical and legal professions had specific rules that proscribed any action that threatened to dishonor law or medicine, but these standards referred to the personal conduct of the individual practitioner. Accountants' interpretation of the concept of acts discreditable expanded the idea to cover areas of technical competence. The principal reason for the difference lay in the recognition that accountants were potentially responsible to third parties—investors and creditors—whereas doctors' and lawyers' primary responsibility was to their clients. Accountants noted that the law had not yet evolved to protect the interest of third parties, whereas the client-professional relationship had been clearly delineated by the courts. The lack of a contractual relationship between the accounting practitioner and third parties prohibited the ultimate user from suing for redress in cases of professional incompetence. Despite demands by practitioners as early as 1908 that the situation be remedied by a broader interpretation of accountants' legal liability, the situation was not remedied until the thirties. Accountants, therefore, attempted to develop their own means of policing the profession and protecting third parties from incompetent practice.

When the institute was organized, a general statement was incorporated into its bylaws which permitted the national organization to control the technical quality of accountants' work. The institute "on the written complaint of any person aggrieved, whether a member or not," could expel or suspend a member "guilty of an act discreditable to the profession" (AAPA, *Yearbook,*1907: 238). This permitted wide latitude in condemning actions which, though not specifically proscribed by the code of ethics, could be construed as harmful to colleagues, clients, or the general public. The council members of the institute took this duty seriously and were not averse to bringing charges against prominent members of the profession. But the lack of power vested in the national body soon became apparent. When James Anyon was suspended, he was furious, and demanded to know what suspension meant. He was told that he could no longer use "member of the A.I.A." on his letterhead. To which he retorted, "I don't use it anyhow," and quit the institute (AIA, *Minutes,* 1918: 25–80; 142–192).

Unfortunately, the only power that the institute might have had—publicity—was closed because of the attitude of some members. There has always been a strong tendency among professionals for "guild selfishness" and "group bias." Within the national organization, a very influential group believed that accountants should not censure their colleagues. A concession made to these opponents of self-policing, which many considered unwise but unfortunately necessary, was that the names of persons or firms found guilty of professional misconduct not be published in the *Journal.* Only the facts of the case and its determination would be reported (AIA, *Minutes,* 1917: 30ff).

The foundation of ethical and educational standards was laid during this trying period, although the issues were not satisfactorily resolved given the institutional framework of the profession. No one body had the power to mandate compliance with professional standards, a problem that was equally perplexing in early efforts to develop accounting theory.

Accounting and Auditing Theory

Accountants began to discuss the need for a "science of accounts" before the turn of the century, but it soon became apparent that the use of the term "scientific" was creating widespread misunderstanding among persons outside the profession. When accountants used the term, they connoted a systematic approach to accounting problems through which judgment, guided by experience and education, enabled the practitioner to arrive at appropriate solutions in each specific engagement. The goal was to develop informal guidelines that would be acceptable to all accountants, rather than the promulgation of absolute rules of procedure applicable in all situations, circumstances notwithstanding. Uniformity bred dogmatic solutions, and this accountants feared would compromise their hard won recognition as professionals.

External Pressure for a "Science" of Accounts

Businessmen and government officials were in the vanguard of the movement for "scientific" accounting theory, by which they often meant development of uniform procedures. Alexander Smith declared that "accounting is, or ought to be, a science, not a system of ethics, amenable to definite axioms and capable, in proper practice, of producing definite and exact results" (Smith 1912: 170). Arthur Lowes Dickinson replied that Smith demanded a "rule book" and retorted that accountants "could never have a rule book, circumstances must rule, you have to use experience, that is why we are professional accountants." Accountants feared that demands such as Smith's were designed to reduce the accountant's function to that of a clerk (AAPA *Yearbook*, 1912: 59ff). They argued that accountancy never was nor could be an exact science. An editorial in the *Journal of Accountancy* stated the position of most practitioners. "The work of the auditor is not an exact science and every profit and loss to which he is asked to certify is in a very substantial measure an expression of opinion and therefore subject to honest divergence of views both as to substance and form" ("Editorial," *Journal of Accountancy*, May 1912: 360).

Practitioners had excellent reasons to be wary of efforts to enforce so-called scientific accounting (uniformity). Public accountants had been displaced by nonprofessionals whenever standard procedures had been introduced. The Interstate Commerce Commission had required uniform reporting in the railroad industry; almost immediately independent audits were dispensed with and CPAs replaced by technicians. Similar losses of clients and engagements closely followed the introduction of uniform audit procedures for banks, insurance companies, utilities and other regulated industries (Carey 1969: 60ff). Accountants, understandably, rejected "scientific" accounting when it was used in the very narrow sense of simply meaning the determination of "fundamental axioms" that permitted "uniform procedures" to be established and applied in all circumstances.[30]

Practitioners started a public education campaign whose central message was that, due to the uncertainty faced by the accountant, the essence of professional work must be the exercise of judgment to find the appropriate procedures in each individual circumstance (May 1915). They argued that financial statements based on blind acceptance of uniform procedures would be more misleading in most cases than if accountants were permitted to choose among alternative accounting methods. Early practitioners believed that, in order to accurately portray the vastly different circumstances encountered in the business world, accounting practice was best viewed as an art.

Accountancy as an Art

A standard definition of an art is "the power of performing certain actions especially as acquired by experience, study, or observation." The artist does not seek fundamental truths but relies instead upon the independent, informed judgment of the individual in the interpretation of phenomena as they emerge through circumstances. As late as 1940, George O. May wrote that "accounting is an art, not a science, but an art of wide and varied usefulness" (May 1943: 189).[31]

Both pragmatism and economic conditions in the United States appeared to support the practitioners' position that accountancy was an art. Pragmatism was suited to the developement of concepts and principles within the context of an art. Truth was perceived as phenomenally relative; ideas must be tested for practicality and attainability; experience enabled each individual to judge the validity of ideas according to specific circumstances. Pragmatic epistemology asserted that "knowledge" emerged through experimental, informed observation and testing of ideas within a "social" context. It dismissed "contemplative knowledge" (which Dewey had labeled a "spectator theory of knowledge") as inadequate to manage in the context of a dynamic environment (Dewey 1910). Pragmatism rejected traditional conceptions of theory and maintained that theory that rested upon abstract or metaphysical truth was without meaning unless its application resulted in some kind or form of social "good." It could be deemed neither "true" nor "false" unless "tested" in the "laboratory" of social context. This pragmatic concept of "adaptive" theory which emerged from the crucible of experience was a foundation of early practitioners' theory. As Seymour Walton explained:

Being based on experience, theory is able to . . . further illuminate a subject. . . . It does so by applying the law to other activities besides those from which it was formulated. . . . Thus, theory, using men's limited experience broadens into a practically unlimited field (Walton 1917: 277).

Accounting theory, consistent with its pragmatic inspiration, became primarily concerned with the subject of the proper interpretation of values. Contemporary economic conditions required that practitioners retain flexibility in valuation. Deflation, which persisted from 1865 through 1897, with some respite between 1879 and 1884, was the most pervasive issue before the turn of the century. From 1898 to 1919, inflation was general but accounting practitioners were reluctant to preclude renewed deflation. Faced with duo-directional price level changes, practitioners had begun to hedge with respect to valuation procedures. Reluctance to make any general assumption about price level disparities became even more pronounced after the depression of 1919-1921 when the nation began to experience deflationary trends which reopened the whole question of price and value adjustments.

The Development of Accounting Theory

The 1904 World Congress of Accountants is identified with the genesis of the profession's intellectual phase. Although both practitioners and academicians had begun discussion of the need to provide a theoretical framework for accountancy before World War I, it is difficult to distinguish between accounting and auditing theory. Practitioners and academicians seemed to have perceived matters related to accounting as coincident to the auditor's concerns. Typically, public accountants functioned in both roles; as auditors they verified accounting information and as accountants they interpreted it. This dual role is important, since today interpretation of information is left largely to the analyst or user (as witnessed by the Cohen Commission recommendation in 1978 that accountants spell out salient facts, but leave interpretation to the user). During this early period, clients and users expected and demanded CPAs to audit, analyze and interpret financial reports. The interpretive function required that accountants consider external factors in developing accounting theory. Pragmatists contended a theory was only valid if it resulted in "useful social consequences," and early accountants seemed to accept this idea. Accounting theory, they argued, could only provide a general framework; the determination of "correct" accounting principles was dependent upon circumstances surrounding each engagement. Proper interpretation of the facts was the major responsibility of the profession.

The Theoretical Framework

Guided by philosophical pragmatism, early accounting theories attempted to define a conceptual framework based upon logic to replace "rationalization" as used in personification of accounts. The first integrative theory to evolve was labelled "proprietary" and most accounting theorists before World War I may be identified as "proprietary theorists." Several previous efforts have been made to develop a "school of thought" thesis regarding proprietary theory.[32] Although this classification and synthesis may be useful, it may also obscure the evolutionary nature of theory and the lingering persistence of certain concepts despite the predominance of other "schools" in later periods.

In the United States, accountants appeared to be responding to demands for corporate publicity to protect investors and creditors. Proponents of corporate secrecy who testified before the Industrial Commission contended that dividends paid provided all the information investors required about corporate operations. Since many corporations that never suspended dividends had, nonetheless, declared bankruptcy (a good number having done so while the commission was collecting its evidence), it was not a notably successful apology. The commission's final report specifically charged accountants with the duty of protecting investors from the erosion of capital as a result of dividends being paid in excess of earnings (U.S. Congress, 1902: 650ff). The English Companies Act required that accountants determine "profits available for dividends" and also made it clear that one of the accountant's primary functions was to ensure that capital was not impaired by illegal payments of dividends (Dickinson 1904).

There appears to be some reluctance in the historical literature to recognize that proprietary theorists considered the needs of both investors and creditors. This situation may be due to the unfortunate conclusion that, since theorists used the term "proprietor," they were unaware of the ramifications of the separation of ownership and control (investor versus manager) for the accounting process. This was not true. Charles Sprague, among the earliest of the proprietary theorists, explicitly noted that with the emergence of the corporation as the dominant form of industrial organization ownership had been separated from control. But Sprague and other proprietary theorists

Congress of Accountants at Louisiana Exposition, St. Louis, September 26, 27, and 28, 1904

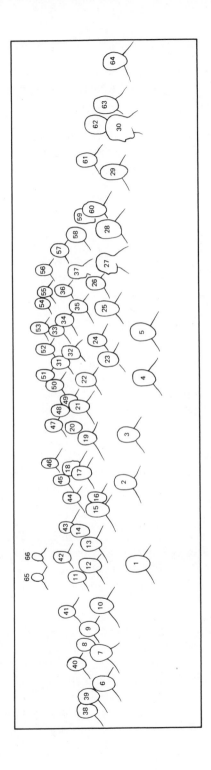

1. Arthur Lowes Dickinson
2. Francis W. Pixley
3. Joseph E. Sterreh
4. James Martin
5. George Wilkinson
(6. *Unidentified*)
7. Robert H. Montgomery
8. Joseph French Johnson
9. J. Porter Joplin
10. John Alex. Cooper
(11. *Unidentified*)
12. George O. May
13. John B. Niven
14. J. E. Masters
15. John Hyde
(16. *Unidentified*)
17. Edward S. Elliot

(18, 19, 20. *Unidentified*)
21. Harvey Stuart Chase
(22, 23. *Unidentified*)
24. Frederick A. Cleveland
(25, 26, 27. *Unidentified*)
28. Frank McPherson
29. Thomas P. Ryan
(30, 31, 32, 33, 34, 35. *Unidentified*)
36. George R. Webster
37. Walter A. Staub
38. E. Shorrock
39. Adam A. Ross
(40, 41, 42, 43, 44, 45, 46. *Unidentified*)
47. J. Albert Miller
(48, 49, 50. *Unidentified*)
51. John Ross
52. A F C Ross

53. J. S. M. Goodloe
54. E. W. Sells
(55. *Unidentified*)
56. H. A. Keller
57. L. O. Fisher
(58. *Unidentified*)
59. Enos Spencer
(60. *Unidentified*)
61. H. R. Jones
(62. *Unidentified*)
63. E. Van Diem
64. David Rolla
65. Henry Mussey
66. Benjamin Franklin, Jr.

167

held that the legal fiction of an economic entity separate from its ownership should be ignored by accountants, since the form of the business did not alter the accounting process (Sprague 1908: 38, 47–48).

William Paton challenged this assumption. He contended that with the emergence of the corporation the goal of business could no longer be simply to maximize the wealth of its owners. He believed that management perceived its purpose to be to increase the return "to all equities" and "not the return to common stockholders" (Paton 1922: 89). Paton used the term equities to encompass all sources of financing for the firm, and entity theory evolved from the basic assumption that management was not primarily concerned with returns to only one group of equity holders. Thus, although it is often suggested that entity theory was an advance in conceptualization, financial theory today is more in line with the assumptions of proprietary (maximize stockholder's wealth) than with entity (maximize the return to all equity holders) theory.

Concepts of Income

The central distinction between proprietarists and later entity theorists lay in their different assumptions about the purpose, not the form, of business. Proprietary theorists argued that the purpose of a business, its organization or form notwithstanding, was to increase the wealth of its owners. Specifically with respect to corporations, the owners—those who bore the risk of business operations—were investors. The accounting function did not change with separation of ownership from control but remained as the measure of net wealth accruing to owners (Hatfield 1909: 195f, 358).

Since the purpose of proprietary theory was to measure "the return to the owner" the accounting equation was posited as *assets = liabilities + equities.* Proprietarists made a careful distinction between liabilities and equities since the most common accounting equation to this time had been *assets = liabilities.* They felt that viewing the creditor and owner in the same terms had led to abuses because there was no account to ensure that the integrity of original capital be maintained. Sprague caustically noted that the opposite of proprietorship was insolvency, which transformed the accounting equation to *assets + insolvency = liabilities.* He suggested that even those who suggested that proprietorship was a liability could not argue "that insolvency is an asset." But, he added, many accountants were willing when capital was impaired "to find some alleged asset

. . . goodwill, etc., and water is added" to the accounts. He argued that clearly distinguishing between capital and liabilities was the mandatory first step for the profession to take (Sprague 1908: 61–62).

Not only was proper segregation of capital and liabilities essential to proprietary theory, but also equally important was the problem of segregating capital and income. Proprietary theory was rooted in classical and neoclassical economics and, much in the manner of Adam Smith, income was defined as "the amount that can be consumed without encroaching upon capital." It is important to recognize that both capital and income were viewed as a "stock of wealth" and proprietarists rejected Irving Fisher's assertion that income be viewed as "flow of funds" over time.[33] Proprietary theory viewed income as "the increase in the beneficial interest accruing to the proprietor."

Because most proprietary theorists felt that the purpose of calculation of profit and loss was "to show the net profits of the concern for the period with special reference to the amount of profits available for dividends," they sought to measure the change in net wealth to ensure that capital was not impaired (Hatfield 1909: 196). However, the desire to measure profits available for distribution to owners did not, by itself, mandate the primacy of the balance sheet. (Residual equity does not require that the balance sheet be viewed as the premier financial statement.) It was the proprietarists' limited view of income as a stock of wealth that appeared to dictate emphasis on the balance sheet.

Development of Proprietary Theory

Accounting theory does not evolve in isolation but in response to the specific problems of any given age. Several different reasons have been advanced as to why the accretion concept of income became central to proprietary theorists. George O. May attributed this phenomenon to the fact that in the United States, which was experiencing great industrial growth, the quickest way to increase one's wealth was through capital accumulation rather than annual earnings. "Ask an American how much it is worth," wrote May, and "he will say x number of dollars. Ask an Englishman, and if he answers you at all, it will be in terms of so many pounds per year"(May 1936A). May was probably correct in his assessment of the American character, but other circumstances seemed to mandate acceptance of the accretion concept of income, with its focus on asset valuation, and the concern with segregation of capital and income given the major financial problems of the era.

The major concern of accountants around 1900 was the development of a theory that could adequately cope with the overcapitalization of industry. The Industrial Commission in 1902 specifically demanded that independent accountants develop methods that would protect investors from the grossly misleading financial reports circulated by some promoters. In 1899, by admission of the promoters, combinations had issued $3,395,000,000 of common stock, of which two-thirds or $2,254,000,000 was "water." (U.S. Congress 1900: 13ff).

Two views existed as to what constituted proper capitalization. The most common practice was to issue preferred stock in an amount equal to the market value (not cost) of tangible assets and common stock equal to the "value" (primarily promoters' estimates of the firm's expected earning power over its life) of intangible assets. The minority opinion was "that the amount of capitalization should be limited to the actual value of properties owned" (U.S. Congress, 1901A: ix f). Accountants preferred the latter view, although they conceded that the value of a going concern was its expected future earning power. They objected to "going concern" capitalization procedures because earning power could not be objectively measured.

The allegation that dividends paid provided sufficient informational content about the quality of earnings had been proved false by evidence given at the Industrial Commission. Thomas Greene, in *Corporation Finance* (1897), addressed the problem of grossly inflated balance sheets and concluded that even if financial reports were made public, investors, probably, would not discern the source of dividends.[34] This suggested to most proprietarists that the major problem facing the profession was to ensure the integrity of the balance sheet, to wring it dry of "water."

Asset Valuation

Although accountants turned their attention to asset measurement, the most obvious omission of proprietary theory was the failure to adequately define the term asset. Assets were defined by most proprietarists as "things owned or for the benefit of the proprietor." Liabilities were "negative assets." Hatfield explained that "in a strict sense, liabilities as well as valuation accounts are a subtrahend from the assets, for debt is merely a negative asset" (Hatfield 1909: 184). The failure to agree on what constituted an asset led to some strange results. The modern reader can only wonder at such items as obsolete machinery, water, and ice pond listed under the broad classification of "other assets." Early theorists seemed more concerned with overcoming the prevalent notion of the time that anything that had a debit balance must be an asset. All discounts (bonds, common stock, etc.) were listed by many accountants as assets and early proprietary theorists were greatly concerned about such classifications.[35] Therefore, they devoted much time to developing the concept of contra-accounts while assuming that all CPAs knew a tangible asset when they saw it (an erroneous assumption in many cases). But, although they did discuss proper classification of all accounts, the bulk of their energy was spent trying to find an acceptable measurement base for assets. The different views of capital maintenance that evolved significantly affected the measurement base deemed correct by early theorists.

Capital Maintenance

One of the most persistent problems of historical analysis is that, as terms evolve, usage and meaning may change, and at any given point in time a single term may have different meanings to different persons or groups. To say that capital maintenance was central to all early theorists is true but may be misleading because the term telescopes three differing concepts into one term.

Most accountants agreed that it was mandatory for investors' and creditors' protection to maintain invested capital intact. This seemed to require that all expenses, including the cost of the expiration of fixed assets be accounted for periodically. Since businessmen viewed such expenses as discretionary, increasing them in profitable periods, ignoring them in difficult times, most accountants believed their first priority should be to gain acceptance of the idea that such costs were not discretionary. Capital maintenance, used in this context to mean preservation of legal capital, required first recognition of all legitimate business costs and second acceptance of the "operating" concept of depreciation discussed below.

Dickinson and Cole were among those who expanded the concept to include not only the maintenance of legal capital but also the maintenance of the physical productive capacity of the firm. They argued that, in addition to annual depreciation charges to record expired costs, a depreciation reserve must be established to provide sufficient funds so that the assets might be replaced. They were not advocating adjustments for price level changes, but suggesting that, since the common practice of the day was to pay out all earnings and dividends, that some earnings be deferred in a depreciation reserve to replace existing assets (Dickinson 1904; Cole 1908: 78f).

A third concept of capital maintenance surfaced during World War I when accountants began suggesting that "real" capital be preserved. By 1918 Livingston Middleditch, William Paton, and Russell Stevenson began questioning the validity of the assumption of a stable dollar. Middleditch argued that financial statements should be adjusted for general price level changes to accurately reflect changes in the purchasing power of the dollar (Middleditch 1918). Paton and Stevenson went one step further and suggested that specific price level changes must be reflected in the accounts if true corporate profits were to be reported (Paton and Stevenson 1918: 462). These early theorists were attempting to carry the accretion concept of income to its natural conclusion: there could be no increase in wealth unless the stockholder or the firm was "better off," as measured in terms of purchasing power, at the end of the period than at the beginning. This concept of capital maintenance implied that the integrity of "real" capital had been maintained.

Although it is possible to say that capital maintenance was central to early accountants, it should not be concluded that there was general agreement as to what this term meant. Theorists used the concept to justify various asset valuation measurement bases. Perhaps the greatest contribution this group made to accountancy was gaining acceptance for modified historic cost for fixed assets. It would have been interesting if the weight of theoretical arguments carried the day, but it appears that the income tax law was far more important in convincing businessmen that deviations from cost were acceptable. Tax considerations seemed to preclude any general acceptance of the natural extension or accretion theory to include appreciation, and this concept never fully evolved.

Asset Measurement

Although some theorists continued to advocate maintenance of original cost for assets on the balance sheet (most notably Esquerré), most accountants agreed that some departure from cost was essential if the balance sheet was to reflect the "true financial condition" of any firm. Both depreciation and appreciation were recognized as valid concepts, but accountants were far more successful in gaining acceptance of the former.

Depreciation

W. Sanders Davies, who taught theory at the short-lived Institute of Accounts, had, as president of the American Association in 1898, urged his fellow members to insist that all firms make an adequate provision for depreciation. Most practitioners agreed that this was theoretically sound but impossible to implement in practice. William Lybrand reflected the mood of accountants in 1908 when he predicted that it would take another generation before CPAs realized acceptance of such charges to income. Lybrand could not foresee that the income tax would have a profound effect on attitudes and would render the accountant's task of convincing businessmen much less formidable (Lybrand, 1908: 255ff).

Although most theorists acknowledged the need for depreciation, two distinct views emerged as to why such charges were necessary. Henry Rand Hatfield, who made the classic statement that all machinery was on an "irresistible march to the junk heap," led those who took an operating view. Citing unfairness to future consumers if prices did not reflect all expenses incurred at one point in time, he used the benefit/sacrifice approach (Hatfield 1909: 121). The Interstate Commerce Commission (ICC), with its insistence that depreciation be based upon historic, not replacement cost, was compatible with the operating view of depreciation. This concept, however, was inadequate to those who perceived depreciation as a means of maintaining capital in terms of physical capacity.

Dickinson and Elijah Watt Sells were very critical of the ICC's position. They believed that depreciation charges should be sufficient to ensure asset replacement. They argued that only in this way could one prevent the erosion of capital through payment of dividends in excess of funds required to maintain the firm's productive capacity (Sells 1908).

The idea that depreciation provided a "reserve" for replacement of assets was a concept that plagued accountants for decades. The operating school clearly stated that depreciation, which they defined as the expiration of value in use of fixed assets, prevailed. Those who referred to a "depreciation reserve" implied to some that depreciation provided funds to a firm. This view of depreciation as a "source of funds" greatly irritated Henry Rand Hatfield. He demanded that accountants quash such an illusion. "That depreciation is a 'retention of profits' is simply not true," he wrote. "A Paul may at one time have been a prosecutor of saints; a Lucifer may have at one time held high rank among the heavenly host. But never, no never, could a 'hole in an asset' have been under any circumstances, a constituent part of profits" (Hatfield 1928: 211). This split among the ranks of theorists was not reconciled before World War I, but those who viewed depreciation in terms of maintenance of physical capital had their arguments extended by appreciation theorists to all values on the balance sheet. The most obvious conservative valuation—lower of cost or market—was almost universally rejected by early theorists.

Lower of Cost or Market[36]

Conservatism is the usual rationalization for acceptance of lower of cost and market. Most proprietary theorists noted the logical inconsistency of recognizing only decreases in market value and suggested it be discarded. The obvious exceptions to this trend were the English-trained (May and Dickinson) or English-influenced like Montgomery (who edited Dicksee's *Auditing* for U.S. publication in 1905). Hatfield, in 1909, was willing to concede the need for "conservatism" in practice, although he noted that this violated the principle of valuation in a going concern (Hatfield 1909: 101f). But by the twenties he had concluded that such a departure was void of theoretical merit and should be precluded in favor of "cost or market" (Hatfield 1927: 274). Paul Esquerré agreed with Hatfield's first assertion, lack of theoretical merit, but concluded that "there is a good reason why market values should not be used at all" and advocated strict adherence to original cost (Esquerre 1920: 171). Roy B. Kester felt that lower of cost or market was not acceptable and favored disclosing market values on the face of the balance sheet while retaining original cost in the accounts (Kester 1917: 13–14). Those who continued to use lower of cost or market noted that "conservatism in valuation of assets, especially in inventory is the safest course since one could otherwise deceive both the banker and the creditor" (Montgomery 1912A: 159f).

But Montgomery's assertions that "conservatism" and the needs of bankers and creditors should guide accountancy were being challenged.[37] Many American accountants felt he placed undue emphasis on creditors and criticized his books (see, for example, Freeman 1914: 341–342). By 1918 Paton and Stevenson had clearly condemned conservatism, writing that this concept was often interpreted to mean management can do what they want. They believed accountants often failed to make a "clear distinction between conservatism and downright concealment," concluding that "understatement of assets" is not warranted since it "hurts stockholders and bondholders" (Paton and Stevenson 1918: 467–468). By the second decade of the twentieth century, a clear trend toward valuation theory seemed to be emerging.

Market

Market value, which would incorporate appreciation as well as depreciation in the accounts, became more widely accepted by theorists as this period progressed. Practitioners, especially within the institute, countered with the objection that accounting profit must be "realized," and a major debate centered on the classification of "unrealized gains."

Two distinct approaches to recognition of appreciation evolved. The central issue became determination of value to a going concern. Those who opposed recognition of appreciated values argued that to a going concern the only value that had any meaning was value in use.[38] Wildman, who discussed the problem during this early period, most concisely stated his position in the twenties. He contended that the value of any firm was dependent upon its future earning power. Therefore, unless an asset's appreciated value enhanced future earning power, that is, unless it became more valuable in use, appreciation should not be recognized in the accounts. He noted that value in exchange was a meaningless concept to a going concern; and certainly, he continued, no one could rationally argue that an increase in the market price of an asset, which would not, and probably could not, be sold, should be recognized in the accounts. Wildman conceded the appreciation of natural resources and certain intangible assets (patents and trademarks) acquired at a nominal cost, which probably did increase future earning power. But he felt it was illogical to hold that a fixed asset, held for use and not for sale, increased earning power while systematically being used up in production (Wildman 1928).

At the turn of the century, it would have been inappropriate for accountants to have accepted "valuation" theory. Overcapitalization was a major problem, and promoters had been overly optimistic in predicting future earnings. One observation, that "promoters were not only discounting the future but the hereafter" seemed appropriate. But by 1918 conditions had changed and so had the direction of accounting theory.

Appreciation theory was gaining widespread acceptance and would become the focal point of heated debate in the following decade.[39] Wildman foreshadowed the direction that debate would take with his clear differentiation between value in use and value in exchange. The most significant conceptual arguments occurred after World War I, and extended discussion of the question is left for the following chapter. But it is important to reiterate that "value accounting" was acceptable to many early theorists, that appreciated values were considered relevant, and that conservatism did not justify procedures totally devoid of theoretical merit. The balance sheet orientation facilitated discussion of asset valuation and as long as income was viewed as a stock of wealth and not as a flow concept there seemed to be little need to determine periodic operating results.

The Seeds of Entity Theory

Unfortunately for any historian facing the inherent limitation of a chronological order, accounting theories do not miraculously emerge to accommodate specific time periods. Most theories have antecedents that predate their formulation and acceptance by years, and they have a lasting effect, a "fallout," on succeeding generations. Although a comprehensive statement of entity theory did not appear until the publication of Paton's *Accounting Theory* (1922), the effects of the separation of ownership and control had been examined in earlier periods. The business entity concept (the fact that the legal entity existed apart from its ownership) was not questioned, only ignored, by proprietarists. Entity theory, as presented by Paton, has never achieved primacy in accounting, since his basic assumption that the purpose of management was to increase the wealth of all sources of financing has never been fully accepted.

Littleton traced entity theory back to the sixteenth century in connection with agency accounting but acknowledged that it did not affect the direction of accounting thought until the twentieth century. William Morse Cole was among the earliest American accountants to ask whether in a corporate era accountants could ignore the need to report on management's effectiveness in the use of assets entrusted to them. He suggested that the profit and loss account could no longer be viewed as residual. He also attempted to provide information as to the sources and uses of funds in his "Where Got—Where Gone" statement (Cole 1908: 101, 178ff).[40] Although Cole approached entity theory, he never fully developed the concept. H.C. Bentley viewed the capital of the corporation as "its capital," not the capital of the owners, and drew fire from home and abroad for his "error." An editorial in the *Accountant* chastised Bentley, stating that "no one ever suggested that they (properties owned) were the capital of the business itself" (September 14, 1914).

Practitioners often implicitly acted on Bentley's assumption when need seemed to dictate abandonment of proprietary theory. Dickinson, working with W. J. Filbert, controller of U. S. Steel, developed consolidated theory based on the entity premise (*Journal of Accountancy* February 1906: 90–91). The methodology of consolidations has changed over the years and today many would say it reflects the assumptions of proprietary not entity theory. But in this early period the methodology was significantly different. Entity theory maintains that the source of financing (debt, stock, minority interest) is immaterial to the corporation and all returns to every supplier of capital are distributions of profits and not "expenses" to the corporation. Since the primary purpose of most early consolidations appears to have been to eliminate intercompany transfers, there was no attempt made to show a minority interest in either income or surplus (see Figure 5-1).

Most accountants agreed that the overriding consideration in financial reporting was that financial statements not be misleading.[41] If it became necessary to abandon any particular theory to more accurately report the financial condition of any enterprise, they did so without hesitation. The idea advanced by early accountants that no single theory or set of procedures could be evolved to handle all situations equally well has remained a fundamental conviction of many accountants.

Although a complete discussion of entity theory is left for the next chapter, it is important to note that at this early stage the fundamental difference between proprietary and entity theorists lay in their views of corporate income. Proprietarists held that the effectiveness of any business, whether controlled by its owners or managers, was measured in terms of the increase of wealth accruing to the stockholders. Paton contended that in a corporate age income must measure the "total return" to all suppliers of funds. Therefore, he argued, "net operating revenue is then the excess of values received over purchase assets utilized in connection with product sold, and represents the increase in capital to be apportioned or distributed among all individuals or interests who have committed cash funds or other property to the undertaking." (1922: 259). But, Paton, at this time, did not exclude appreciation from earnings calculations nor did he view accounting purely as a cost allocation process. The revenue-expense orientation which became familiar to accountants of the thirties was not simply an extension of entity theory, but an adapta-

Condensed General Balance Sheet, December 31, 1902.

ASSETS.

PROPERTY ACCOUNT:

Properties owned and operated by the several companies			$1,453,635,551.37	
Less Surplus of Subsidiary Companies at date of acquirement of their Stocks by U. S. Steel Corporation, April 1, 1901		$116,356,111.41		
Charged off to Depreciation and Extinguishment Funds		12,011,856.53		
			128,367,967.94	
				$1,325,267,583.43

DEFERRED CHARGES TO OPERATIONS:

Expenditures for Improvements, Explorations, Stripping and Development at Mines, and for Advanced Mining Royalties, chargeable to future operations of the properties. **3,178,759.67**

TRUSTEES OF SINKING FUNDS:

Cash held by Trustees on account of Bond Sinking Funds. **459,246.14**

($4,022,000 par value of Redeemed bonds held by Trustees not treated as an asset.)

INVESTMENTS:

Outside Real Estate and Other Property	$1,874,872.39	
Insurance Fund Assets	929,615.84	
		2,804,488.23

CURRENT ASSETS:

Inventories	$104,390,844.74	
Accounts Receivable	48,944,189.68	
Bills Receivable	4,153,291.13	
Agents' Balances	1,091,318.99	
Sundry Marketable Stocks and Bonds	6,091,340.16	
Cash	50,163,172.48	
		214,834,157.18

$1,546,544,234.65

Audited and found correct.
PRICE, WATERHOUSE & CO.,
Auditors.
New York, March 12, 1903.

LIABILITIES.

CAPITAL STOCK OF U. S. STEEL CORPORATION:

Common	$508,302,500.00	
Preferred	510,281,100.00	
		$1,018,583,600.00

CAPITAL STOCKS OF SUBSIDIARY COMPANIES NOT HELD BY U. S. STEEL CORPORATION (*Par Value*):

Common Stocks	$44,400.00	
Preferred Stocks	72,800.00	
Lake Superior Consolidated Iron Mines, Subsidiary Companies	98,714.38	
		215,914.38

BONDED AND DEBENTURE DEBT:

United States Steel Corporation Bonds	$303,757,000.00	
Less, Redeemed and held by Trustee of Sinking Fund	2,698,000.00	
Balance held by the Public	$301,059,000.00	
Subsidiary Companies' Bonds	$60,978,900.75	
Less, Redeemed and held by Trustees of Sinking Funds	1,324,000.00	
Balance held by the Public	59,654,900.75	
Debenture Scrip, Illinois Steel Company	40,426.02	
		360,754,326.77

MORTGAGES AND PURCHASE MONEY OBLIGATIONS OF SUBSIDIARY COMPANIES:

Mortgages	$2,901,132.07	
Purchase Money Obligations	6,689,418.53	
		9,590,550.60

CURRENT LIABILITIES:

Current Accounts Payable and Pay Rolls	$18,675,080.13	
Bills and Loans Payable	6,202,502.44	
Special Deposits due Employés and others	4,485,546.58	
Accrued Taxes not yet due	1,051,605.42	
Accrued Interest and Unpresented Coupons	5,398,572.96	
Preferred Stock Dividend No. 7, payable February 16, 1903	8,929,919.25	
Common Stock Dividend No. 7, payable March 30, 1903	5,083,025.00	
		49,826,251.78
Total Capital and Current Liabilities		$1,438,970,643.53

SINKING AND RESERVE FUNDS:

Sinking Fund on U. S. Steel Corporation Bonds	$1,773,333.33	
Sinking Funds on Bonds of Subsidiary Companies	217,344.36	
Depreciation and Extinguishment Funds	1,707,610.59	
Improvement and Replacement Funds	16,566,190.90	
Contingent and Miscellaneous Operating Funds	3,413,783.50	
Insurance Fund	1,539,485.25	
		25,217,747.93

BOND SINKING FUNDS WITH ACCRETIONS	4,481,246.14
Represented by Cash, and by redeemed bonds not treated as assets (see contra).	

UNDIVIDED SURPLUS OF U. S. STEEL CORPORATION AND SUBSIDIARY COMPANIES:

Capital Surplus provided in organization of U. S. Steel Corporation	$25,000,000.00	
Surplus accumulated by all companies since organization of U. S. Steel Corporation	52,874,597.05	
		77,874,597.05*
		$1,546,544,234.65

* NOTE.—In preliminary Report submitted to stockholders at the First Annual Meeting, February 17, 1902, the accumulated surplus of all subsidiary companies to November 30, 1901, was shown as $174,344,229.32. This total, however, included the surplus of the subsidiary companies at time of the original acquisition of their stocks by United States Steel Corporation in 1901, which surplus in this balance sheet is stated in diminution of Property Account.

Figure 5-1

Condensed general balance sheet of U.S. Steel Corporation, December 31, 1902.

tion of only selected elements of that theory. Proprietary concepts, such as earnings per share, became firmly rooted in the subsequent development of accounting. Finally, the rejection of institutional theory cast doubts on two popular interpretations of proprietary theory of this period, namely, a lack of concern for investors and acceptance of "conservatism" as the guiding light for the profession.

Institutional Theory

Francis Pixley introduced institutional theory to American accountants at the 1904 World Congress. In a paper delivered before the congress, Pixley argued that "the duties of an auditor of a company were to the company as an institution, not to the individual stockholder." He argued that accountants should permit the accumulation of secret reserves to assure the continuance of business in times of distress (Pixley 1904: 34). Certainly Pixley had legal precedent on his side, for there were clear examples in case law that accountants had no liability when they understated assets.

The *Newton v. Birmingham* small arms case (1906) granted accountants absolute immunity from prosecution in cases where the value of assets were understated. The judge ruled that

> Assets are often by reason of prudence, estimated and stated to be estimated, at less than their probable realizable value. The purpose of the Balance Sheet is primarily to show that the financial condition of the company is as least as good as there stated—not to show that it is or may not be better. (*JA*, 1913, 335)

Although settled in an English court, the opinion was widely known in the United States, and English law was regarded as providing precedent. (There is little to be said about American legal precedent at this time, for despite practitioners' urgent request for clarified legal liability, American courts had not acted.)

American accountants could not so completely disregard investors (Pixley was British), and they rejected institutional theory. J. Porter Joplin, president of the American Association from 1914 to 1916, provided the clearest exposition of contemporary views on the subject. Joplin held that no convention, not even conservatism, could justify understatement of assets to create secret reserves. Accountants, he believed, must "stand firm for principle—no understatement or overstatement of assets." Like many early practitioners, he argued that the most obvious danger in the United States was excess optimism and overstatement of assets. In most cases, convervatism was beneficial to prevent abuses. But, consistent with the attitudes of early practitioners, Joplin was most concerned that reports should not mislead any user. To that end, he suggested that "increased values in assets must be shown on the Balance Sheet (parenthetically) or in another schedule" to provide the reader with all relevant information (Joplin 1915).

That is not to say that accountants objected to establishment of such reserves. Seymour Walton probably typified the views of most CPAs when he wrote of the merits of the "objective to provide out of prosperous years, a fund which can be drawn upon to increase profits of less prosperous ones, a sort of governor to make the machinery at least appear to be running at a nearly uniform rate. *No one can dispute this is good policy.*" Walton continued that the real question is not a matter of policy, but whether or not such reserves should be kept secret. He concluded that they should not; for the present owner of stock could be harmed if he wished to sell his stock and had no knowledge of the accumulated reserve strength (Walton 1909). Dickinson hedged on this issue, perhaps in an attempt to reconcile British and American views. For corporations, he recommended publicity of any such reserves. For banks, which were subject to sudden unexpected losses, secret reserves should be tolerated so that "losses can be met without any apparent disturbance of normal conditions, so investors would not panic" (Dickinson 1914, 113–114). Full disclosure became an accepted concept among American accountants, and they generally rejected contentions that management had the right to conceal assets. Paton and Stevenson were adamant on this point: there was no justification for understatement of assets to create secret reserves since stockholders would be misled (Paton and Stevenson 1918: 468).

But it is perhaps equally important to note that although management's right to create secret reserves was challenged, there was acceptance of the contention that earnings should be regularized by increasing or decreasing discretionary reserves. There was little if any discussion about the propriety of making income appear to be relatively stable when it was not. The idea that accountants should encourage such stabilization was accepted and would have a definite impact on the later development of accounting theory. That it did not become the subject of debate at this time is perhaps a reflection of the minor status of the profit and loss account.

Profit and Loss

Whereas proprietary theorists could and did dismiss the "entity" fiction, they found it more difficult to answer criticisms that their treatment of profit and loss was totally inadequate to provide any information about the efficiency of management's operations. Most proprietarists agreed with Hatfield that the Profit and Loss account was "a subdivision of the Capital account . . . [that indicated] current changes in net wealth." Income determination was merely another aspect of asset valuation (Hatfield 1909: 197). They ignored the earnings process and concepts such as revenues and expenses. Hatfield defined expense as "negative proprietorship" and did not address the question of what is revenue. He was content to explain the revenue account as a "temporary, collective account, recording the changes in net wealth due to business operations of a stated period" (Hatfield 1909: 72f, 195ff).

Modern accountants would find it difficult to visualize an accounting theory in which income determination was not of primary concern let alone of a very crude nature. Accountants' propensity to totally disregard the Profit and Loss Statement had been criticized prior to the turn of the century. In 1899, an editorial in *The Bookkeeper* chastised the profession, claiming that "the profit and loss account is the most absurd in the whole . . . system, it is positively a kind of back door ash heap, where people throw their refuse and nobody clears it away" ("Editorial," May, 1899: 1). Most early theorists simply viewed profit and loss as a residual of the asset valuation process. Despite references one finds in the thirties to the return to "orthodoxy" of early theory, it seems clear that there was no single, acceptable procedure for profit determination in this time period.

As late as 1928, Howard Greer noted that accounting textbooks often referred to two nominal accounts, the mixed merchandise and the expense account (Greer 1928). He pointed out, the use of only two accounts did not lend itself to accuracy in determination of profits. The mixed merchandise account was debited for purchases (at cost) during the year, and credited for sales. At year end, the closing inventory was debited at sale price, which resulted in some startling annual profit figures. This problem had long been the subject of debate without successful resolution.

In 1917 the institute charged Maurice Kuhns with a violation of its bylaws (committing an act discreditable to the profession) for certifying a misleading statement due to technical incompetence. Robert

Montgomery, acting as the council's "prosecutor" presented the following schedule as evidence.

Gross Sales	$ 16,000
Beginning Inventory	6,000
Purchases	47,000
Ending Inventory	98,000
Profit	50,000

(AIA, *Minutes, 1917:* 219–220)

Caustically, Montgomery asked if some doubts did not arise concerning the statement's validity. (Since the expense account was not shown in the minutes one can only assume that since the mixed merchandise account showed a gross profit sales and ending inventory of $61,000 that there were $11,000 of expense in the other nominal accounts. No "cost of good sold" could have been calculated). Kuhns retorted that the client only wanted a balance sheet audit and besides, he argued, "since it had been held in courts that accountants are not considered detectives . . . (he) had done all that is necessary." Montgomery replied that at least since 1905 accountants knew they should not certify a misleading statement. The council suspended Kuhns, but it would be fair to say that the peculiar method of income determination Kuhns used was common (AIA *Minutes,* 1917: 250f).

Paton and Stevenson wrote that although it was fallacious to argue that recognition of appreciation in the accounts was to anticipate profits, there could be no question that "to use selling price in taking inventories—in other words to capitalize the services of the firm before those services are performed, is to anticipate profits." The cost of inventory replacement, they argued, only mirrored relevant changes in economic events and felt that accountants should record all changes if they hoped to show "a true financial posture" of the firm (Paton and Stevenson 1918: 462f). It is interesting to note that those who suggested that appreciation be recognized in the accounts were accused of reverting to the dark ages of single entry bookkeeping (Littleton 1933A: 578f).

One finds little discussion of the need for income determination, and although the concept of realization was addressed, it was not fundamental to the development of most early theory. Implicit in the early debate was the enduring belief that accountants must view either the income statement or balance sheet as fundamental, and the other residual. It was during this period that the perplexing enigma of double entry was recognized. If financial statements were to articulate, one had to choose up sides by opting for a proper income statement or a proper balance sheet, the belief being that you could not have relevant values in both.

A significant discussion of income was generated by cost accountants (led by Clinton Scovell of Scovell and Wellington who insisted that profits accrued only after all factors of production received payment for their factor shares, including payment for the use of capital). Thus, they argued that imputed interest on equity should be a cost of production (AIA, *Minutes*, 1917: 156ff).

Minutes of the institute (1912–1919) and issues of the *Journal of Accountancy* during those same years show that the debate was indeed heated. Cost accountants (who took an entity view) claimed that it was immaterial to management whether investors or creditors provided funds. There was a cost for use of such funds, and all cost should be included in production. Had the debate continued it might have been effective in raising some pertinent questions in the twenties, but it was rendered moot by the appearance of *Uniform Accounting* (1917), which specifically precluded interest on capital as a cost of production. Scovell, addressing Robert Montgomery, who had been one of his steadfast opponents, asked what this meant. Montgomery told him that as a member of the AIA he was prohibited from including such charges in audited financial statements. Scovell became enraged and indicated he just might ignore such a prohibition which, in fact, many practitioners did.[42]

Developing Technical Standards

Although Scovell's reaction was understandable, the institute welcomed the chance to gain some authority within the profession with the issuance of *Uniform Accounting*. Prior to 1917 each practitioner determined his own audit procedures and there were no authoritative pronouncements. The problem had been recognized early in the century and various remedies suggested.

An Accounting Court

Seymour Walton supported a "supreme tribunal which can pass on questions about which there is honest difference of opinion." Adding, "lawyers have their Supreme Court, why should not CPAs" (Walton 1909). A decade later, a similar idea surfaced when Vannais complained at a meeting of the institute that because so many contradictory opinions existed as to proper treatment of accounts, the practitioner had no direction.

He cited Montgomery's statement that treasury stock was an asset, and Paton's contrary opinion that it was not. Why, he asked could not the institute establish a Court of Appeals (AIA, *Minutes*, 1919: 258). Unable to resolve such problems, the institute readily acceded to a request that it cooperate with governmental officials to establish technical standards.

Uniformity-The Simple Solution

Uniform Accounting was the culmination of a trend which began around the turn of the century, namely, to look upon uniformity as the panacea for accounting problems. Accountants themselves had contributed to the growing "faith" which politicians placed in uniformity. In an attempt to respond to progressive reformers' demands for greater accountability by elected officials, public accountants helped to design municipal accounting systems which won the profession widespread praise and recognition in the financial press. They also were instrumental in developing more sophisticated accounting systems for rate regulated industries.

In 1904 Robert Montgomery delivered an historic paper, "The Importance of Uniform Practice in Determining Profits of Public Service Corporations Where Municipalities Have the Power to Regulate Rates," at the International Congress in St. Louis (Montgomery 1904: 34–38). The association immediately appointed a committee to study the recommendations made in the paper and to report to Congress any suggestions that would facilitate rate regulation. The advocacy of uniformity when statements were to be used for a specific purpose in homogeneous, regulated industries became a common posture for the profession.

By 1906 the AAPA became an active participant in the movement to establish uniform systems for municipal accounts. At the conference on Uniform Municipal Accounting (called by the U.S. Census Bureau, 13–14 February 1906), a tentative schedule of uniform accounts was presented. The association responded to this event by appointing a committee "to consider the practical application of true accounting principles in connection with standard schedules for uniform reports on municipal industries and public service corporations" (AAPA, *Yearbook*, 1906: 2).

Harvey Chase, chairman of the committee and widely acknowledged as a leading authority on the subject of municipal accounting, conducted an extensive campaign to secure adoption of the association's system (see Exhibit 5-2). The schedule that was devised did improve the quality of municipal reporting and was adopted by several major cities. The National Municipal League had long advocated such a system. It was suggested that the "one great advantage in having a uniform standard system of accounts is that by means of the same it becomes possible to compare" revenues and costs and the efficiency of public officials in handling public funds (*Chronicle* November 18, 1905: 1463). Accountants readily acknowledged the merit of such arguments, but they were not prepared to have them extended to the private sector without considering the different circumstances involved—primarily multiple users and the multiple objectives of financial reporting. But, uniformity had struck the fancy of federal officials as the solution to all reporting and accounting problems.

Schedule for Standard and Uniform Reports
For Municipal Industries and Public Service Corporations
As Amended by Committee of Seven

Suggested Form For Standard Schedule

Revenue from Operating

Gross Earnings from Public Services	$
Gross Earnings from Private Consumers	$
Gross Earnings from By-Products, etc.	$_____
Total	$
Deduct Rebates, Refunds, Discounts, etc.	$_____
Total Revenue from Operating	$

Expense of Operating

1. Expense of Manufacture	$
Operation	$
Maintenance	$
Product Purchased	$
2. Expense of Distribution	
Operating	$
Maintenance	$
3. General Expense (Salaries, Office Supplies and Expenses)	$_____
Total (1, 2 and 3)	$
4. Taxes (Real Estate and Other)	$
5. Franchise Taxes (paid or accrued annually or otherwise)	$

Expense of Operating—cont.		
6. Rentals (Leaseholds, etc.)	$	
7. Insurance (Fire, Accident & Fiduciary)	$	
8. Damages (including Extraordinary Legal & Other Expenses and Losses)	$	
9. Guaranty (Bad Debts Written Off and Reserve for Doubtful Accounts)	$	
10. Depreciation (Deterioration Written Off & Reserve for Depr'n.	$_____	
Total Expense of operating		$_____
a. Net Revenue from Operating (or Deficiency)		$
b. Other Revenue, or Income, net (from Sources other Than Operating)		$
c. Appropriations for Operating, Provided by the Municipality from General Funds		$_____
Total Available Income		$

DISPOSITION OF AVAILABLE INCOME		
11. Interest on Funded and Floating Debts		$_____
Remainder of Available Income		
12. Reserve for Sinking Funds	$	
13. Reserved for Amortization Funds	$	
14. Reserve for Other Funds	$_____	
Total Reserves	$	
15. Dividends (Private Plants)	$	
16. Appropriation to Gen'l City Funds (Public Plants)	$_____	
Total Disposition of Available Income		$_____
Credit (or Debit) Balance Transferable to Surplus		$

Source: Report of the Committee upon Standard Schedules for Uniform Reports on Municipal Industries and Public-Service Corporations. 1906 Annual Meeting Papers. New York, AICPA Library.

Figure 5–2

Fortunately, perhaps for independent accountants, the next extension of this concept came in the area of cost accounting. Edward Hurley, chairman of the Federal Trade Commission, was convinced that the lack of knowledge of costs caused most businessmen to underprice their products which led to disastrous competition.[43] Certainly in firms with no cost systems there were definite advantages to be obtained in introducing any cost system that permitted the manager to more effectively determine an adequate selling price. But

Hurley's main objective seemed to be to introduce uniform cost standards for every industry to prevent "cutthroat" competition. The AAPA worked willingly with the FTC; the concept of uniformity did not appear threatening since these systems did not advocate proscription of choice in accounting principles, only uniform classification of the various charts of accounts.[44] Hurley, however, apparently became enamored of this idea and missed the subtle distinction between uniformity in classification as opposed to principles. Suddenly, he began to suggest that "uniform" accounting would be beneficial to creditors who used audited financial reports. His proposal included development of "standard financial statements for all purposes, a set of rules and regulations for the valuation of assets and liabilities," and, as discussed previously, verification of such statements by accountants registered by the Federal Reserve Board or by federal banks (Hurley 1916: 175).

Although the national association was obviously disconcerted by Hurley's suggestion of federal registration, the AAPA decided to try to placate his other demands. The association, it appears, acted precipitously when it chose to simply present a statement called *Uniform Accounting* rather than attempting to explain its opposition to uniformity. Hurley, and later Frank Delano of the Federal Reserve Board, implied that a "scientific" methodology could be used to develop an "accounting rule book." It seems to have been most unfortunate that institute leaders, admittedly under intense pressure, chose to acquiesce. *Uniform Accounting* (later reissued under the more appropriate title "Approved Methods for the Preparation of Balance Sheet Audits") (1918) neither advocated uniformity nor did it deal with accounting. It was primarily a statement of auditing procedures. It cannot even be considered reflective on the prevalent auditing practice of the day, since it was a simple adaptation of an internal control memorandum prepared by J. Scobie for Price Waterhouse (Demond 1951: 140f). In the area of audit standards, the document did little to enhance uniformity, in fact, it left almost all choices to the "professional judgment of the practitioner." As Maurice Peloubet observed prior to the issuance of this document, most firms routinely confirmed accounts receivable and physically inspected inventory. *Uniform Accounting* made such procedures optional and suggested that in many cases they were unnecessary extensions of the audit. Management now had an "authoritative" source to prohibit such procedures as too costly and they fell into disuse in the twenties.[45]

Whereas *Uniform Accounting* provided wide discretion to the practitioner in choice of audit procedures, the institute attempted to

UNIFORM ACCOUNTING
Form for Profit and Loss Account

Gross sales	$ _____
Less outward freight, allowances, and returns	_____
Net Sales	$ _____
Inventory beginning of year	_____
Purchases, net	_____
Less inventory end of year	_____
Cost of sales	=====
Gross profit on sales	=====
Selling expenses (itemized to correspond with ledger accounts kept)	_____
Total selling expense	=====
General expenses (itemized to correspond with ledger accounts kept)	_____
Total general expense	=====
Administrative expenses (itemized to correspond with ledger accounts kept)	_____
Total administrative expense	=====
Total expenses	=====
Net profit on sales	=====
Other income:	
Income from investments	_____
Interest on notes receivable, etc.	_____
Gross income	=====
Deductions from income:	
Interest on bonded debt	_____
Interest on notes payable	_____
Total deductions	_____
Net income—profit and loss	_____
Add special credits to profit and loss	_____
Deduct special charges to profit and loss	_____
Profit and loss for period	_____
Surplus beginning of period	_____
Dividends paid	_____
Surplus ending of period	_____

Source: Federal Reserve Board, *Uniform Accounting* (Washington, D.C.: Government Printing Office, 1917).

Figure 5–3

189

dictate many accounting procedures that did not have widespread support. Most academics were alienated by the arbitrary announcement that only "lower of cost or market" could be used for inventories, a proposition they had specifically rejected as void of any theoretical merit; cost accountants were incensed by the position taken on interest as a cost of production. *Uniform Accounting* may have foreshadowed later developments within the profession, especially the conservatism of the thirties, but in 1917 it was not widely accepted. It failed to deal with many of the significant problems of the day, most notably, the proper classification of surplus, a major problem when income was viewed as the change in assets minus capital contributions. Although the institute was successful in forestalling federal intervention, the profession paid a price. By issuing a document that did not have widespread support, a false illusion—that there was an established and accepted accounting and auditing theory—had been created.

Many practitioners ignored this document as they felt it was simply the opinion of a few accountants. *Uniform Accounting* provides a classic illustration of the almost impossible task that accountants face when they attempt to settle questions of principle by acting defensively; this pamphlet provided little protection to the public or direction for the profession, while alienating many practitioners and reinforcing the belief held outside the profession that "uniformity" was *the* solution to all accounting problems.[46]

Summary

Accounting theory evolves in response to the major problems that exist in any given era. Prior to World War I, the most pressing problem in the United States was to introduce reality in the balance sheet valuations. Proprietary theorists made a significant contribution to accounting theory by developing the concept of modified historical cost. There is evidence that CPAs were concerned with both investors and creditors, and inroads were being made to find a comprehensive basis for asset valuation.

A very small number of men had made extraordinary progress in gaining recognition for the profession. CPA legislation had been secured in many states, business courses had been introduced into university curricula, and the question of professional standards had been seriously addressed. Most of the efforts in these early years were designed to promote the independent nature of the profession; that is not to say that accountants were not active in the cost or not-for-profit area, but simply a recognition that the major efforts were concentrated in the auditing area.

The major social demands of the day, greater corporate accountability and publicity, implementation of a progressive income tax, and better control of municipal finances placed accountants firmly in the vanguard of progressive reforms. It was an era of significant accomplishment for the profession. In the next decade there would be a significant shift in the demands made on the profession, which would serve to cloud its social obligation to the public.

NOTES

1. See Thomas Cochran, "The History of a Business Society," *The Journal of American History*, June 1967 pp. 5–18, for a discussion of the pervasiveness of business values in the United States.

2. See Andrew Carnegie, *The Gospel of Wealth and Other Timely Essays*, ed. Edward C. Kirkland (Cambridge: Harvard University Press, 1962). Carnegie originally published an essay in two parts in *The North American Review* in 1899 (June, pp. 663–664; December, pp. 682–698). William F. Steed, editor of the *Pall Mall Gazette* supplied the headline "The Gospel of Wealth."

3. Accounting journals were not averse to adding their voices to the growing criticism of the "money trust." One has only to scan the pages of *The Bookkeeper* and *Commerce, Accounts and Finance* to find repeated references to the "evils" being perpetrated by such a concentration of power.

4. See John R. Commons, *Myself* (Madison, Wis: The University of Wisconsin, 1963), p. 56, for discussion for the minority report he wrote for the Industrial Commission recommending governmental audits. Specific rejection of this proposal is found in U.S., Congress, House, *Final Report of the Industrial Commission.* H. Doc. 380, 57th Cong., 1st sess., 1902, pp. 649ff.

5. See Alfred Chandler, "The Origins of Progressive Leadership," in *The Letters of Theodore Roosevelt*, ed. E.E. Morrison (Cambridge: Harvard University Press, 1954), Appendix III. Chandler prepared a profile of progressives and concluded that reformers were primarily middle class, native-born Americans living in urban areas and having a distinct business orientation.

6. For a contemporary discussion of the Keep Commission, see C. H. Forbes Lindsay, "New Business Standards in Washington—Work of the Keep Commission," *The American Review of Reviews* (February 1908), pp. 190–195. For accountants' reaction see AAPA, *Yearbook* (1907), p. 31f. All correspondence referring to the Committee on Economy and Efficiency in this chapter can be found in the National Archives, R.G. 51, Sec. 131, Washington D.C.

7. See U.S., Congress, House, Industrial Commission, *Reports of the Industrial Commission*, 56th and 57th Cong., H. Docs., 19 vols., 1900–1902. The three volumes cited here are *Preliminary Report of the Industrial Commission*, H.

Doc. 476, 56th Cong., 1st sess, 1900; *Report of the Industrial Commission on Transportation*, H. Doc. 178, 57th Cong, 1st sess, 1901; *Final Report of the Industrial Commision*, H. Doc. 380, 57th Cong., 1st sess., 1902.

8. See U.S., Congress, House, *Report of the Industrial Commission on Trusts*, H. Doc. 182, 57th Cong., 1st sess. (Washington, D.C.: Government Printing Office, 1901) for testimony of business leaders. See testimony of A.S. White, president of National Salt Company and Charles Schwab, president of U.S. Steel, who admitted that management could mislead investors by dividend policies. They advocated publication of annual reports and that independent audits or government supervision be employed.

9. See correspondence from accountants to George W. Wickersham and replies from Wickersham, (Deloitte, Haskins & Sells Archival Collection, New York). For the most comprehensive statement of the problems created by this law, see A.M. Sakolski, "The Federal Corporation Tax and Modern Accounting," *The Yale Review* February 1909, pp. 372–389. Treasury Regulations No. 31, December 1910, permitted the use of accrual accounting but the law was not changed.

10. See Simon Patten, *The New Basis for Civilization* (New York: MacMillan Co. 1907; Thorstein Veblen, *The Portable Veblen* (New York: Victory Press, 1950); and John Commons, *Institutional Economics* (Madison, Wis.: The University of Wisconsin Press, 1959) had the most obvious influence upon accounting literature through the work of his student, DR Scott. But Patten published frequently in the *Annals of the American Academy of Social and Political Science* which prior to the turn of the century carried many articles dealing with accounting topics, and, therefore, it must be presumed that some accountants were familiar with his work.

11. See "Scrapbook—Elijah Watt Sells", Haskins & Sells Archival Collection, New York. In a letter dated February 2, 1908, Herbert G. Stockwell criticized Sells's position but most of the voluminous correspondence is laudatory. The scrapbook includes a letter from Oliver Wendell Holmes who commends the author for publication of the pamphlet mentioned above.

12. For interpretation of this absence of federal support, see Michael Chatfield, *A History of Accounting Thought* (Hinsdale, Ill.: The Dryden Press, 1974).

13. A letter from C. W. Haskins to Dr. Henry McCracken of New York University, December 11, 1898, states: "We recall with regret the attempts that have heretofore been made to establish independent schools of accounts. We believe the failure of these attempts has been due to the absence of this very university foundation which we honor to suggest to you." See NYSSCPA, *Ten Year Book* (New York: NYSSCPA, 1907), p. 24.

14. See, for example, L.G. Battelle, *Story of Ohio Accountancy* (Columbus: Ohio Society of CPAs, 1954), for a description of the difficulties faced by most midwestern accountants where populist sentiment was strong.

15. All references to NYSSCPA are to New York State Society of Certified Public Accountants, *Minute Books of Meetings of the Members and of the Board of Directors*—1897–1910, bound handwritten manuscripts; 1911–1920, bound typescripts (New York: NYSSCPA).

16. See AAPA, *Yearbook* (1907): pp. 215–218 for Cooper's "Draft of a Model CPA Law to Regulate the Profession." This is similar to the model law he presented to the Federation (1902) as a guide for uniform CPA legislation.

17. See "Public Accountants in the United States," *The Accountant* (October 17, 1903 pp. 1251–1253), which contains excerpts from Cooper's address, "National Legislation for the Public Accountant," to the Illinois State Society (1899).

18. AIA, *Minutes - 1916*, p. 115ff and AIA, *Minutes - 1917*, p. 30f discuss Hurley's suggestion. Robert Montgomery, who acted as the Devil's advocate, labeled Hurley as an "unknown" quantity in 1916. But by 1917, with federal regulation no longer a serious threat, he lamented the loss of "our boy in Washington" when Hurley resigned. The zone expert scheme can be found in an editorial, *Journal of Accountancy*, August 1915, pp. 129–134.

19. The plan was devised by E. W. Sells and J. E. Sterrett and can be located in the AAPA, *Minutes* (1916), 50ff and in the 1916 *Yearbook of the Institute of Accountants in the United States of America*. Fortunately, the above name was shortened after approximately three months to the American Institute of Accountants (AIA).

20. The AIA modeled its entrance exam on that of New York State. One of its stated objectives was to gain acceptance for a uniform CPA examination in all states. From 1917 to 1919, the institute's examination was comprised of five fields— practice, theory, auditing, business law, and actuarial science. Many states objected to the inclusion of actuarial science and the AIA dropped that section. But, despite this compromise a uniform national exam was not to be realized for more than three decades.

21. This section places heavy reliance on the writings of the presidents of the AAPA and AIA from 1906 to 1918: E.W. Sells, J.E. Sterrett, E.L. Suffern, J.P. Joplin, R.H. Montgomery and W.S. Davies. Establishing professional standards was a responsibility the national organization attempted to assume. Therefore its leadership was extremely influential.

22. See Irvin G. Wyllie, "Social Darwinism and the Businessman," *Proceedings of the American Philosophical Society*, October 1959 p. 633. Wyllie notes that Vanderbilt waited until age 70 to read his first book. Similarly, Daniel Drew wrote that "Book learning is something, but thirteen million dollars is also something, and a mite sight more."

23. See AAPA, "Report of the Committee on Education," *Yearbook* (1912), p. 137ff. The plea was most explicit in this source and the committee had similar requests from 1907 forward.

24. See Robert Montgomery, "An Accountancy Laboratory," *Journal of Accountancy* (June 1914), pp. 405–411 for a discussion of the need for a "practical" orientation in the classroom.

25. For an opposite view which existed as to the merit of such policies, see "Editorial," *Journal of Accountancy*, April 1910, pp. 448–449. The *Journal*, while under the control of Joseph French Johnson, Dean at the School of Commerce and Accounts, New York University, did *not* advocate increasing

experience requirements. The *Journal's* editorials until 1912, when the AAPA took control, often reflected academic opinion that conflicted with practitioners' views.

26. Sterrett's paper, although viewed as a "classic" by John Carey, shows evidence of a decided British influence; see the New Zealand Code of Ethics. E. W. Sells, in his "Inaugural Address," *Journal of Accountancy*, November 1906, pp. 39–41, suggested American auditing and educational standards were far superior to those in Great Britain, but he conceded that the British were far ahead in the field of ethics.

27. Cooper probably lost the 1912 election for President because of his reputation as a scold. AAPA, *Yearbook* (1912), p. 78ff details this election. Cooper was the Association's official nominee (Montgomery seconding his nomination). Arthur Young nominated Alan Smart from Illinois. Montgomery emerged as a compromise candidate and won on the fourth ballot. Since Montgomery suggested in his autobiography that he was the youngest President to that time and this has been widely quoted and his rise sometimes referred to as meteoric in previous histories, it should be mentioned that he was not, in fact, the youngest man to have been elected. Sterrett in 1908 had been younger (38) and Davies in 1887 had been only 35. The age differential is not significant in itself but it is important to note that young men could and did achieve power within the profession quickly at this time.

28. When one reviews only the written rules, conclusions significantly different with respect to both independence and confidentiality are reached. See, for example, Carey 1969, pp. 84–93, and AICPA, Committee on Long Range Objectives, *Profession–1975*, pp. 256–258, 540–549, which suggest little was done during this period with respect to independence or confidentiality.

29. Robert H. Montgomery, "Professional Ethics," *Journal of Accountancy*, December 1907, p. 148. The author suggested that "the only penalty of practical effect is one which would deprive a man from making a living in his profession," a power which the association did not have, only state boards had the authority to revoke a CPA certificate.

30. See "Public Accountants' Audit vs. the Interstate Commerce Commission," *Commercial and Financial Chronicle* (January 1914).

31. See David Green, "Evaluating Accounting Literature," *Accounting Review*, January 1966, pp. 52–64, for a discussion of the constant debate over "art vs. science." Green suggests that this debate provided little direction and it would be better to explore the question of human knowledge and ways to improve accounting's contribution to that knowledge. But if the art-science issue has been useless, and that seems true, it has permeated the literature.

32. The conception of "schools" of accounting thought can be found in much of A.C. Littleton's early work. See, for example, "What is Profit?" *Accounting Review*, September 1928, 278–287, where he outlines the different views of profit in the balance sheet and income statement "schools."

33. This concept can be traced from Adam Smith to John Stuart Mill to Alfred Marshall. See, for example, Alfred Marshall, *Principles of Economics*, 8th ed. (London: MacMillan & Co., 1964), p. 62ff. Marshall viewed profits as the

difference in the value of the owner's stock at the beginning and end of a year. Charles Sprague (1908), p. 61f, explicitly rejected Irving Fisher's contention that a business entity is "a fictitious person holding certain assets and owing them all out again to real persons." Sprague wrote "even admitting there is a fictitious entity it owes nothing to its owners."

34. Greene, president of the Audit Company of New York, was called to testify before the Industrial Commission as a railroad expert, not as an accountant, but he took the opportunity to advocate publication of corporate reports. See U.S., Congress, (1901A), p. 467ff for Greene's testimony.

35. See for example, Charles Sprague, "Premiums and Discounts," *Journal of Accountancy*, August 1906, pp. 294–296; G.O. May, "The Proper Treatments of Premiums and Discounts on Bonds," *Journal of Accountancy*, July 1906, pp. 174–186.

36. As with many accounting conventions, the antecedents of "lower of cost or market" have been traced to prior centuries by historians. See, for example, A.C. Littleton, "A Genealogy for 'Cost or Market'," *Accounting Review*, June 1941, pp. 161–167 and R.H. Parker, "Lower of Cost and Market in Britain and the United States: An Historical Survey," *Abacus*, December 1965, pp. 156–172.

37. It should be mentioned that conservatism was accepted by Montgomery in this period and, again, in the thirties. But in the twenties he would join with those who rejected conservatism as a basic concept. See Robert Montgomery, "Accountants' Limitations," *Journal of Accountancy*, October 1927, pp. 245–259. Montgomery writes "not courage but fear started conservatism," adding, the "so-called conservatism of the accountant hides understated value which can never harm anyone to know or hides overstated values which it would be useful to know." He concluded accountants did not have a "moral right" to conceal information (p. 251).

38. The going concern concept has had an interesting evolution. Dicksee in his classic, *Auditing* (1892), wrote "the basis of valuation will be a going concern." But, he acknowledged that the meaning of the phrase was unclear, adding that, insofar as any definite meaning is possible, "the term is an elastic one." He first used this concept to support depreciation, but carrying the idea to its natural conclusion required recognition of increases as well as decreases in current assets but not of fixed assets because they are held for use. Hatfield was forced to the same conclusion despite his initial acceptance of "lower of cost or market" for inventories. Thus, although the going concern and "value in use" supported conservative valuation for fixed assets, it proved "inadequate" for practitioners purposes for current assets. For a review of how this problem was "overcome," see Reed K. Storey, "Revenue Realization, Going Concern and Measurement of Income," *Accounting Review*, April 1959.

39. See Paton and Stevenson (1918), p. 454ff, for one of the most explicit statements on the topic. See also Seymour Walton, "Fixed Assets at Cost or Market," *Journal of Accountancy*, November 1915, pp. 482–483, who states that cost should always be maintained, the definitive position of the institute.

40. See L.S. Rosen and Don T. DeCoster, "Funds Statements: A Historical Perspective," *Accounting Review*, January 1969, pp. 124–136 for earlier examples of funds statements.

41. See AIA, *Minutes, 1917,* p. 16ff, where the Park-Potter case was discussed and practitioners indicated that suppression of a contingent liability which was both material and misleading was a violation of the code of ethics under the concept of acts discreditable to the profession.

42. Montgomery's attitude toward cost accounting was enough to make many cost accountants bristle. He told Scovell, "I not only will say I know nothing about cost accounting, I claim it." He contended that there are "certain broad principles we can adhere to . . . and I don't think that in industrial cost accounting, we are obliged to depart them for the sake of expedience." AIA, *Minutes, 1917,* pp. 158–159. In 1919, when the National Association of Cost Accountants was being promoted, Montgomery refused to see this as a challenge telling the Council that, "I think the Institute, as an Institute for professional accountants, need fear no specialized, technical organization, no matter how large and powerful it may be." AIA, *Minutes, 1919,* p. 178.

43. See Edward N. Hurley, *Awakening of Business* (New York: Doubleday, Page & Co., 1916), for a comprehensive statement of Hurley's position. For a discussion of Hurley as a champion of business see Gabriel Kolko, *The Triumph of Conservatism: A Reinterpretation of American History, 1900–1916* (New York: The Free Press of Glencoe, 1963). Although Kolko's major thesis has been challenged, it does seem clear that of all the FTC commissioners, Hurley was the most sympathetic to business.

44. See for example, FTC, "Fundamentals of a Cost System for Manufacturers" (Washington, D.C.: Government Printing Office, 1916) and FTC, "A System of Accounts for Retail Merchants" (Washington, D.C.: Government Printing Office, 1918).

45. In a series of editorials the *Journal of Accountancy* supported this idea. See "Responsibility for Inventories," April 1927, pp. 286–288 where George O. May is quoted with his assertion "that I do not believe the verification of physical inventories is within the competence of auditors," and further stated they were unnecessary. Montgomery (1927), p. 256 and Nichols (1927), pp. 448–449 dissented but the *Journal* subsequently continued to support May.

46. See Merino and Coe 1978 for discussion of the evolution of the concept of uniformity.

6 THE CLASSICAL PERIOD: ACCOUNTANCY COMES OF AGE

The business of America is business.
[Calvin Coolidge]

Background Factors

World War I had a profound effect on public attitudes toward the business sector. Many people attributed the Allied victory to the creativity and ingenuity of American business people. Present day readers may find it hard to visualize a period when "business" enjoyed near apotheosis from almost all elements of society. But that was the case throughout most of the 1920s. Accountants saw the image of their profession enhanced by the volunteer services of such groups as the Dollar-a-Year Men, who provided administrative aid to the government during the war years. Many individual practitioners received personal accolades for their war efforts, which brought the profession to public attention.[1] Because of a widespread belief that business had reformed and that no external regulation was necessary, the accountant's role changed dramatically from protector of third parties to conserver of the interests of business, a change that did not have salutary effects on the development of the profession.

Urbanization of America

The decade of the 1920s has received extensive examination by historians in all fields. Yet, in many respects, analysis and interpretation appear inadequate. Perhaps this is due to the contradictions inherent in periods when major social changes occur. The 1880 census had marked the passing of the frontier. The 1920 census alerted Americans to the urbanization of the nation—for some time after 1915, the rural majority had become a minority (Mowry 1965: 2f.). Urban America certainly presented a less homogeneous population with different values than had existed in a rural nation. Yet, the definitive political solution was to seek a reaffirmation of the "traditional American creed." After World War I, President Warren G. Harding's policy of returning to normalcy inaugurated the so-called Golden Age of Business (Harding 1920). Normalcy promoted economic individualism, rejected the concept of positive government, and held that financiers and businessmen were primarily responsible for the nation's progress, which was, in effect, a return to the traditional American creed.

Government appeared to view the right to own property as absolute and to assume that social progress would be enhanced by a policy of nonintervention. President Coolidge perhaps best expressed this sentiment when he said that the right to accumulate property is "founded on the constitution of the universe" and concluded that business had been the "greatest contributing factor to the spiritual advancement of the race." The ascendancy of business had important ramifications for the accounting profession. Since government adopted a laissez faire attitude toward business, there was little call for corporate accountability and none for external control. Perhaps even more important is the inconsistency in governmental calls for individualism. In the 1920s the regulatory agencies, such as the Federal Trade Commission (FTC) and the Federal Reserve Board (FRB), were in the hands of administrators recruited from the business sector that they were designed to control. Paternalism rather than individualism characterized government policy. One historian concluded that politicians

> were keenly for maintaining the individualistic social ideas and values among the masses. But, for themselves and their fellow businessmen, especially in economic matters, they had to a startling degree become collectivists who depended upon a restricted kind of governmental paternalism (Mowry 1965: 62–63).

And the government did not hesitate to demand that accountants view their primary role as protecting business interests. Regulatory agencies became only residually concerned with public protection.

Immediately after the World War I, the FTC was still attempting to restrain unfair methods of price competition. But the Department of Commerce, under Herbert Hoover, worked with business to standardize products, to establish uniform pricing policies, and to form trade associations and cooperative groups. The Supreme Court interpreted "unfair methods of price competition" very narrowly and looked with sympathy on Hoover's arguments that antitrust legislation be relaxed with respect to trade associations, which, by joint cooperation, aided competition (Dorfman 1959: 42ff.).

The shift was actually one of emphasis, from the prewar concern with the prevention of monopoly to the postwar desire to prevent cutthroat competition.[2] The Northern Securities anti-trust case demonstrated that the courts did not construe bigness per se as unfair or illegal. During the 1920s the courts frequently prevented vigorous prosecution of industrial or corporate abuses. But there was an inconsistency about judicial theory. Louis Brandeis, part of the liberal minority in the Court, disagreed with the concept expressed in Northern Securities. He wrote that "the proposition that mere bigness cannot be an offense is false, because . . . our society, which rests upon democracy cannot endure under such conditions. Something approaching equality is essential" (Dorfman 1959: 153). Oliver Wendell Holmes, a progressive jurist, thought that preserving a democratic competitive economic system was not only unnecessary but inefficient. "What difference does it make," he asked, "whether Rockefeller or the United States owned all the wheat so long as the people consumed it" (Persons 1958: 273).

By 1925, when William Humphreys became FTC chairman, business had acquired a virtually free hand in eliminating price competition. Senator George Norris expressed the disillusionment of reformers when he lamented the passing of FTC authority to Humphreys, whom he called "one of the greatest reactionaries of all times" (Davis 1962: 439).

Thus, regulatory agencies, which had been established to monitor the business community and had in the past encouraged audits to protect the public interest, became less interested in corporate control. Businessmen were left to regulate their own affairs; accountants were now asked to assist management in preparing information on costs, production, and sales to be forwarded to the Commerce Department. The department distributed this information among producers to prevent price competition.

Corporate Social Responsibility

Certainly one might expect reformers to denounce government's abdication of control to the business community, if there had not been some evidence that the businessman would accept the concept of social responsibility. It has often been overlooked, or perhaps dismissed as mere rhetoric given the debacle of 1929, but the 1920s marked the beginning of the debate over business's responsibility to society. Even as rugged an individualist as Henry Ford admitted that in a corporate era no one person would have the absolute right to use property only for his own benefit. He wrote that

> A machine belongs neither to the man who purchased it nor to the worker who operated it but to the public. . . . [I]t advantages the worker and the proprietor only as they use it to the advantage of the public. (Mowry 1969: 8–9)

Were Ford and other businessmen who made such statement sincere? The answer would seem to be yes, even if not for altruistic reasons but because it made good business sense to protect the consumer and worker, given the change in strategy of American business.

Prior to the war, most businesses kept wages low and prices high ("buy cheap, sell dear"), and that policy continued in Europe. In the United States, a mass production-consumption society emerged. Businessmen increased production, cut costs, and decreased prices to attract the mass market. Perhaps the advertising revolution, along with the technological advances in radio and film, made such a policy feasible. But, if one plans to appeal to the masses, then it is good business to provide some protection to wage earners. In most instances businessmen supported pensions, minimum wage, child labor laws, and so forth. Why were such laws not enacted? The answer seems twofold. While businessmen accepted them in principle, there seemed to be no rush to enact such legislation, given the aura of general prosperity. But what was perhaps more important, the Supreme Court continuously declared such legislation unconstitutional during the 1920s.[3]

Accountants became involved in efforts to humanize the scientific management revolution of previous decades. Left to the efforts of engineers, scientific management and cost accounting techniques evolved to measure efficiency. In the 1920s, the question of "rational industrial democracy" emerged. Perhaps most illustrative of the shift in thought was the growth of organizations such as the Technical

Alliance, which sought to ally technicians and labor. H. A. Scott, the organizer, thought that the mission of the alliance should be "to collect data, design or co-ordinate systems, and to give progressive bodies the data of the present mechanism with no sympathy toward any ideal" (Dorfman 1948: 98f.).

Stuart Chase, if not the first, was one of the earliest social accountants. He led a minority group within the alliance which objected to such neutrality as inadequate for public protection in a corporate era. Chase continuously argued that the technician had to assure "that waste was not narrowly defined as inefficiency of the plant" (as did Taylor, Gantt, and others) "but must include the greater waste of undesirable goods, unemployment, and even war" (Chase 1921). Chase, a CPA but more widely known as an economist, was instrumental in generating demands for consumer protection. He foreshadowed later calls for corporate accountability, but most political leaders ignored this movement in the 1920s.

Since the public sector generated few demands for audited financial reports, accountants promoted other services that they could provide the businessman. Budgeting, implementation of standard cost systems, and other management accounting techniques were extremely important in gaining acceptance for public accountants during the 1920s.[4]

During this decade, formalized management services became an accepted function of the independent accountant. In those early years, however, there was a significant difference in the services provided from those provided today. Clients often had no accounting staff, and the CPA firm furnished the staff for internal management control. Smaller firms also turned to CPAs to interpret financial statements, suggest operational improvements, and design new control systems. S.D. Leidesdorf, a leader in the field of management services, believed that it was during this period that the image of the CPA as a nearly infallible advisor to the client became widely accepted (Kent 1975). Although serving as advisors to small businessmen enabled some small practitioners to survive, there is little doubt that income tax legislation had a more profound impact and significantly changed the image of the profession. The tax law of 1924, which created the Board of Tax Appeals, gave both lawyers and CPAs the right to represent clients; thus, accountants became advocates.

In 1911 Edward L. Suffern, AAPA president, had reminded his colleagues that as independent accountants they had a duty to see that all parties, including government, shared equitably in corporate profits (Suffern 1912). Such ideas were no longer entertained in the

1920s. Early debates about the CPA's role and obligation to both the client and the public became infrequent. The philosophy of Andrew Mellon, secretary of the Treasury from 1921 to 1930, prevailed. A bitter progressive described Mellon as the only secretary "under whom three Presidents served." Mellon believed that the most effective tax program was one that minimized taxes on the rich. He reasoned that the wealthy must be better able to manage economic resources than the poor. And, therefore, the more the rich controlled, the better off the country would be. The poor would benefit residually as the enhanced national wealth flowed downward. The social role of accountants came to be seen as minimization of taxes. Although some reformers questioned Mellon's synergistic approach, which assumed that the wealth of the rich would eventually filter down to the poor, social thought appeared to support Mellon.[5]

After 1929, when economic conditions and social attitudes no longer supported Mellon's view of the wealthy class's superior ability to administer the national welfare, accountants did not reopen the question of their role. Nor did academicians question practitioners about the propriety of maintaining an advocate's role. Tax planning and preparing tax returns became the accountant's chief functions, a much narrower role than that perceived by the earliest practitioners. With tax work and management services being the main avenues of survival for many accountants, the audit function became less important. Many new practitioners remained oblivious to, if not totally unaware of, any obligation to third parties.

Before World War I, the FRB had been influential in the original efforts to develop accounting and auditing standards. From the appearance of "Approved Methods for the Preparation of Balance Sheet Statements" in 1918 until the aftermath of the stock market crash more than a decade later, the board did little about financial reporting standards. And other regulatory agencies also ceased to ask for independent audits as a form of corporate control. The social demand generated in the progressive era for corporate accountability vis-à-vis greater publicity had sustained CPAs in their original claim to professional status. During the 1920s that claim was significantly weakened by public indifference and a reaffirmation of the traditional American Creed. (See Chapter 5, pp. 128ff.) Economic theories, which focused on competition as the most effective means of promoting social welfare, suited officials in Washington well, for then they had no responsibility.

That is not to say that new theories were not evolving. It was obvious to many that old economic and social theories did not adequately cope with the social conditions in a corporate age. John Dewey called for a "social macroscopic" method of analysis to replace the "microscopic" approach, which focused on profits to the individual (Dewey 1929: 261–263). Dewey believed that legislation was mandatory and concluded that "the basic legislative remedy would require full public disclosure of operations of modern large-scale corporations. In this way the fear of adverse public opinion would serve as a deterrent to the unbridled pursuit of profit." Certainly, the institutionalists, such as Veblen and Commons, also demanded government control and questioned the assumption that the social good would be best promoted by allowing individuals to maximize their own wealth. The institutionalists, especially Veblen, did influence some accountants (see, for example, the work of DR Scott). But by and large accounting practitioners accepted the position that microscopic, rather than macroscopic, reporting was their role. They, like many economists, never viewed the 1920s as a watershed and certainly never considered the problems inherent in an economy of abundance.[6]

The Accountant's Legal Liability

Legal theory had failed to adapt to changing social conditions and afforded little protection to security holders. The courts continued to stress individual rights, especially the right to own property and the privity of contract. Despite the frequent dissents of Holmes and Brandeis, most of the Supreme Court justices interpreted the constitution to explicitly sanction laissez faire economics and forbid government regulation (Link 1967: 335–338).

The law that had served well for an agrarian society in the nineteenth century did not readily adapt to the industrial realities of the twentieth. Accountants noted the inadequacy of the law to protect security holders, and an early editorial in the *Journal of Accountancy* advocated that the laws be amended "to fix legal liability upon the auditor" (July 1912: 56–57).[7]

The liability of accountants evolved primarily from three theories of law—negligence, fraud, and breach of contract. Judicial interpretation of those theories had established that accountants had very limited liability. Green wrote that the broader theory of negligence was of limited use, perhaps inoperable with respect to intangible property such as securities (Green 1937: 5). Negligence did not encompass misrepresentation, and interpretation of its four elements (duty, duty violation, casual relationships, and damages) had made it difficult for security holders to litigate successfully against CPAs.

A 1905 legal decision held that as members of a skilled profession, accountants must exercise reasonable care. Relying on English law, the court ruled that one could not "expect more than reasonable care for the accountant was not an insurer." By 1918 it had become clear that judges would interpret reasonable care leniently; the auditor had to verify cash but not receivables or other assets. But most important, "accountants could assume the honesty of management and could rely on their representations." Contributory negligence on the part of the client gave accountants an absolute defense. Finally, a causal relationship had to exist. It was not sufficient to merely show that the defendent was negligent and the plaintiff suffered an injury. Even when the auditor was found negligent, the amount of damages was limited to the amount of loss that flowed from breach of duty.[8]

In *Landell* v. *Lybrand* (1919) the Court found that, although the accountants were careless in preparing their report, there was no duty to the plaintiff—an investor who had relied on financial statements—and therefore the theory of negligence was inapplicable. In *Craig* v. *Anyon* (1925) a jury found the auditors guilty of negligence and awarded damages of $1 million. But the Court disallowed the award, citing contributory negligence on the part of the plaintiffs (based on the negligent manner in which they ran their business) and required that only the audit fee of $2000 be remitted. Until the Cardozo decision, security holders had little redress if audited financial statements misled them.

In 1931, perhaps unintentionally, the accountant's legal liability was extended. In the Ultramares case, New York Supreme Court Justice Cardozo noted that accountants could be held liable for gross negligence tantamount to fraud. According to reports of a conversation between S. D. Leidesdorf and Cardozo (who was related to Leidesdorf's wife) the judge thought this was of benefit to accountants because it clarified their position. Leidesdorf, on the other hand, was horrified and felt it was the worst thing that had happened to the profession. He felt that few juries would be able to distinguish the subtle difference between simple and gross negligence (Schur 1976). Perhaps, without intending to, Cardozo had served to remind accountants of their public responsibility.

Until the 1933 and 1934 federal securities acts, public demands for audits decreased, and the profession's obligation to third parties was obscured. The direction and growth of accounting practice was in the area of credit reports to bankers, as advisors to businessmen, and as tax experts. The New York Stock Exchange consistently refused to acknowledge the need for independent audits of listed companies before 1929. Only after the crash did accountants receive the full support of the exchange.[9] Perhaps a strong, united profession could have generated demands for protection of investors and developed standards to insure that all practitioners were aware of their responsibilities as professionals. But amid a wave of speculative fever unparalleled in American history which created a need for strong control and leadership in accountancy, the profession was bitterly divided. The lack of a unified, authoritative institution through which accountants could exercise strong leadership in the financial community persisted until 1936.

A Profession Divided: The AIA and the ASCPA

The 1916 reorganization of the AIA had accomplished the immediate goals of allaying external criticism and retaining self-regulation of the profession. But the institute appeared to have abandoned the CPA certificate as an absolute requisite for membership. When the leadership of the institute failed to challenge organizations such as the National Association of Certified Public Accountants (NACPA), which was accused of "selling" CPA certificates, bitter hostility developed.

The American Society of Certified Public Accountants (ASCPA) was established in 1921, creating what John L. Carey called "The Great Schism."[10] Available historical literature is not consistent in its analysis of the institute and the society and may simply reflect the biases of each side of the dispute. Accountants who experienced the rift often refer to the bitterness and recrimination that accompanied it, either in their own autobiographies or memoirs or in personal interviews. They suggest that important philosophical differences existed within the profession which made unification impossible.

The ASCPA presented a direct challenge to the leadership of the AIA. One of the clearest and most dispassionate expositions of the differences between the two groups appeared in an editorial in The *Certified Public Accountant,* written by Frank Wilbur Main, the society's president. He wrote that the institute embraced national control of the profession, uniform CPA examinations and grading procedures, regional associations, strict rules of conduct, a decided emphasis on auditing, and national publicity of the profession. He contrasted this with the society's perspective, which included state promulgated and administered examinations, which reflected state standards; no formal rules of conduct; an emphasis on broader accounting services, and state publicity of the profession (Main 1923). It may be apt to describe the institute and the society as being, respectively, federalist and states' rights in orientation.

Institute membership tended to be concentrated in urbanized states, and its leaders were often connected with large, well-established, and prosperous firms. The institute represented, to use a modern phrase, an Eastern Establishment. Homer Dunn believed that the institute did not even make an attempt to understand regional differences. "Why," Dunn had asked, "do you need uniform standards for commercial ventures in agricultural and mining states?" He alleged that the institute simply sought to establish "a professional body above the regulatory laws of any state" to gain personal satisfaction for its leadership clique (Dunn 1922). Dunn's particularism was in sharp contrast to the institute's demands for uniformity and was basic to the misunderstandings which arose.

Many felt that the institute's organizational design restricted entry into the profession. The apparent abandonment of the CPA certificate as the sole requirement for admission in favor of membership by invitation was thought to be undemocratic.[11] In an age when many young people were attracted by the monetary rewards of accounting practice, any restriction on entry was viewed with hostility. Leo Levanthal and Ira Kirkstein, both Wharton graduates, vividly recalled the difficulty that young men had in obtaining employment. They, like most others starting out, were totally dependent on bookkeeping and tax work for small clients. The evidence is clear that auditing alone would not support a new practice. Accountants often served as secretaries to the clients' boards of directors. Independence from such involvement in a client's business was a luxury not many could afford (Kirkstein 1972). The AIA's emphasis on auditing seriously impaired its claim to be the national voice of the profession.

An important factor in the erosion of the institute's authority was its failure to respond to threats to the legitimacy of state CPA certificates. Organizations like the National Association of CPAs (NACPA) proliferated and threatened the very existence of CPAs in less urbanized states. State societies like those in Texas and Michigan, which in 1920 had memberships of 20 and 47, respectively, were threatened by open sales of meaningless CPA certificates. William Dolge, in an attempt to discredit the NACPA, submitted an application in the name of I. A. Duarf. After paying $25, he received a CPA certificate, with no questions asked. Dolge pointed out that Duarf was "fraud" spelled backwards (Herrick 1969). Struggling state societies in the Midwest and the South simply could not tolerate the proliferation of CPAs given the lack of sophistication among their clients. The AIA did finally secure an injunction against the NACPA in August 1922. But, although the NACPA existed for little more than a year, the issuing of its bogus certificates had polarized opposition to the AIA, especially in the Midwest and the South. The prevailing opinion was that the AIA had done too little too late. In many states, such as Texas, the financially hard pressed state societies had fought the legal battle earlier and more effectively (Tinsley 1962: 29f.). To say that the split would not have occurred if the AIA had acted more expeditiously would be mere speculation. But one can say that the delayed response exacerbated sectional differences and rendered less viable the AIA's claim for national attention. Nevertheless, personality clashes among practitioners appeared to have made a split inevitable.

The effect this division had on the profession cannot be understood without a glimpse at some of the serious estrangements that developed among leading practitioners, such as the enmity between Eric Kohler and George O. May. Kohler, who was inclined to attribute all major contributions to the ASCPA and often ignored specific documentary evidence to the contrary, reflected the bitterness that remained even after the organizational division was healed (Kohler 1975). He strongly disliked May, whom Kohler felt represented the "embodiment of the Eastern establishment." May, brilliant and undoubtedly one of the leading spokesmen for the profession through the institute, was unfortunately unable to accept criticism. Even those who admired his abilities admitted that weakness and acknowledged that he often raised the hackles of contemporaries so that Kohler's reaction to him was far from unique.[12]

Similar resentment existed toward A. P. Richardson, secretary of the AIA and editor of the *Journal of Accountancy*. Many agreed with one Midwest practitioner's complaint that Richardson, who was neither an accountant nor an American, had far too much influence in professional matters. Durand Springer, secretary of the ASCPA, and Richardson were constantly at odds, and some of their confrontations became legend. Carey concluded that each secretary

personified his organization in the eyes of CPAs . . . the conflict [was] between aristocracy, an exclusive organization, the elite [Richardson] and a democracy [Springer] a grass roots organization devoted to the common man (Carey 1975A).

John Forbes felt that both May's and Richardson's demeanor lent credence to the belief held by many California practitioners that the reorganization was merely a ploy to keep the "bahstads" (pronounced with a broad English accent) out (Carey 1975B).

Thus, from 1921 until 1936—when it became imperative to present a united front to the obvious threat of federal intervention through the securities acts and the establishment of the Securities and Exchange Commission (SEC)—the accounting profession was in chaos, divided within and having no authoritative body to provide leadership. From its inception, the AIA lacked authority, and its leadership was severely challenged. Several of the institute's leaders adamantly refused to consider the kinds of compromise necessary in the politics of any profession. If accountants are to be assigned any responsibility for the financial debacle of 1929, perhaps it would be just to say that their inability to work together as professionals hampered the development of accounting standards and precluded acceptance of self-regulation, which a viable institute might have

A. P. Richardson, secretary of the American Institute of Accountants.

Durand Springer, secretary of the American Society of Certified Public Accountants.

provided. This lack became painfully apparent in the failure of the profession to delineate and enforce stringent ethical and educational standards.

Professional Standards

The AAPA had provided positive and early leadership in the development of both ethical and educational standards. The institute faced significantly different environmental pressures. Politicians were demanding the cessation of all cutthroat competition, and the institute was forced to address the issue of limiting competition. Cultural constraints prior to World War I had precluded the promulgation of any rules that would restrict competition. The sophisticated differentiation between ordinary business competition for the presumed benefit of the public and the potentially damaging effects of competition among professionals was not universally understood or accepted. Accountants seemed unable to gain an appreciation of the subtle distinction between business and professional competition. The ensuing debate over ethical standards to limit competition further divided the profession.

Ethical Standards

The American Society had a very democratic (perhaps anarchic) position toward ethical standards: Each practitioner would be guided by his own conscience and no rules would be enacted (Main 1923: 3). The AIA continued to try to promulgate rules of conduct, essentially in the area of Other Responsibilities, Responsibility to Colleagues, and Responsibility to Clients. From 1918 to 1936, only two new major rules, dealing with contingent fees and advertising, were incorporated into the Code of Ethics. Both issues were volatile, arousing strong emotions that increased tensions among practitioners.

Contingent Fees

As early as 1907, John A. Cooper introduced a rule at the annual meeting of the AAPA that stated "no member shall perform accounting services payment for which is by arrangement upon the contingency of the result of litigation or other form of adjustment." Views polarized, and Robert Montgomery and Cooper were continuously at loggerheads. Cooper contended that "a client could persuade an accountant to sign a dishonest certificate in a case where the latter is interested in the results." "If he'd sign one on a contingent basis," retorted Montgomery, "he would just as likely sign one on a fixed fee" (AAPA Yearbook 1907: 60ff.). But, with the spectre of the FTC's demand for greater competition within the profession, it would have been political suicide for accountants to have banned contingent fees in the progressive era; however, with the advent of "normalcy" it appeared mandatory that accountants enact rules to prohibit unseemly competition.

After the war emphasis changed from the attest function to tax and other client-oriented services and politicians viewed excessive competition as being harmful to profitable operations. And the Treasury took the lead in demanding rules that would cut competition. The institute's council banned contingent fees in 1919 after pungent debate. The rule read as follows:

> No members shall render professional services, the anticipated fee for which shall be contingent upon his findings and results thereof. (This rule shall be construed as inhibiting only services in which the accountant's findings or expert opinion might be influenced by consideration of personal financial interest.) (AIA, *Yearbook, 1920*, p. 72).

The sentence in parentheses was deleted in 1920 because some practitioners contended that it permitted tax work by accountants on a contingent fee.[13] This rule still did not serve to halt acceptance of contingent fees. And in 1923 a new rule banned contingent fees absolutely: "Members and associates should neither render nor offer to render services for which the fees are contingent" (AIA, *Yearbook, 1924*: 95, 145–146). It was interpreted to mean that no such fees could be accepted for any kind of work an accountant might do, a more stringent rule than presently applies.

It soon became apparent that the rule would not be observed; in the 1923 edition of *Auditing Principles*, Robert H. Montgomery and Walter Staub mentioned its enactment, concluded it was too strict to be enforceable, and even suggested that tax work be accepted on a contingent fee basis (Montgomery and Staub 1923: 9–10). Normally, one such as Montgomery, who was a recognized leader of the AIA, would be expected to comply with its norms. But during the free-wheeling 1920s, with the profession sadly divided, deviations were tolerated. The ASCPA condemned the rule, and it was widely ignored, seriously threatening any claims the AIA made to national leadership. As divisive as the debate over contingent fees had been, the subject of advertising was even more so.

Advertising

No debate was more damaging to the interests of a united profession than the one over advertising. Institutional publicity was not only considered permissible, it was mandatory, to educate the public about the scope and value of accountants' services. Personal advertising was considered by many, however, to be unethical. As early as 1893, W. Sanders Davies had introduced a resolution in the AAPA banning advertising. Davies, through continual attendance at monthly meetings, succeeded in getting the resolution passed in 1894 when only a few members were in attendance. But Davies' position had no widespread support; two weeks later, a special meeting was called and members voted overwhelmingly to repeal the advertising ban (Webster 1954: 121–125).

One of the problems that plagued practitioners was the definition of advertising. Solicitation, circularization, publications, and the like, had all at one time or another been condemned by one or all of the leadership of the AAPA and, later, the AIA. Smaller practitioners, struggling to establish practices, did not hesitate to question the motives of the opponents of advertising, who tended to be well-established, prosperous, and affiliated with the better known accounting firms.

Many persons entering the profession as tax experts viewed accounting purely as a business service and advertised accordingly. There was a rapid proliferation of use of the self-granted title Income Tax Expert, which graced many a business card and newspaper column.[14] Cooper, disgusted with the universal claims of expertise, chided his fellow practitioners saying they should emulate Sheridan and announce, when asked their profession, "I am sir, a practitioner of the panegyric, or to speak more plainly, a professor of the art of the puffery" (Cooper 1914).

By 1919 abuses, especially in the tax area, became so widespread that the AIA could vacillate no longer. Fred R. Angevine, assistant solicitor for the Bureau of Internal Revenue, who spoke for the commissioner, told the AIA that if its members and officers did nothing to curb misleading advertising, the federal government would. Davies was asked to be chairman of a Committee on Ethical Publicity to enforce a new rule that all "proposed circulars or instruments of publicity" be forwarded to the AIA for evaluation. This was a half-measure at best. Davies wrote suggesting that "the only thing worthwhile to say is that the Institute will now allow its members to advertise" (AIA, *Yearbook, 1920:* 88–89). The institute suffered added humiliation from the compromise; after being asked to submit promotional material for evaluation, some members elected to resign from the AIA.

In 1921 the Treasury announced that unless a clear ban on misleading advertising were enforced, the federal authorities were prepared to step in and take the initiative. The Committee on Professional Advancement (Davies, chairman; J. E. Sterrett; Arthur Teele) drew up and submitted the following rule:

> Accounting is a profession. Self-praise is unprofessional. All advertising must be characterized by a certain amount of self-praise, therefore all advertising is unprofessional and accountants should abstain from it (AIA, *Yearbook, 1922:* 74–75).

This proposal might have been defeated if Angevine, present at the AIA's annual meeting, had not announced that the Treasury was prepared to promulgate regulations that proscribed advertising, with respect not only to tax matters but also to simple declarations of available services. The recommendation passed, 150 to 68, and the following year a rather long and tedious rule was incorporated into the code of ethics (AIA *Yearbook, 1922:* 71ff.). Many accountants ridiculed the AIA for enacting such a rule, and some prominent practitioners withdrew from the institute. Even those who accepted the rule expressed sardonic reservations concerning its fairness and effectiveness. Thus, while the rule met the demands of the Treasury, it precipitated cynicism among practitioners and rendered cooperative efforts in the profession more difficult than ever.

Accountants during the 1920s reflected the mood of the times: little was done to curb individual freedom, but efforts to deter competition were sanctioned. Rules became more proscriptive, limiting certain specific activities, such as forbidding CPAs to deal in securities and prohibiting AIA members from associating with schools practicing discreditable methods of operation (1929). Conceptual issues, however, were not hotly debated. Independence, a major concern of early accountants, received little attention. In 1931 Frederick Hurdman attempted to gain support for a resolution mandating an accountant's independence from his client. Defeated in 1932, the resolution was reintroduced and enacted in 1934 when pressure from the financial press and the government made its acceptance almost involuntary.

A struggling profession, its social obligations obscured during the heyday of normalcy, became concerned above all with justifying its services. Tax work and managerial services offered breadth to accountancy and enabled many practitioners to survive. Education reflected the tendency to train business advisors, and the CPA examination guided the content of accounting programs. Some accountants questioned whether universities produced professionals or technicians.

Educational Standards

The movement to establish accountancy in universities was an overwhelming success, if one is content to look at the rapid growth of programs offering accounting education. In 1900 there were no schools offering a B.A. in accounting. By 1930 over 300 schools awarded such degrees in accountancy, at both the undergraduate and graduate levels (Allen 1927). But, although these statistics may appear impressive, concern with the content and direction of accounting programs was clearly evident throughout the period.

The original objective of most accounting programs had been to train assistants working in accounting firms, but early practitioners had always advocated a broad curriculum. Unfortunately, in the opinion of many, pragmatism; which had given the original philosophic justification for inclusion of accounting in schools of higher education, began to be interpreted to mean vocationalism. Concurrently, it became clear that schools of business, where other disciplines had become firmly entrenched, perceived accounting as the mere tool of business requiring little more than memorizing techniques. Ironically, accountants who provided the initial impetus for many university programs were considered less scholarly than their colleagues in other business disciplines (Marshall, L. C., 1926).

When one examines the proliferation of accounting courses, one must conclude that teaching how to account for specialized fields had become more important than normative approaches to accounting. The laboratory method prevailed, and the student learned by doing rather than by understanding. By the mid-1920s over ninety different accounting courses were being offered in universities, often reflecting specific questions that had appeared on previous CPA examinations. Although one might understand the need in certain regions of the country for courses in mine, farm, and forestry accounting, over forty such courses in the area of financial accounting seems to indicate that little thought was given to basic principles of accounting (Allen 1927).

The Role of Accounting Education

The academic literature is replete with discussion of the need for "a philosophical orientation" for accounting.[15] In 1925 Raymond Blight noted that there existed a "popular fallacy that an accountant should have what is known as a mathematical mind—that is he must be an expert with figures, be able to perform prodigious feats in addition and multiplication, have a deep knowledge of the esoteric meaning of professional mathematical formulas and be a prestidigitator of numbers." Blight concluded that "This is a grave error," adding that specific knowledge would not produce professionals, only technicians. He contended that "accountancy requires a philosophical mind" and required broad, general education as its base (Blight 1925). Russell Stevenson, William Gray, and other academicians echoed this same argument. The disillusionment with accounting programs led to a call for "professional schools of accountancy" by 1936.

Roy Kester and Roswell McCrea outlined a plan for a professional school at Columbia University. They surveyed the existing accounting curricula in 1935 and concluded that "too many schools and to too great a degree at the present time accounting has been taught from the standpoint of the mechanics or techniques of the art rather than from the science on which it rests." In 1929 New York State amended its standards for certification, requiring that by 1938 all candidates present evidence of having satisfactorily "completed the course of study in a college or school of accountancy." McCrea and Kester believed that the time had come for a five-year accounting curriculum. The program they proposed to institute at Columbia incorporated two years of study in liberal arts and three years in accounting and related business fields. The graduate would then receive a Master of Science degree in accountancy (McCrea and Kester 1936).

McCrea and Kester had a very pragmatic view of the science of accountancy, writing that "accountancy as a science will always be in a state of flux, ready to adapt its laws and principles to the needs of the business society and the civilization in which it functions." Like many others, they viewed the professional practice of accountancy as an art but said that the art must rest "upon a body of organized knowledge that will be called a science" (McCrea and Kester 1936). Their conclusion that the science of accounts could only be taught effectively through the case and problem method is not developed in their article. And this approach is at odds with analysis by other academicians and practitioners who hoped to move away from the methodological orientation that existed within the discipline.

Seymour Walton gave a great deal of attention to the merit of existing educational methods and concluded that accounting educators taught the "how" not the "why" of accountancy. He felt this was due to a fundamental misconception of the role of education and practical experience in the training of a professional accountant (Walton 1917). Practitioners, like Francis Belser, believed that, although "it was all right to learn theory in school," practice and application was as important as theory. He suggested that educators "duplicate practice" because, he implied, the role of education was to provide technically competent men who had been exposed to various factual situations (Belsar 1927). Walton would have strongly disagreed with this sentiment because he thought that the role of education was not to produce a competent accountant, but to enable the young person to become competent. Facts per se are meaningless, Walton wrote, unless one can systematically order those facts. Education, as the first step, should ground the young person in fundamental scientific principles so that he can effectively use his practical experience. The interaction Walton posited between experience and theory was that "experience is necessary to furnish the foundation on which theory is built and theory is necessary to guide experience." If educators stressed theory, then the young man could use his future experience to adapt his response to cases with differing facts. But if the student was exposed only to various factual cases, then he would be helpless when he encountered a new condition (Walton 1917). But it would seem that with the development of numerous specialized courses, the dominant trend in accounting throughout the period was toward presenting as many facts as possible. As one educator noted, this may have been due, not to the lack of theoretical merit in demands for a broader scope in accounting education, but to the "lack of gold" (i.e., monetary reward) available to the educator who pursued this course.

The Role of the American Accounting Association

Organized in 1916 as the American Association of University Instructors in Accounting (AAUIA), the first national body of academicians did not initially address itself to the problems of research but focused on curriculum development. This orientation is understandable, given the rapid proliferation of schools offering accounting courses and the lack of uniform educational standards. By the mid-1920s, 36 percent of all native-born practitioners had college degrees (as opposed to only 9 percent of foreign-born accountants), but the quality of education varied widely (Higgins 1965: 164). Prior to 1936 only two schools, New York University and Harvard University, ever graduated more than ten prospective CPAs in any given year. Twelve other schools were producing professional accountants at the rate of four to seven a year, but over 50 percent of those entering public accounting graduated from schools with very small programs. The quality of many of these programs was suspect, and the organizers of the AAUIA hoped to provide some direction for curriculum development. The papers read at the first annual meeting clearly reflected this concern. J. E. Treleven's paper considered "The Present Status of Instruction in Higher Education Institutions," and F. H. Elwell was concerned with "The Problems of Standardizing University Courses in Accounting."

Even in choice of the name of the organization, it was apparent that organizers of the AAUIA did not view with sympathy the rapidly growing nonuniversity "business" schools. They limited admission to the association to university instructors specifically to ban teachers in "fly-by-night" business schools. There was little friction between educators and the AIA as long as educators focused on curriculum development and the association was not perceived as a competing national organization. But in 1921 when Paton suggested changing the name to the American Accounting Association, relations with the institute cooled. Montgomery, in order to preempt such a change, took out incorporation papers in several states to prevent the use of the name. In 1924, the institute, relenting somewhat, moved to admit educators with five years' teaching experience and a CPA certificate. (AAA 1966A: 8f, 36f)

Calls for an Academic Publication

As early as 1919 Dewing introduced the idea of an independent journal, the *Journal of Accountics*, to foster academic research. Hatfield opposed this move, not because he did not favor scholarly research, but because he believed that accountants should strive for one good journal rather than two mediocre ones. The plan was temporarily abandoned, but in 1926 the AAUIA agreed to sponsor *The Accounting Review*, naming Paton as the first editor (AAA 1966A: 14f, 24f). One of the more interesting facts about these early issues is that, despite demands for scholarly research, most articles have no citations, obscuring the historical trail. Littleton was a notable exception to this general trend. When Eric Kohler became editor of the *Review* in 1928, he attempted to direct the orientation of the publication toward normative research. But despite these early efforts, academic research in accounting tended to lag behind, not lead practice. Prior to the mid-1930s academics had little influence on the development of accounting principles.

The academic organization was restructured in 1935, and the name was changed to the American Accounting Association (AAA). Academics issued a direct challenge to practitioners with the new stated objectives of the group. In March 1936, publication of a "Statement of Objectives" served notice that academicians sought to take the lead in the development of accounting theory (AAA 1936A). Practitioners did not empathize with the AAA's attempt "to develop accounting principles and standards, and to seek their endorsement or acceptance by business enterprises, public and private accountants and governmental bodies." Practitioners had long assumed this to be their function and were reluctant to cede this privilege to any group, whether within (academics) or outside of (the SEC) accounting.[16]

With the publication of "A Tentative Statement of Accounting Principles," also, in 1936, the AAA left little doubt that they had adopted a new strategy. But the institute was not prepared to abandon the matter of developing of accounting principles to academics, for clearly there was much at stake in the matter. Prior to 1936 there were no standardized accounting curricula and very little uniformity of course coverage among schools. Research, despite the excellent efforts of certain individual academicians, continued to lag behind other disciplines in terms of normative theory.

Accounting Theory and Practice

Stephen Gilman evaluated accounting theory in the post–World War I period and found it inexplicable that income determination had not become the focal point of financial reporting. He concluded that the maturity of large corporations, the income tax laws, and rapid advances in cost accounting ought to have led to the primacy of the income statement. That this was not the case, Gilman believed to be one of the paradoxes of accounting (Gilman 1939:27ff.). But, if one examines other environmental factors in the 1920s, the continued emphasis on the balance sheet is understandable.

Most accountants believed that any theory must be pragmatic (useful, practical, leading to desirable social consequences) and adaptive (to meet the changing demands made upon the profession). During the 1920s there is little evidence that any user group would have supported efforts to report only income from operations. To do so would have limited, or at least dampened, the wave of optimism which swept the country.

Accounting in the 1920s

The demands for accounting information being made by various user groups—political, financial, and managerial—changed dramatically during the 1920s. Government leaders, having adopted a paternalistic attitude toward business, suggested that there was no need for the accountant to police the business community—the integrity of management was not only assumed, it was eulogized as well. Accountants, political leaders appeared to feel, should work closely with businessmen to limit cutthroat competition. One of the primary responsibilities of the accounting profession was to ensure that business received a "fair return" on its investment.

Reporting to Creditors and Investors

A second factor that seemed to negate the importance of income determination in financial reporting was the relatively weak position of bankers with respect to corporate business. Prior to the 1920s, accountants had argued that, since most firms paid out all reported earnings as dividends, "conservatism" and "sound values" should be reflected in the balance sheet. But after World War I business management adopted a new financing strategy—the regularization of dividends (Sobel 1969: 32f.).

The regularization of dividends had two important ramifications. Businessmen turned to the small investor, who during the war had become accustomed to investing in Liberty bonds as a source of equity capital. The rationale was that if business could pay out regular dividends, akin to interest, it could attract these investors. The strategy was extremely successful in luring new capital. Most firms maintained a surplus cash position ($3 billion in 1921; $9 billion in 1929), and corporate demand for bank loans plummeted accordingly (Sobel 1969: 262).

Bankers, forced to seek new outlets for their funds, became active participants in equity markets. No longer did sound value accounting or conservatism seem attractive. Bankers, like all other sectors of the nation, had a vested interest in fostering the illusion of prosperity. During the 1920s banks increased their purchases of stocks and bonds by two-thirds, and their affiliated holding companies floated $19 billion in equity issues. Keeping the investor happy was as important to bankers as it was to business management, and nothing that would have dampened investor expectations was likely to be countenanced.

The Emergence of the Small Investor

One might expect that the emergence of the small investor as a major source of equity capital might have brought increased demands for greater "accountability" on the part of management and extended the stewardship function of the accounting profession. But there is little evidence that investors considered financial reporting and independent audits important. Investors ignored warnings that pure speculation was a nonproductive function that was dangerous and potentially destructive when unregulated and fed by low margin requirements.

Corporations were attracted to a guaranteed return of 20 percent on money lent to speculators. Many businessmen could see no reason to expand productive facilities that could never realize a similar return. Thus productive capacity remained dormant while corporate and banking funds fueled the speculative fever. Those who urged caution went unheeded. In 1928 the financial report of International Harvester advised that too much money was being spent on stock and that the direction of investment was dangerous. Corporate funds were being diverted to nonproductive uses that would not support economic growth (Frantz 1950). It would be foolhardy in view of this attitude to suggest that accountants had the authority or the mandate to limit reported earnings to "realized operating income." As a rule, management would not support such an accounting model, and there was no user group demanding conservatism or sound value accounting.

The Primacy of Business

Critics of accounting theory and practice during the 1920s have suggested that accountants abdicated the stewardship role and placed greater emphasis on the needs of management, permitting too much flexibility in financial reporting. In examining the development of accounting thought and practice during this period, it is important to remember that accountants worked in an era marked by massive official indifference. One early practitioner noted that "every businessman used his own accounting principles and fought like hell to sustain them." The prerogative of management to instruct the accountants might have been questioned (primarily by accountants), but the principle was never in jeopardy. The profession simply did not have the authority or the power to handle corporate abuses.

Even regulatory agencies were powerless to turn the speculative tide. The Federal Reserve Board has often been blamed and more often exonerated for the financial collapse of 1929. But the FRB probably cannot be credited with either "Coolidge prosperity" or that which followed because it did not have sufficient power to be responsible for either event (Schumpeter 1946). In 1928 the FRB raised the rediscount rate from 3.5 to 5.0 percent with little effect. A year later, seriously concerned over speculation, the board raised margin rates to 12 percent, but the banks refused to heed the signals. Charles A. Mitchell, a class A director of the Federal Reserve Bank of New York, was determined to frustrate efforts to reduce available funds. Immediately after the announcement of the increased margin rates, Mitchell announced that his bank, National City, would advance $25 million to investors to take up the slack created by the board's decision (Allen 1931:308).

Perhaps the atmosphere of the decade was most succinctly captured by Sobel as he traced the Piggly Wiggly Corner in 1923 and concluded that, "It is fitting that the first major corner of the bull market began with a Livermore-Bliss victory, the wreck of a businessman, avoidance of responsibility on the part of the Exchange, all this in connection with a stock named after a pig" (Sobel 1969:264).

The Contributions of Academic Theorists

In the 1920s, the call for a fair return to business (a return based not on cost incurred but on the current value of assets employed) and the emergence of the attitude that "capital growth" was as important, if not more important than operating results seemed to mandate that the balance sheet, which reflected both economic (operating) and financial (holding) gains, continued to be considered the most important of the financial statements.

The appearance of the first comprehensive statement of *entity theory* (Paton's *Accounting Theory*, 1922) still focused on the balance sheet. Paton wrote that "In the study of the theory of accounts, the income statement is of little importance, showing as it does the elaboration of an element already incorporated in the balance sheet" (Paton 1922:20). As noted earlier, Paton criticized early proprietary theorists for implying that the "earnings" process was not real. But, as long as he accepted the accretion concept of income, he could not deny the primacy of the balance sheet.

Paton's concept of entity theory never received widespread

acceptance among accountants. His assertion that management no longer sought to "maximize stockholder's wealth" but, rather, the return to all equity holders (including creditors), was not in accord with contemporary financial or economic theory. His concept of "enterprise income" was rejected by most accountants who did not believe that one could disregard the source of financing and view both interest and dividends as distributions of profit. (Paton 1922:84ff, 259). Given the income tax laws, few practitioners favored the suggestion that interest was not an expense. But more important to the rejection of enterprise income was that it was incompatible with existing theories of finance. Despite Paton's criticism of proprietary theory or, as he called it, "residual equity" theory, most financial theorists were placing more emphasis on such *proprietary concepts* as earnings per share, book value per share, and net book value as methods of analysis throughout the 1920s.[18] The concept of enterprise income was rejected; but the significance of Paton's work was his focus on income as a measure of managerial efficiency.

The Nature of Income

Early proprietary theorists were content to measure income as the change in net assets during a given time period. This measurement procedure was consistent with their assumptions that (1) wealth accrued to the owners (shareholders) and that (2) the owners had absolute control over corporate assets. The theorists' primary objective was to differentiate between capital and liabilities (negative assets) to measure the change in proprietary wealth. Because the corporation was assumed to distribute all reported income, accountants sought to ensure that the firm was not unintentionally liquidated and that the concept of capital maintenance was critical to early theory. (See Chapter 5, p. 171 for discussion of capital maintenance.)

In the 1920s, two phenomena, the acceptance of management's right to retain earnings and the call for a "fair return" to the corporation, seemed to undermine the assumptions of early proprietary theory. Paton's work recognized the relevance of dual income measures to report corporate wealth and operating profits. He assumed that total income (wealth) accrued to the entity itself—not to the stockholders. Measurement of corporate wealth was important to determine the value of resources entrusted to management and the annual increment in value. Paton advocated recognition of specific price level changes (holding gains and losses) as well as operating profits in calculation of total income. But, wealth change (total income), he asserted, was irrelevant to the stockholders.

Stockholders, he argued, wanted an income number that would serve as (1) a measure of managerial effectiveness in the use of assets entrusted to them and (2) an indicator of expected future earnings (Paton 1922: 167ff). Paton assumed that revenue associated with a particular set of enterprise operations (realized revenue) was of major importance to stockholders. He implied that earned (realized) income was not only a good indicator of future earnings but also future distributions to stockholders. Recognition of the need for segregation of income into two distinct flows (financial and operating) by accounting theorists seems to have been the result of the increasing sophistication of the economics literature dealing with income determination and not, as some have suggested, a natural result of the adoption of entity theory. Paton, and John Canning, a proprietary theorist, seem to have been significantly affected by Irving Fisher's work.

The most perplexing problem for both Canning and Paton was development of a model that defined revenue independently of asset valuation. Canning simply defined gross income (revenue) as:

> the summation of gross operating income (the fruition in money, or the equivalent of money, effected within a period, of all those elementary services which are components of enterprise operations) *plus* the amount of gross financial income (the higher earnings, effected within the period arising from the grants of monied funds made by one person, persons, to another) (Canning 1929: 100)

Paton defined revenue as "benefits accruing to the firm" and expenses as "sacrifices made in the generation of benefits." But, since he recognized that "benefits accrued" throughout the production process, the above definition was unsatisfactory for determination of earned (realized) income. He never resolved the issue of what is revenue. Instead, he concentrated on explaining when revenue was realized and developing a model that matched revenues and expenses to determine operating income (Paton 1922: 257ff). Canning more explicitly outlined the matching process, listing three conditions that must be met to determine operating income:

(1) The future receipts of money within one year has become highly probable
(2) The amount to be received can be estimated with a high degree of reliability

(3) The expenses incurred or to be incurred in the cycle can be estimated with a high degree of reliability (Canning 1929: 103).

But he, like Paton, never resolved the question of benefits accruing that increased asset values but were not realized.

There was surprising unanimity among academic theorists about how to measure operating profits; the key question, still unresolved, was how, given the constraints of double entry, could the accountant adequately report both an increase in corporate wealth and earned income. As Alexander was to point out, three decades later, the idea that operating income could be measured to facilitate predictions of future receipts to shareholders required definitions of revenues and expenses that were antithetical to wealth measurement (Alexander 1950: 57ff). The debate that has raged over the balance sheet vs. the income statement schools, and, more recently, the "asset/liability" vs. "revenue/expense" views, indicates the difficulty the profession has had in resolving the issue. During the twenties, theorists were exploring various measurement models and reporting schemes that would enable them to report a relevant income number to stockholders and to present an adequate statement of corporate wealth.

The Nature of Profits

As early as 1918 accounting theory reflected the influence of Fisher's definition of wealth adjusted for changes in purchasing power. Paton and Russell Stevenson suggested abandoning the assumption of a stable dollar as unsound. Accountants, according to the authors, could not hope to show the "true financial condition" of any firm if they persisted in using an inappropriate measurement assumption. If income was to reflect the well being of the firm, then Paton and Stevenson insisted that accountants consider price-level changes. They were equally adamant that "specific, not general, price-level changes" must be reflected in the accounts. They advocated price-level adjustments for two specific purposes. They believed that "the most important function of accounting is to provide data to management . . . [and therefore] accounts should reflect the most relevant values, present values." And they believed that accountants had a duty to ensure capital maintenance (in terms of "real capital," defined by Fisher in terms of productive capacity) and therefore could not ignore the effects of inflation in calculating income (Paton and Stevenson 1918: 462ff). .

The second argument became a central issue among accountants in the 1920s. A. C. Littleton rejected the idea that accountants should concern themselves with the "preservation of capital," which was and should be the responsibility of management. He wrote that accountants should be content to do what they could do, namely, measuring the flow of earnings to the stockholders (Littleton 1928). Henry W. Sweeney reflected the views of those who disagreed with Littleton and contended that capital maintenance should be a major concern of the profession.

Surprisingly, perhaps, there was little debate over definitions of capital. Most theorists accepted the idea that capital was "the present advantage of a right to receive future benefits" (Sweeney 1933A). There was even a consensus that capital value must be measured in terms of productivity. Accountants, however, could not agree on two basic issues. First, which type of productivity—past, present, or future—should capital valuation reflect; second, did capital maintenance mean maintaining actual physical productive capacity or simply that the firm continue to be in a position to provide a stock of services, irrespective of the type of physical capital employed in the future. Given these basic divisions, numerous measurement bases were advocated by theorists. Proponents of historical cost, replacement cost, and price-level accounting sought and found economic theories to support their measurement preferences.

Measurement and Capital Valuation Theory

Those who advocated historical cost bolstered their arguments by referring to such works as Kemper Simpson's *Economics for the Accountant*.[20] Simpson believed that "the value of capital goods arises only from their productivity" and that capital investment should not be measured in terms of economic sacrifice but "in relation to postponement of claims on consumption goods." He cautioned accountants to beware lest they confuse the value of capital goods with the value of capital. He argued that if you recognized a gain owing to appreciation, you simultaneously must infer that capital investment had increased. This was wrong, Simpson wrote, because "the rate of interest on capital is fixed at the time of investment, and no additional sacrifice was required." He would permit only one valuation—original cost (Simpson 1922: 121f.).

Littleton cited Simpson to support his argument that appreciation did not lead to increased capital values. But he relied on classical economic theory to justify deviations from original cost, that is, depreciation. Accountants, according to Littleton, should be content to measure the "value in use" of capital assets. At the date of purchase, cost reflected expectations about "future productivity." Littleton suggested that while economists might say that the value of assets is determined by supply (cost of production) and demand (for both consumer and productive goods), accountants should concern themselves only with the measurement of the supply side. (Littleton: 1926). To Littleton and other historical cost theorists, the suggestion that accountants attempt to measure replacement or reproduction cost by focusing on present or future estimates of productivity based on demand seemed fanciful and was totally rejected.

The Replacement Cost Debate

Canning was most vehement in his denunciation of any efforts to attempt to measure replacement cost. He thought that basic to the misunderstanding among accountants was the failure to clearly differentiate between the cost of replacement of capital goods with other capital goods of like kind and quality (maintaining physical productive capacity) and replacing a stock of services. The latter, not the former, should be the primary concern of the accountant, he wrote. If accountants attempted to measure replacement cost, they would incur costs that could not be justified on a cost-benefit analysis. He warned that

> The consequential difficulties and losses from substituting one instrument for another, whether they are like or unlike in physical characteristics, are in general so great, that the actual cost of the unused stock of services is nearly always more appropriate. (Canning 1929: 242).

More important, he wrote, was the misleading nature of any attempt to approximate replacement cost. Any attempt "to smuggle in, consciously or unconsciously, a preconceived value of the capital instrument and then capitalize the service series is worse than guesswork," he cautioned.

> Confessed guesswork misleads no one, but to express a valuation process in the form of a capital valuation process when the essential data are fictitious, or derived from the value to be found, is statistically vicious (Canning 1929: 243ff)

Since it was rare, according to Canning, to have an establishment reproduced in kind, the only value that a measure such as "cost of reproduction less depreciation" might have was as a working rule for a damage suit. But it was invalid as the sole rule for a going concern whose primary objective was to reproduce a stream of *services*, not actual physical capital in any specific form (Canning 1929: 255f).

Sweeney's *Stabilized Accounting* was the most comprehensive work on price-level accounting to appear during this period. In the early 1930s, Sweeney published a series of articles (later presented in book form) advocating general price-level adjustments of financial statements. He criticized accounting practitioners who allegedly demonstrated no interest in measuring income but, rather, chose to measure only "realized" income (Sweeney 1933B).

In his series of articles, Sweeney first dealt with the question of capital maintenance, concluding that "the basis for maintenance" that is probably most often in harmony with the fundamental purpose of economic activity is the maintenance of absolute general purchasing power, that is, the maintenance of real capital (Sweeney 1930). Like other theorists of the period, Sweeney viewed productivity as the determining factor in capital valuation. The most relevant value, he believed, was future productivity. Since this was impossible to measure or implement, then the proper surrogate would be replacement or reproduction cost. He contended that, according to marginal economic analysis, in the long run, replacement does approximate future productivity.

Whereas Sweeney argued that replacement cost was the best surrogate for future productivity, he did not advocate specific price level adjustments. He argued that any specific price level index was too unstable, subject to violent fluctuations, to be recorded on the books. Instead, he recommended that general price level adjusted statements be adopted. Perhaps, under the influence of his dissertation advisor, Roy Kester, Sweeney invoked the hallowed accounting doctrine of conservatism to gain acceptance for his proposal. His argument was that, because most producers are not marginal producers, their expected future productivity would be higher than that expected by the marginal producer and, therefore, application of general price level changes would understate assets (for the nonmarginal producer) and be decidedly conservative (Sweeney 1933). Because Sweeney's works usually discuss concepts normatively but implementation practically, they probably contributed to the failure of the profession to adequately differentiate among price level adjustments (both specific and general), replacement cost, and current value measurements and what they purport to show for many years.

The attempts of accounting theorists to develop measurement

procedures to report the "total" income of corporations is probably the most widely remembered characteristic of theory in the 1920s. It seems unfortunate that these other issues have been too often overlooked, perhaps because the rejection of value theory led to a disregard of theory per se. There are references to the post–World War I period providing the "hard historical evidence" that deviations from historical cost-based, conservative accounting led to the crash of 1929. Many accountants empathized with George O. May's statement that

> in the 1920's accountants fell from grace and took to adjusting capital values on the books . . . to an extent never before attempted. . . . In extenuation they might plead unsound laws, unpractical economics and a widespread if unfounded belief in the new order of things combined to recommend such a course, but . . . the wiser course is to admit the error and not be misled again   (May 1936A).

During the early 1930s there was an effort to divorce accounting from economic theory on "practical" grounds. Topics such as the accountant's function in a regulated society, the need for multiple valuations, and the problems of articulation introduced in the 1920s were subsequently ignored as the work of "valuation theorists."

The Function of Accounting in a Corporate Age

Littleton analyzed the evolution of accounting theory, writing that "accounting is relative and progressive" and concluding that, "as older methods become less effective under altered conditions, earlier ideas become irrelevant in the face of new problems" (Littleton 1933A:361). He suggested change mandated acceptance of the "historical cost allocation model," which became the dominant theory of accounting in the late 1930s. But it is unfortunate that in justifying the new model, Littleton implied that previous accounting valuation theorists had not been aware of the ramifications of the separation of ownership and management. Therefore, previous literature was no longer relevant. This implication seemed not only to justify disregarding questions raised in the 1920s but also to assert that once the corporate entity was accepted, theorists had no choice but to accept the historical cost allocation model.[21]

Not the entity theory as delineated by Paton, nor the proprietary restatement of Canning, nor the cost allocation model of Littleton comprehensively examined the ramifications that separation of ownership and control might have for expanding the use of accounting data to facilitate economic planning and control. The assumption underlying all of these theories was that the accountant was primarily responsible to report to those directly interested in corporate operations, namely, management, investors, and creditors. The subsequent dismissal of much of the literature of the 1920s resulted in accountants disregarding one of the more interesting debates of the period, which concerned the accountant's function in a regulated economy.

The Role of Accounting Data in a Regulated Economy

One question frequently asked was: What would the function of accounting information be in a noncompetitive economy? Assuming that in a corporate age competition had ceased to be an effective means of economic control, such theorists as C. Rufus Rorem concluded that there "would be a shifting of responsibility to the accounting processes of adjustment and organization of economic control around accounts." Would any model that focused solely on the profits to owners (whether creditors or investors) be adequate to meet the need for efficient allocation of economic resources if this function could no longer be presumed to be regulated by competitive forces (Rorem 1928A)?

DR Scott examined the same question, asking "what will happen if regulation becomes the rule rather than the exception and the authority of the competitive market dwindles into relative inconsequence?" The answer, he felt, was obvious. Accounts would replace competition as the primary mechanism of economic planning and control. What ramifications did this have for the profession? Scott believed that accountants would have to abandon the old theories based on double entry because they would be too narrow. And concepts such as conservatism, which might conceivably (although erroneously, according to Scott) be justified by the assertion that they protected the stockholder and the creditor, would be totally inadequate if accounting data were to be used for economic planning and control (Scott 1931A:206ff.). The 1920s found widespread discussion of the need for multiple valuations and the inadequacy of formulating theory based on the constraints of double entry, issues which were dismissed in the late 1930s but which have been subsequently reexamined.

The Constraint of Double Entry

It can be suggested that most theories of accounting have been attempts to rationalize double entry. Accountants, somewhat curiously, have appeared to accept the idea that they cannot prepare two adequate financial statements; that is, if the statement of financial condition or the income statement is considered predominant, the other statement is viewed as residual. In the 1920s some theorists began to examine the question of whether or not "articulation" was a necessary constraint. H. C. Daines asked why accountants "were willing to sacrifice the accuracy of the balance sheet in order that the two statements might mathematically tie up with each other." He warned that this led to "a rather artificial showing of values on the balance sheet," with the strange justification that such values were proper, if inaccurate, for a going concern (Daines 1929). Although there is no suggestion that accountants were willing to abandon the mathematical precision afforded by double entry, questions such as those asked by Daines did lead to considerable discussion of the benefits to be achieved by multiple valuations in financial reports.

Multiple Valuation Models

H. C. Greer, in response to Daines' article, suggested that accountants prepare a two column balance sheet—one column showing original cost, the other showing present value (Greer 1929). But most accountants were fearful that investors would be confused by having two sets of figures and implied that investor confidence would be eroded if financial reports contained more than one valuation. It has been characteristic of the profession that accountants decry the fact that investors view accounting measurement as having a degree of precision which no accountant would ever claim. But when suggestions have been made that accountants reflect their uncertainty by multiple valuations, the response has been unfavorable.[22]

Canning attempted to develop a multiple valuation model for accounting. Dismissing specific productivity as impossible to measure, Canning suggested that accountants must (1) determine what series, having a sufficient number of terms, can best be correlated with "future series of receipts and disbursements" with respect to various assets; and (2) define the relationship between the surrogate series and the future series of receipts and disbursements (Canning 1929: 219). This would permit different measurement bases for different assets. It could also, in Canning's opinion, support multiple measurement bases for specific assets. For example, he believed that inventory valuation might require three different measurement bases to convey all relevant information to users. Canning wrote that "cost has great significance," but cost and income series, although related, are not identical; it is but one of the values of interest to the user. Market was also significant because it showed the spread between market and selling price—an important factor in determining the future mix of goods to acquire. Yet, Canning warned, the significance of acquiring goods is quite different from the significance of selling goods. Probably to the dismay of practitioners, Canning suggested that primary valuations should be based on a "going concern" selling price—adjusted for any change of future selling price annually, or the change implied by altered states of market conditions—as the most reliable valuation. One key to understanding Canning's multiple valuation approach seems to be his interpretation of the term "going concern value." He maintained that the value of any asset "should be dependent solely upon the contemplated use of the valued thing in operation of the enterprise" (Canning 1929: 202ff.). With the advent of the Depression and the search for stability, arguments favoring variety were dismissed, a phenomenon perhaps fostered by the Depression mentality. However, suggestions that the 1920s and early 1930s were void of theoretical scholarship should be challenged; despite the practical problems of that age, significant conceptual advances were made.

Zeff examined price-level theory from 1928 to 1935 and concluded that accountants subsequently chose to ignore a classic body of literature. This raises the question: At what cost to the profession? As Zeff points out, "In Paton's 1918 article on appreciation, one finds an outline of the thesis for which Edwards and Bell, in the *Theory and Measurement of Business Income* would be celebrated forty-three years later" (Zeff 1976: 3ff.). In this early work by Paton, the two components of net income, "current operating profit" and "realizable cost savings" are clearly defined but are generally ignored until their incorporation into the later study.

The debate over the accountant's role in a regulated economy foreshadowed contemporary concerns—the question of articulation has recently been reopened, and the whole subject of multiple valuations is of concern today. The preoccupation with economic recovery following the crash of 1929 distracted from further developments in these areas, and the literature of this decade was overlooked by the profession for many years. Perhaps an examination of the practical problems encountered during the 1920s best explains why "objectivity" became central to the subsequent evolution of accounting theory.

The Problems in Accounting Practice

A major practical problem in the 1920s was related to accounting for no-par stock, which presented opportunities for manipulation to financiers and promoters. Initially no-par reform was welcomed by accountants as a means of halting previous abuses in the manipulation of par stock (Hurdman 1919). Accountants were faced with a curious dilemma with par value stock. The law required that capital be stated at par value; if stock was sold at a discount, accounting theory was inadequate to handle the debit balance. Paton in "Theory of the Double Entry System" (1917) attempted to explain the accounting in terms of Assets (properties) = Equities (rights in properties). But he conceded that "to the extent the stock is overstated" (par is greater than property received), "the amount of discount [appears] among the property items" (Paton 1917). It was through this method that "water" was usually introduced into the balance sheet, and many investors did not recognize this.

But no-par stock was not exempt from manipulation directly affecting surplus. Accountants generally agreed on the means of classifying surplus. This posed no theoretical problem. They argued that paid-in capital, capital surplus (gains from disposal of capital assets), surplus from appreciation, and earned surplus should be segregated. Legal statutes complicated the issue. Charles Couchman warned that it was

> held by some that surplus attaching to no-par might be credited to the capital account on the theory that the very purpose of no-par stock is to show unit ownership *only*, without differentiation as to contributed value and earned value.

He said accountants must say an absolute No to such procedures (Couchman 1921). The problem was that the law said Yes.

Robert Montgomery explained this dilemma of accountants in the proper treatment of surplus. First, there had been the problem of appreciation. He noted that when accountants first began writing up fixed assets, there was "almost unanimous agreement" that unrealized appreciation should be credited to a separate account. Then came no par value stock, stated capital, paid-in capital, initial and capital surplus complications coupled with formidable legal opinions that accountants should mind their own business and *not* use such terms as earned surplus.

He concluded that legal pressure had forced accountants to use a single surplus account, an unwise and dangerous procedure (Montgomery 1927). The debate on this complicated issue continued throughout the 1920s.[23]

John Wildman and Weldon Powell, recognized authorities on the subject of no-par stock, comprehensively examined this problem in their book *Capital Stock Without Par Value* (1930). They defined three basic principles: (1) capital must reflect consideration received, (2) dividends cannot be paid out of capital, (3) cash dividends must come out of earned surplus. Although accountants may have agreed on these principles, examination of financial reports during the 1920s would lead to the conclusion that they were either not applied or could not be applied. One of the most striking examples of the failure in this area can be found in the financial reports of Dodge Brothers, Inc.

When Dodge Brothers was reorganized in 1925, the corporation paid $246 million for assets with a fair market value of $85 million.[24] One question rarely asked in subsequent decades but which might be asked is how historical cost would have aided accountants in this kind of transaction. The assumption underlying acceptance of cost as an original valuation is that exchange price is a "reasonably prudent act" (Canning 1929:231). Accountants would have had verifiable, objective evidence of $246 million being paid for the assets of the firm; they probably could not have coerced management into showing a loss under the lower-of-cost-or-market valuation concept. When examining the financial chicanery of the 1920s, one must remember that accountants were operating in an economic arena where conduct which would be regarded as unethical today was condoned by the markets and government. Insider trading, preferred stock lists (which included most of the important government officials), and a pernicious bonus system were all accepted. It is also well to remember that the following maneuvers of Dodge Brothers were legal at the time.

After the initial sale of the assets by the Dodge family to the corporation, the firm went public. The corporation received $90 million for 2 million shares of common stock and 850,000 shares of preferred stock. The preferred shares sold for $100 per share ($8.5

million) but were reported at the nominal figure of $1 per share ($850,000) on the balance sheet; $7.65 million had simply disappeared. Similarly, the two classes of common stock (no-par) sold for approximately $81.5 million were capitalized at $.10 per share ($200,000), and $81.3 million disappeared from the books. Some juggling of the surplus account, combined with the understatement of $89 million of invested capital, permitted the corporation to list its assets at $85 million, or approximate market value. Obviously, the accountants did not follow Wildman's principles, and the question remains whether it would have been better to overstate assets at their original cost or to understate capital. Such transactions were legal, and accountants were in no position to force management to comply with theoretical principles by properly classifying the surplus account.[25]

In many states during the 1920s a corporation could include only a portion of the proceeds received from stock in the capital account. Having only one surplus account, corporations would issue dividends from surplus as they saw fit, regardless of the origin of the funds. One interesting, if unresolved, issue was linked to both no-par stock and the new management policy of retention of earnings. It was not clear that society desired or expected managers to exercise such economic control. Accountants questioned the propriety of this policy. Charles B. Couchman mirrored the feeling of the day when he wrote that "profits retained by a corporation *above* the amounts necessary for preserving its commercial and financial arrangements are the equivalent of reinvestment of capital by the stockholders without his individual consent" (Couchman 1924). Accountants were unsure of their role. Could the profession exclude from surplus those amounts legally available for dividend distribution?

Wildman felt that accountants must be guided by economic principles, not law. But he conceded that there was little an auditor could do to enforce any principle with a client, except to use moral suasion, which was not notably successful in the 1920s (Wildman 1928A). Modern accountants can perhaps empathize with the position of these early practitioners. It was by no means clear what the auditor's position should be when a client acted legally (law is commonly supposed to reflect social values) but with questionable ethics. The most perplexing question for practitioners was whether or not the accounting profession had the right or the mandate to insist that clients do more than comply with the law. Ripley obviously believed they should. But with no support from the federal government, it is questionable if the profession would have been able to enforce proper accounting principles.

The irony of historical analysis is that those practitioners who warned investors that income and surplus accounts, although legally correct, were misleading often faced the severest criticism. Ripley condemned one "auditing house" for issuing an audit certificate that said "the profit and loss account, read in conjunction with the statement of no-par value stock attached to the balance sheet, sets forth the results of operations for the year." The company reported a profit (by refusing to recognize certain discretionary expenses, such as depreciation, and by deferring operating expenses to future years), increased surplus through refinancing and then wrote off those "discretionary expenses" directly to surplus. The auditors were not able to follow an "accepted accounting theory." But by referring the reader to the increase in surplus owing to the no-par issue, it became apparent to Ripley and presumably to other readers, that a substantial operating loss had been incurred (Ripley 1927: 197f.). If the auditors had not qualified their certificate, they would not have received any criticism. The reader probably would not have been aware of the refinancing transaction. Certainly by today's standards, the auditors' actions were not sufficient, although one could argue that the requirements of full disclosure had been met. Finally, it should be mentioned that during this decade businessmen could and did advocate corporate secrecy on the grounds that dividends provided the investor with all the information he needed about corporate operations.[26] Although this argument had been totally rejected during the progressive era, it was now acceptable. Ivar Krueger, the "Match King," provides a classic example of how some promotors were able to avoid all *accountability.*

Krueger, who attributed his success to "secrecy, more secrecy, and even more secrecy," simply refused to tell anyone anything. Yet he was fawned over by bankers.[27] He adamantly refused to even speak to an accountant. Joseph J. Klein, whose accounting firm was called in at the demise of the Krueger empire, recalled in his memoirs that Krueger would not answer any questions. If any banker had the audacity to question him, Krueger would simply threaten to withdraw his proposed new issue from that bank. Even after the stock market crash, International Match stock and bond sales were strong. It was among the few companies that never suspended dividend or interest payments, which, as Klein notes, is understandable. Since dividends never had been based on operating profits, how could the Depression have an effect? Kreuger had simply rolled over his financing, paying dividends and interest from the proceeds of each new issue. Surplus was not stratified (it included operating profits as well as additional paid-in capital and premiums on bonds), and the investor had no way of penetrating this financial thicket (Klein 1969: 76).

The Krueger pyramid was bound to topple, as finally it did. But not before thousands were victimized by the scheme, their own blind speculation and greed. Why did bankers fight to promote Krueger's bond issues; why did they accede to his demands for continued secrecy? Krueger, Samuel Insull, the utility wizard and other promoters had no fear that independent auditors would be called in. The reaction of the stock exchange was disinterest when the AIA attempted to devise a plan for audits of all corporations; no one wanted to tamper with the "prosperity of the times." Subsequent criticism of the accounting profession has often suggested that accountants could have done more. But, given the massive indifference to investor protection in both the governmental and financial sectors, that criticism would appear to be unfair.

An Analysis of Criticism of Accounting in the 1920s

Given the inability or disinclination of governmental regulatory agencies to curb financial speculation, the total indifference toward investor protection and a legal system that venerated the "rights" of the individual, it is not difficult to understand why accountants were not successful in curbing abuses in financial reporting. Statements by such eminent practitioners as Leonard Spacek "that accountants should bear to a great degree responsibility for the depression" are not only damaging, they appear to be untrue as well (Lauss 1970).

Current critics, like Robert Chatov, suggest that accountants should have taken more positive action. He contends that practitioners ignored Ripley's criticism because he was not a member of the "club." Chatov's evidence was the condescending nature of George O. May's reply to Ripley and the lack of references to Ripley in accounting journals (Chatov 1975: 18–20). The first contention is hardly evidence as May adopted a condescending attitude toward most people, including fellow accountants.[28] One must ask why May's reply was so curt and derogative.

What were Ripley's main criticisms? He was primarily concerned with manipulation of surplus and no par stock (Ripley 1927: 46ff). None of the problems he cited was new, and accounting journals had contained a wide variety of articles on the very evils that Ripley condemned. The criticism was neither new nor revolutionary to accountants; they had pointed to the same problems as dangerous. Ripley had no workable solutions, but he did suggest that the Federal Trade Commission (FTC) provide guidance and leadership in improving financial reports and regulating corporate business (Ripley 1927: 115). If accountants did not dismiss this as a publicity gimmick, then they certainly did not or could not take such a suggestion seriously.

It is hard even for the present-day historian to imagine the FTC under the leadership of William Humphreys, the father of governmental "paternalism" toward business, leading a crusade to protect the investor. Certainly Ripley could not have expected support from President Coolidge. The president had issued a statement to the press that (1) he did not believe that the FTC had the authority to intervene in corporate affairs; (2) corporate reporting was controlled by the states; (3) blue-sky laws gave more than enough protection to investors; and (4) since "it is difficult to tell a good stock from a bad one, why bother" (*The Chronicle*, September 4, 1926: 1201). May did refuse to debate with Ripley over the quality of corporate reporting, conceding that it left much to be desired and asking for positive reforms. May noted that, since financial statements were the representations of management, accountants had little authority to specify "correct treatment" and, in a decade that exalted the freedom of the businessman, absolutely no power to compel business to use any principles they did not wish to employ. Ripley had no answer to May's arguments, except for federal control, which was not a feasible solution, given the attitudes then current in Washington.

Today, in part because of the increased sophistication of investors, it is easy to misunderstand the functions and capabilities for action which existed in the capital markets in a previous era. Politicians, like investors, indicated a lack of understanding of the market place. For example, one U. S. Senator did not hesitate to offer a solution in response to the October 29 break in the market, wiring the New York Stock Exchange the following message:

> Today's activity in your Exchange demonstrates the absolute necessity for immediate adoption of a rule limiting the amount of loss on any one stock during any one session. This country is not prepared to withstand the effect of a repetition of what happened today. Unless a rule is adopted and published establishing a reasonable amount of depreciation in any one session, campaign for reform will immediately take shape with the possible result of either closing the Exchange or placing the same under Government supervision (*The Chronicle*, July 22, 1933: 581).

That statement suggests that some of the assumptions made in the next decade about the reasons for the spectacular market failure may have overestimated one significant factor—the intelligence of the investor. The remedial legislation of the 1930s assumed that investors had been misled by financial reports and that legislation would have prevented most of the abuses. The evidence, however, is unclear on this point. And there are those who contended that the country was in the grips of a mass psychosis fanned by a "casino" environment in the market and that no amount of information could have dampened the sincere belief of many that indeed the millennium had come and "everyone ought to be rich."[29]

The Depression Years

It is a formidable task to assess the impact of the stock market crash in 1929—historical evidence suggests that contemporary observers did not foresee the lasting impact that event would have. Yet it seems clear that the crash had a profound effect on the subsequent evolution of accounting practice. Politicians could no longer argue that Americans would prosper under a business system managed—or unmanaged—as it had been in the 1920s. But reaction was slow, and political leaders neither blamed accountants for the debacle of the 1920s nor looked to the profession for protection in the 1930s. Accountants worked diligently to convince the political sector that there was a need for corporate audits to protect investors. The leaders of the profession sought to convince both businessmen and politicians that a strong, independent accounting profession could prevent future abuses.

In 1929 the AIA, with the support of the FRB, issued the *Verification of Financial Statements*. This pamphlet is fondly remembered as the "auditor's bible" by some older accountants. Although it was an attempt by the institute to provide guidelines to the profession, practitioners made clear that they were not attempting to revive the concept of uniform accounting. Many accountants seemed to believe that the issuance of the document "Uniform Accounting" had created an illusion that there were accepted accounting and auditing procedures in widespread use which led to complacency on the part of both the public and the profession. An editorial in the *Journal of Accountancy* condemned any suggestion "for uniform systems of accounting and auditing for all sorts of business conditions" as extremely dangerous because that implied to many investors a degree of assurance that could not be given by auditors faced with the uncertainty that existed in the business sector ("Editorial," *Journal of Accountancy* May 1929: 356–357). Accountants emphasized the need to permit the auditor some flexibility in determining appropriate accounting methods and stressed the importance of professional judgment in any engagement.

As the possibility of government intervention in the corporate sector grew, accountants found business leaders more receptive to pleas for cooperation. The financial press began to laud the profession. A 1932 article in *Fortune* claimed that accountancy was "the youngest, least known and most responsible of professions" and that accountants were "a race of watchdogs guarding the corporation from its hopes, [and] guarding the stockholders against misstatement." The article implied that only the reserve and modesty of those in practice prevented the profession from receiving the accolades it deserved (1932: 64-66). Accountants took advantage of this growing support for the profession.

At the 1930 annual meeting of the AIA, J. M. B. Hoxsey opened the door for cooperation between the New York Stock Exchange and CPAs. May, who had served as advisor to the exchange, became chairman of the Special Committee on Cooperation with the New York Stock Exchange. The committee presented its first draft of accepted accounting principles in 1933 and submitted six recommendations to the institute and exchange for approval the following year.

The exchange agreed to five of the six recommendations. They rejected the requirement that "all listed companies . . . disclose the accounting methods employed" (AIA Minutes 1932: 62f.). Cooperation resulted in the publication of *Audits of Corporate Accounts*, which listed five basic principles that dealt with the most overt abuses of the 1920s: (1) no unrealized profit; (2) no charges of expenses to surplus to relieve the income account; (3) earned surplus prior to an acquisition is not earned surplus of the parent; (4) dividends on treasury stock are not income; (5) notes and accounts receivable due from officers or employees must be shown separately (AIA, 1934: 14). A sixth principle —(6) donated capital does not result in earned surplus—was added at the annual meeting of the Institute in 1934 (AIA, *Yearbook*, 1934, pp. 196–197). *These basic views indicate that accountants had recognized the validity of the argument that the inability, or perhaps unwillingness, of the profession to properly aggregate capital and income had been one of the major reasons for unsatisfactory reporting in the previous decade.*

Despite the many theories about the nature of capital and income, there was general agreement among accounting practitioners that dividends should be paid from earned surplus. But there was no generally accepted procedural approach to this problem. Eric Kohler became a leading spokesman for the "revenue-expense," income orientation, which came to dominate accounting theory in the 1930s. One of the more interesting assertions made by historical cost-oriented accountants was that bankers had influenced accounting standards and had oriented accountants toward liquidation values. Kohler said that this had greatly reduced the worth of accounting information and suggested that, if accountants attempted to trace values rather than costs, they would not find a satisfactory solution. Perhaps the most significant change occurred in the rationale advanced to justify accountants'placing total reliance on cost. Kohler contended that "the intent of management must play a prominent part in the definition of assets and liabilities." Therefore, he argued "since an accountant should not substitute his judgment for that of management," the profession must focus on the objective elements—revenue and expense (Kohler 1935). The idea that assets and liabilities were subjective— that is, dependent on the intent of management—and could not be accurately measured gained widespread support within the profession. And it had a lasting impact on the subsequent evolution of accounting principles and auditing practice.

Faced with a direct challenge from academics with the American Accounting Association's publication of "A Tentative Statement of Accounting Principles" (1936) and the specter of federal intervention with the establishment of the SEC, practitioners united. In 1936 the AIA embarked on a new research program. Accountants were successful in their efforts to keep the standard-setting process in the private sector and in retaining their right to set those standards despite demands from some that the federal government assume absolute control over the financial reporting process. For example, William Schluter's proposal, contained in his *Economic Cycles and Crises* (1933), called for entire federal control of accounting. Schluter advocated an institute of accountance and pricing or valuation that would require *all* business enterprises to keep accounts according to standards set by the federal government. Although Schluter would permit some latitude, standardized systems would be adapted to the needs of different industries. He believed that such rules would permit the "elimination of the present day system of certifying individual public accountants" and allow the government to do this important work. His proposed national institute of accountancy would be analogous with respect to accountancy to the Supreme Court of the United States. He posited three divisions within the government to handle accounting data: first, there would be a division of accounting theory, methods, and procedure, empowered to develop accounting theory and principles; second, a division of reports for uniform classification and compilation of data; and, third, a division of examination and audit, whose duties would be similar to those now performed by public accounting firms.[30] Given such proposals, the SEC, with its emphasis on disclosure, was not as onerous to the profession as has sometimes been suggested.

The Specter of Federal Intervention

Accountants would benefit by demands for reform in the 1930s as they had in the Progressive Era. The Pecora investigation, the federal securities acts, and the establishment of the Securities Exchange Commission (SEC) clearly established that the government would insist on greater protection for investors. At first Congress did not advocate independent audits as a means of improving financial reports. But when Arthur Carter, as president of the New York State Society of CPAs, testified before the Congressional Committee on Banking and Currency, he pointed out that the failure to require audits was a major omission in the suggested reforms. As a result of his testimony, it is generally acknowledged that Congress became convinced of the need for independent audits. The establishment of the SEC in 1934 had initially sent tremors through the financial community, but the concern of the business sector diminished significantly when Franklin D. Roosevelt named Joseph P. Kennedy as the first chairman of the SEC. Kennedy's appointment was generally acceptable to the financial community because he was "one of their own." Reformers lamented the choice, so typical of Roosevelt, who sponsored revolutionary reform and then modified the impact by making conciliatory appointments.

The Federal Securities Acts

The 1933 and 1934 federal securities acts marked the beginning of the development of a "social consciousness" with respect to business and financial reporting in the United States (Greer 1964). Although that statement may eventually be proved to be historically true, since this legislation did acknowledge the importance of financial information for economic and social control, its immediate impact upon the accounting profession seemed to narrow somewhat the traditional concepts of the independent public accountant's responsibilities. Despite the fact that the image of the profession was enhanced by the call for independent audits, these acts were not regarded as salutary for the profession. Many CPAs were frightened, not as some have suggested *purely* by the increased legal liability, but also by the extravagant claims being made by some reformers about the efficacy and reliability of accounting information.

This is not to say that the Truth-in-Securities Act (1933) did not cause grave concern with respect to its liability provision. May, who recognized that "securities legislation was natural, perhaps inevitable" in the 1930s, vigorously attacked the original law. He felt that it was unfortunate that this act not only abandoned the old rule that "the burden of proof is on the plaintiff" but also rejected the "doctrine of contributory negligence and the seemingly sound theory that there should be some relation between the injury caused and the sum to be recovered." But he was not paralyzed by fear; he believed, correctly, that this unfortunate section would be repealed.[31]

Assertions about the factual and accurate nature of accounting also concerned accountants. Wide publicity had been given to Ripley's statement that "the balance sheet is an instantaneous photograph of condition of the company" (Ripley 1927). As early as 1932, the AIA had shown the direction its future efforts would take by the title selected for its correspondence with the New York Stock Exchange, "Value and Limitation of Corporate Accounts and General Principles for Preparation of Reports to Stockholders," referred to previously in this chapter by its official title *Audits of Corporate Accounts.*[32] This document clearly stated that a balance sheet was merely a "reflection of opinion . . . subject to a possibly wide margin of error" (AIA 1932: 3–4). Perhaps Clem Collins, AIA president, best summed up the prevailing sentiment within the profession when he wrote:

It is altogether possible that accountancy has been oversold. That is, a general belief has apparently developed that accounting procedures are infallible. Medical science may have its defects, the principles of engineering may fail because of unforseeable conditions, justice may miscarry because of malevolent human ingenuity, and even our spiritual destination might be uncertain as a result of the diversity of human understanding and belief, BUT, in the minds of many, accountancy seems to stand as the one science against which the machinations of the human mind shall not prevail (Collins 1939).

Throughout the 1930s accountants stressed the limitations of financial reports. Many practitioners believed that claims being made for the efficacy of accounting information were absurd. Ironically, accountants themselves had helped to create the image that they were seeking to overcome.

Establishing Realistic Objectives

Accountants had not been caught totally unaware by the passage of federal legislation to control the securities markets. During World War I the profession had been actively involved with the Congressional Capital Issues Committee, which had proposed a federal securities bill.[33] But, despite the obvious precedents for such legislation, they were uncertain about the expectations of Congress with respect to an auditor's responsibility. Both Arthur Carter and George May stressed the limitations of audits. Carter warned that "investors are too prone to regard balance sheets and income accounts as positive and indisputable statements of fact . . ." while accountants knew they were simply a matter of opinion (U.S., Congress, 1933: 62). Carter and May argued that financial statements were simply representations of management, and Carter totally rejected the suggestion that officers of corporations be required to verify under oath that "the statements . . . are correct." Neither management nor the accountant could make such an assertion, Carter said.

The desire for certainty seems to have been one of the characteristics of the "depression mentality." Accountants could not give legislators all the assurance they demanded. Over the years, it had become apparent to most practitioners that there were no simple rules in accounting. What might conceivably be viewed by others as a simple question (Does an asset exist?) was not elementary for the CPA who believed that managerial intent was an important consideration in asset recognition. Assessment of managerial intent was not an objective matter, according to practitioners. And professional judgment continued to be a most important attribute of the CPA.

Congress showed a lack of understanding about the distinction between the accountant's and the auditor's roles during the 1933 Senate hearings. This was attributable to the fact that accountants themselves had not made a clear distinction between the two. At the beginning of the twentieth century, when CPAs were struggling to gain initial recognition, it was common to find a hierarchy of financial reporting roles—the clerk, bookkeeper, auditor (who was a member of the firm), and an accountant (the independent practitioner). The auditor's work was inspective; the accountant's, analytical (Moxey 1902). Since much of the profession's attention had been directed at securing legislation for accountants and little had been done in the areas of cost accounting (which seemed to be ceded to industrial engineers) and municipal accounting (which was dominated by economists), there was no clear conception of an accountant as anything other than an auditor. By 1933, in fact, many felt that the terms "accountant" and "auditor" were synonymous. Walter Staub attempted to clarify the picture, explaining that auditing "has been sometimes described as the analytical phase of the accountant's work and accounting *per se* as a synthetic phase." But he admitted that the two areas overlapped to such an extent that this division was very obscure (Wiesen 1978: 26).

The confusion among congressional leaders is understandable. Accountants had come full circle in their attitude toward financial reports. At the turn of the century, when reformers demanded publication of corporate accounts to prevent or deter alleged corporate abuses, accountants had been very cautious and stressed the limitations of financial reports. Anson Kittredge might have been speaking in 1933 when, in response to political demands being made, he said "it could happen that the most skilled accountant may examine the books" yet the reports may have "little value as a basis upon which to estimate earning power." He explained that "bookkeeping is [simply] a statement in tabular form of the *opinions of management.*" A report, he continued, "may be technically correct yet essentially untrue" (Kittredge 1901). As it became apparent that independent audits were not being required, accountants began to emphasize the benefits of independent audits to various user groups.

By 1910 accountants were using such terms as "consulting economist" and "financial advisor" and indicating a breadth of service that future auditors would deny in their discussion of the analytic aspect of auditing. Edward L. Suffern had explained the concept of "analytic accounting" by describing the CPA as a financial advisor. The accountant checked the internal control system, the compliance with that system, and noted its weaknesses and strengths. He then considered external factors, asking such questions as was there "a good and continuous demand" for the product, did a "reasonable supply of labor exist" and how would "political considerations" affect the business. The goal, Suffern suggested, was that

> the accountant does become, or has the opportunity to become an advisor to a large clientage, to the stockholder primarily, and to the supervising authority, State or National (Suffern 1910).

CPAs accepted such statements as plausible in the early part of the century; nonaccountants considered such performance improbable, if not impossible. In the 1930s these two views still existed; only the positions of accountants and nonaccountants had become reversed.

The SEC and Full Disclosure

When the federal securities laws were first enacted, accountants feared that the SEC might insist on draconic accounting rules that would significantly circumscribe the use of professional judgment. Robert Montgomery had expressed earlier the opinion of most practitioners when he wrote: "Our most precious asset is our independence in thought and action. Our method of expressing the use of our asset is by means of opinion or judgment." He contended that "slavish adherence to definitions or precedents would reduce our usefulness to a vanishing point" (Montgomery 1927). The profession therefore welcomed the SEC's emphasis on achieving full disclosure, as opposed to dictating numerous specific accounting rules.

The emphasis on disclosure was an interesting one because it rested on the assumption that investors had been misled previously by inadequate disclosure. The historical evidence is not clear on this point, although it is probable that other practices (e.g., insider trading, preferred stock list, managerial bonus system) were more harmful to investor interests than lack of disclosure. It has yet to be established that the investing public was in fact misled by financial reports in the 1920s. One early study points out that promoters were *not* reluctant to disclose even negative information, even though there was no pressure to do so. The author suggests that promoters had an abiding faith in the "stupidity of the investor." George Edwards surveyed major bond issues of the 1920s and concluded that there was only one case that could possibly be construed as fraud. After examining a number of prospectuses, he wrote that

> again and again the prospectus stated that the earning power was insufficient, security pledged was inadequate, the past financial record of the corporation was bad, or that the corporation was reserving for itself powers which might adversely affect the investment position (Edwards 1939: 312ff.).

Thus, although the conclusion that disclosure was the proper response to the debacle of 1929 may have been erroneous,[34] it was welcomed by accountants as a "workable" solution. Once again, independent public accountants were among the prime beneficiaries of reformers' demands for greater investor protection and activist government policy. A young profession, which had been bitterly divided, unified itself in response to these new laws. And CPAs acquired a legally defined social obligation—*to assist in creating and sustaining investor confidence in the public capital markets.*

NOTES

1. The most obvious example was Joseph Sterrett, who served as the transfer agent of the Dawes Commission for reparations. Sterrett was decorated by several foreign countries for his work. See also AIA, *Yearbook, 1917*, pp. 84ff, for a discussion of the work of the Dollar-a-Year Men.

2. See George Rublee, "The Original Plan and Early History of the Federal Trade Commission," *Annals of the American Academy of Political and Social Science*, January 1926, pp. 115–117.

3. In the area of social legislation the dichotomy between liberal-conservative jurists becomes pronounced. Conservatives viewed the corporation as a federal citizen, a doctrine first accepted in 1882 and finalized with the *Smith* v. *Ames* case in 1898, which gave federal courts the right to review not only federal but also state regulation of corporations when regulation might be deemed unreasonable. The courts consistently overturned child labor laws, protective legislation for women, and mandatory pension and other social welfare plans enacted by the States. The rationale was that such laws impinged on the freedom of either the individuals or the corporation.

4. See George O. Newlove, "In All My Years . . . ." *The Accounting Historian*, 1975, 2–3, for a discussion of the advances in budgeting. He cites J. O. McKinsey, *Budgeting*, and H. W. Maynard "Flexible Budgeting," *NACA Bulletin*, 1928, as examples of the new technical expertise. Another important issue was the separation of fixed and variable costs (see J. H. Williams, *Taylor Society Bulletin*, April 1922.)

5. See Andrew Mellon, *Taxation: The People's Business* (New York: MacMillan Co., 1924). Montgomery (1927, p. 252), wrote that Mellon's conservative tax estimates (revenues were grossly underestimated throughout Mellon's tenure) were the secretary's way of dealing with an "extravagant" Congress. In effect, Mellon curbed the power of the legislative branch by saying "Boys, that's all you have to spend."

6. See A. A. Berle and Gardiner Means, *The Modern Corporation and Private Property* (New York: MacMillan & Co., 1933), for a discussion of "the new corporate era." Berle and Means questioned the applicability and adequacy of traditional economic theory to cope with the problems encountered in the modern industrial state.

7. The editorial closely parallels the speech by Joseph Sterrett, "Present Position and Probable Development of Accountancy as a Profession," *Proceedings of the*

Annual Meeting of the American Economic Association, December 1908, pp. 85–96. This is not surprising as Sterrett was chairman of the AIA's committee on the *Journal.* A. P. Richardson remarked that Sterrett took a keen interest in the editorial policy and was, in fact, primarily responsible for writing many of them.

8. For an overview of legal liability in this period, see William R. MacMillan, "Sources and Extent of the Liability of a Public Accountant," pamphlet reprinted from *Chicago-Kent Review,* December 1936 (New York: American Surety Co., 1939).

9. See the editorials in the *Journal of Accountancy,* November 1924, pp. 365–366; January 1926, pp. 40–41; March 1925, pp. 201–202; and July 1925, pp. 37–39. The *Journal* expressed regret that the New York Stock Exchange had refused to sanction audited reports when it made it mandatory for members to publish financial statements. It also noted that the offers by both the AIA and NYSSCPA to help and work with the exchange to curb abuses were summarily dismissed.

10. John L. Carey, secretary of the AIA for many years, played an important role in healing the schism. His many works about accounting history and, especially, his definitive study of the institute provide a contemporary view of the problems of administering a "national" organization.

11. See AIA, *Minutes, 1916,* pp. 105ff. Although membership was by invitation, which could be viewed as "elitism," the rationale expressed in the *Minutes* is that by administering its own examination, the institute could (1) admit people from the nine states whose CPA laws were not recognized by the institute and to whom membership had been closed and (2) admit people who were qualified but lived in New York and Illinois, where examinations were considered "unfair" and where few people passed.

12. See John C. Carey, "The CPA's Professional Heritage," Part II, Working Paper no. 5 (The Academy of Accounting Historians, 1975), p. 6. Carey, one of May's contemporaries at the institute and an admirer of his mental abilities, acknowledged that "his [May's] greatest weakness . . . was an egoism which made him impatient of any disagreement . . . he offended people by brushing aside their ideas brusquely."

13. See AIA, *Yearbook, 1920* (New York, 1921), pp. 70, 118–119. The rule adopted in 1919 was expected to permit management services, e.g., installation of cost systems on a contingent basis. But it was interpreted to permit tax work on a contingency basis. The Committee on Ethical Publicity said abuses were "so flagrant that they bid to bring scandal upon this Institute and the entire body of the profession."

14. See the editorial in *Journal of Accountancy,* Feb. 1919, pp. 134–136, and AIA, *Minutes, 1917,* pp. 35ff for discussions about the problem of self-styled income tax experts.

15. See Leverett S. Lyon, "Accounting Courses in Universities," *Journal of Accountancy,* December 1924, pp. 422–429. Lyon said that there was too much emphasis on bookkeeping in most accounting curricula.

16. Some practitioners were scornful of the sophistication of accounting educators; see, for example, F. W. Thornton, "Teaching Them to Think," *Journal of*

Accountancy, August 1928, pp. 81–85. Thornton wrote that academics "think they think, whereas they have become ready-made word tailors using hand me down phrases which they substitute for thought."

17. See Dorfman 1959:286f for discussion of warnings issued by Leonard Ayres, President of Cleveland Trust Company, that were ignored.

18. Simultaneously some accountants advocated that more emphasis be placed on earnings per share to overcome what they felt was undue reliance on dividends paid as an indicator of corporate performance. See Leo Greendlinger, *Financial and Business Statements* (New York: Alexander Hamilton Institute, 1923). It should also be noted that discussions of the concept of "cost of capital" tended to reinforce the proprietary view.

19. See Paton (1922: :253ff; 443ff) for his discussion of the concept of revenue, which does not really provide a definition of the concept but does focus on the *content* of the revenue accounts and discusses revenue in operational terms.

20. Most theorists accepted only parts of Simpson's thesis and rejected original cost in favor of some modified system of historical cost, i.e., they would recognize the decline in value due to depreciation. An exception to the rule was Paul Joseph Esquerre who was a staunch original cost advocate (see *Applied Theory of Accounts*, New York: Ronald Press, 1914).

21. We will examine the evolution of this model in Chapter 7.

22. Many early writers considered various forms of multiple reporting; see Cole (1908), who advocated presentation of more than one balance sheet. But few early writers would accept multiple measurement.

23. The Institute published a prize essay on this topic in 1924. See S. Gundelfinger, "Principles Which Should Govern the Determination of Capital and the Amounts Available for Distribution of Dividends In the Case of Corporation With Special Reference to the System of Capital Stock Without a Par Value," *Journal of Accountancy*, May 1924, pp. 321–48; June 1924, pp. 420–431; July 1924, pp. 31–41.

24. See William Z. Ripley, *Main Street and Wall Street* (Boston: Little Brown and Company, 1927), pp. 195ff for details of the Dodge manipulations. Ripley, a Harvard economist, was widely known through his articles in the *Atlantic Monthly* in 1926.

25. Although the details presented by Ripley appear to be correct, see George O. May "Letter to the Editor" *New York Times*, 27 August 1927, for consideration of Ripley's motives. May accurately states that one of Ripley's main theses is that "disclosure, itself, is the vital thing; the form of disclosure is of little importance" (an argument that the SEC was to accept). May agrees, and he asks why condemn the Dodge report; although it may have been technically unsatisfactory, the concept of full disclosure was followed. In fact, the disclosure may have totally confused the reader.

26. For a more passionate view of corporate abuses of the period, see I. Maurice Wormser, *Frankenstein Incorporated* (New York: Whittesey House, 1931).

27. See *Time*, 23 October 1929. Krueger was on the cover as an example of the successful financier. J. J. Klein, in his memoirs, said that all one could say about investors and bankers was "that they were honest but damnably dumb" (Klein 1969: 119).

28. See Carey (1975B: 6), who recalls that May's aloofness is perhaps best illustrated by the fact that "Even his partners called him Mr. May. Nobody called him George."

29. For an historic review of the 1920s, see F. L. Allen, *Only Yesterday* (New York: Harper & Bros., 1931), 290ff. Allen contended that "if stocks started upward the public would buy, no matter what the forecasters said, no matter how obsure was the business prospect." (296).

30. For a more detailed synopsis of Schluter's proposals, see "Accountancy Under Economic Self Government." *Accounting Review*, December 1933, pp. 279–384.

31. See *Securities Exchange Act of 1934* (Washington, D.C.: Government Printing Office, 1934), pp. 5–44, which amended the original act so that the plaintiff had to at least prove he had sustained a loss as a result of reliance on audited statements. CPAs could also defend themselves by proving they had "acted in good faith and had no knowledge that statements were false or misleading." For a discussion of earlier attempts to develop securities regulation; see G. Edwards, 1938, pp. 308–318.

32. The document was printed but never distributed by the AIA with the original title. No other changes were made after it had been introduced into testimony by the New York Stock Exchange in the Senate hearings. It was subsequently released in the AIA as *Audits of Corporate Accounts*. Copies of the original printing are in the AICPA library, but the document is not listed in the *Accountants Index*.

33. See U.S., Congress, House, *Report of the Capital Issues Committee*, 65th Cong., 3rd sess., 1918, H. Doc. 1485. See also Jeremy Wiesen, *The Securities Acts and Independent Auditors: What Did Congress Intend* (New York: AICPA, 1978), for a discussion of the bill introduced by Edward Taylor (1919), which closely paralleled the subsequent securities acts.

34. For a more recent criticism of the SEC's policy of disclosure, see George J. Benston, "The Effectiveness and Effects of the SEC's Accounting Disclosure Requirements," in *Economic Policy and the Regulation of Corporate Securities*, ed. Henry G. Manne (Washington D. C.: American Enterprise Institute, 1969), pp. 23–78.

7 EXPANSION AND CONTROVERSY: ACCOUNTANTS IN AN AGE OF UNCERTAINTY

The ideological debates of the past began to give way to a new agreement on the practicalities of managing a modern economy. There . . . developed a new consensus which gave hope of harnessing government, business and labor in a rational partnership for a steadily expanding American economy.
[Arthur Schlesinger, Jr., *A Thousand Days*, 1966]

The Great Depression of the 1930s and World War II and its aftermath were, in terms of their impact on American society, second in importance only to the years 1776–1789 (from the war of independence to the inauguration of George Washington as president). Before 1936 and the so-called Keynesian revolution, the most common attitude toward business was that, apart from some obvious ameliorative legislation (child labor laws, and so forth), the overall performance of the nation's economy was best left to the private sector. In the absence of calls for a positive government policy with respect to the economy, the accountant's role had primarily been one of "information processor" for the business sector. The New Deal was perceived by many contemporaries as profoundly altering demands being made upon the profession. But it is questionable whether or not New Deal policies significantly altered the traditional financial reporting process.

Throughout the 1930s and 1940s political reformers were attempting to integrate capitalism and administrative theory. At first it was assumed that regulation could not be reconciled with capitalism because regulation rejected the fundamental belief in the efficacy of competition in the market place. But it soon became apparent that administrative theory did not negate the need for a self-regulating mechanism, it simply shifted the focal point from the individual to groups—from self-regulation through economics to self-regulation through politics (Lowi 1969: 29f). Scott believed that with the recognition of the ineffectiveness of competition in an industrial society, accounting information would become the chief means of social control (Scott 1939). This prediction appears to have been premature. The theory of "bargaining" evolved slowly, and for many years accounting information continued to be used primarily for economic control within the business sector.

The New Deal and Accountancy

The attitudes of historians toward Roosevelt's New Deal have changed over the years. Yet even those who question the degree of true reform that the Roosevelt era accomplished continue to agree with the assessment that he "unlocked new energies in a people who had lost faith" in the ability of the old order to manage the economy (Schlesinger 1959: 20). While federal officials sought to regulate the economy, especially with respect to employment and growth, New Deal leaders continued to look to accountants to restore investor confidence in the private sector, not to assume responsibility for broader social programs. CPAs were forcefully reminded of their obligation to investors and were asked to aid in the government's efforts to revitalize the capitalist system by developing more reliable financial reporting standards.

Roosevelt's desire to stimulate investment and restore investor confidence was clear. Undersecretary of Commerce Edward Noble addressed the annual meeting of the AIA and told the assembled practitioners that the government felt that the basic problem of the age was "finding ways and means of stimulating the flow of new investment." He added that new investment "depends entirely upon the prospects of return on that investment" (Noble 1939). There was an implicit message in Noble's speech, apparently not lost upon accountants. Risk deterred investment, fluctuating income patterns increased perceived (if not actual) risk, and such uneven income streams could be detrimental to economic recovery. Acceptance of these ideas, with the related acknowledgment that the government viewed the financial reporting process as a means of stimulating investment, appeared to have a decided impact on the evolution of accounting theory. Income smoothing and write-downs of asset values could result in more stable reported income and higher returns on investments after the initial round of asset write-offs.[1]

Accountants, like many others in the business community, may have felt that the politics of the New Deal were extreme, but it soon became apparent that federal officials sought cooperation with and not control of the corporate sector. The Employment Act of 1946 clearly indicated that the financial resources of the federal government would be used to stabilize the economy by supporting the corporate system. The Council of Economic Advisers, created by the employment act, was expected to

> develop and recommend to the President, national economic policies to foster and promote free competitive enterprise, to avoid economic fluctuations or to diminish the effect thereof, and to maintain employment, production, and purchasing power.[2]

"Depressionless" Capitalism

The 1946 Employment Act was indicative of the optimism (after an initial period of fear that the post–World War I depression experience would be repeated) throughout the country after World War II. Americans seemed to believe that the government would and could underwrite the economy. Some economists, most notably Alvin Hansen and Stuart Chase, argued that the United States had entered a period when there would be no further economic growth. They cited the disappearance of the frontier, the decline in population, and the use of highly advanced technology as evidence that the industrial era had ended. Victor Stempf reflected the mood of most Americans when he criticized the "dismal" economists for failing to recognize the existence of "unlimited technological frontiers" that would sustain future economic growth (Stempf 1944B). The political sector had given implicit recognition to *pluralism* in the employment act—the idea that various interest groups could and would make self-regulation possible through the bargaining process. John K. Galbraith was to more formally delineate the theory underlying this policy when he wrote that "private economic power is held in check by the countervailing power of those who are subject to it." "The first begets the second" (Galbraith 1955: 111). Few questioned whether this system of decision-oriented bargaining ("logrolling") would, in fact, result in effective standards or direction for future social policy. Yet pluralism was deemed to be working because the economy seemed stable and healthy, a major governmental objective.

During the 1950s, despite several recessions, it seemed plausible to most Americans that the economy could be permanently stabilized and security assured. Survival did not seem to be a major problem for most corporate businesses; in fact, during this decade, few large firms failed.[3] Managers, perhaps in an attempt to increase their bargaining power, showed a marked preference for equity financing. Diversification was sought, but usually through merger or acquisition, not by internal expansion (Vatter, H., 1963: 191ff.). In the 1960s management's search for security, combined with an apparent desire to solidify its bargaining position, led to a subtle shift in managerial attitudes that would reopen the question of accountants' responsibility to society. But throughout the 1940s and 1950s the emerging social philosophy, which acknowledged the countervailing power found within various interest groups and the concomitant need for social control vis à vis accounting information, seems to have been largely overlooked by both accountants and politicians.

The Managerial Revolution

Although the acceptance of positive government had the most obvious impact on the development of accountancy after 1936, the rise of an independent managerial class also had a significant effect on the responsibilities of the profession. Adam Smith had held grave reservations about hired managers, believing that they would be "disputatious, uninformed and lazy." But most analyses conclude this was not the case. Managers were viewed as reputable, hard-working, and able (Bird 1966: 248f.). Accountants implicitly accepted this latter view and assumed the integrity of management.

The goals of the accounting profession and of management were not dissimilar; each hoped to deter government intervention in establishment of financial reporting standards. But there were early conflicts between the two groups. Professional managers, sensitive to perceived challenges to their control and judgments and faced with the task of rescuing shaky corporations in a questionable economic climate that seemed to encourage federal intervention, had a vested interest in the development of accounting principles. Auditors, on the other hand, were extremely sensitive to the charge that they were "tools" of management and had to be very careful not to appear to be compromising their independence. Accountants found themselves in an unenviable position—they were criticized by managers who felt they were systematically excluded from the decision process while simultaneously being cautioned to free themselves from the clutches of management (Landis 1935; Phillipe 1963). Despite criticism of the close alliance between accountants and management, few questioned the assumptions that management sought to maximize stockholders' investment or that financial reports designed solely to record economic data were relevant to contemporary needs.

Surprisingly, Joseph Schumpeter, the conservative Harvard economist, was among the first to question the adequacy of economic analysis in the corporate age.[4] Schumpeter found that capitalism was economically viable but still concluded that the system was doomed. He believed that the demise of the entrepreneurial spirit with the creation of a managerial class—"private bureaucrats"—meant that capitalism would decay internally. Managers, he wrote, sought security and a steady income and were risk averse; willingness to take risks, he felt, had been the key factor in the success of capitalism. Whether this thesis is correct or not is unimportant, but his recognition that noneconomic factors must be considered in analyzing the effectiveness of corporate operations had clear implications for financial reporting.

Heilbroner, in his assessment of Schumpeter's work, concluded that Schumpeter had, in effect, challenged a basic assumption underlying economic theory for over 200 years. Namely, if *"one could divine the nature of economic forces, one could foretell the future"* (Heilbroner 1961: 280). Financial reporting has been based *on the acceptance of this premise;* namely, if one reported events, then the user could predict future results.

Sociologists and political scientists were also developing new theories in the late 1940s and 1950s which would have important ramifications for accountancy in the 1970s. But from 1937–1966, the financial reporting objective outlined in the New Deal—stimulating investment in the private sector—had not been superceded by broader social goals. Social philosophies evolve slowly, and to suggest that the accounting profession anticipated the need for developing more reliable information for social control would be erroneous. Financial reports continued to be geared toward two primary user groups—investors and creditors. This chapter examines the evolution of accounting thought in light of the prevalent view within the profession that accounting data can facilitate regulation and order via the market place (economic control) but that it is not designed to provide information for self-regulation by the administrative process (political control).

Response to Federal Regulation

The passage of the securities acts of 1933 and 1934 marked the end of the complete autonomy of the accounting profession with respect to financial reporting standards. The FTC and later the SEC were authorized to establish accounting principles, if they so desired. Typical of the New Deal reforms that established agencies to protect the "public interest," the SEC sought cooperation from the private sector.

The SEC and legislators initially advocated "uniformity" as the most effective remedy for the overt abuses in financial reporting. Accountants sought to modify this demand, and a report of a joint committee of the AIA and the ASCPA transmitted to the SEC foreshadowed the approach the profession would take in attempting to codify accounting principles. The committee believed that uniform accounting was unrealistic and ineffective, its primary virtue being simplicity. "Uniformity has been greatly overemphasized," the report contended, adding "it may be more misleading than informative." Consistency in applying alternative procedures was suggested as the objective of financial reporting. The committee advocated that uniformity be limited "to a few general principles so broadly stated that they will permit wide variation in application to meet different circumstances" (AIA and ASCPA 1934: 5–8). For many years the profession would debate the merits of "flexibility" versus "uniformity" in developing accounting standards, which, in the opinion of one practitioner, significantly retarded progress. The debate, he suggested, should have centered on middle ground not extreme positions, with the goal being the elimination of *needless* variation to enhance comparability—an objective defined by Robert Trueblood as "making like things look alike, and unlike things look different" (Lawler 1969).

A second conclusion reached by the joint committee proved more beneficial in providing direction to the profession. The report outlined the impact that viewing the investor as the "primary" user of financial statements would have on the development of accounting principles. Investors were interested in future earnings; therefore,

since "past performance" provides the best indicator of future earnings, the focal point of accounting should be the income statement.[5]
But, the committee warned, neither the SEC nor investors should
assume that accounting information would be sufficient, by itself, to
predict future earnings. Such things as the ability of management,
changes in technology, and shifting markets affected earnings and
were not assessed in financial reports (AIA and ASCPA 1934: 9).

It was not clear prior to 1937 which group, academicians or
practitioners, would take the lead in the area of accounting standards.
Judge James Landis spent most of 1936 vehemently attacking
accounting practitioners. He was widely quoted in the press when he
said, "The impact of almost daily tilts with accountants, some of them
called leaders of their profession, often leaves little doubt that their
loyalties to management are stronger than their sense of responsibility to the investor. . . . Such an experience does not lead readily to
acquiescence in the plea recently made by one of the leaders of the
accounting profession that the form of statement can be less rigidly
controlled and left more largely to professional responsibility alone"
(Demond 1951: 238). In 1937 there was a precarious 3 to 2 majority
among the SEC commissioners favoring standard setting in the
private sector.[6] A year later Commissioner Robert Healy suggested to
accounting academicians that accounting principles be established by
"disinterested" parties. He asked members of the American Accounting Association to join forces with the SEC to assume leadership in
this area. Healy categorized practitioners "as special pleaders for their
most lucrative clients" and claimed that they waffled whenever asked
to take a definite stand on any issue. He contended that the SEC
should force CPAs to state *clearly* whether accounting procedures
used by their clients were appropriate. "Not," he warned, "in ciphers
that would stump Francis Bacon himself." Healy supported those
who suggested that the SEC's Accounting Series Releases (ASRs)
should be the definitive source for establishing accounting principles
(Healy 1938). But, the external attacks on the profession had a
unifying effect. In 1936 the ASCPA and the AIA merged (the latter
name was retained) and the academic community rejected all suggestions that they ally themselves with the SEC.

Organizing the Profession

Accounting practitioners, now united in one national organization,
sought recognition of the AIA as the authoritative voice of the
profession. The earlier cooperative efforts with the New York Stock

Exchange, which resulted in a few broad principles, had been well received. George May consistently prodded the leaders of the national organization to continue the efforts begun by various special committees of that body. But available time was short, and many CPAs did not believe that the AIA should codify accounting principles. Therefore, while an effort was being made to convince practitioners that the profession should act, an AIA committee on auditing procedure issued *Examination of Financial Statements*, which incorporated the principles established by the AIA and the New York Stock Exchange in 1934 plus all SEC disclosure requirements at that time. No one questioned the right of the AIA to set audit standards. Samuel Broad recalled that "we felt, in our own minds, although it was not expressed, that we were in effect setting forth the common law for accounting practice, for the next few years" (AIA, *Minutes, 1936:* 84). But by 1937 it became apparent that, if practitioners were to provide the leadership in the area of accounting "theory," the work could not be left to special committees or to postscripts to audit bulletins.

1937–A Year of Challenge

Nineteen thirty-seven marked the fiftieth anniversary of the AIA, and many older practitioners must have been dismayed when they surveyed the number of demands being made on the profession. Clem Collins, dean of the University of Denver and president of the AIA, traveled throughout the country in 1938 and 1939 trying to gain support for the national organization. He warned his fellow CPAs that the securities acts, the Revenue Act of 1936, the Robinson-Patman Act, and the Borah-O'Mahoney Bill (Federal Corporation Act of 1937) were indicative of the increased interest in and influence on the evolution of accountancy that the political sector would have. The autonomy of the profession was in danger unless practitioners could unite.

The most obvious threat came from the Borah-O'Mahoney Bill, which included a provision for audits by "certified corporate representatives" of all interstate corporations (not unlike Hurley's 1915 zone expert proposal). The representatives would be licensed by the federal government after passing a civil service examination in corporate accounting and business law. Collins reminded his colleagues that there was no longer any debate over whether or not the government had the right to exercise such control. In the 1930s, the belief became widespread that it was the duty of government to assume an active role. Collins' message was simple—historically, once any government agency began to examine corporations, independent audits were no longer required. He cited "banks, railroads, public utilities, and savings and loan associations" as examples of areas in which auditors had been displaced (Collins 1938). If the SEC assumed powers similar to those of the ICC, the public accounting profession might cease to exist.

Developing Audit Standards

During the 1920s, political leaders had not called for auditors to guard against exploitation of investors and the public by business interests; most politicians believed in the integrity of financial capitalists. Roosevelt, in his 1932 inaugural address, left no doubt that political perceptions of the business community had changed. He said, "the rulers of the exchange of mankind's goods have failed through their own stubbornness and their own incompetence." Admitting that they had tried, the president added that they failed because they "have been cast in the pattern of an outworn tradition." He concluded that "stripped of the line of profit, . . . they have resorted to exploitations . . . [because] they know only the rule of a generation of self-seekers." This, he believed, would be the demise of the business system as it had existed; new leadership was to come from the political sector to insure the welfare of the people (*New York Times*, March 5, 1933).

While most accountants probably did not accept Roosevelt's indictment of business, the profession recognized that effective control would have to be established in the private sector if future federal intervention was to be deterred. Surprisingly, the SEC expressed little interest in promulgating auditing standards, and accountants acted quickly to retain this prerogative.

The AIA appointed a Committee on Auditing Procedure, under the leadership of, first, Frederick Hurdman and, later, Samuel Broad, to establish auditing standards for the profession. *Examination of Financial Statements* outlined standards and did not attempt to dictate specific auditing procedures. Unlike the Committee on Accounting Principles, which worked under the threat of SEC intervention if it did not limit alternatives, the Committee on Auditing Procedure was under no such pressure. It was therefore able to outline broad standards while permitting the practitioner considerable latitude (the use of professional judgment) in applying those standards. The lack of procedural specificity seemed to have resulted in less antagonism toward audit standards within the profession than that generated by similar attempts to define accounting principles.

The committee, having been given the opportunity to define auditors' responsibilities and duties, emphasized that management, not auditors, had primary responsibility for financial statements (AIA, *Minutes, 1936:* 82ff.). Given the political climate of the 1930s, one can

AIA Speakers' Party for Wartime Accounting Conferences, held by the state societies of Pennsylvania, Louisiana, Texas, Oklahoma, Missouri, Nebraska, and Minnesota in April 1944. Standing, left to right: John Carey, Victor Stempf, and Jay A. Phillips. Seated, left to right: George Bailey, Samuel Ellis, and Samuel Broad.

understand the desire of the profession to limit its responsibilities. But the stress on limitations seems to have had unfortunate ramifications. In subsequent years, the emphasis continued to be, not on what auditors can do, but on what they cannot do. This negative orientation has raised serious question about the willingness of the profession to effectively meet social demand. The McKesson-Robbins scandal contributed to the defensive posture that the Institute seemed to adopt.[7]

The McKesson-Robbins Case

The McKesson-Robbins case brought to light the ineffectiveness of audits in detecting fraud involving collusion. Early in the century the profession had conceded that audits could not be designed to specifically detect fraud; the costs would be too high (Sells 1906). But this message was not fully understood. The AIA leadership, although greatly concerned by the McKesson-Robbins case, did not act precipitously. Most accountants believed that this was a most unusual case of collusive fraud but that it did not require a wholesale restatement of auditing procedures ("Editorial," *Journal of Accountancy,* Feb. 1939, pp. 65–69).

The press treated the case in a sensational manner, and New York Attorney General John Bennett conducted a series of hearings at which both the New York State CPA Society and the AIA were represented. Bennett called accountants to task, citing the "*Whitney case, Interstate Hosiery, McCaffrey and Co., and Coster-Musica* (McKesson-Robbins)" as reflections of certain fundamental weaknesses in the preparation of financial statements by large corporations (Bennett 1939: 1f.). The CPAs responded that "in most, if not in all, of the cases cited by the attorney general . . . in which questions of auditing have been involved, it has been human behavior which has failed rather than the procedures commonly followed" (Bennett 1939: 14). Despite the unfavorable publicity, the AIA decided not to revise the 1936 statement but, instead, to extend accepted auditing procedures.

"Extensions of Audit Procedures" (1939A) acknowledged the need for confirmation of receivables and verification of inventory. But, more important, it recognized the relationship among internal control, risk, and evidence. The document stated that "it is the duty of the independent auditor to review the system of internal check and accounting control so as to determine the extent to which he considers that he can rely upon it." A contribution of the postwar years was clarification of the relationship between internal control and the scope of the auditor's work.

Internal Control

The suggestion that internal control and auditing procedures were related was not new. In 1904 Walter Staub had written that "when an audit is being made for the first time it will be of great advantage . . . to go thoroughly over the system in force." And in 1912 Montgomery recommended that the first step in any audit should be to ascertain the system of internal check (Staub 1904; Montgomery 1912A: 53f.). But despite the early recognition of the importance of internal control, the auditor had no formal guidelines establishing the degree of assurance that one could place on a managerial system.

Since accountants were disclaiming responsibility for financial reports, it became imperative that they assess the reliability of a firm's internal control system. In 1948 the AIA issued "Internal Control— Elements of a Co-ordinated System and Its Importance to Management and the Independent Public Accountant," which became an authoritative source for most auditors.[8]

In 1951, the AIA Committee on Auditing Procedure issued *Codification of Statements on Auditing Procedure*, a condensation of the twenty-four statements issued between 1939 and 1950. But, during the postwar years into the 1960s, little normative discussion occurred with respect to audit standards and auditors' responsibilities. Although the 1960s were to renew interest in the latter question, most of the Institute's and the profession's attention was directed toward the more difficult task of establishing financial accounting standards.[9]

Establishing Accounting Principles

The AIA had organized a seven member special Committee on Accounting Procedure (CAP) in 1936, but it soon became apparent that this approach was totally inadequate. May, who has to be regarded as one of the most influential members of the accounting profession at this time, sent a letter to the Executive Committee of the AIA (September 22, 1937) saying that a committee with no research staff, no power to initiate discussion of problem areas, and no authority was totally absurd. He asked that the committee be greatly expanded, a research capability be established, and the committee's duties restated to give it the authority to initiate discussion on any problem area. May characterized this as an ambitious but necessary program, and the Executive Committee agreed to all his suggestions. Academicians were invited to join in this effort, and William Paton, A. C. Littleton, and Roy B. Kester were appointed to the expanded group.

The first issue discussed was what approach should CAP take in its effort to limit accounting alternatives. Committee members quickly rejected the idea that the first duty should be "to formulate a comprehensive statement of accounting principles" (Werntz 1959). This decision resulted in the criticism that the committee was "narrow-sighted" and had adopted a "brush-fire" approach. But most members of the committee did not believe that they had the time to develop a conceptual framework.

Jacob Taylor recalled that "the choice was not entirely ours." He said he had asked Healy at the 1937 AAA convention if the SEC "would wait until accountants reconcile their differences" and develop a broad framework. Healy's answer, "Absolutely, no." This might have been expected, given Healy's views. But, Taylor indicated that when Carman Blough concurred and indicated that if accountants did not find satisfactory answers to pressing issues, the SEC would act, and quickly, he became convinced that the profession did not have the time necessary to develop a theoretical framework (Taylor, 1938). Having decided not to attempt to define a comprehensive statement of accounting principles, it may have been unfortunate that the institute agreed to publish the Sanders, Hatfield, and Moore study, *A Statement of Accounting Principles*. The institute, somewhat naively perhaps, intended to disassociate itself from the work by saying it was not an official pronouncement. Many accountants, however, did view this as an authoritative source for the establishment of accounting principles, being a survey of existing practice.

The Impact of A Statement of Accounting Principles

The publication of this work produced an immediate reaction from the academic community, most of it critical. William Paton expressed the feeling of many when he wrote, "In view of the distinguished authorship of this statement, I was expecting a report which would be outstanding in scholarly approach, in clarity of expression, and in sound and constructive formulation." But, he found the work "has little or nothing to offer . . . by way of substantive recommendations" and concluded that what the authors "seem to be saying to business management is, 'Give the problem careful consideration and then do as you think best, subject to legal limitation.' " (Paton, 1938) Andrew Barr concurred with Paton's sentiment suggesting that "a better title for their statement would have been *A Statement of Accounting Practices* with a footnote referring to Professor Hatfield's book for a statement of principles." (Barr, 1938). The criticism, while just, is interesting because according to Arthur Carter the Haskins and Sells Foundation had commissioned "three eminent academicians to survey existing practice and write *a definitive statement of the best practice.*" (emphasis added) (Carter, 1937). This, the authors had done.

It was not until the manuscript was complete that Carter approached the institute about the feasibility of bringing the statement out under the institute's auspices "without necessarily committing the Institute to the adoption of principles stated" (Carter 1937). The Executive Committee, perhaps motivated by the desire to counter the effect of the 1936 American Accounting Association statement, agreed.

The apparent inaccuracy in the title of the study reopened charges that practitioners did not want to establish accounting principles but, rather, to perpetuate existing practice. The study was used by some practitioners to justify existing practice. The correspondence file from CAP's early years and the annual meetings of the institute from 1937 to 1941 show that the study was cited by many as an authoritative source.[10]

One of the reasons for the vehement reaction against the *Statement of Accounting Principles* in academia may have been because it bore the imprimatur of Henry Rand Hatfield, who was considered an eminent accounting scholar. Hatfield, after publication of the work, tried to make it clear that he disapproved of any effort to "tabulate the practice of many corporations and swear by the results." This procedure for establishing accounting principles, he said, "rests on the dictum":

> . . . spite of pride, in erring reasons spite
> One truth is clear; What ever is, is right.

This he clearly rejected. The problem, Hatfield implied, was that the profession did not know what a principle was. "The search goes on," he lamented, "for the still undiscovered accounting principle," suggesting that "perhaps some day an AIA President will come upon it, extend his hand, and say 'Ah, Major Accounting Principle, I presume" (Hatfield 1939). But despite Hatfield's protestations, the appearance of the original statement, combined with the appointment of Thomas Sanders as the research director of CAP, convinced some that accounting principles need to be no more than reflections of existing practice.

Having first decided that time would not permit an exhaustive study of accounting theory, then having issued a statement of principles based on practice seemed to negate CAP's intention to seek theoretical as well as "practical" solutions. Since May urged his fellow committee members to adopt a pragmatic approach, there was widespread belief that CAP gave only lip service to theory.

The CAP Approach

May recognized that a "pragmatic" theory would have negative connotations for many academicians. But he used the term in its philosophic sense, explaining that "I feel very distinctly that unless accounting is pragmatic in the sense of being practical and giving results that are satisfactory from the standpoint of practical results, it will cease to perform the function which it should perform." He asserted that "the results must be judged from the benefits or ill effects upon society at large" (May 1938). While May did not advocate simply justifying practice, his approach did allow considerable latitude. For example (since it was clear that the "social good" would be enhanced by increasing private investment, an obvious goal of the New Deal) should accountants accept smooth income figures so that investors might perceive less risk? Clearly, a pragmatic theory could support many alternative practices, and the CPA was free to make subjective value judgments.

It seemed apparent that an organization whose membership encompassed less than a third of all CPAs had to at least acknowledge existing practice.[11] Most of those who listened to May's appeal conceded the need for practicality, perhaps not in a pragmatic but in a realistic sense. The AIA simply did not have the authority to force compliance with any of its opinions, and most practitioners ignored CAP when the principles stated were unacceptable to them.

Even among members of the Committee on Accounting Procedure there was no agreement that the institute pronouncements should be considered authoritative. Accounting Research Bulletin No. 1 contained the seemingly harmless statement that "accounting research bulletins are rules which may be subject to exception." But a modifying clause was added: "the burden of proof is on those departing from the bulletin." Frederick Andrews, a member of CAP, was upset at what he believed were the "unwarranted dictatorial tactics," not of the committee, but of Thomas Sanders as research director. Andrews asserted that the committee had never, and would never, agree to the research bulletin statement (Andrews 1939: 1). The clause had been added at the urging of Charles Couchman, then president of the institute, who said he did so "to reduce or avoid the appearance of dictation." "It is not," Couchman argued, "the habit of dictators to recognize in advance that there might be exceptions to their own rules" (CAP 1939: Couchman).[12]

It is not surprising that CAP decided it "would consider special topics, to recommend one or more alternative procedures and reject unacceptable procedures." The attempt would be to narrow alternatives. Once again a long debate ensued attempting to justify this decision in terms of accounting as an "art." George Bailey expressed the beliefs of most of the committee when he noted a tendency to view accounting "as an art rather than a science, and as an art it should be subject to the necessity of proper observance of many fundamental practices, but leave room for other procedures involving judgment, emphasis, and experience" (CAP 1940: Bailey). This "framework" certainly did not provide much guidance to committee members. Fortunately, all members of the committee were able to agree that they must view the investor as the primary user of financial reports. And this did give some direction to the committee's work.

Investor Protection

The impetus for the codification of accounting procedures came from the SEC, which left little doubt about the objective it sought to attain. "The major purpose of annual reports is to provide guidance to investors" to aid in "prediction of future earnings," SEC Chairman Frank told accountants (Frank 1939). Paton recalled that at early meetings of CAP, it was proposed and agreed that "we take as a 'golden rule' the proposition that the most important purpose of corporate accounting is the periodic measurement of income" (Paton 1939). Practitioners and academicians agreed that "the principal and almost the only use to ordinary readers of a single accounting period is its use as a basis of estimating—or perhaps we should say guessing—the probable earnings for the immediate future" (Nissley 1940). But, as the above statement indicates, many practitioners were leery of the claims being made for the predictive power of a single-period income statement.[13]

May felt that Frank and the other SEC commissioners viewed income in simplistic terms as "something to which a multiplier could be applied to provide a guide to capital values." If they expected accountants to determine a single income figure to which a multiplier can be applied, then, May concluded, all unusual and nonrecurring gains must be excluded from the income statement (CAP 1939: May). Although accountants agreed that income determination was central to the reporting process, they disagreed about what constituted income.

Concepts of Income

The SEC's emphasis on "earning power" seemed to be a formidable barrier to any conceptual debate with respect to the nature of income. Earning power, in an economic sense, can be viewed as the discounted present value of future receipts to be generated by total corporate assets, including the "going value" of the corporation itself. Accountants had always disclaimed any attempts to make them responsible for determining the capitalized value of a firm based on expectation, a position that was not unreasonable given the uncertainty of the business environment. But, throughout the 1920s, theorists were trying to approximate economic income and were still examining the relationship between asset valuation and income, at least with respect to tangible assets.

In the 1930s, income determination (focusing on *matching* of revenues and expenses with a strict definition of realization) seemed to some theorists to make the question of asset valuation irrelevant. The direction the profession took is clearly shown by such statements as "the balance sheet is nothing more than a vestige of double entry which acts as a repository of our income statement maneuvers." (Defliese 1964) Accounting income, it was assumed, could be discussed without reference to economic concepts, and, as might be expected the ensuing debate was trivial. Accountants debated what should be reported on the income statement—not what is income.

There were two basic concepts about what should be reported on the "bottom line": current operating income and all-inclusive income. There was a division over which concept was correct, which has been depicted as an academic–practitioner schism. Although there are obvious exceptions to such a generalization, it is basically valid.[14] The suspicion existed that practitioners may have been pandering to management; this, unfortunately, obscured much of the real debate. Most accountants agreed that current operating income was the best surrogate for future earnings. What they disagreed about was the ability of investors to understand financial reports. Academics saw no reason why an investor would focus on the bottom-line figure alone when there was a classified income statement. Current operating income would be shown, but not as the last figure on the report. Practitioners argued that investors were not that sophisticated and that the financial press had conditioned people to look at the bottom line. Accountants, they contended, could not effectively educate users of financial statements to do otherwise (CAP 1939). The debate quickly disintegrated (failing to focus on such basic questions as what is income or what effects reporting "all-inclusive" versus "current operating" income had on investors' perceptions of future earnings) into a series of accusations about the motives of practitioners.

Paton, one of the leading proponents of the all-inclusive concept, told his fellow committee members that the "income sheet should be from 'Genesis to Revelation'—start with sales and end with surplus." He warned that if the profession did not adopt this position, practitioners would face extreme pressure from management to "tuck away, through the back door of the surplus account, charges or credits which management finds it inconvenient to disclose explicitly" (Paton 1939A). At least one practitioner, Warren Nissley, felt that Paton's assessment was correct. Nissley criticized the Sanders, Hatfield, and Moore study for stating that "some charges could be made directly to surplus to facilitate prediction of current earnings." He predicted that this assertion would cause "many grey hairs for auditors" because management certainly would prefer a "private burial in surplus which was much less noticeable than a public funeral in the income account" (Nissley 1940). There was a notable lack of acceptance of the contention that the primary motivation for reporting "current operating" performance was to avoid misleading investors. The desire to "hide" losses was the most common allegation made, but critics did not overlook the fact that the current operating concept facilitated income smoothing.

Two external factors—the desire of the government to stimulate investment and the undistributed profits tax incorporated in the 1936 federal income tax law—suggested to some accountants that, practically, it would be most beneficial to report as smooth an earning pattern as possible (Crandell 1938). These factors, combined with the argument that recurring income streams were better predictors of future earnings, served as justification for adopting the current operating concept of income within the institute. Although accountants agreed that proper income determination should guide the CAP members in establishing principles, adopting the current operating approach made the task of limiting alternatives very difficult. It became a matter of judgment about whether items should be reported on the income statement or through adjustments to the surplus account. Whether losses should be reported or deferred in some instances was left to the discretion of the accountant. This led to some decidedly nontheoretical conclusions.

Establishing Principles of Accounting

It is impossible in a general history to examine and evaluate all the opinions and related issues promulgated by CAP. But an examination of the debate over proper treatment of "Unamortized Discounts on Refunded Bond Issues" (ARB no. 2), the first major issue referred to the committee by the SEC, exemplifies the problems encountered by CAP in trying to gain a consensus in the absence of a theoretical framework. Once the SEC indicated that an immediate resolution of this issue was mandatory to gaining greater consistency in treatment of unamortized bond discounts, CAP members submitted opinion papers to either May or Sanders. Littleton felt that the committee must attempt to be guided by two major questions:

> will the balance sheet contain an item that cannot be called an asset and will the income statement fail to report an item now, which if it had been known when the bond was issued, would have been amortized during past periods?   (CAP 1939: Littleton).

But the committee was most concerned with limiting existing alternatives and consequently surveyed existing practice, finding three procedures that they proceeded to debate.[15]

Those who felt that refunding of the bond issue indicated that the accounting transaction was complete supported a write-off of the discount to surplus. For advocates of the current operating approach, the alternatives suggested by CAP posed little theoretical problem. May explained that he favored a direct write-off because "I feel it would be most unfortunate for the Institute to initiate this service by putting forward as a preferable procedure the carrying forward of a non-existent asset" (CAP 1939: May). May could accept the propriety of charging the loss to surplus as unusual and nonrecurring.

Paton, who agreed that refunding represented a completed transaction and that no asset existed, was placed in the untenable position of having to choose from three alternatives, all of which he felt devoid of theoretical justification. As a proponent of the all-inclusive income statement, he could not accept a write-off to surplus. He tried to convince the members of the committee that the loss was "real" and that all economic events must be reflected in the income account. (CAP 1939: Paton)

Proponents of amortization argued that direct write-off distorted income and surplus and that an asset did exist because the transaction was not complete. George Bailey contended that, although it was a basic concept in accounting that "losses should not be carried forward after they are determined, . . . premature retirements are not losses. . . . They are deliberate investments made for future benefits" (CAP 1939: Bailey). Some committee members used the Sanders, Hatfield, and Moore study to justify amortization by citing that work's statement that "it is reasonable to defer abnormal losses which are not convenient to write off" (Sanders, Hatfield, and Moore 1937:114). Since direct write-off could impair a firm's ability to pay dividends, it might be decidedly inconvenient to do so.

Although proponents of amortization advanced some theoretical arguments for deferral of the loss, they were hard pressed to justify what CAP recommended as the preferable solution—amortization over the life of the old bond issue. Paton and Henry Horne joined forces on this issue, although Horne, unlike Paton, believed amortization was correct. Horne argued that no loss occurred because "a normal refund was constructive . . . not a lamenting over borrowing badly done." But how, he asked, could you contend that the future benefits accrued to a nonexistent bond issue? (CAP 1939: Horne). Paton said he could conceivably support the assertion that the discount should be amortized because the transaction had not been completed. But he doubted that anyone could contend that the transaction ended with the expiration of the retired issue (CAP 1939: Paton). The only theoretical argument advanced in this instance was the doctrine of conservatism.

Once the committee had agreed to the primacy of the income statement, conservatism was advocated because it would enhance the balance sheet. Littleton, an ardent advocate of conservatism, suggested that the "amortization period should be over the old *or* new issue, whichever is shorter" (Littleton 1939: 4). Bailey remarked that "I am not quite prepared to accept the shorter period as theoretically preferable." But, he added, "the difference can hardly be material" (CAP 1939: Bailey). The obvious reason that could be advanced for the shorter period was to reduce risk; that is, many practitioners feared that amortization over a longer period would lead to constant refunding and pyramiding of refunded debt issues.

The decision about the period for amortization, which was the subject of heated debate, was less divisive than the decision to permit a direct write-off to surplus (an acceptable alternative procedure in ARB no. 2). This issue presented a fundamental theoretical conflict; namely, should the effects of all transactions be reported in the income statement. Frederick Andrews was displeased by the acceptance of this method. He dismissed the contention that a write-off to income would distort the income statement, asking "how can an income statement be distorted if it truly reflects what happened during a period?" He challenged anyone to show him the wisdom of trying "to approximate uniformity of successive income accounts if they lack conformity with reality." He totally rejected the concept of amortization. "No good can come from a procedure which would result in surplus where there will not be assets. . . . This is real distortion" (CAP 1939: Andrews).

Paton and Kester found ARB no. 2 so theoretically unacceptable that they formally dissented. The negative vote of two academicians did not go unnoticed, and Kohler suggested that perhaps practitioners were not really seeking theoretical solutions but simply justifying what they did. He asked why the dissents were not printed, implying that the two academicians were probably silenced by CAP because they were right (*Accounting Review*, 1939: 445) May, in his usual diplomatic style, responded in a letter to the editor of the *Review* that the only thing jaded was Kohler's "critical faculty." He said that Kester dissented because he advocated amortization over the life of the new issue, while Paton objected to direct write-offs to surplus. The debate over this issue foreshadowed the difficulty CAP would have when it discussed principles that affected the determination of income and financial condition.

If one examines this issue, or the many others discussed by CAP, purely with respect to theoretical considerations, then CAP is found wanting. The only alternative that everyone agreed had theoretical merit in this case—amortization over the life of the new bond issue—was the one alternative prohibited. But one must ask the question, what would have been the reaction in the political sector to direct write-offs to income, an approach preferred by many academicians. Roosevelt's messages constantly reiterated the need to overcome the depression mentality and what he believed to be the pervasive but unwarranted economic pessimism of the day. Regulatory agencies usually required direct write-offs, but to surplus where they could be hidden. Even with "uniform" procedures, these agencies were not hesitant to permit any of the alternatives suggested by CAP, if it was inconvenient for a company to absorb the loss currently.[17] If losses did not impair a company's ability to pay dividends and did not affect the current income, then direct write off would meet with no objection from the political sector.

Amortization was obviously the more attractive alternative to those who hoped that investors could be persuaded to enter the capital markets. Surplus would be only nominally impaired; income would not be greatly affected; and, in most cases, net assets would increase. Practitioners, perhaps influenced by their sensitivity to their increased legal liability, might argue that the "loss" was really an asset since it had future benefits. But they were not anxious to expose themselves to the potential liability that could be incurred if a company consistently refunded its debt issues, pyramiding its asset structure. May was quick to note that accounting principles could not be developed in isolation without regard to their practical consequences. And, although one may question the theoretical merit of CAP's work, it should be recognized that most of its decisions were in line with the desire of the government to stimulate the economy.

Moonitz, in his survey of the various CAP and later Accounting Principles Board (APB) opinions, concluded that opinions dealing with the form of presentation, the extent of disclosure, or the amount of detail were accepted readily. But "those opinions which bear on valuation of assets or liabilities, and, therefore, recognition of revenue and expenses" failed (Moonitz 1974: 23–24).

It is not surprising that accountants should have experienced difficulty in reaching accord on those areas cited by Moonitz. These issues had an impact on the market valuation of securities, and opposition could be expected from groups who might be adversely affected. Practitioners seemed reluctant to take a unilateral stand; compromise earmarked CAP deliberations. The work of the committee established that determining accounting principles was a political as well as a theoretical process.

Despite its inability to resolve key issues, CAP did play an important role in the evolution of accounting theory. The committee met political demands and enabled accountants to retain the right to establish accounting principles. Its failure, in some cases, to derive principles that could be theoretically justified led to calls for conceptual research, which had been markedly absent in the principle-setting process before the establishment of the Accounting Principles Board.

Recent commentators have suggested that the SEC should have assumed control of the standard-setting process in the 1930s, the

Eric L. Kohler

Thomas H. Sanders, Research Director, Committee on Accounting Procedure.

George Oliver May.

Source: From a portrait painted by Paul Irebilcock in 1945.

presumption being that there would have been a more consistent and equitable resolution of issues. Certainly that agency could have forced compliance with its pronouncements (a power that CAP lacked); but there is little evidence to suggest that the SEC would have been more effective or able to withstand lobbying and management pressure. Since the resolution of these difficult issues would have had a significant market impact at a time when a major political objective appeared to be to restore investor confidence, it seems unlikely that a federal agency would have enacted standards on a purely theoretical basis that ignored the economic impact of such standards. Moreover, the SEC did not encourage conceptual debate. The agency's attitude seemed to be that any attempt to deviate from the historic cost allocation model would introduce too much subjectivity into the income determination process. Thus, the SEC rejected efforts to introduce alternative measurement procedures into financial reports in the post World War II decade.

The Replacement Cost Controversy

While the accretion concept of income was irrelevant to income determination within the framework of the historic cost allocation model, accountants could not totally ignore (although they may have preferred to) valuation problems. In the late 1930s, the issue was a procedural one. Namely, how could the profession handle appraised values introduced into financial reports in the 1920s. CAP never found a satisfactory solution to the problem of amortizing such "appraisal values." Most members agreed that the "increased" depreciation (depreciation on appreciation) must be charged to current operating income, presumably to deter future write-ups (CAP 1939: Nissley). Paton advocated using different values on the balance sheet and income statement, that is, calculating depreciation on original cost for the income statement and charging the "excess depreciation" to surplus (CAP 1939: Paton). But ARB No. 5, "Appreciation on Depreciation," never resolved the question of the nature of appraisals and CAP discouraged conceptual debate.

But, in the post World War II era inflation once again became a serious problem and the relevance of historic cost was questioned. Managers complained that accountants overstated corporate profits by failing to recognize the decreasing purchasing power of the dollar. In the late 1940s William Blackie expressed the views of management and chastised accountants for their inability, or unwillingness, to accurately measure income and for the total disregard of the needs of users of financial statements. Greer, in discussing this issue, had written: "The correct solution to this problem lies in the education of the public in the problems of business economics and the way in which they are affected by fluctuations in money values." He concluded that "this requires not a revision of accounting statements but a thorough exposition of their significance as stated" (Greer 1948). Blackie was notably skeptical, remarking that the "unchanging continuance of present accounting practice would seem to call for a change in people," which would be a bit more difficult for accountants than resolving their own reporting problems (Blackie 1948). He advocated "economic accounting" (recognition of current values) as the solution to accountants' major function, the evaluation of stewardship, which had become more important as society demanded greater accountability from management. Blackie wanted "to preserve the integrity of the balance sheet while making the income statement also serve its purpose effectively." Recognition of current cost levels would not only enhance stewardship, according to Blackie, it would also move "towards an increasingly desirable coordination of financial accounting, economics, national statistics . . . and, not least, valuation" (Blackie 1948). More important, Blackie foreshadowed future assertions that, while each individual business may for some purposes be regarded as a separate entity, for economic and social progress, each business was part of a social system, and accounting should play an important role as a means of social control.

By 1947, corporations were trying to show the impact of inflation by making additional charges to income to augment depreciation based on original cost. But attempts to charge these "additional" costs to current revenues were rejected by the SEC and companies like U.S. Steel (1949) were forced to conform to traditional reporting practice.[18] A compromise, acceptance of accelerated depreciation (not unlike the previous concession to accept LIFO [last in first out] for inventory valuation) stilled the harshest criticisms of management. But, this issue did result in excellent academic research into the concept of business income through study groups organized by the AIA with the cooperation of the National Bureau of Economic Research.[19]

Academic Research Efforts

The AAA, through the work of various committees and its sponsorship of research monographs, sought to provide a conceptual framework for financial accounting theory. The AAA, a national organization for collegiate accounting educators, until quite recently, virtually ignored managerial accounting. The National Association of (cost) Accountants (NAA) provided much of the research support for academics interested in the cost and managerial accounting areas. This division is significant because for many years it was assumed that the type of information useful to managers had little significance for external users. In assessing the impact of the contributions made by academics in each area, one must keep in mind that the NAA did not attempt to prescribe accounting methods. Acceptance of academic research depended primarily on its utility and relevance to management. In this scenario, it is quite likely that standards could be established through academic research. In the financial accounting area, the situation was not the same. Principles were set by authoritative bodies to meet specific needs; although academic research might influence the development of principles, academic research did not establish standards.

Financial Accounting

The AAA issued a series of statements between 1936 and 1948 that clearly moved accounting toward the historical-cost valuation model: "A Tentative Statement of Accounting Principles Affecting Corporate Reports" (1936), "Accounting Principles Underlying Corporate Financial Statements" (1941), and "Accounting Concepts and Standards Underlying Financial Statements: 1948 Revision." The 1936 statement asserted that "accounting is . . . [concerned with] . . . the allocation of historical cost." But a concession was made for deviations from historical cost for amounts "not recoverable in the course of future operations." The most significant departure from accepted accounting practice was the support found for the all-inclusive concept of income in these early statements. Although these AAA statements sparked debate, they did not appear to significantly influence CAP.[20].

In 1940 the AAA issued *An Introduction to Corporate Accounting Standards*, by W. A. Paton and A. C. Littleton, a monograph that has been considered a classic by accounting educators. The study purported to be the first integrative theory of accounting, a claim that some feel is open to challenge. But the authors made several important contributions to the evolution of accounting literature. They defined revenue—a notable omission in AAA statements until 1948 and in CAP discussions—and they were among the first to differentiate between "realization" and "earnings." The authors believed that while earnings obviously accrued throughout the production process, they should not be realized as revenue until conversion occurred through the legal sale *or* a similar process and was thus validated by the receipt of liquid assets. The early AAA studies had closely allied realization with the passage of legal title, which Paton and Littleton felt unduly restrictive. The authors advocated that accounting be viewed as a cost-allocation model and that matching of revenue and expenses was the key to income determination. (Paton and Littleton 1940) The monograph provided an accounting model that found widespread favor in contemporary textbooks. Unfortunately, the assertion that propositions were logically derived from concepts was accepted without being first tested.

This led to confusion, especially in respect to the ramifications that the acceptance of the "entity concept" had on the development of accounting theory. Paton and Littleton wrote that "with the entity concept as a basis, there is no difficulty in accepting the proposition that all costs legitimately incurred by the enterprise are properly included, in the first instance, in the total of assets." Chambers, Deinzer, and others contend that this is an attempt to rationalize the later assertion that "costs attach" and not a logical deduction. The entity notion is neutral with respect to cost or value, critics suggest. And they deny that this theory mandates the use of historical cost. There is, however, ample evidence that many accountants have accepted the proposition that entity theory supports the cost-allocation model advanced by Paton and Littleton.

An Overview of Theories

In 1938 George Husband attempted to show that despite accountants' eager acceptance of entity theory, accounting principles and practices were not consistent with either entity or representative theory. Husband felt that, although both theories were capable of supporting a theoretical framework, it would be more realistic for the development of accounting principles to be based on representative theory. He warned that, if the statutes in various states do not afford proper protection to the investor and the public, then the law should be changed rather than relying on the "application of so-called good accounting principles" to protect the corporate stockholder (Husband 1938). But with the appearance of Paton and Littleton's monograph, accountants disregarded Husband's claim that many accounting procedures—i.e., computation of book value, treatment of a holding company's investment in a subsidiary, and the accounting decision about the nature of the stock dividend—were of a proprietary nature. The rejection of proprietary theory, despite its evident use, has been one of the consistent paradoxes of accounting theory.[20]

Merely changing the accounting equation to Assets = Equities did not signify acceptance of entity theory. The key question, never resolved, was the relationship of equity holders to the entity. The AAA publication, *Accounting and Reporting Standards for Financial Reporting–1957 Revision* attempted to separate "enterprise net income" from "net income to stockholders" to resolve some of the logical inconsistencies in earlier pronouncements. "Interest charges, income taxes, and true profit sharing distributions are not determinants of enterprise net income," the revision declared but added that, in "determining net income to shareholders . . . [they] . . . are properly included." The document was criticized for this stand with the assertion being made that business custom considered the first two costs (a view management undoubtedly wanted to perpetuate with regard to interest given income tax legislation). Arthur Kelley wrote that "it would seem highly desirable for accountants to follow business custom and adhere to one concept of corporate income, namely, net income to stockholders" (Kelley 1958). A more interesting criticism of this document was "that if the Committee had started the report by identifying the users of financial statements . . . and a discussion of the informational needs of one group of users [investors], the entire document probably would have been more oriented to the reasons why accounting is done" (Staubus 1958:11). The latter point is important since it gave recognition to the growing body of thought that suggested that the starting point of accounting theory was the development of decision models for particular user groups. It should have become clear that most accounting theories differed with respect to the enterprise-stockholder relationship.[21] By and large, proprietary concepts have significantly influenced the development of accounting principles, perhaps as a result of the proprietary nature of finance and microeconomic theory.

Sidney Alexander surveyed existing accounting and economic concepts of income and concluded that much of the debate was useless since there was no agreement on the nature of income. He outlined three basic income concepts as follows:

> Economic income—change over the period in capitalized value of dividends of this and future periods.
>
> Tangible income—economic income—change in value of good will over the period = total change in value of tangible equity

Accountant's income—tangible income—change in value of tangible assets not realized in the period, + change of value of tangible assets accrued in other periods and realized in this period = proceeds of all assets sold—costs assigned to those assets. (Alexander 1950)

He criticized accountants for their rigid adherence to objectivity and conservatism. And, most important, he clearly delineated three major issues which should become the focus of debate. He suggested that principal differences among concepts of income were (1) real versus the money measure (2) inclusion versus exclusion of capital gains and (3) accrual versus realization as the criterion for timing of a gain or loss. His suggestion that realization was dependent on the "critical" event, not necessarily sale, would encourage others to broaden that concept. (Alexander 1950) And, he divorced his discussion from traditional constraints of "proprietary" vs. "entity" theory.

William Vatter's *Fund Theory of Accounting and Its Implications for Financial Reports* (1947) challenged the focus on the right-hand side of the balance sheet. He argued that the dialogue between the enterprise-stockholder relationship was essentially fruitless. Accountants, he believed, should be indifferent to the question of to whom revenues accrue. Neutrality with respect to users, according to Vatter, would enable the accountant to focus on statistical summaries of changes in accounts. Fund theory did not require that the firm as a whole be regarded as the "entity." Instead, any separate group of assets, equities, or operating activities associated with the performance of a function or the attainment of a managerial goal could be viewed as a fund. Although Vatter's theory has been dismissed by many as inapplicable to corporate accounting, he has had, perhaps without acknowledgement, a definite impact on the evolution of accounting thought.

Most accounting theories prior to Vatter's work had been user oriented and had focused on the right hand side of the balance sheet. Given the constraints of double entry, the segregation of assets and expenses became a function of what the theorist considered the primary needs of users and which statement he felt was most important. The spate of literature discussing the "income statement" vs. "balance sheet" school gave implicit recognition to the arbitrariness of allocation within the accounting model and, somewhat inexplicably, the profession accepted the assertion that it could not develop two realistic statements simultaneously (Littleton and Zimmerman 1962: 158f). Vatter introduced a new consideration—the managerial view. Accountants seemed to assume that managerial and financial accounting theory were almost totally divorced; Vatter challenged that assumption. By focusing on separate entities within the firm, the question of the usefulness of allocation was reopened. But, most important, Vatter's work influenced other accountants who began to ask why, if management used information to predict future events, that same type of information would not be equally useful to investors who were trying to predict future earnings. Vatter's book reawakened interest in the managerial decision process and its applicability to financial accounting theory.

Managerial Accounting

Academic accountants did not exhibit much interest in managerial accounting prior to the 1950s. Despite the appearance of John M. Clark's *Studies in the Economics of Overhead Costs* (1923), which could have provided conceptual support for the development of managerial accounting theory, accountants showed little interest in developing principles of managerial accounting in the postdepression years. Most of the early research took place under the auspices of the National Association of Cost Accountants (NACA, which later became NAA). But research usually took the form of surveys of existing practice. This is not surprising as management was primarily concerned with survival in the 1930s; cost accountants focused on cost control, product costs, and defining cost elements (Bergstrom 1974). Especially popular were studies examining the methods used for allocation of costs. Walter McFarland writes that it soon became clear that such studies "gave the impression that accounting practice consisted of an unordered variety of different methods and procedures." In the 1940s, research was extended to find out not only what practice was being used but also why such practices were chosen (McFarland 1961). As managerial research began to focus on the reasons and utility of existing practice, attention was directed toward the managerial decision process.

Accountants had seemingly ignored the implications of Clark's assertion that there were different costs for different purposes. But they had suggested that perhaps allocation of costs was not particularly meaningful to managers. As early as 1936 Jonathan Harris published what appears to be the first technical paper on direct costing in an N A C A Bulletin. The interest in direct cost continued, with a proliferation of articles on the subject in the early 1950s. NAA Bulletin no. 23, "Direct Costing," was published in 1953; more accountants began to suggest that the procedure was relevant not only to management but to investors as well. Vatter and Hill dissented from the 1957 revision of the AAA statement on financial reporting standards because they believed that "direct costing is at least as acceptable in accounting theory as is the full cost concept."[22] They did not have widespread support in the late 1950s. But their views did not seem quite so radical, given the spate of research that occurred in the next decade.

Despite these initial efforts in the managerial area, Maurice Moonitz and Carl Nelson were able to conclude as late as 1960 that there was little theoretical literature in the field of managerial accounting (Moonitz and Nelson 1960). But interest was developing, as evidenced by the trend in Ph.D. dissertations in the late 1950s, when the amount of research in the managerial area surpassed that in the area of financial accounting theory. (Kirchner 1961)

American practitioners in the area of cost accounting, despite the "lack of managerial theory," had come to be regarded as having the most dynamic and aggressive approach to the subject in the world. The Organization for European Economic Co-operation looked to the United States to attempt to improve cost accounting methodology and, especially, to finalize methods of reducing operating costs.[23] Scientific management had spurred interest in efficiency, and industrial engineers and accountants had successfully introduced cost control into American business. But in accounting education, as well as in academic research, the primary focus had been on external reporting until the mid-1950s.

The trend in education had a significant impact on the subsequent development of the accounting profession. To fully understand the evolution of accounting theory and the demands for greater accountability and responsibility on the part of the profession, it is necessary to examine the change in business education.

Accounting Education

Despite persistent efforts by the AIA and the AAA to upgrade formal educational standards for CPAs, accountants continued to lag behind the traditional professions with respect to education. In 1934 the institute instructed its Committee on Education to conduct a survey of accounting education with special attention to college and university courses. The following year, the committee published partial results of its survey. One hundred and twenty three schools offered accounting courses, but only nine had programs that went beyond two years.

The committee suggested that the institute's goal be to implement a four-year college requirement, with at least 120 semester hours of study, divided into 60 hours of cultural study and 60 hours of professional subjects. Although the cultural studies were not prescribed, professional subjects had to include thirty-eight hours of accounting, supplemented with eight hours each in finance and commercial law and six hours in economics. The report also suggested that the institute develop standards to evaluate accounting programs—courses, faculty, libraries, resources, and so on—and begin enforcing such standards by 1940 (AIA, *Year Book 1936:* 46). As might be expected, a plan that gave practitioners authority to develop curriculum and, in fact, become the accrediting agency for accounting education did not find widespread support in the academic community.

The Response of the Academic Community

The AAA responded by outlining a 60/60 model curriculum correlated with the AIA's in 1937.[24] Not all educators were convinced that undergraduate training would be sufficient; but to have called for graduate training at a time when only one state (New York) had succeeded in convincing state legislators that a bachelor's degree should be the minimum requirement would have been foolhardy. Even New York's law would not be implemented until 1939. The call for a "liberal" education was not new and had repeatedly, if ineffectively, served as the model for designing accounting programs.

One of the enduring beliefs within the profession seems to have been that a CPA must be a "well rounded" person. One is able to find almost constant references to this as the objective of higher, and more particularly, accounting education. Kester and McCrea based their call for professional schools upon this objective. Anyone, they wrote, "who expects to enter a profession, should have a sufficiently broad knowledge of the so-called arts and sciences to give him a proper appreciation of present day civilization. He should know the major scientific facts about the world he lives in and should have an appreciation of the richer fruits of civilization, usually known as the fine or liberal arts" (McCrea and Kester 1936). T. E. Ross, in his address "What the Practitioner Looks for in the College Trained Accountant," reflected the same view. Education should instill in the prospective practitioner such attributes as character, integrity, discretion, judgment and industry, he said: thus liberal arts were fundamental to the training of any professional (Ross, T., 1940). Any historian encountering the repeated references to the value of the liberal arts must question whether that was not implicit recognition that accounting "professional" programs were viewed as mere technical proficiency and the accounting educator as the technician par excellence. Since accountants have a long tradition of denouncing mere "technical virtuousity" as insufficient training for a CPA, accounting academicians were not in an enviable position. The major debate centered on the amount of time to be devoted to "cultural" versus "professional" courses and "practical" versus "conceptual" approaches. One hypothesis is that there was a reluctance to accept the idea that accounting itself could or should be handled in a conceptual manner. Therefore, the profession looked to other disciplines to instill in the student the professional attributes it considered mandatory, while the accounting educator would fill the much more practical need for technical skill.[25]

There are many reasons that the profession can cite for the limited success in upgrading accounting programs (including the resistance of state legislators to promulgating higher standards). But a major factor seems to have been the pride many accountants had in being considered the most "open" of the professions. As late as the 1950s the desire to remain open seemed to continue. Arthur Cannon felt that a B.A. should be the normal prerequisite for entry, yet he still called for an "escape clause": "I'm still enough of a believer in the Abraham Lincoln or American Boy concept," he explained, "to want to leave some way for the occasional underprivileged or handicapped but otherwise qualified individual who may gain a[n] education by less common means" (Cannon 1956). Perhaps this belief in the viability of self-education was a heritage from the profession's early years when most practitioners had been self-taught.

Raising Educational Standards

The war years had the effect of suspending debate over the quality of accounting education. But a natural process did occur that, in fact, raised the level of education of those entering the profession. The GI Bill, combined with the ever-increasing number of white-collar jobs within the postwar economy, created an enrollment explosion in collegiate education. Therefore, despite the inability of accountants to establish uniform minimum educational requirements, the percentage of college graduates entering the profession rose from 60 percent in 1936 to 75 percent in 1955. By the latter year, the institute once again began examining means of improving the training process for CPAs.

The Commission on Standards of Education and Experience for CPAs issued its report in 1956 (commonly referred to as the Perry report after its chairman, Donald Perry) and renewed interest in the certification process. The commission recommended five criteria— college graduation, a qualifying entrance examination, a professional academic program, an internship, and completion of the uniform CPA examination—for admission to the profession. The educational requirements did not provoke great controversy because the commission suggested that accreditation of accounting programs be left to the joint efforts of the American Assembly of Collegiate Schools of Business and the Standards Rating Committee of the AAA.[26]

Practitioners, however, voiced strong opposition to the abandonment of a formal experience requirement. The Association of Certified Public Accountant Examiners had debated this issue the previous year and concluded that there was little support for such a measure. The examiners had formulated a compromise measure, a two-tier system, whereby a person would receive a certificate as a public accountant upon completion of the CPA examination and a CPA certificate after completion of three years' practical experience. The Perry commission concluded, however, that the CPA certificate signified no more than entrance-level competence, not attainment of professional competence. Henry Hill countered that if one expected other professionals (doctors and lawyers) to have practical experience, then certainly one "should support the idea that the newest and most recently made certified public accountant must have experience" (Hill 1956). Most of the commission members who dissented from the Perry report accepted this argument as valid.[27] They attacked what they believed was a basic inconsistency in recommending an internship if practical experience had no benefit.

The chief factor that mitigated against abandonment of the experience requirement seemed to be the inability of educators to measure the "quality" of academic programs. Diversity in standards had long plagued the profession, and disagreement existed about how one judged quality in any case. The director of research of the AIA had a simple solution. He conducted a survey and concluded that in "good" schools the percentage of people passing the CPA examination was eight times higher than in "bad" schools (Pedelahore 1956: 6). Academicians were not ready to agree that this was a significant test of quality. This issue was never resolved, and the experience requirement remained. But the profession shortly received a shock when two external studies suggested that the basic problem was inherent in the accounting curriculum, which was erroneously oriented toward CPA training. Academics and practitioners had rarely questioned whether or not accounting education should be directed toward the potential CPA. The profession had assumed that this was the primary function of university training. This certitude faced a provocative challenge with the issuance of the Pierson and the Gordon-Howell reports.[28]

External Pressure to Improve Business Education

Educators in all business disciplines were affected by the appearance in 1959 of the Pierson and the Gordon-Howell reports. Both studies concluded that mediocrity and vocationalism permeated business education, that students were not as bright or motivated as their liberal arts counterparts, and that faculties did not have proper academic credentials. Accountants could take some comfort from the fact that accounting students were generally considered superior to others within schools of business. But both academicians and practitioners viewed with dismay the suggestion that the study of accounting should be perceived primarily as an instrument to aid management in their day-to-day decisions. Academics felt that the reports failed to recognize the broad social role that an independent profession had and the social obligation that management had in a corporate economy. Raymond Dein felt that the reports were not "aware that accounting is the only discipline that supplies such vitally useful (if somewhat imprecise) information on the net income of business enterprises" which would facilitate social control (Dein 1961). Although it is true that neither the Pierson report nor the Gordon-Howell report recognized the social role of accountancy, it should be remembered that the same criticism had frequently been leveled at accounting educators.

The least difficult problem addressed by the reports was the upgrading of credentials for accounting faculty. By 1965 the AAA resolved that the doctoral degrees would be the standard academic credential, while a CPA certificate was considered beneficial but not essential. The association recommended a broad theoretical base for doctoral programs, with an emphasis on research (AAA 1965: 415–416). But academics did *not* deny the need for professional or technical training, they simply stated that such work should be completed prior to admission to the doctoral program.[29]

Academics did not respond quickly to the demands that undergraduate curriculum abandon its emphasis on financial accounting and auditing in favor of a managerial orientation, and the suggestion did not meet with widespread support. Practitioners explicitly rejected this proposal when a 1960 conference was held to study the issue, concluding instead that the university must remain "the principal seat of CPA training" in the United States and that the institute should issue a statement of objectives for accounting education. The objective statement, released in 1961, advocated that university education prepare a student "to learn to be" and not "to be" a CPA. The statement recognized that social, economic, and business theory were important and that accounting education must be oriented to "broad problem solving" and not to "specialized competence." The student, it was conceded, must be able to intelligently address managerial problems. But, not unexpectedly, practitioners concluded that future programs must be based on a "hard core of accounting, tax and auditing principles" (Bach et al. 1961: 18ff.).

Spurred by external criticism, the AIA, working with the Carnegie Mellon Foundation, sponsored a research study to determine a "common body of knowledge" for accountants. Robert Roy, an engineer, and James MacNeill, an accountant, undertook this study. By 1963 Roy was able to report that a comprehensive survey was being undertaken to determine the components of this body of knowledge. In 1967 the institute published *Horizons for a Profession* by Roy and MacNeil as a definitive statement on the training process for accountants. The authors outlined a broad academic program and endorsed a five-year educational requirement as well as the need for professional schools of accountancy. The latter recommendation, while not new, was given added impetus by the "new" look in business school curriculum that appeared to threaten the traditional CPA orientation of accounting programs.

The new emphasis in universities was on planning, management, and quantitative analysis. The prospect of students being educated through programs that deemphasized accounting, viewing it primarily as a "tool" of management, was not well received by CPAs. The profession had been responsible for introducing business disciplines into university curricula in many states; now it appeared that they would be ignored. Charles Horngren warned that the accounting curriculum must meet the challenge. He warned of "a takeover of the internal accounting function by mega-information specialists" and of the "disappearance of financial accounting as a legitimate subject worthy of study" unless accountants could provide a more conceptual, interdisciplinarian approach (Horngren 1971). The simplest solution to avoid encroachment was to establish professional schools with separate identities to ensure continuation of student identification with the public accounting profession. But that does not absolve accountants from answering the question of what is meant by professional education, an issue which has yet to be resolved.[30]

Leonard Spacek criticized the common-body-of-knowledge study because he believed that it was useless to "glibly address ourselves to such a fundamental task, [while] failing to recognize that the very premise of such an objective prevents its realization. . . . Until we can define the objectives of accounting principles, we cannot define the knowledge and intellectual habits or technical skills needed to apply them" (Spacek 1964B). Although the profession committed itself to the development of a conceptual framework with the establishment of the APB in 1959, there was validity in Spacek's charge that the objectives of accounting had been ill-defined.

Accounting Thought in Transition

Criticism of CAP and its method of determining accounting principles became more pronounced in the 1950s. Steady post–World War II inflation had renewed interest in replacement-cost accounting. And, although CAP did address itself to some of the practical problems that carried over from the 1920s (depreciation on appreciation, and so on), the committee failed to discuss the theoretical basis for departures from cost.[31] In 1948 SEC Chief Accountant Earle King called for a "definitive statement of principles" and avoidance of "optional treatments." His admonition that the AIA join with academicians to derive a statement as comprehensive as that of the AAA to leave no doubt about what is meant by generally accepted accounting principles seemed to go unheeded (King 1948). The institute did initiate an effort to develop a comprehensive theory in 1953 but soon after abandoned it.

Academics joined in the growing criticism of the "practice" orientation of practitioner-theorists. "Blueprint for Accounting Theory," by Raymond Chambers, challenged accountants to build up a theory without any reference to the practice of accounting (Chambers 1955). But perhaps the most stinging indictment, from a practitioner's point of view, came from one of their own, Leonard Spacek. In 1956 Spacek began to command attention in the popular press with his attacks on financial reporting practices. He termed CAP pronouncements as "generally accepted and antiquated accounting principles." Headlines that read "Accounting Has Failed to Prevent Major Misrepresentations" did not endear him to the profession (Carey 1969: 74). What was perhaps his most devastating criticism was his assertion that if CPAs had bothered to follow the objective standards that already existed, 95 percent of the abuses wouldn't have occurred. (Spacek 1958A) It became evident to the leaders of the AIA that unless they adopted a more satisfactory approach to developing accounting principles, self-regulation was threatened. Marquis Eaton, president of the Institute in 1956, established a committee on long-range objectives for the profession and suggested that a new program be designed to counter external criticism. It was left to Alvin Jennings, who succeeded Eaton, to outline the new plan.

Jennings, who has been described as one of the few CPAs who could bridge the gap between academicians and practitioners, seemed ideally suited for that task (Schur 1976). At the 1957 annual meeting of the institute, Jennings explained that CAP provided little, if any, opportunity for sound experimentation. Accounting principles, he said, should be regarded as arising from pure research. He suggested establishing a formal research organization within the institute which would seek the active cooperation of the academic community (Jennings 1957). The function of this research body would be to conduct a continuous examination and re-examination of accounting assumptions in order to develop authoritative principles. After some delay, Jennings' proposal was accepted and formed the basis for the organization of the Accounting Principles Board (APB), which came into existence in the fall of 1959.[32] The by-laws of the APB endorsed the idea that research studies precede official pronouncements, whenever possible, to provide guidance to the board. But these studies, although informative, were to be considered "tentative only" and the board was to issue "a clear statement" with each study indicating whether "it has been approved or disapproved by the institute" (AICPA 1959: 20) But despite this original endorsement of normative research, it also became clear that practitioners would continue to insist that theory be "practical."

The Primacy of Practicality

Throughout the turmoil in the late 1950s, as accountants sought to find a way to curb criticism of financial reporting practices, there

John W. Queenan.   Alvin R. Jennings, Carman Blough.

Source: AICPA.   Source: AICPA.

continued to be resistance to change. May was somewhat skeptical
about the call for reform. He said that forty years in the profession
convinced him that every proposal for material change met with one
of two objections: "Either, the proposal is inadequate and nothing
should be done in the matter until the subject is dealt with comprehensively (e.g. ARB 33) or that the proposal is too sweeping and
that the subject should be dealt with piece by piece" (May 1957A).
Although the APB advocated normative research studies, May was
probably correct in his belief that major changes would be difficult to
implement. The leaders of the institute still stressed practicality as a
vital element of "good" accounting theory. Jennings issued what
could be deemed a pragmatic restatement when he said, "where
science looks within the fact to discover the principle, accounting
looks, or should look, to the desired end result" (Jennings 1958A).
Weldon Powell, the first chairman of the APB, quickly moved away
from earlier contentions that the development of accounting principles should be regarded as pure research. By 1961 he emphasized

that "research in accounting is more in the nature of applied research than of pure research, an important criterion is the usefulness of its results." Since the APB had placed great emphasis on examining four levels of broad problems of financial accounting (postulates, principles, rules, or other guides for applying principles in specific situations and research), Powell probably surprised some accountants by suggesting that the first step in any research program should be to study prevailing practice (Powell 1961). This statement foretold the reception that Accounting Research Studies (ARS) no. 1 and no. 3 would receive from practitioners and the APB.

Postulates and Principles

In 1958 the institute's Special Committee on Research issued its report. The committee recommended that early research be directed toward identifying postulates and principles of accounting: "Postulates are few in number and are the basic assumptions on which principles rest." The committee recommended that "a fairly broad set of co-ordinated principles should be formulated on the basis of the postulates." The report concluded that "the principles, together with the postulates, should serve as a framework of reference for the solution of detailed problems." (AIA, "Special Committee on Research" 1958: 62) Maurice Moonitz agreed to undertake a study of accounting postulates and then joined with Robert Sprouse to define accounting principles. No. 1, *The Basic Postulates of Accounting* (1961), met with a very subdued response.[33] An editorial in the *Journal of Accountancy* noted that "few accountants should find any difficulty in agreeing with these and other postulates . . . most are self-evident" (September 1961: 36). It was precisely this point that led William Vatter to question whether the study served any useful purpose. He argued that most of the so-called postulates were not basic assumptions of accounting but, rather, "general descriptions, rationalizations of double entry, and/or statements of existing conditions" (Vatter 1963). But most accountants appeared to be reserving judgment on this study until after the principles statement was completed.

ARS No. 3, *Tentative Set of Broad Accounting Principles for Business Enterprises* (1962), probably signaled the demise of any attempts to adopt a normative research orientation for the APB. The board issued the following statement with respect to the research studies on principles and postulates. "We are treating these two studies as conscientious attempts by the accounting research staff to resolve major accounting issues, which, however, contain inferences and recommendations in part of a speculative and tentative nature. . . . [W]hile these studies are a valuable contribution to accounting thinking, they are too radically different from presently generally accepted accounting principles for acceptance at this time."[34] Members of the APB were widely divided on the advisability of releasing the study. Nine comments by board members were attached to the monograph, only one being completely favorable. The dissents covered a broad range of view, from Leonard Spacek's assertion that there need only be one concern for accountants, "fairness," to Paul Grady's contention that one must begin the search for principles by summarizing generally accepted accounting principles as of the present time, the "inventory approach," which the APB ultimately endorsed.

William Shenkir's analysis of ARS No. 3 concludes that "the study's focus on the measurement of assets and liabilities shattered tradition and differed from the cost and revenue allocation model that the APB had inherited from CAP" (Shenkir 1974). Raymond Marple deplored the willingness of the authors to abandon historic limitations on concepts of profits, that is, profits "available for dividends" and "subject to taxation." He predicted that if practitioners failed to address themselves to such specific needs, two events would occur. First, management would be convinced that accounting data were useless and, second, financial analysts would simply begin focusing on cash rather than accounting profit. Marple suggested a very narrow role for the accountant: "if accounting is to serve the business and financial community—and it has *no other use*—its practitioners must never forget that the only test of good practice is its usefulness in developing information for the purpose for which the information is to be used" (Marple 1963). But the greatest antagonism was generated by the suggestion that historical cost was not the bedrock of accounting measurement.[35]

John Queenan, president of the AICPA in 1962, hoped that his fellow practitioners would offer "constructive criticism" of these research studies. But his pleas seemed to go unheeded as most of the dissent could not be labeled "constructive" (Queenan 1962). Jennings indicated that the lack of enthusiasm for these studies "was largely responsible for a definite, if subtle shift, in the direction of the Board's efforts." The APB decided to take a less "risky" approach and place "greater stress on solutions of particular problems" (Jennings 1964). Paul Grady was commissioned to do an inventory, identifying principles that appeared to have achieved general acceptance. Surprisingly, the APB did not examine the previous ramifications that such a policy had had on the development of acceptable principles. Grady's study, although comprehensive, was not unlike the Sanders, Hatfield, and Moore work, which had surveyed existing practice in the 1930s.[36] It had been conceded that the latter effort had provided inadequate guidance for CAP; yet practice, once again, became the starting point for theory.

The Decline of the APB

Attempting to establish "principles" from generally accepted practice that differed markedly among firms proved to be no easy task for the APB. The board had little power to force compliance with its pronouncements. As Weldon Powell noted, it had to rely on persuasion rather than compulsion (Powell 1961). Since the SEC had indicated, over a number of years, that it sought to reduce the alternatives in accounting practice, one might have expected the commission to have supported all efforts by the APB to narrow alternatives. But the investment credit issue seriously undermined the authority and viability of the board.

The investment credit was a tax incentive designed to stimulate capital investment. The APB, forced to act quickly, could not gain a consensus on the proper treatment of this item and, perhaps precipitously, prohibited the "flow through" method, thereby preventing the full income impact of the credit from being reported in the year of investment. Since the motivation for passage of such a credit was to improve the economic outlook, policy leaders in Washington were not pleased. Management was distressed because their earnings, they believed, would be understated, and the SEC had to reconcile the interests of these various groups. Manuel Cohen explained that the SEC, consistent with its administrative policy, found substantial authoritative support for using alternative treatments to the board's preference for a "deferred" treatment. Indeed, three of the Big-Eight firms announced they would not follow APB No. 2.[37] Thus the SEC decided it would not bind registrants to APB No. 2 (Cohen 1964). Given the direction of earlier SEC pronouncements, which indicated that the agency would support all efforts to reduce alternatives, this announcement seriously undermined the APB's claim to authority for the establishment of accounting principles.

Accountants must have been surprised to read SEC Commissioner Bryon D. Woodside's statement that "I believe . . . it is better to have some looseness—the creaking of a joint, if you will—some sacrifice of the ultimate in consistency and uniformity and acceptability under such a system than to seek a rule." He admonished the APB that the "task you set for yourselves to force conformity on matters of accounting principle where there is not in fact acceptability of conformity, I think, is an impossible one." Woodside made it clear that the APB must rely on education and persuasion, not on the SEC. "Those who wish to compel conformity, or rather seek to have us compel conformity, for only we have the tools," he wrote, "are no doubt less than happy with the approach." But he made clear that the SEC would not compel compliance (Woodside 1964). In retrospect, even those associated with the SEC would acknowledge that the strength of the APB had been undermined by the government agency. John C. Burton has characterized the association of the SEC and the AICPA as a "partnership" designed to provide federal support for accounting principles established by the profession. Although accountants are not so sanguine, as one practitioner stated, "There are *partners* and there are *Partners.*" Burton considered the investment credit episode as a conspicuous exception to the rule. He explained that the SEC "concluded that it would not support an opinion when representatives of leading accounting firms had not only voted against it but that they would not require their clients to abide by it." Burton said that the "commission was not enforcing a view contrary to the Board but rather refusing to enter a dispute among major firms on the side which the Board favored." "In retrospect," Burton concluded, "it is the judgement of most parties involved that the Commission made an error in declining to support the Board," adding "it is certainly clear than neither the profession nor the Board benefited from the episode which ultimately culminated ten years later in an act of Congress which enshrined the diverse practices which had been used" (Burton 1974: 269). The board, forced to yield in this matter, found it even more difficult to gain general acceptance of its authority to set standards.

The AICPA attempted to strengthen the rules of professional conduct to enhance compliance with APB opinions. In 1965 a resolution was passed making it a "requirement to disclose deviations from generally accepted accounting principles in an auditor's certificate." But the AICPA had no effective sanction to impose upon any accountant who failed to disclose departures from the Generally Accepted Accounting Principles (GAAP).[38] By 1962 the need for compromise in order to gain a consensus on every issue seemed to mandate that accounting principles were to be defined in terms of existing practice and not based on normative considerations.

Academicians began to raise serious questions about the effectiveness of principles derived in such a manner.

Academic Research Efforts

Littleton's *Structure of Accounting Theory* (1953) attempted to use the "scientific method" to establish a new theory of accounting. Littleton defined the central objective of accounting in traditional terms: "the central purpose of accounting is to make possible the periodic matching of costs (efforts) and revenues (accomplishments)." He described this concept as the "benchmark" that affords a fixed point of reference for accounting theory (Littleton 1953: 30). Criticism of Littleton's work was widespread, not only for his alleged failure to fully understand the scientific and deductive process, but also for his narrow conception of accounting's role. Chambers contended that Littleton described the center of accounting as it then existed. The important question, he suggested, was not how but why income is calculated. Accountants had to be concerned with "all fields of human action," if they hoped to be able to communicate relevant information to various user groups. People need information for decision making, and the accountant's job was to convey information concerning both income and financial condition (Chambers 1955).

The reunification of managerial and financial accounting theory had introduced new questions with respect to the role of financial reporting. The charge was made that arbitrary financial reporting practices, designed to measure "realized" not "economic" income, had intruded upon the economic decision making process and had an adverse effect on the rational allocation of resources. Sidney Davidson asked how accountants could justify retaining a theory (or set of practices) that, in some cases, "penalized" management for making rational economic decisions (Davidson 1963A). The question of allocation was being reexamined. But perhaps more important, accountants began to ask why certain "basic" concepts had evolved and if these accepted concepts were, in fact, fundamental to the financial reporting process.

"Realization," which justified in the minds of many the differences found between accounting and economic income, came under attack. Why, many people were asking, must accountants report realized income? Did this enhance users' abilities to make decisions? As these types of questions were being raised, it became apparent that accountants should, perhaps, be concerned with a more fundamental dispute, namely that the accepted concept, realization, meant different things to different people.

The AAA's Committee on Realization issued a report in 1965 that stated realization occurred when "a change in an asset or liability has become sufficiently definite and objective to warrant recognition in the accounts." The important factor was that the Committee reunited asset valuation with income determination by broadening the concept. They recommended that the change in value of all assets except goodwill which was supported by adequate evidence be recognized. (AAA, 1965, 312f) By attempting to reconcile accounting income with economic concepts of wealth, the AAA moved toward discussion of fundamental conceptual issues.

The call for normative research accelerated and accountants began to reexamine basic concepts. Despite the fact that Sprague and Canning had recognized the primacy of answering such questions as what is an asset, the profession had not effectively addressed this issue. With the primacy of the matching model, assets had become residuals and one finds nondefinitions such as the Institute's description of an asset, accepted.[39]

George Sorter and Charles Horngren challenged conventional theory and suggested that "relevancy" could be the primary determinant of whether or not an asset existed. They argued that Paton and Littleton's dictum that "costs attach" had been widely misinterpreted and that their subsequent statement that "accounting is concerned with economic attributes and [concern over] measurements, . . ." had been largely overlooked. They wrote that if one is concerned primarily with economic attributes, then the asset-expense measurement problem becomes dependent on two factors—future expectations and relevance. The authors concluded that, if this were so, then only one rule was necessary for asset determination, namely, that "a cost is carried forward, if, and only if, it has a favorable economic effect on total future costs or total future revenues" (Sorter and Horngren 1962). This idea did not go unchallenged, but it did foreshadow the direction that the next definitive work of the AAA, *A Statement of Basic Accounting Theory* (1966) would take.

This AAA study attempted to examine accounting theory without regard to existing practice, and its four basic standards provided direction without prescription for the development of theory. Throughout the early 1960s accountants were attempting to reconcile economic and accounting theory and presenting new ideas on ways to develop a "scientific" accounting theory. One of the early leaders in the drive for a more rigorous accounting methodology was Richard Mattessich. He advocated in one instance a "mathematical theorem," gradually expanding his methodology to develop a general theory of accounting by using the methodology of any applied science (Mattessich 1957, 1972). Simultaneously, accounting academics were being introduced to more sophisticated quantitative tools. W. W. Cooper, A. C. Charnes, and Yuji Ijiri significantly influenced the future direction of academic research with their early work, which would be widely used in later empirical research.[40]

The argument that accounting theory must be "useful" and give practical results was being challenged from all sides. Determining what is "useful" and "to whom," it was suggested, had substituted the accountant's judgment for that of users. The assertion being made was that traditional accounting theory produced little reliable information for outside judgments (since the data had been censored) which afforded effective control over business (Hylton, 1962). The whole question of the financial reporting process came under scrutiny, with serious criticism being raised about the viability of an approach that presumed that accountants knew "user's needs" when, in fact, that was simply not true. Carl Nelson, like William Morse Cole fifty years earlier, contended that accounting information is unsatisfactory if "the profits of the accountant have no economic significance." Nelson concluded that continuation of the traditional historic cost approach was justified only if people were looking at accounting "as a more expensive Miltown, a non-oral tranquilizer" (Nelson 1967).

Accounting Practice: The Challenge of the 1960s

An historical analysis of accounting practice in the 1960s remains importantly inchoate. Although it is possible to examine new ideas and philosophies, their ramifications will not be discernible for many years.

Subjugation of Shareholders

In the late 1950s there was a proliferation of literature challenging the viability of capitalism. One thesis that has caused a reassessment of the public accountant's role is that of "subjugation of stockholders." Edith Penrose argued that managers did not care any more about stockholders than they did about creditors or any other supplier of funds (a thesis developed by Paton in *Acccounting Theory* in 1922 and generally ignored by the accounting profession). Penrose wrote that the stockholder was viewed as a "quasi-creditor" who must be paid enough to keep silent and content, so as not to interfere with management's major objective of retaining within the firm as large a portion as possible of funds generated by operations. The aim was to control corporate assets without interference (Penrose 1959). One finds a considerable acceptance of this thesis as the literature becomes more critical of accounting for failing to fulfill what now was perceived as a traditional role—investor protection.

Howard Greer wrote that the investor finds "his hired help has no intention of letting him share fully in any earnings . . . since earnings, he is told in paternal tones, must be re-invested for growth and development, for protection in industry position, for social welfare projects, which improve the corporate image." Greer criticized accountants for not being able to aid the confused investor to determine how his firm was doing, for he was told that income could be figured six different ways, all having official sanction (Greer 1964). The problem of income determination, always complex because of the uncertainty in the business environment, became more controversial as a steady inflationary trend continued and reopened questions about the relevance of "reported" income.

Auditing in the 1960s

Expectations have a decided impact on the perceived adequacy of financial reports. Despite years of disclaiming that auditors could or did "certify" to exact results, public expectations differed markedly from those of the auditor. As early as 1939 John Haskell (New York Stock Exchange) warned that what the public expects the auditor to do (especially with respect to defalcations) and what the auditor believes is feasible to do are widely divergent (Haskell 1939: 12f.). In the 1960s criticism of the profession accelerated as various interest groups expressed widely differing conceptions of the scope of the auditor's role.

One survey showed that the general public, bankers, and investors delineated a broad role for CPAs, while corporate executives viewed auditors as "non-questioning reporters" working within the confines of GAAP. The SEC may unwittingly have fostered this latter view by insisting that independent accountants state that financial statements were in accordance with GAAP. Although accountants have never been absolved from assessing risk and determining that a particular practice, permissible under GAAP, was appropriate in a given circumstance, there seems to have been, during the 1950s, a general impression among managers that auditors could not reject the use of an "accepted" principle. Indeed, the profession had little power to force management to use any specific procedures. And a few auditors seemed to believe that one of the most fundamental concepts of the profession—that financial statements not be misleading—had somehow been superceded by GAAP. It took a court case to vividly remind auditors that fairness was still an essential quality, and that "fairness" could not be modified by the words "in accordance with GAAP."

Bankers began complaining in the 1960s that GAAP had become almost a cliché. They argued that accounting practices, while they may have been appropriate to previous generations, failed to recognize the changing needs of creditors. In the early decades of the century, most loans were short term and, therefore, working capital analysis and conservative valuations of accounts receivable and inventories were applauded by bankers. But by the 1960s most major banks were engaged in long-term or "cash-flow lending." Bankers wanted to predict future cash flows and maintained that this was impossible given the inconsistencies in GAAP. Moreover, they noted that the flexibility of GAAP made it impossible to compare company reports even within the same industry (Laeri 1966). Despite the SEC's emphasis on disclosure, there was some merit to the bankers' claims that inadequate information was being provided for both bankers and small investors. Auditors had, to some extent, become reporters; and the accounting profession was chided for placing too much reliance on GAAP.

Corporate Social Responsibility

Although accountants have attempted to respond positively to government demands for disclosure for investor protection, they have been reluctant to extend their activities to become societal "watchdogs."[41] In the early 1940s accountants contended that "if the social aspects of accounting had not been recognized in the past, the fault, in a measure, at least, lay in the fact that accountants did not occupy a sufficiently independent position" (Dohr 1941). But during the Roosevelt years, accountants continued to view their role as enhancing social welfare by facilitating the accumulation of capital within a manufacturing oriented society. An accounting framework had developed based on microeconomic theory and, generally, social measurement was left to economists. This is not an indictment of the profession, for there is little evidence to suggest that politicians or the public expected more. The Temporary National Economic Commission turned to economists in its attempt to stimulate interest in social statistics. Accountants, viewing their work as practical, considered the notions in the commission's Monograph No. 7 ("Measurement of Social Performance of Business") with disbelief. Social analysis of corporate performance was not considered to be within the traditional scope of the profession's responsibilities, and it seemed that many practitioners hoped that that would continue to be the case.

During the 1960s the question was raised about whether CPAs should be making implicit value judgments or simply reporting economic events for use by others in society for control over business (Hylton 1962). There was evidence of a growing recognition within the profession that accounting theory could not be divorced from broad social considerations.

Carl Devine, writing in 1960 ("Research Methodology and Accounting Theory"), supported the scientific method but indicated that by itself, it would not solve the problems facing the profession. He noted that although accountants could not be expected to significantly alter the ethical standards of society, they must still consider their social responsibilities and develop a practical structure to help fulfill social goals (Devine 1960).

Accountants spent most of the 1960s trying to define the concept of "corporate social responsibility."[42] Whenever specific standards had been set in the political sector (i.e., war on poverty, city planning, environmental reporting) to implement specific social goals, the profession could and did respond.

The Implication of Administrative Theory

The crusade of the gospel of efficient markets as applied to accounting disclosure suggested to some that the furor over financial statements was meaningless. The market, it was held, could not be "fooled" by accounting information that was not timely since it had, in any case, been already discounted by the market. But the theory, although applicable to the market as a whole, is not applicable to the individual investor, the specialist, or the creditor. With the rise of institutional investors, large international corporations, and powerful organized exchanges, politicians were feeling the popular pressure of consumerism and became more, not less, concerned with the individual. Traditional concerns for individual rights and public protection from the abuses of big business were rekindled. The accountant, once again, was called upon to protect the individual. The auditor's role became more complex as some demanded that the profession assess and disclose the economic "power" and social conduct of various interest groups, not merely "report" on cold financial statistics.

It was becoming apparent during the 1960s that the accounting profession would have to acknowledge and participate in the achievement of broader corporate accountability. A basic problem seems to have been that the profession did not know how to respond to these new expectations because it lacked understanding of its role within the constraints of administrative theory.

Administrative theory posits that a unification of pluralism (recognition of various competing interest groups) and capitalism, once having been completed, leads to alienation and discontent when Congress delegates authority to administrative agencies. With little day to day control being vested in the "visible" public sector, government becomes but one of the many interest groups in society and cannot provide the leadership necessary to regulate the economy except in so far as it can bargain with other interest groups. Lowi contended that delegation of responsibility from Congress to an independent agency was once viewed as a problem but has now become a virtue in its own right. It places big government on an equal basis with other interest groups and preserves the illusion of democracy (Lowi 1969: 67). Whether this analysis is correct or not is open to question. But it can be seen that the proliferation of regulatory agencies, each with a mandate to protect certain interest groups, makes it more difficult for the accounting profession to respond to popular demands for data that can assist in fulfilling the "social control" objectives following from administrative theory. Within the realm of social measurement, it is not clear what the accountant's duties are or how financial reports can serve multiple, and often antagonist, interest groups.

The challenge to traditional assumptions about managerial motives did not cause a significant change in accounting practice in the early 1960s. But in the latter half of the decade questions were being asked about the reliance on "traditional" theory in the new corporate era. Carl Nelson predicted the implications that administrative theory would have for accounting in this era of political awareness when he wrote that accountancy must be guided by the "social purposes that society expects our profession to fulfill." Therefore, he noted,

> our measurement and decision rules are influenced by conflicting group pressures and the profession must, therefore, exhibit enough stubborn honesty to "preserve equity," at least in the measuring and reporting sense, among the groups according to the hierarchy of worthiness established by social attitudes. (Nelson 1960: 56).

NOTES

1. For a discussion of the problems created by the depression, see William Paton, "Accounting Problems of the Depression," *Accounting Review* (December 1932), pp. 258–267. Paton explains the concept of income smoothing as developing "accounting and statistical procedures to result in the averaging of operating data, the elimination of modifications of the peaks of prosperity and the valleys of depression so far as the showing of net profits are concerned . . ." (p. 261). For an overview of the recent literature on the topic, see Joshua Ronen, Simcha Sadan, and C. S. Snow, "Income Smoothing: A Review," *The Accounting Journal* (Winter 1976), pp. 11–22.

2. For an accountant's view of the impact this law had on financial reporting, see Herman W. Bevis, *Corporate Financial Reporting In A Competitive Economy* (New York: Macmillan, 1965), pp. 20ff. The Employment Act of 1946 was Public Law 340 of the 79th Congress.

3. See Frank A. Kottke, "Mergers and Acquisitions of Large Manufacturing Companies, 1951–1959," *Review of Economics and Statistics*, November 1959, pp. 430–433. Kottke surveyed 1001 manufacturing firms in existence on January 1, 1951: 854 survived the decade; of the 147 that disappeared, 138 were in operation, having been acquired by larger firms. This gave a survival rate of better than 99 percent for large firms in the decade.

4. See also A. A. Berle and Gardiner Means, *The Modern Corporation and Private Property* (New York: The MacMillan Co., 1933) and A. A. Berle, *Twentieth Century Capitalist Revolution* (New York: Harcourt Brace & Co., 1954). But, while Berle and Means question managerial motives, they, unlike Schumpeter, do not conclude the system cannot survive.

5. The conclusion may have been new, i.e., the focus on the income statement; but the idea that predictions of future earning power was of major importance to investors had long been accepted. For an overview, see Richard Brief, "Assets, Valuation and Matching," in *Proceedings of the Charles Waldo Haskins History Seminar, 1976* (New York: Ross Institute, New York University, 1977).

6. See William Douglas, *Go East Young Man*, vol. 1 (N.Y.: Random House, 1974), pp. 27ff., for a description of the division within the commission. The chief accountant was instrumental in maintaining the balance for standard setting in the private sector, according to some reports. For an analysis of legislative intent, see Wiesen, 1978, 110ff.

7. See, for example, Victor Stempf, "The Post War Challenge " (AIA 1943: 1–8). For details of the case and accountants' views of McKesson-Robbins, see "Testimony of Expert Witnesses at S.E.C. Hearings." *Journal of Accountancy* (April, May 1939), pp. 199–203, 279–297.

8. Although the subject of internal control and audit scope has been widely discussed in the postwar years, some practitioners feel the issue has not been resolved. One commentator has said that, despite the various pronouncements, "the definition of internal control has been in a penumbra, and criteria for evaluation have yet to be set."

9. The AIA spent much of the 1940s examining existing auditing procedures. Paul Grady was a leader in this area. In 1947 a "Tentative Statement of Auditing Standards—Their Generally Accepted Significance and Scope" was published. The contemporary format of dividing standards into three areas—objective standards for (1) field work and (2) reporting, and subjective standards (3) personal and general guidance—was adopted. The same format was used in the 1954 statement "Generally Accepted Auditing Standards—Their Significance and Scope." The SEC had solidified the auditor's position when in 1941 it required that the scope paragraph be extended to include a direct representation of compliance with basic auditing standards, thus giving the institute's pronouncements legitimacy.

10. Maurice Moonitz, in *Obtaining Agreement on Standards in the Accounting Profession*, AAA Study in Accounting Research, No. 8 (1974), p. 20ff., contends that the Sanders, Hatfield, and Moore study was largely ignored, and that was probably true of academics after the initial criticism. But it is not equally clear that the practitioners ignored the work.

11. On January 1, 1938, 22,632 people held CPA certificates; 17,030 of these people were in practice. The total membership of the AIA, associate and full, was only 4989, and membership in all state societies totaled only 8507. The majority of CPAs did not choose to affiliate with professional organizations. And the AIA could not even control its own members and force compliance with opinions issued in these early years, since no effective penalty for noncompliance existed.

12. All references to CAP refer to letters and memoranda found in the Committee on Accounting Procedure correspondence on file at the AICPA library in New York.

13. Carter (1933: 55ff.), in his testimony before the House Committee on Banking and Currency, warned that statements for a single year could be misleading because of the artificial time constraints and suggested that the SEC require comparative statements for at least a three-year period to facilitate prediction.

14. The AIA pronouncements adopted the current operating concept of income that excluded from the income statement all unusual and nonrecurring gains and losses. The AAA 1936, 1941, and 1948 statements advocated the all-inclusive concept of income that favored reporting all gains and losses on the income statement. Somewhat inexplicably, the 1957 AAA statement departed somewhat from the all-inclusive concept and was severely criticized. See, for example, George Staubus, "Comments on 'Accounting and Reporting Standards for Corporate Financial Statements—1957 Revision,'" *Accounting Review* (January 1958), pp. 11–24.

15. The three procedures were: (1) amortization over the life of the old bond issue, (2) amortization over the life of the new bond issue, and (3) direct write-off to surplus.

16. Although practitioners could be accused of yielding to clients in this case, it should be mentioned that after the economic downturn in 1938, political leaders would not have looked favorably on any method that might cause a decrease in reported corporate earnings.

17. See Herbert Freeman, "Unamortized Discount and Premium on Bonds Refunded," *Journal of Accountancy*, December 1939, for a discussion of the

question of unamortized bond discount as handled by California regulatory agencies with a "uniform" system. Accounting convenience justified departure from direct write-offs to surplus in the minds of public utility commissioners, who permitted, within a three-year period, all three methods discussed by CAP.

18. For a discussion of corporate financial reports that departed from historic cost, and examples of such departures, see Arthur H. Dean, *An Inquiry into the Nature of Business Income Under Present Price Levels*. New York: AIA 1950.

19. Percival F. Brundage was chairman of the study group. Accountants had always worked closely with the bureau. Sterrett had been one of its founders and one of the original directors. He had been succeeded by his partner May, who had been an active force within the bureau. One position on the bureau had been reserved for accountants through an agreement made upon the founding of the bureau, and the institute retained close ties with the bureau.

20. For an analysis of the cost-allocation doctrine as developed by the AAA studies, see Harvey T. Deinzer, *Development of Accounting Thought* (New York: Holt, Rinehart and Winston, 1965), chaps. 6 and 7.

21. This study cannot hope to review all the theories that have been forthcoming in academia, but the reader may wish to consult Eldon S. Hendriksen, *Accounting Theory* (Homewood, Ill.: Irwin, Inc., 1976), for a more extensive overview.

22. Quoted in Sidney Davidson, "Old Wine in New Bottles," *Accounting Review*, April 1963, p. 280. In this article Davidson's reviews Clark's book, mentioned above, and notes that it had had little impact for many years. He also states that he probably should have joined Hill and Vatter in their dissent, having been convinced by subsequent work of the appropriateness of their position.

23. See *Cost Accounting and Productivity, the Use and Practice of Cost Accounting in the U.S.A.*, Organization for European Economic Cooperation, 1952.

24. The AAA did not limit itself to one program, outlining programs ranging from a minimum of thirty-three hours to a maximum of eighty-seven. See Hermann Miller, "A Suggested Program of Education for the Accountant," *Accounting Review*, June 1937, for a discussion of the need for graduate education.

25. The remedies suggested from 1936 to the present day have not been dissimilar. Accountants have periodically determined that a five-year program would be beneficial, that liberal arts studies are beneficial, and that education makes the experience requirement obsolete. See, for example, the AIA 1936 Committee on Education Report; AIA 1956 Committee on Education and Experience.

26. For an overview, see Donald F. Perry, *Public Accounting Practice and Accounting Education* (Boston: Houghton-Mifflin, 1955), which, not unexpectedly, parallels the institute's report.

27. For a summary of dissenting opinions, see J. Earl Pedelahore, "Case for the Dissent," Address at the Annual Meeting of the AIA, September 23, 1956 (AICPA Library, New York).

28. See Franklin Pierson et al., *The Education of American Businessmen* (New York; McGraw Hill, 1954), and R. A. Gordon, and J. E. Howell, *Higher Education for Business* (New York: Columbia University Press).

29. Issues that create a schism between academicians and practitioners seem to have broad popular appeal. Thus one finds articles such as Paul J. Aslanian and John T. Duff, "Why Accounting Teachers Are So Academic," *Journal of Accountancy*, October 1973, pp. 47–53, which quotes this particular AAA committee as stating that "there should be no auditing, CPA review, federal income taxation, governmental accounting, and accounting systems . . ." in doctoral programs. Although the quote is accurate, it probably creates an erroneous impression, since the authors neglect to say that the AAA committee on doctoral programs said that, if a person did not have this type of technical skill, then such courses should be required but as remedial work, not as part of the doctoral program.

30. There has been a proliferation of articles on the topic of professional schools. But despite the frequency with which such articles appear, there is some doubt that "professional" schools signify acceptance of "professional" academic training. In the late 1950s there appeared in the *Accounting Review* a wealth of articles on the topic of the future of accounting education, which ask some questions that have remained unanswered. See for example, Peter A. Firmin, "Educating Tomorrow's Accountant," October 1957; R. J. Canning, "Training for an Accounting Career," July 1958; and P. Fertig, "Organization of an Accounting Program," April 1960.

31. For an overview of the long debate over replacement cost, see the CAP correspondence file for 1940, which includes memoranda on the subject from William Paton, Gilbert Byrne, A. C. Littleton, Henry Fernald, and others. Only Fernald supported adjustments for inflation, but it became clear that the academic community seriously questioned the ability of the profession to handle this problem. See, for example, *Proceedings of the International Congress* (1948).

32. See AICPA 1959 and AICPA, *Minutes, 1959*, p. 50ff., AICPA Library, for a discussion of the basic organization and approach of the APB. The APB's first meeting was held on September 11, 1959.

33. Only Leonard Spacek of the advisory board felt strongly enough to have a formal comment published in the research study. See "Comments of Leonard Spacek," ARS No. 1, pp. 56–57.

34. See "News Report," *Journal of Accountancy*, April 1962, pp. 9–10. A "Statement by the Accounting Principles Board," April 13, 1962, was attached to each copy of the research study issued publicly and contained the above disclaimer.

35. This antagonism toward the proposal to abandon historical cost and stabilized earnings was understandable in the light of the phenomenon of "going public" in the 1960s. Numerous small corporations chose that course under the SEC's Regulation A; therefore, large numbers of persons had an interest in maintaining stable earnings.

36. See Paul Grady, *Inventory of Generally Accepted Accounting Principles for Business Enterprises* (New York: AICPA, 1965). Grady had apparently begun lobbying for such an approach with the issuance of ARS No. 2. See also Paul Grady, "The Quest for Accounting Principles," *Journal of Accountancy*, May 1962.

37. The largest eight public accounting firms in the United States are known as the "Big Eight." Alphabetically, they are Arthur Andersen; Arthur Young; Coopers & Lybrand; Deloitte, Haskins and Sells; Ernst and Ernst; Peat, Marwick and Mitchell; Price Waterhouse; and Touche Ross.

38. See "News Report," *Journal of Accountancy*, January 1970, pp. 29, which discussed the defeat of a proposal to make failure to disclose departures from GAAP a violation of the code of ethics of the institute. Woodside expressed the view of most of the opponents when he said that the opinions must stand on their own merit; if they could not, they deserved to be ignored, without penalty, by any practitioner.

39. ARB No. 43 defined an asset "as something represented by a debit balance that is or would be carried forward upon the closing of the books of accounts according to the rules or principles of accounting (provided such a debit balance is not in effect a negative balance applied to a liability) on the basis that it represents either a property right or value acquired, or an expenditure made which has created property rights or is properly applied to the future."

40. See for example, Y. Ijiri, "Break-Even Budgeting and Programming to Goals," *Journal of Accounting Research*, Spring 1963.

41. Accountants in the 1960s began to address these issues. The reader should examine the work of the AICPA's Committee on Social Measurement.

42. See David Linowes, "Development of Social Economic Accounting," *Journal of Accountancy*, November 1968, pp. 37–42.

8 THE AGE OF POLITICAL ACCOUNTANCY: ACCOUNTING FACES AN IDENTITY CRISIS

> *Recent developments suggest that accounting is a series of political decisions which we now call accounting principles.*
>
> [Herbert E. Miller]

The Mystery Profession[1]

Alistair Cooke observes that the object of Columbus' venture, which would lead him to the American continent, was two-fold: "For Gospel and for Gold " (Cooke 1973: 32). In short, Columbus chose to be known as both a missionary and a merchant. Yet he came to fame as an explorer and discoverer, not in one of his prechosen roles.

During the 1960s, the American accounting profession faced a similar identity confusion. Is accounting a profession or is it an industry? Is its primary concern the well-being of its users or its own revenue and profit? In a society so dependent upon capital formation and confidence in the capital markets, what functions should accountants perform? Will they one day be noted for something other than that which they now seek to provide? (*Wall Street Journal*, October 30, 1973:18)

The roots of this identity confusion can be traced, in part, to the unprecedented growth of CPAs, accountants, and auditors since the post-World War II period. Table 8–1 provides population statistics for several disciplines in the United States from the period 1950–1977. Of particular importance, from 1960 through 1977, membership in the AICPA increased from 37,000 to 134,000. This expansion in the ranks of the AICPA in less than two decades suggests that the contemporary self-view of the modern professional warrants reexamination and reidentification.

Practitioners in Selected American Disciplines, 1950–77 (in Thousands)

	1950s	1960s	1970s	1977
Accountants and auditors	390	496	713	n/a
CPAs[a]	39	59	117	179
AICPA members[a]	16	37	74	130
Engineers	543	872	1,230	n/a
Lawyers and judges	184	218	274	n/a
Physicians and surgeons	195	234	282	n/a

[a]Data from the American Institute of Certified Public Accountants. The number of CPA's in 1957, 39,123; 1962, 59,490; 1972, 117,070; and 1977, 179,500 are as of June 30 of those years.

Source: Historical Statistics of the United States, Colonial Times to 1970, Bicentennial Edition, Bureau of the Census, U.S. Dept of Commerce, VOL. I, p.140. (1975), [A Statistical Abstract Supplement].

Table 8–1

What do so many new CPAs have in common? What is their view of the role of the professional accountant? Aside from their education and their professional examination, what are the common points of their identity as professionals? How is this role to be specified? In 1967 the financial press noted that the accounting profession was "being forced out of their very private world into the public spotlight" (*Forbes,* May 15, 1967).

Yet in 1977 *U.S. News & World Report* noted that accounting was "America's Mystery Profession." Accountants were being called upon to acknowledge the pervasive impact of their practice upon the American economic system and culture (Mayer 1977). Some significant events and their implications at this stage of the profession's development are the subject of this chapter.

The Social and Political Environment

The complexity of the fast-paced, space age culture of America in the 1970s defies description. Yet certain ideas and events of the 1960s, more than others, portray a spirit of the period. From the media-focused disenchantment of Vietnam and Watergate to the overflowing pride found in the Bicentennial Celebration, Americans experienced troubling depths and exhilarating heights.

Increasing frictions were to be found between federal and state systems in matters of resource allocations, civil rights, state rights, and fiscal responsibility. America's urban life style emphasized that it was no longer a land of immigrants and farmers but, rather, one that had become a capital-intensive business civilization, with an economic policy taunted by inflation and geared to almost endless consumption. Americans walked on the moon, sought ways to offset price increases and acknowledged the need for new energy sources. There has been a shock wave of instant access to communications, credit, and travel. Three instruments of modern culture—television, bank charge cards, and the jet airplane—have had a profound effect on people's expectations as individuals and on our society.

At the center of this culture is the computer, a device used by many but understood by few. As computer technology passes through successive generations of increased capability, it has created new opportunities for the sharing of knowledge and enhanced decision-making ability by providing instant access to vast quantities of data. As it enhanced the standard of living, it caused increasing interdependencies between the sectors of the economy, thereby creating challenges for the accountant. The computer's complexity challenges the profession's ability to trace the computer's logic and insure the propriety of its operations. The computer's dependence on electronic messages erases the paper audit trail that had conventionally served as a basis for audit evidence. Ease of access to the computer in the business world has created the need for new accounting skills and for team auditing. In the near future, it promises to provide the means to create a checkless or cashless society based on the electronic transfer of funds between financial institutions.

Capital Markets

Considering that a market economy represents hundreds of millions of personal value judgments embodied in the bases of investment decisions, it seems reasonable to suggest that the economic heart of a capital intensive business civilization is its capital markets. Two ingredients of the capital market process are reliable information and investor confidence. To the extent that the confidence of investors is enhanced by reliable financial information and other disclosures provided by the activities of the accounting professional, the capital market structure of society is strengthened.

The forces of change began to affect the capital market structure in the 1960s just as those forces have worked their effect on all other institutions. The world is no longer dominated by nations, but is witnessing the expansion of the role of the transnational corporations. Their appetite for capital will speed the integration of financial markets from London to Tokyo. The problems inherent in accounting for the international capital investment structure of such organizations suggest the central political and economic problems of the future. To the extent that this integration has been occurring for several decades, a reference to the significance of this development is essential to a consideration of modern accounting and its environment. Another important change affecting the post-Watergate capital market is a return to an emphasis on "fair dealing" in order to promote confidence.

Two centuries ago Adam Smith identified the operational necessity and advantages of economic specialization. During the 1960s, practicing public accountants began to realize that specialization had manifest itself in their own discipline as well (Samuelson 1962).

Today a general practitioner is becoming more the exception than the rule. Accounting is beginning to be taught by functional specialization, that is, by subject area, to include not only financial accounting and auditing, but also managerial accounting, taxation, not-for-profit and governmental accounting, advisory services, and regulatory accounting. Accounting developments are now directed not only by these specialty functions but also by practice in specialized industries, from steel and automobiles to energy and transportation. The environment in which this specialty practice is taking place is being significantly influenced by a number of important institutions to include private-sector professional associations and their self-regulatory actions; public-sector federal and state government agencies and regulations; court decisions; and academe, to include the personal influence of noted professors, their writings, and research. How important are the particulars of these institutions and their influence on accounting practice?

The formation of the AAA's Commission to Establish Accounting Principles and the subsequent formation of the Wheat Committee of the AICPA, both in 1971, signaled the start of a series of efforts by academics and practitioners to reevaluate the process for establishing accounting standards. The APB's failure to capture the confidence of the profession and gain the support of the SEC, beginning with the investment credit issue, indicated that the APB lacked the necessary stature to influence the outcome of debates over accounting principles. The deliberations of the Wheat Committee led to the establishment of the Financial Accounting Standards Board (FASB), which began operations in 1973 (Seidler 1973). The recommendation for such a board confirmed the preference for an autonomous, appointive, due-process approach to private-sector standards-setting versus a legalistic court system approach, as had been suggested by Seymour Walton as early as 1909 and revitalized in the speeches of Leonard Spacek in the late 1950s.

The formation of the FASB was the profession's response to the many criticisms directed toward the APB. Lobbying and political pressure on Congress at the time of the reinstitution of the investment tax credit in 1971 resulted in the enactment of a law specifying either the flow-through or the deferral technique for financial accounting of the credit as appropriate. This excursion by Congress into the realm of financial accounting standard-setting awakened accounting professionals to the fact that congressional legislation in other matters related to the specification of financial accounting principles was not impossible. The political message was clear: The APB had ignored or misinterpreted the intention of Congress. The political and economic consequences of modern accounting rules were closely perceived by corporate and government officials. The investment credit decision was a manifestation of this development. The profession could not act without addressing the economic concerns of the business community, which was a part of its constituency.

Public Control

SEC, FTC, GAO, CASB, OSHA, IRS, ICC, FCC, FTC, HUD, ERISA, DOD? What do all of these have in common? They represent the acronyms of various federal government agencies or the legislation that directly influences financial and management accounting practice and thereby shapes its environment.[2] The increased volume of financial reporting and the peculiar specifications established by each of those agencies has spawned a cost-benefit backlash, including the suggestion by Commerce Secretary Juanita Kreps that programs be required to demonstrate effectiveness by means of a cost-benefit budget (Kreps 1978). Whether or not this proposal will receive support is unknown. But the actions of regulatory agencies themselves are not likely to conform to any specific pattern of development. For example, although the ICC announced a decision to maintain its accounting regulations in accordance with GAAP, the CASB betrays a continuing posture of activism, accenting the prospect that this agency, formed to create uniform cost methods for defense contracts, could wind up making rules for corporate accounting.

The fact that those agencies create specialized information demands on the practice of accounting affects the discipline and is causing accountants to modify their practice and to review the adequacy of the education and testing of those appearing at entry level. Accounting, tax and auditing services, although still at the heart of professional activity, now are strongly complemented by "comparative advantage" specialties in management advisory services, governmental, and not-for-profit accounting. These functional specialties are further refined within specialized industries.

Management Services, an Old "New" Specialty

American public accountants have been offering advisory services since the inception of the profession before the turn of the century. Attention of the national public accounting and regional public accounting firms on management advisory services (MAS) as a "specialty" dates from the post–World War II era. Recent AICPA studies suggest that a need exists for modification of traditional education, training, and competence requirements in order to serve this area. Furthermore, separate general and technical standards for management advisory services work will soon be forthcoming under a resolution approved by AICPA council in October 1978. These standards will be enforced under Rule 204 of the recently amended AICPA Code of Professional Conduct.[3]

A fundamental question remains, however. Can certified public accountants provide advisory services and remain independent with regard to audit relationships with a client? Although MAS activities for major publicly held companies may be performed by nonauditing staff under conditions of different responsibilities, there may be an appearance of loss of independence and a question about the willingness of the firm to point out its own faults should the auditing team discover subsequent weaknesses in the performance by their MAS team. These situations create the impression that the public accounting firm may be incapable of objectively evaluating a system they recommended.

From one point of view, the comparative advantage maintained by accounting firms which enables them to efficiently provide advice to their clients is a social asset. In the process of conducting an effective audit, the public accountant is likely to become intensely familiar with the strengths and weaknesses of a client system and, therefore, is in a position to make recommendations that the client may acknowledge and implement to improve the service or product of the firm and thus pass the cost savings of new efficiency on to the consumer. By eliminating the CPA firm as a source of technical advice, society loses the potential beneficial efficiency effect that would come from the auditor's talent as an advisor. The risk of sacrificing the fact or appearance of audit independence because of MAS involvement must be balanced against the loss of this advisory resource. Can the accounting firms offer both advisory services and audit services to the same client and not sacrifice an independent view of the fairness of the financial statements? Can society afford not to have the advice of the expert accountant available in nonaudit matters?

Accounting for Taxation

On the eve of World War II the United States income tax affected fewer than 5 million people. In 1975, 82 million tax returns were filed. The complexity and enormous impact of tax accounting have led to a series of tax "simplification" acts enacted by the Congress since the 1960s. These acts were intended to reduce the financial burden on low-income taxpayers and to simplify filing and reduce loophole advantages that had developed as a result of the provisions of complex tax regulations and court decisions. Tax reforms were also implemented in an attempt to accomplish various social objectives, including eliminating tax inequities between the very rich and the very poor, providing stimulation for acquisition of capital goods and the formation of capital, and encouraging a more efficient use of energy in households. It is not clear that such policies have been successful, but it is likely that the intention to use tax policy as a means of achieving social objectives will persist.

Tax law, as with all legislation, is subject to interpretation, reinterpretation, trial, and appeal. Expert tax advice, with the accountant serving as an advocate to all classes of personal and corporate taxpayers, has become an increasingly important and necessary function. Recent modifications in collegiate accounting curricula indicate the development of special courses and degrees to meet the highly technical knowledge requirements for competence in tax practice.

Certified Management Accounting and Internal Auditing

With the inception (1972) of the Institute of Management Accounting's initial award of the Certificate in Management Accounting (CMA), accountants have access to a form of competence testing that serves to advance the professionalization of management accounting. The Certified Internal Auditor (CIA) designation was also established in the early 1970s under a program sanctioned by the Institute of Internal Auditors (IIA). The CMA reflects an increase in stature and maturity of management accounting. Furthermore, research conducted by financial executives and participation by management accountants in the deliberations on accounting standards and policies boards and agencies have increased.

Recently internal auditors have gained stature as they acquire added responsibilities for operational auditing within large corporations. Furthermore, the SEC's chairman has noted that the approval of the IIA's "Standards for the Practice of Internal Auditing" increases the prospects that internal auditors will be asked to perform tasks resulting in public reports on internal controls and to serve to aid the growing responsibilities of the corporate audit committee of the board of directors. The audit committee is viewed as an internal safety valve that operates to equalize accountability pressures between internal and external auditors and to signal compliance by management with the policies and goals of the corporation which are consistent with investors' interests. The audit committee is an attempt to provide a significant modification to the corporate governance process. It is not yet clear that it will provide the balance needed between corporate management and owners and also satisfy the demands of external parties such as consumerists and the government.

Governmental and Not-for-Profit Accounting and Auditing

Perhaps the least understood and fastest growing area of specialty accounting is governmental and not-for-profit accounting. Prior to the mid-1960s, the AICPA had recognized, but not focused on, the need to develop a coherent body of ideas applicable to not-for-profit and governmental agencies. A research study sponsored by the AICPA in the early 1960s was terminated before being published. Meanwhile, the Municipal Finance Officers Association (MFOA) had asserted its authority in the area through a document entitled *Governmental Accounting, Auditing and Financial Reporting*. In the late 1960s, the AAA sponsored a series of committees to study the need for developments related to reporting and disclosure in this area. In 1974 the National Council on Governmental Accounting, with 21 representatives, was formed to replace the ad hoc National Committee on Governmental Accounting, which had operated in a fashion similar to the APB.

More recently the AICPA again turned its attention to not-for-profit matters, issuing a number of items including audit guides that acknowledged the importance of the MFOA document. A revision of that document has been undertaken, in part as a response to the demands by investment analysts for more information about the financial status of local governments, particularly major cities.

With the amount of resources committed to public-sector governmental and not-for-profit agencies increasing, the need for the involvement of CPAs in their traditional role as attestors to reports of public-sector management has increased. Because of the situation of major city governments and the need for a more complete accounting of the resources at their disposal, increasing public pressure has been brought for revision or replacement of the traditional fund approach to governmental and not-for-profit agencies accounting. In 1978 the FASB released a research report, *Financial Accounting in Nonbusiness Organizations* by Robert N. Anthony, in an attempt to explore the conceptual issues related to the controversy over proper approaches to public-sector and nonbusiness accounting.

Audited information requirements that are included in the provisions to federal grants have also created an increased demand for professional accounting services. These federal requirements, coupled with the increased needs for security analysts for information to compare the quality of municipal investments with competing commercial and industrial company investments, have resulted in a market pressure for reporting reforms in the governmental accounting area. At the same time, federal legislation is being considered that would place the reporting and accounting rule-making authority for governmental agencies seeking funds through public capital markets in the hands of the SEC. This approach is less likely to occur because of the issue of conflict between the roles of state and federal governments with regard to the Tenth Amendment (a constitutional question about the federal government limiting or governing the ability of other governmental units to raise money and maintain their own financial integrity).[4]

The technical bankruptcy of New York City in the early 1970s crystalized the concerns of many for more information about municipalities and other governmental institutions. Although several congressmen have sponsored legislation to require that local governmental agencies and municipalities who enter the securities market be subjected to federal securities laws, the constitutional question remains. Does the federal government have the right to "regulate" other political entities' attempts to raise capital?

Within the federal government, it is estimated that paperwork and internal reporting processes cost about $2 billion a year. Management audit and review responsibilities for this process have been the task of the GAO and the controller general since 1921. "Accountability" investigations by the GAO, based on *Standards for Audits of Governmental Organizations, Programs, Activities and Functions* (June 1972), have gained favorable acknowledgment as providing useful "watchdog" information to Congress and society. The burgeoning federal budget and the proliferation of government programs have, however, called into question whether any single agency can hope to properly oversee and review the vast array of financial activity represented by federal budget expenditures of $400 billion annually.

Accounting for One World: From Generally Accepted Accounting Principles (GAAP) to Geo-Accounting Principles (GAP)

Business internationalism, as has been noted, is one of the forms of change having increasing influence on the capital market. FASB Opinion no. 8 (1975), which attempted to address the reporting of gains and losses from foreign currency translation, has served to highlight the difficulty of resolving differences of a fundamental nature among diversified multinational corporations. Today corporations work in the legal form of a single entity but operate in economic substance as multiple individual operations in various foreign and domestic locations.

"Accounting and Auditing in One World," the theme of the eleventh World Congress of Accountants (Munich, October 1977), suggests the importance that accountants place on achieving harmony in accounting practices in industrial countries throughout the world.

The formation of the International Accounting Standards Committee (IASC) in 1973 and the recent founding of the International Federation of Accountants (IFA), headquartered in New York City, will provide means for institutions and individuals to discuss the means of resolving the financial measurement and reporting differences that exist between countries with different economic systems and accounting customs.[5]

Among the basic issues to be resolved is the blend of the host nation's accounting principles and the guest company's accounting principles to be followed when there are differences. If there is a need for comparable financial information to be made available for an internationally integrated capital market system, there will be a corresponding need for international standards to provide comparability of financial disclosures throughout the world. Although it would appear to be an almost impossible task to cut through the cultural, language, monetary, and legal differences among multinational industrial societies, the necessity for cooperation and a spirit of accounting professionalism on a national and international scale affords an excellent opportunity to make progress with these difficult matters. Furthermore, since systems of accounting are based on the double-entry method, there is, at the heart of all commercial accounting systems, that common element of procedure from which an internationally responsive and comparable system of accounting can be developed. Recent efforts by the Committee of Experts working with the Organization for Economic Cooperation, and the forthcoming accounting position statement of the European Economic Community attest to the greater awareness of and progress being made in international accounting matters.

Professional Self-Reform: A Market Solution

In an attempt to better manage their own affairs, CPAs established two major fact finding committees in the early 1970s and subsequently formed a commission to study the change in public expectations with regard to auditors' responsibilities. The Wheat Committee (1971), the Trueblood Committee (1971), and the Cohen Commission (1974) represent the profession's attempt to address the need to govern and direct its own standard-setting activities, to identify the reporting population to which it holds a prime responsibility, and to report to society in view of the expectations of the latter. In forming these groups and addressing these issues, the accounting profession began to acknowledge its diverse constituency and the "political" implications thereof.

The Wheat Committee recommended the formation of the Financial Accounting Standards Board (FASB) consisting of seven full-time members who would articulate decisions relative to financial accounting and reporting standards.

The Trueblood Committee's report maintained that the primary purpose of published financial statements was to provide information useful for making economic decisions by those who were primarily dependent on annual reports and who had limited resources, authority, and ability to obtain such information. The Trueblood report thereby identified the profession's constituency to be the broad and nonspecialized group of financial statement readers.

The Cohen Commission established in October, 1974 addressed the matter that, through custom and other influences, had long been represented in the legal maxim "The auditor is a watchdog and not a bloodhound"—that is, if the auditor takes reasonable care, he is justified in believing that the management of the company in whom he has placed confidence is in fact honest, and that he, as an auditor, may rely upon management's representations.[6] However, in the wake of the massive computer fraud underlying the collapse of Equity Funding and the creative accounting manipulations in the National Student Marketing case, the question that became most common was, "Where were the auditors?" In each case, prominent auditing firms were directly or indirectly involved in the filing of the financial statements of these publicly held companies. These concerns, accented by the post-Watergate revelations of questionable political and business payments, have made it important to reconsider whether the auditor is expected to accept a responsibility to be both watchdog and bloodhound. With a view toward establishing and identifying the role of the auditor in today's society, the Cohen Commission considered several key issues. Are society's expectations of auditors realistic? Are all auditors' views about their role somewhat identical? Do they differ from society's? The tone of the Cohen Commission's report is sobering. If auditors are to address the needs of society, they must begin by amending their own deficiencies by reexamining the process by which auditing standards are established and by seeking to improve the fundamental education and continuing education processes applicable to auditor training.

Social Expectations and Responsibility: Regulation and the Law

Have accountants maintained their integrity as professionals? Have they insured that competence and independence have not been compromised or impaired? How are the expectations of society determined?

There are two sources from which we can gain information about societal expectations of the profession. The first comes through the actions, rulings, and activities of governmental agencies created to oversee the activities of the accounting profession. The second comes by way of the courts and case law.

The governmental agencies cited earlier are involved directly or indirectly in establishing accounting measurement and reporting requirements. Since the end of World War II, they have increased their activity. Most prominent among these agencies is the SEC and its office of the chief accountant, which serves as the principal advisor to the commissioners in accounting measurement and disclosure matters. Under the Securities Act of 1933 and the Securities Exchange Act of 1934, the SEC has the authority to set accounting principles and reporting standards for reports filed with the commission by companies who trade their securities in the public capital markets at national, regional, or over-the-counter locations.[7]

Under customary interpretations of the requirements of the federal securities law, audited financial statements are included as part of both initial filings and annual filings. From the outset, as in Accounting Series Release (ASR) no. 4 (1938), the SEC has stated its policy that financial statements prepared in accordance with accounting practices for which there was no substantial authoritative support were presumed to be misleading and that footnotes or other disclosure would not avoid this presumption. The commission has also stated that when there was a difference of opinion between the commission and the registrant about the proper accounting to be followed in a particular case, disclosure would be accepted in lieu of correcting the financial statement, only if *substantial authoritative support* existed for the accounting practices followed by the registrant and that the position of the commission had not been previously expressed in rules, regulations, or other official releases.

In 1973 the SEC took steps to further define its relationship with the accounting profession in such matters by issuing a statement of policy on the establishment of accounting principles and standards in ASR no. 150. For purposes of clarifying the policy previously stated, the commission indicated that standards, principles, and practices promulgated by the FASB in its statements and interpretations would be considered by the commission as having substantial authoritative support and that policy, principles, standards, and practices that were contrary to such FASB promulgations would be considered to have no such support. At the same time, the commission noted that previous statements by the APB and by CAP, which had preceded the FASB, would be considered as continuing in force with the same degree of authority as pronouncements of the FASB. ASR no. 150 establishes the relationship between the government agency primarily charged with the responsibility for overseeing the adequacy of financial reports filed by corporations who trade in the public markets and the members of the accounting profession who act as independent professionals. ASR no. 150 was unsuccessfully challenged in the courts over whether it represented proper delegation of authority to a nongovernmental agency. Its existence and the potential for cooperation between the government agency and the profession now seems to have been enhanced. (McCraw 1975)

The issuance of ASR no. 150 was only one of the important developments that occurred during the four years (1972–1976) that John C. Burton was chief accountant of the SEC. Not all of Burton's actions have been viewed as serving to aid the profession in establishing a positive sense of self-identity and social responsibility. In background, training, and temperament, Burton was well suited to the job of chief accountant during the turbulent years of the profession's "identity crisis." The son of a former senior partner of Arthur Young & Co. and a professor of Accounting at Columbia University, Burton brought to his job an appreciation of both the practitioner and academic views of accounting in the contemporary environment. Through his exhortations and his insight into the complicated nature of disclosure and regulation, Burton strove to implement meaningful disciplinary actions and innovative reporting requirements (Burton 1973). In a series including ASR no. 173, no. 196, and no. 207, Burton sponsored commission sanctions of accounting firms with broad public responsibilities, inferring that these firms had not adequately regarded their professional responsibility. During this four-year tenure, Burtonian policies provided the basis for peer review, interim reporting, replacement-cost disclosure, and voluntary forecasting. He artfully blended the "carrot" of his brand of progress with the "stick" of SEC authority, providing a watchfully sympathetic but firmly enforced set of precedents for professional change. Burton's management of the office differed in style and in philosophy from his predecessor, Andrew Barr. Both were men of integrity whose critical

oversight of the accounting profession combined to provide a disciplinary technique and mechanism that the profession itself had been
unable to implement even after the establishment of Rule 203 of the
AICPA Code of Professional Ethics.[8]

The Congress

Congress's concern with the role of the accounting profession was
evidenced in the hearings called by Congressman John Moss and
Senator Lee Metcalf during the sessions of the 94th Congress. These
hearings provided the profession with an opportunity to respond to
criticism and to address the expectations of federal legislators about
accounting and society's needs. The hearings also inquired into the
effectiveness of the oversight functions of the SEC as to accounting
principles and the attest function. Each of these congressional
committees in turn has questioned the effectiveness of certified
public accountants in detecting and disclosing management fraud,
wrong doing, and particular violations of the law as now related to
illegal payments under the Foreign Corrupt Practices Act of 1977.
The staff report of the Metcalf Committee further asserted that public
accountants have not maintained an independent relationship
with large publicly held clients. This alleged lack of independence, it
contended, raises the prospect of a breakdown in confidence in the
auditor's attest function. Congressmen have also observed that management advisory services further impede independence and diminish the value of the attest function because they raise the question,
noted earlier, about whether "auditors as advisors" can objectively
review their own advisory service work in a client operation. In
addition, Congress questioned the placement services and executive
search practices of some large firms to include accounting firms
placing their own former staff audit personnel in executive positions
with clients. Such placement policies, they argued, further diminished the appearance of independent relationships between the
firm and responsible financial executives of clients. In June 1978 the
SEC acted to reduce the concern over auditor independence relative
to such situations—it required that registrants disclose services
performed by the auditor for the firm and the percentage of the total
fee paid to the auditor for each service if the percentage exceeds 3
percent of audit fees. (ASR no. 250)

Another concern advanced by the Congress was that there was
insufficient turnover of audit firms among major public clients.
Prolonged auditor-client relationships, the congressmen inferred,

tended to diminish the appearance of independence and reduce the ability of the accountant to be alert and skeptical in familiar surroundings, particularly when amicable personal relationships had developed and could compromise an auditor's objectivity. In brief, congressional concerns include the prospect that accountants had become advocates, not independent adversaries. The congressmen argued that since the fee paid to the auditor was either directly negotiated with or indirectly controlled by management, this was sufficient means for management to influence the performance of the auditor. The criticisms of "the accounting establishment" by the Congress centered on allegations that the profession lacked integrity and independence, in part because of such alleged close, long-term relationships with corporate management.

A remedy in the government regulatory view would be to "restore competition" to the area, since there is an apparent lack of turnover and therefore insufficient competition. Yet, from the accountant's point of view, there is a high learning-curve cost to society for unwarranted auditor turnover and too rapid a turnover aids management in concealing fraudulent or unauthorized activities. Furthermore, the existence of professional standards and SEC requirements to disclose disagreements between auditors and firms, as set forth in ASR no. 247, creates an environment sufficiently conducive to insure that the independent auditor is able to obtain the cooperation of management to achieve meaningful disclosures when there is a dispute. Assuming a professional's competence and integrity, long-term relationships work to the benefit of both the firm and society by reducing costs and increasing competence on the part of the auditor because familiarity with the firm eliminates the need for the costly process of relearning a particular sophisticated financial system each time an engagement is undertaken.[9]

The SEC

Additional criticisms of the accounting, reporting, and disclosure process made at congressional hearings included comments that in certain areas the SEC's oversight function of the profession was ineffective. Critics pointed out that, although the SEC had been active in developing accounting principles, there was no clear evidence that auditing standards, another critical element in the development of reliable and useful financial information, were being similarly scrutinized by the SEC. The critics contended that therefore new legislation should be considered to extend SEC authority to mandate auditing procedures as well as accounting principles, since the commission's authority to regulate auditing standards was not currently specified in the law. The SEC's response to this suggestion noted that through its disciplinary and enforcement proceedings, it effectively had exercised appropriate controls over auditors with regard to filings with the SEC. The commission also noted its recent record number of disciplinary actions against accountants, including those that had barred several large public accounting firms from accepting new SEC clients for several months. This approach, the SEC argued, afforded a clear message about acceptable audit practices. The SEC's response also indicated that it worked to improve the quality of audits by requiring auditors who had been sanctioned to undertake extended periods of continuing or remedial education as part of the settlement in enforcement actions.

In July 1978 SEC Chairman Williams reaffirmed the SEC's support of the process of allowing the accounting profession to continue its efforts at self-regulation and reform. This support, in the face of pending legislation introduced by congressman John Moss (H. R. 13175, June 16, 1978, "The Public Accounting Regulatory Act"), affords the profession additional time to implement the reorganization that was voted on at the 1977 AICPA annual meeting. An important aspect of the profession's ability to accomplish meaningful self-regulation will be tested as the newly formed Public Oversight Board of the SEC Practice Section of the AICPA Division of Firms begins its activities. The five member public board includes, as chairman, lawyer/diplomat John J. McCloy; other members are former SEC chairmen Ray Garrett and William L. Carey, John D. Harper, retired chairman of the Aluminum Company of America and Arthur M. Wood, former chairman and chief executive officer of Sears, Roebuck & Co.

The Courts

The 1960s witnessed an increasing number of complex litigations involving accountants. To the extent that each of these cases evidences a particular social expectation, the courts have reoutlined a view of accountants' responsibilities. Practitioners who are cynical about the ability of the courts to resolve the matter on the basis of legal principles indicate that case law is nothing more than a rationalization of a preconception of the judge's decision. That is, the courts will look for available resources to redress the grievance and then develop a legal rationale to support the economic outcome of the preconception. This "deep pocket" liability theory is based on the belief that accountants' earnings are sufficient to withstand the cost of suit. Table 8–2 suggests that such incomes are modest on the average, however salaries paid to partners in large firms, and the capitalization of such firms, are more likely the basis for this theory than the "average" accountant's earnings or wealth. A recent disclosure in the financial press notes that "partners in most . . . Big Eight firms seem to earn between $90,000 and $100,000" per year. More specific information on accountants' incomes will be forthcoming from the results of the economic census being conducted by the Department of Commerce in which CPA practitioners are included for the first time.

Average Net Income of Certain Professionals, 1972

	CPAs	Lawyers	Physicians	Dentists
Sole practitioner	$10,700	$15,000	$28,955	$25,790
In partnership	27,595	34,975	39,540	22,000

Source: "Tax Report" *Wall Street Journal,* January 8, 1975, p. 1.

Table 8–2

The 1136 Tenants decision suggests that the courts expect the public accountant to operate as a "financial detective." This case was decided in favor of the owners of a cooperative apartment complex against a small practitioner who had not, in the court's view, clarified the scope and responsibility of the engagement that he had agreed to undertake.[10] This decision demonstrated a technical deficiency, that is, the need to specify, in the form of engagement memorandum, the nature of accounting services to be provided. Both small and large practitioners have therefore been made aware of the need to educate specific clients about the variety of services that they provide other than the audit. The decision was more important, however, in that it further evidenced the public's expectation that when a CPA was involved in an engagement, an investigation of basic discrepancies is anticipated. Whether or not such a view is justified is, of course, subject to argument, particularly in the light of the distinct traditional difference between private company services offered by some practitioners (financial statement compilation and review) and the audit of financial statements. The 1136 Tenants case highlights social expectations that amplify the need of private company practitioners to be distinguished from auditors whose clientele are predominantly publicly held international and SEC reporting companies. If private company practitioners are expected to conform to the disclosure standards followed by major public company–SEC accounting firms, this might eliminate the essential unaudited financial statement service of the small practitioner. The implications of this decision for the social role of the small client practitioner suggest a fundamental duality of CPA practice between private and public companies. Recently, in recognition of this "duality burden," the FASB acknowledged that certain earnings-per-share data (APB no. 15) and certain segment disclosures (FASB no. 14) would not be required of small, privately held companies.

A set of decisions by the Supreme Court of the United States in 1976 may also have significant consequences for the practice of CPAs. In a June 1976 decision *(TSC Industries, Inc. et al. v. Northway, Inc.)*, Justice Thurgood Marshall defined the notion of a "material fact" for the purpose of complying with disclosure requirements of Federal Securities Law proxy filings (Rule 14a-9, 1934 act). Since the adequacy of disclosure in SEC terms tends to be based on this notion, the Supreme Court definition is important. The Court noted: "An omitted fact is material if there is a substantial likelihood that a reasonable shareholder would consider it important . . ." in deciding how to vote.

Accountants' liability under federal securities law is specified under Section 10b-5 of the 1934 act, which governs the annual reporting requirements of registrants. In 1976 a Supreme Court decision *(Ernst & Ernst v. Hochfelder)* led to a reconsideration of the extent of the auditors' liability in cases when there is a contention that false and misleading financial statements have been filed with the SEC. In this case, the Supreme Court ruled that there must be proof that the auditor knowingly intended to deceive if there is to be remedy under the law. Negligence alone does not provide a basis for relief under Section 10b-5.

Because of the difficulty of proving intent to deceive, accountants believe that this interpretation will reduce the number of attempts to secure judgments against them in matters involving SEC disclosures. The significance of the Hochfelder decision as a precedent in federal securities law, however, remains untested. Other courts may, in future decisions, infer *scienter* (i.e., knowing intent) as an element of deception if, in fact, the accountant is adjudged as having been grossly negligent. Furthermore, the Hochfelder decision may fail to reduce the vulnerability of public accountants to suit under state laws that are not necessarily influenced by federal court decisions.

In part because of the rapid changes in accounting reporting and disclosure standards in the 1960s, there have been increasing attempts by third parties to establish their right to recover damages from professional accountants when a question about the adequacy of financial disclosures arises. Case law precedents indicate that small and large practitioners are equally vulnerable in such an environment. Although recent federal case law precedents may be interpreted as not having increased the exposure of public company (SEC) practitioners, the 1136 Tenants case, as it involves both groups of practitioners, suggests that when a CPA is involved in financial presentations, some degree of skeptical investigation into the integrity of the financial statements is expected. If continued to be acknowledged by the judiciary in light of the expanding numbers of practitioners, such expectations can only lead to frustration. The auditor, through his professional organizations, will have to better educate the general public about the capabilities and limitations of the professional practice if that frustration is to be avoided.

Perhaps the most significant purpose to which the profession can address itself in the coming years is the enhancement of its communication relationships with the general public. Such posture would better equip the professional to anticipate the needs of society and to acknowledge the validity of criticisms directed by various segments of the public audience. In an attempt to "open" the profession and to stimulate competition and contact between firms and potential clientele, the AICPA has dropped its ban on advertising, although the ban on uninvited direct solicitation remains.

The basis of the reliability of the financial reporting system is, in essence, one of cooperative effort among owners, their board representatives, management, public accountants, and analysts. To the extent that apathy, indolence, fraud, incompetence, and conflicts of interest exist on the part of any party in such an arrangement, the free capital market system is threatened. The new structure of the AICPA board of directors, which expanded the representation to include three members from the general public, is an apt step. The restructuring was a result of recommendations of the committee chaired by Russell Palmer instituted by the Financial Accounting Foundation (FAF) in early 1977. The findings of the Palmer Committee, among other recommendations, have led to an end of the required majority representation on the FASB of practicing CPAs and to the adoption of a simple majority approval rule for passage of a proposed standard.

The response of the profession to its critics has not been limited to changes in the number and makeup of the AICPA board of directors or to the makeup and procedures of the FASB. The institute also made an important internal realignment acknowledging the difference between the privately held company CPA firm and the national and regional CPA firm which has as a primary client the publicly held and SEC registered company. In September 1977 the membership at the institute's annual meeting authorized a reorganization plan that would permit practicing firms to identify and enroll as members of either or both the SEC and private companies firms divisions of the AICPA. At the same time, the institute took steps to establish a senior technical committee to deliberate matters relating to accounting principles for privately held companies. In addition, in 1978 the FASB instituted a "feedback" review process designed to assess reaction to its first twelve statements and to consider whether modifications of any statements were warranted.

The profession has also responded to the criticisms and concerns of politicians about specific areas of accounting responsibility, and the FASB has also shifted research resources to focus on the subject of accountants' responsibility for the economic consequence of accounting standards. Additionally, the national accounting firms, in cooperation with an institute-sponsored program, have undertaken a candid peer review program designed to provide a vehicle for constructive interpractice criticism in the United States and in overseas affiliates as well.

Golden Age of Academic Individualism

While practitioners and politicians have been embroiled in debating the social and political consequences of auditing and accounting, the academic arm of the profession has been reassessing its identity in relationship to society and the practicing professional. The existence of a gap between academic and practitioner views has been noted. Yet background, interest, training, and reward-structure differences between academics and practitioners necessitate that each group reflect such differences in their view of the profession's role. However, practitioners note that the responsibilities of the profession, taken as a whole, require that the important intellectual resources of the accounting academic community be available to assist in solving the many and complex application problems.

A growing emphasis on applied research that would be useful in practice has become apparent. The establishment of several professional schools of accountancy at major universities since the early

1970s also evidences the extent to which practitioners have begun to influence academics about the validity of their concerns. The educational views and objectives of professional schools tend to vary widely from the objectives sought by accounting faculties within graduate schools of management. Each of these educational approaches will continue into the future, but it would seem that the trend toward professionalization of accountancy programs will direct the educational environment in the coming years. As the recognition of the need for specialized education increases, professional schools can be structured to offer the particular focus equivalent to the educational opportunities that are now offered to such professions as law, engineering, and medicine. Within a professional school, it is held, the faculty of accounting will be increasingly responsive to developing curricula along specialty lines, including taxation, advisory services, not-for-profit and governmental accounting, information systems, management accounting, financial reporting, and auditing. Each of these areas in turn would address the regulatory and specialty issues that bear on effective practice. This attention to specialization, however, must not be at the expense of narrowing interdisciplinary training in other business and liberal arts subjects. (AICPA 1978)

In recent years there appears to have been an increase in the influence of practitioners on the shape of the vehicle of accounting education; so, too, the importance of academic influence on the formation of accounting policies and principles from 1965 to the present should be recognized. Academics, such as David Solomons, as a member of the Wheat Committee, which recommended the formation of the FASB; George Sorter, as a member of the Trueblood Committee on objectives of financial statements; and Robert Sprouse, as vice chairman of the FASB, had significant influence on accounting practice. Similarly, both Robert Mautz—a former professor at the University of Illinois and at the time a partner of Ernst & Ernst and charter member of the Cost Accounting Standards Board—and John Burton, as Chief Accountant of the SEC, have significantly influenced the accounting profession and the public through their service in regulatory agencies.[11]

The history of accounting theory in the late 1960s and the 1970s warrants more attention that can be given here. Many of the theoretical propositions advanced in this time period remain to be tested, although they have been widely discussed and debated in academic journals, at conferences, and in workshops. If there has been increasing academic concern over the drift toward legal formalism in a codification of accounting via the regulatory and quasi-legislative posture of practicing accountants' boards and government agencies, accounting academics and theoreticians have not acknowledged this concern by relenting in the development of proposals for normative systems to improve the content of accounting information and reports. The importance of these different views and the continuing fresh input of ideas has seemed to benefit the thoughtful practitioner and the standard-setting process. Perhaps the frequent quibbling among some academics is viewed by practitioners as a sign that academics simply can't agree on anything. Such a view is unfortunate and naive.

Academics should learn of problem situations by observing the practitioner. An academic's role is to propose ideas and to test them; this role does not ordinarily extend to implementation. Practitioners would be primarily involved in implementation such that the problem-solving process, from beginning to end, is one of communication and of working in areas of comparative advantage. The comparative advantage of the academic is in the realm of developing "ideas," and this role of intellectual stimulus to the profession should not be terminated. The multiple alternatives offered by contemporary accounting theorists should not be criticized but commended. It is to the existence of alternatives that the profession owes progress. Alternatives create the opportunities to select the most suitable approach to deal with the changing and particular needs of a vast array of clients. The mania that seeks to eliminate alternatives as the solution in the search for accounting "truth" is popular, but it is based on the misconception that there is such a thing as a "penny-precise" answer or a single interpretation of "value" or "income" determination issues.

Within the conventional double-entry model, there exist several academic schools of thought on value and measurement. Ray Chambers argues that continuously contemporaneous accounting, that is, cash value accounting, is appropriate for the reporting process. Others, including those identified with efficient markets and information economics theories, might contend that the justifications for such an approach are not as warranted as those that concentrate on assessing the availability and cost of information provided to potential users. Information economics theorists have argued that it is relatively impossible to develop a meaningful normative standard given the myriad expectations that the population of investors develop from their individual social value judgments. The primary resource for learning the appropriate reporting requirements, in an environment concerned with the efficient market and information economics, they assert, is to tabulate the reporting activities of information producers and assess the influence of changes in informational content upon the trading price of securities. Accounting theory should respond to the needs of an efficient market and provide predictive information useful to analytical investors. This contrasts with the traditional view of supplying information based on historical cost for purposes of stewardship and "scorekeeping."

Also prominent among contemporary approaches to accounting theory formulation is the view that accounting should be more "sciencelike." Proponents argue that so long as accountants accept accounting as led by convention, they will seek to address issues as if accounting were an art and not a science. Advocates of accounting science see the need to redefine the nature of accounting and the process by which accounting problems are solved; they suggest adhering to a scientific approach (Sterling 1976).

Although skeptics remain unconvinced that the nature of accounting can be changed simply by changing the way in which the profession views itself, there is credibility to the notion that accounting problems cannot be overcome by the use of scientific techniques alone if there is no recognition that accounting problems must first be defined in a scientific manner. Advocates of accounting science argue that the scientific method fails accountants because their problems are not developed in scientific terms. Critics of the accounting science approach point out that accounting is more like law and economics (the social sciences) than it is like physics or chemistry. They assert that to consider accounting as a hard science is absurd. Accounting scientists respond by noting that the history of hard science suggests that "soft" stages of theory agreement are a part of the evolution of a discipline toward the state of "hardness." Accounting, they argue, has just begun to take on the properties necessary to supply it with this "firmness." Therefore, it is now appropriate to address problems "scientifically" and remove from the definition of accounting problems and prior solutions the bias of habit and social convention.

In light of the diversity of academic opinion about the proper structure of accounting, it is not a surprise that the impact of academic research on accounting practice has been adjudged to be minimal, if not nonexistent, in the 1970s. Perhaps it is too much to expect that in the crush of events that occurred in the late 1960s and the 1970s there would be a serious reordering of practitioners' acceptance of new views. There was an avalanche of technical and procedural pronouncements, political intrigues, and a period of unparalleled growth, all of which professional leaders had to address, in turn, with little time to assess them. Perhaps the traditional view of accounting, as a past-oriented, stewardship function remains at the heart of the schism between academics and practitioners, with the latter group preferring to continue to recognize the value-in-use and scorekeeping role of accounting.

To the extent that all accounting theories represent a rationalization of the limitations of a conventional double-entry system of reporting, they all afford a basis for conceptual comparability. Beyond the point of this rationalization, arguments for the preference of one accounting theory over another often are reduced to the mere desire to institutionalize subjective preferences under the guise of "rational and systematic" approaches. If, over time, accountants' functions transcend the system of accounting based on the double-entry model, and accountants begin to take on reporting responsibilities not primarily limited to financial measurement, then there will be an expanded dimension of accountants' social reporting obligation. To the extent that theorists have defined broader accounting goals under the headings of "social accounting" and "human resource accounting," that is an indication of the potential for theory that transcends conventional financial measurement (Nelson 1967). Yet the recent view of the Cohen Commission tends to reaffirm that the accountant is concerned with matters controlled by the accounting system, a reaffirmation of the double-entry theme.

The AAA—an organization representing accounting educators, not only nationally but to an increasing extent, internationally—accented the importance of the variety of theories and the relative impossibility of reconciling competing theories in its most recent study of the state of accounting thought. In 1977 the AAA issued a *Statement on Accounting Theory and Theory Acceptance*, which is an attempt to assess the developments and theories of accounting relative to the AAA's 1966 study entitled *A Statement of Basic Accounting Theory*. The 1977 document is an important milestone in the academic evaluation of progress in theory development. It is a readable exposition that attempts to identify the main streams of thought and assess their differences without judging the merit of one approach over another.[12]

This statement reaffirms the association's "golden rule" about theoretical preferences and alternatives that followed a debate and resolution at the 1973 annual meeting in Quebec. The debate concerned whether the association spoke for the academic accounting community at large or for the individual or executive committee preparing the particular statement. The outcome of the Quebec debate reaffirmed the importance of the individual academic's view and limited the association's endorsement of general statements. As such, it provided increased impetus to theoretical experimentation by individual researchers; if the association were precluded from taking a definitive position, then alternative individual positions would merit equal opportunity for exposure, recognition, and acknowledgment, based on the ability of the individual to convince the community as a whole of the merit of the proposition. It requires a degree of academic self-confidence to propose and maintain alternative and competing theories in the face of popular and equally well articulated theories. To the extent that this self-confidence exists, a new degree of academic freedom has been achieved. Heretofore, the prospects for the survival of such alternatives may have been limited, particularly if a new view tended to oppose the view sanctioned by the AAA.

The encouragement of diversity of thought in the academic community and the corresponding recognition of the pursuit by individuals to perfect competing theories of accounting, suggests a maturing of the academic community and a resolution of the concern brought about following the publication of the 1966 *Statement of Basic Accounting Theory* as the model for accounting measurement and reporting.

The Heritage and the Future of Accounting

How much of the past remains true today? How much has changed over the profession's history? If there is any conclusion to be drawn, it would be that, while accounting has achieved a position of unquestioned importance in the economic and social order, it continues to face growing accountability to investors, management, clients, employees, and society as a whole—on a global scale. The challenges facing accounting today are an enlarged reflection of the issues of the past and the character of contemporary institutions and societal demands—this is, as it was in each preceding generation since the profession became recognized. What has changed is, not the nature of the problem faced by accountants, but the form of the response and the substance of the institutions of accountancy.

Today's readers, when examining the major issues facing the profession in the earlier progressive era, can find significant parallels to the issues in modern debate. If one accepts the thesis that accounting must be pragmatic—that it must meet social demands and result in positive social consequences—then one must consider that

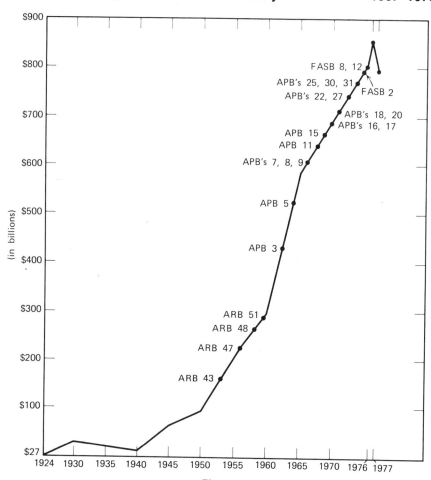

Figure 8–1
Market value of all listed stocks, 1924–1977.

Source: *New York Stock Exchange 1978 Fact Book,* p. 77.

there is a tendency for accounting problems to recycle. External forces, rather than accountants themselves, seem to define the profession's role. Therefore, as attitudes change, one must expect criticism of the profession during periods of readjustment to signal new demands.

The attitudes found in the progressive period and among reformers today are remarkably similar. Both periods seem to have been characterized by hostility to big business and demands that accountants protect the public from the *expected* abuses in the corporate sector. Questions of independence are paramount as the policing function becomes more important. Progressive practitioners convinced the political sector that an advocacy role in tax service and independent auditing were not incompatible. Accountants made a subtle distinction between business and professional competition and argued that, to ensure professional competence, they must have at least minimum entrance requirements via restrictive legislation. Similarly, the profession warned of the precarious effects that "price" competition (advertising, soliciting) would have on the quality of work. The arguments did not convince critics and accountants faced charges of attempting to create a monopoly and following a policy of deliberate exclusion. Most of those issues have again found their way to the surface in the 1970s—the age of political accountancy.

Finally, one might be tempted to draw a parallel between the proprietary theory of the progressive era, with its emphasis on asset valuation, and the contemporary direction being taken by the FASB. Certainly one could hypothesize that in a period during which any suggestion that cooperation between management and the accountant is suspect, accountants will focus on a measurement model (asset valuation) and on the objectively determined elements of financial reports, for accountants prefer to be viewed as unbiased "reporters" of facts. This may be a response to overt demands by reformers which attempt to extend the profession's responsibility—that is, to interpret such facts and to indicate preferability of accounting treatment. But contemporary theory is not a reversion to proprietary concepts. Progressive theorists had only begun to explore the concept of operating income, and most did not view income as a flow concept. Today the realm of theory has expanded beyond such limited views.

It appears that accounting is on the threshhold of resolving its most recent series of challenges and reassuming control and responsibility for its role in American society. An effective implementation of the restructured FASB, the reorganization of the AICPA, and the successful modification of the auditor's role as suggested in the report of the Cohen Commission suggest that the profession is capable of directing its own future.[13]

The prospect for the rebirth of a profession dedicated to society's service in the current age of intensified accountability is even more promising now than in the 1960s, especially when one considers that directors of public corporations, investors, management, and analysts as well, are taking steps to reaffirm the principles of responsible relationship among society, corporations, and the capital markets.

Furthermore, the opportunities for individuals, regardless of sex, race, religion, or creed, to advance in the ranks of professional accounting and to gain significant status has been characteristic of the profession from the earliest years. Accounting has long been viewed as an "open" profession in America. The first black CPA, John W. Cromwell, passed the CPA examination in New Hampshire in 1921; women have been increasingly successful in public accounting and have received added opportunities in management accounting and education, particularly since the end of World War II.

The consumer movement of the 1970s, as represented by increased advocacy of the individual investor, also promises to increase public awareness about and involvement in accountability for all business and financial affairs, to include estate planning and personal financial matters.

The accounting profession is on the threshhold of a new and greater role to serve society, and the new accountant has a better education and a larger audience and market than ever before. At the same time, the factors of change, legal responsibility, specialization, and government regulation are likely to set higher performance requirements for the new accountant and the profession. Among the greatest challenges facing the profession today are the requirements to develop accounting information which is conditioned to inflation and which will aid in making decisions about resource allocations in such areas as energy research, urban growth, operation, and preservation, and assist in the management of social programs conducted at the national level.

In 1931 DR Scott wrote *The Cultural Significance of Accounts*, bearing witness to a perception that accounting had become an important thread in America's social fabric. Today accounting is a fundamental aspect of the American way of life *(Novus Ordo Seclorum)*, and the bottom line is as essential to the identification of American culture as are baseball, hot dogs, and apple pie.

NOTES

1. The signal events of American accounting history which have occurred in the decade since 1967 are less subject to satisfactory historical analysis than episodes in the periods preceding it, if only because several of the principal issues continue to be in complex transition and debate.

2. (SEC, Securities and Exchange Commission; FTC, Federal Trade Commission; GAO, General Accounting Office; CASB, Cost Accounting Standards Board; OSHA, Occupational Safety and Health Act; IRS, Internal Revenue Service;

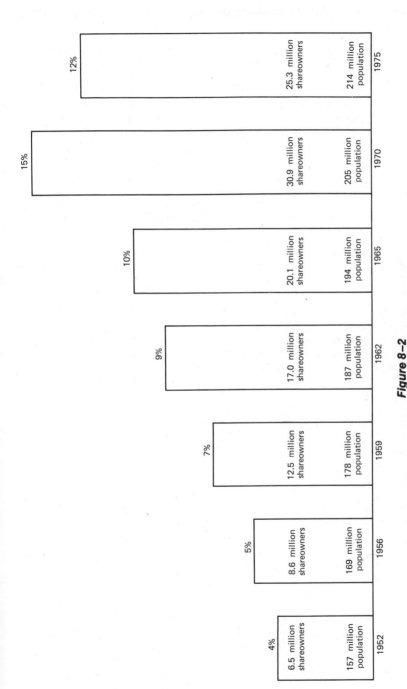

Figure 8-2
Post World War II market data (1952–1975). New York Stock Exchange shareowners as a percentage of U.S. population.

Source: Shareowner data from the *New York Stock Exchange 1978 Fact Book;* population data from U.S. Dept. of Commerce, Bureau of the Census, *Statistical Abstract of the United States,* 1977, p. 5.

ICC, Interstate Commerce Commission; FCC, Federal Communications Commission; FPC, Federal Power Commission; HUD, Department of Housing and Urban Development; ERISA, Employee's Retirement Income Security Act; DOD, Department of Defense).

Although it might be inappropriate to single out any one of these agencies as being more or less influential than another, practitioners have been most influenced by the policies prescribed by the IRS, SEC, and CASB. The potential for an "exponential explosion" of regulatory accounting policy, given the influence of and tradition for prescribed accounting in regulated industries, is a matter of increasing concern to the profession.

3. *Statements on Management Advisory Services*, AICPA, Management Advisory Services Executive Committee, January 1975. E. L. Summers, "Academic Opportunities Related to MAS in the CPA Profession," in *Emerging Issues*, ed. G. J. Previts, Proceedings of the 1976 Alabama Accounting Research Convocation, pp. 91–111.

4. The Tenth Amendment, one of the Bill of Rights of the Constitution, was enacted to take effect on December 15, 1791. It states: "The powers not delegated to the United States by the Constitution, nor prohibited by it to the States, are reserved to the States respectively, or to the people."

5. IASC has issued a number of standards to date, which are recognized by the professional accounting bodies in over forty countries. In addition, the Accounting International Studies Group has sponsored and published a series of comparative studies on accounting thought and practice in Canada, Great Britain, Ireland, and the United States.

   The differences that exist between countries can be many. For example, in the treatment of research and development costs, FASB Statement no. 2 mandates that in all cases, expenditures should be charged to expense. Other industrial nations account for research and development costs on a deferral basis when benefits are expected to be derived. The American accounting standard requiring expensing is so singularly opposite that of other nations, it creates a basis for questioning the validity of the American approach. Similar instances in other accounting treatment exist between nations; however, the contrast in the case of research and development accounting is striking.

6. This statement paraphrases the wording of the decision handed down by Lord Justice Lopes in the decision involving the Kingston Cotton Mills (1896).

7. Corporations of sufficient public consequence to capital market activity must file financial reports with the SEC. Generally speaking, privately held corporations, those with less than 500 shareholders, are exempt from SEC filing requirements.

8. Rule 203 of the AICPA Code of Professional Ethics provides that it is acceptable to depart from the accounting principles promulgated by the body designated by the council of the AICPA if, because of unusual circumstances, failure to do so would result in misleading financial statements.

9. Practitioners note that it is no more necessary for a client to periodically replace his auditor in order to insure independence than it would be for a patient to replace his doctor to insure achieving an independent relationship. Turnover is

not in itself necessary or sufficient to insure competence and independence. Professionalism based upon self-discipline, dedication to public service, and integrity is the basis for achieving society's trust.

10. *1136 Tenants' Corporation* v. *Rothenberg & Co.* [36 A.D. 2d 804, 319 N.Y.S. 2d 1007 (1st Dept. 1971)]. The outcome of this suit has caused a review of the procedures employed for unaudited statements and focused the attention of the profession on the need to address problems in this area.

11. The list of such influential academics is more extensive: Other notable parties include Sidney Davidson, University of Chicago; Paul Garner, University of Alabama; Charles T. Horngren, Stanford University; Norton Bedford, University of Illinois; Wilton T. Anderson, Oklahoma State University; James Don Edwards and Herbert E. Miller, University of Georgia; Charles Zlatkovich and Glenn Welsch, University of Texas at Austin; and Maurice Moonitz and George Staubus, University of California at Berkeley.

12. See R. S. Kaplan, "The Information Content of Financial Accounting Numbers: A Survey of Empirical Evidence," Symposium on the Impact of Research in Financial Accounting and Disclosure on Accounting Practice, Duke University (December 1975); and R. K. Mautz, "Some Thoughts on Applied Research," in *Bridging the Gap, Proceedings of the 1975 Alabama Accounting Research Convocation*, ed. G. J. Previts (The University of Alabama, University, AL , 1976) pp. 1–14.

13. The Cohen Commission's recommendations cover the following areas:
    1. Role of the independent auditor in society
    2. Forming an opinion on financial presentations
    3. Reporting on significant uncertainties
    4. Clarifying responsibility for the detection of fraud
    5. Corporate accountability and the Law
    6. Boundaries of the auditor's role and its extension
    7. The auditor's communication with users
    8. The education, training, and development of auditors
    9. Maintaining the independence of auditors
    10. The process of establishing auditing standards
    11. Regulating the profession to maintain the quality of audit practice

BIBLIOGRAPHY

"Accounting: A Crisis Over Fuller Disclosure." *Business Week*, April 22, 1972: pp. 55–60.

Adams, Daniel. 1817. *The Scholars Arithmetic or Federal Accountant.* Keene, N.H.: John Prentiss.

Aitken, Jr., J. N. 1938. "The Future Relationship of the Certified Public Accountant and the Public." In AIA, *APP*, pp. 200–206.

Alexander, A. DeWitt. 1939. "Procedure in Accounting Research." In AIA, *PAP*, pp. 242–244.

Alexander, Sidney S. 1950. "Income Measurement in a Dynamic Economy," in AIA, *Five Monographs*, pp. 1–96.

Allen, C. E. 1927. "The Growth of Accounting Instruction Since 1900." *Accounting Review*, June, pp. 150–166.

Allen, Frederick Lewis, 1931. *Only Yesterday*, New York: Harper & Co.

American Accounting Association. 1936A. "A Statement of Objectives of the American Accounting Association." *Accounting Review*, March, pp. 1–4.

————. 1936B. "A Tentative Statement of Accounting Principles Affecting Corporate Reports." *Accounting Review*, June, pp. 187–192.

————. 1944. "Accounting Principles Underlying Financial Statements." *Accounting Review*, June, pp. 51–58.

————. 1948. "Accounting Concepts and Standards Underlying Corporate Financial Statements; 1948 Revision." *Accounting Review.* October, pp. 339–344.

————. 1957. *Accounting and Reporting Standards for Corporate Financial Statements and Preceeding Statements and Supplements.* Madison, Wisc.: AAA.

————. 1965. "Doctoral Programs in Accounting." *Accounting Review*, April, pp. 414–421.

————. 1966A. *The American Accounting Association Its First 50 Years.* Evanston, Ill.: AAA.

————. 1966B. *A Statement of Basic Accounting Theory.* Evanston, Ill.: AAA.

————. 1977. *A Statement on Accounting Theory and Theory Acceptance.* Sarasota, Fla.: AAA.

American Association of Public Accountants. 1906. "Collected Papers, 1906 Annual Meeting." Manuscript file, AICPA, New York.

————. 1906–1915. *Year Books of Annual Meetings*, 10 vols., various publishers.

American Institute of Accountants. 1916–1956. *Minutes of the Annual Meetings and Meetings of the Council.* Bound annually, New York: AICPA.

————. 1916–1956. *Yearbooks of Annual Meetings*, 40 vols., New York: AIA.

————. 1921. "Confidential Communication—National Association of CPAs." Manuscript file. AICPA, New York.

———. 1931. "Resume of Special Report of the Accounting Procedures Committee of the AIA." Manuscript file, AICPA, New York.

———. 1932. "Value and Limitations of Corporate Accounts and General Principles for Preparation of Reports to Stockholders." New York: AICPA. (Released subsequently as *Audits of Corporate Accounts.*)

———. 1934. *Audits of Corporate Accounts.* "Correspondence between the Special Committee on Cooperation with the Stock Exchanges, AIA and the Committee on Stock List of the New York Stock Exchange, 1932–4." New York: AIA.

———. Circa 1935. "How to Read a Financial Statement." Manuscript file, AICPA, New York.

———. 1936A. *Examination of Financial Statements by Independent Public Accountants.* New York: AIA.

———. 1936B. "Proceedings of the Advisory Council of State Society Presidents, January 6." New York: AICPA.

———. 1937. "Correspondence File: Sanders, Hatfield and Moore Study." New York: AICPA.

———. 1938. *Papers on Accounting Principles and Procedures* (cited as *APP*). New York: AIA.

———. 1939A. "Extensions of Auditing Procedure." *Journal of Accountancy,* June 1939, pp. 342–349.

———. 1939B. *Papers on Auditing Procedure and Other Accounting Subjects* (cited as *PAP*). New York: AIA.

———. 1940. *Experiences with Extensions of Auditing Procedure and Papers on Other Accounting Subjects* (cited as *EAP*). New York: AIA.

———. 1941. *Accounting, Auditing and Taxes* (cited as *ATT*). New York: AIA.

———. 1943. *Accounting Problems in War Contrast Termination, Taxes and Postwar Planning.* New York: AIA.

———. 1944. *Termination and Taxes and Papers on Other Current Accounting Problems* (cited as *TPP*). New York: AIA.

———. 1946. *Professional Ethics of Public Accounting.* New York: AIA.

———. 1947. *Tentative Statement of Auditing Standards–Their Generally Accepted Significance and Scope.* New York: AIA.

———. 1948. *New Responsibilities of the Accounting Profession.* New York: AIA.

———. 1949. *Accounting and Tax Problems in the Fifties.* New York: AIA.

———. 1950. *Five Monographs on Business Income.* New York: AIA.

———. 1953. *Accounting Research Bulletin* No. 43 ("Restatement and Revision of Accounting Research Bulletins"). New York: AIA.

———. 1954. *Generally Accepted Auditing Standards: Their Significance and Scope.* New York: AIA.

AIA and ASCPA. 1934. "Financial Statements Under the Securities Act and the Securities Exchange Act—Report Submitted by a Joint Committee of the AIA and ASCPA," August 8. Manuscript file, AICPA, New York.

American Institute of Certified Public Accountants. 1957–1966. *Minutes of the Annual Meeting.* Bound annually. New York: AICPA.

———. 1959. "Organization and Operation of Accounting Research Program and Related Activities," October. Manuscript file. New York: AICPA.

———. 1974. *Statement on Auditing Standards No. 4–Quality Control Considerations for a Firm of Independent Auditors.* New York: AICPA.

———. 1975A. "Report of the Special Committee on Equity Funding." New York: AICPA.

————. 1975B. "Statements on Management Advisory Services." New York: AICPA.

————. 1976. *Standards for Professional Accounting Programs and Schools.* New York: AICPA.

————. 1977A. "A Response by the AICPA to the Study of the Subcommittee on Reports, Accounting and Management, U. S. Senate Committee on Government Affairs, entitled *The Accounting Establishment*," April. New York: AICPA.

————. 1977B. Social Measurement Committee. *Measurement of Corporate Social Performance.* New York: AICPA.

American Institute of Certified Public Accountants. 1977C. *Annual Report of the American Institute of Certified Public Accountants.* New York: AICPA.

————. 1978. *Education Requirements for Entry into the Accounting Profession: A Statement of AICPA Policies.* New York: AICPA.

Andersen, Arthur A. 1926. "Accountant's Function as a Business Advisor." *Journal of Accountancy*, January, pp. 17–21.

Anderson, E. H. 1962. "The Evolution of Management." *Industrial Management*, June, pp. 1–4.

Anderson, J. A. 1928. "The Historical Development of Bookkeeping in the First Half of the Nineteenth Century." Master's thesis, University of Illinois.

Andrews, Wayne. 1941. *The Vanderbilt Legend: The Story of the Vanderbilt Family 1794–1940.* New York: Harcourt, Brace & Co.

"The Annual Audit." 1925. *LRB&M Journal*, April, pp. 15–18.

Anyon, James T. 1909, "Sinking Funds and Reserve Accounts." *Journal of Accountancy*, November, pp. 185–191.

Anthony, Robert. 1963. "Showdown on Accounting Principles." *Harvard Business Review*, May-June, pp. 99–106.

"Architects of the U. S. Balance Sheet." 1932. *Fortune*, June, pp. 64–66, 101–102.

Aslaman, Paul, and Duff, John. 1973. "Why Are Accounting Teachers So Academic?" *Journal of Accountancy*, October, pp. 47–53.

Bach, G. Leland; Davidson, H. J.; and Trueblood, R. M. 1961. *The Future of Accounting Education.* Pittsburgh: Carnegie Institute.

Backer, Morton, ed. 1969. *Modern Accounting Theory.* Englewood Cliffs, N.J.: Prentice-Hall.

Badger, Ralph E. 1923. "Interpreting Financial Statements." *Administration*, May, pp. 595–604.

Baggs, George E. 1928. "The Historical Development of American Bookkeeping in the Last Half of the Nineteenth Century." Master's thesis, University of Illinois.

Bailyn, Bernard, ed. 1964. *The Apologia of Robert Keayne, 1653, The Self Portrait of a Puritan Merchant.* New York: Harper & Row.

Barden, Horace G. 1957. "What Do We Mean by Auditing Standards?" Collected Papers of the Annual Meeting. Manuscript file. New York: AICPA.

Barr, Andrew. 1938. "Comments on 'A Statement of Accounting Principles.'" *Journal of Accountancy*, April, pp. 318–323.

————. 1959. "Disclosure in Theory and Practice." *New York CPA*, September, pp. 633–643.

————. 1968. "Accounting Yesterday, Today and Tomorrow." *California CPA Quarterly*, June, pp. 38–39, 41.

Barzman, Sol. 1975. *Credit in Early America.* New York: National Association of Credit Management.

Battelle, L. G. 1954. *Story of Ohio Accountancy*. Columbus: Ohio Society of CPAs.

Baxter, W. T. 1945. *The House of Hancock*. Cambridge, Mass.: Harvard University Press.

——. 1946. "Credit, Bills and Bookkeeping in a Simple Economy." *Accounting Review*, April, pp. 154–166.

——. 1951. "A Colonial Bankrupt: Ebeneezeer Hancock." *Bulletin of the Business Historical Society*, June, pp. 115–124.

Beaver, William H. 1973. "What Should Be the FASB's Objectives?" *Journal of Accountancy*, August, pp. 49–56.

Beck, Herbert C. 1903. "The Value of Auditing to the Business Man." *Annals of the American Academy of Political and Social Science*, November, pp. 433–444.

Bedford, Norton, ed. 1977. *Accountancy in the 1980's–Some Issues*. Urbana, Ill.: University of Illinois.

Bell, Hermon F. 1959. *Reminiscences of a Certified Public Accountant*. New York: privately printed.

Bell, William H. 1923. "Audit Reports—A Tool for the Executive." *Administration*, June, pp. 727–734.

Belser, F. C. 1927. "How the Universities Can Aid the Accounting Profession." *Accounting Review*, March, pp. 37–42.

Bennett, James. 1842. *The American System of Practical Book-keeping*. New York: Collins & Hannay.

Bennett's Business College. 1889. *The Countinghouse Arithmetic*. Baltimore: W. H. Sadler.

Bennett, John. 1939. "Transcript of Conference with John Bennett, Attorney General of New York State the AIA and the New York State Society of CPAs, January 6." New York: AICPA.

Bennett, R. J. 1922. "A Brief History of the Pennsylvania Institute of Certified Public Accountants," in PICPA, *Biographical Sketches*, pp. 41–77.

Benston, George. 1969. "The Effectiveness and Effects of the SEC's Accounting Disclosure Requirements." In *Economic Policies and the Regulation of Corporate Securities*, edited by Henry G. Manne. Washington D.C.: American Enterprise Institute.

Bentley, Harry C. 1911A. *Corporate Finance and Accounting*. New York: Ronald Press.

——. 1911B. *Science of Accounts*. New York: Ronald Press.

——. 1929. *A Brief Treatise on the Origin and Development of Accounting*. New York: privately printed.

Bentley, Harry C. and Leonard, R. S. 1934–1935. *Bibliography of Works on Accounting by American Authors*. Vol. 1, 1796–1900; Vol. 2, 1900–1934. Boston: H. C. Bentley.

Bergstrom, Kenneth. 1974. "Looking Back." *Management Accounting*, March, pp. 47–50.

Berle, A. A. 1938. "Accounting and the Law." *Journal of Accountancy*, May, pp. 368–378.

——. 1954. *The Twentieth Century Capitalist Revolution*. New York: Harcourt, Brace & Co.

Berle, A. A., and Means, G. 1933. *The Modern Corporation and Private Property*. New York: Macmillan.

Bevis, Donald. 1958. "Professional Education for Public Accounting." *Accounting Review*, July, 445–459.
Bevis, Herman W. 1961. "Riding Herd on Accounting Standards." *Accounting Review*, January, pp. 9–16.
————. 1965. *Corporate Financial Reporting in a Competitive Economy*. New York: Macmillan.
Bird, Caroline. 1966. *The Invisible Scar*. New York: David McKay Co.
Blackie, William. 1948. *What Is Accounting For? A Consideration of the Nature and Measurement of Income In a Changing Price Economy*. New York: NACA.
Blight, Reynold E. 1925. "Cultural Value of Accountancy Studies." *Journal of Accountancy*, May, pp. 385–392.
Bloodworth, A. J. 1941. "Case Study in Auditing of Internal Check." In AIA, *ATT*, pp. 10–13.
Blough, Carmen G. 1937A. "The Relationship of the Securities and Exchange Commission to the Accountant." *Journal of Accountancy*, January, pp. 23–39.
————. 1937B. "Some Accounting Problems of the Securities and Exchange Commission." *New York Certified Public Accountant*, April, pp. 3–14.
————. 1939. "Accounting Reports and Their Meaning to the Public." *Journal of Accountancy*, September, pp. 162–168.
————. 1941. "The Work of the Committee on Accounting Procedure." In AIA, *ATT*, pp. 125–136.
Böer, Germain. 1966. "Replacement Cost: A Historic Look." *Accounting Review*, January, pp. 92–97.
Boockholdt, James L. 1977. "Influence of Nineteenth and Early Twentieth Century Railroad Accounting on the Development of Modern Accounting Theory." Working Paper No. 31, July. Academy of Accounting Historians.
Brandeis, Louis D. 1914. *Business–A Profession*. Boston: Small, Maynard & Co.
Brewer, H. Peers. 1976. "Eastern Money and Western Morgages in the 1870's." *Business History Review*, Autumn, pp. 356–380.
Bridenbaugh, Carl. 1966. *Cities in the Wilderness*. New York: Alfred Knopf.
Brief, Richard P. 1964. *Nineteenth Century Capital Accounting and Business Investment*, Ph.D. dissertation, Columbia University.
————. 1966. "The Origin and Evolution of Nineteenth Century Asset Accounting." *Business History Review*, Spring, pp. 1–23.
————. 1967. "A Late Nineteenth Century Contribution to the Theory of Depreciation." *Journal of Accounting Research*, Spring, pp. 27–38.
————. 1970. "Depreciation Theory in Historical Perspective." *The Accountant*, November 26, pp. 737–739.
————. 1976. *Nineteenth Century Capital Accounting and Business Investment*. New York: Arno Press.
————. 1977. "Assets, Valuation and Matching." In *Proceedings of the Charles Waldo Haskins History Seminar*. New York: Ross Institute, New York University.
Briloff, Abraham J. 1964. "Needed: A Revolution in the Determination and Application of Accounting Principles." *Accounting Review*, January, pp. 12–14.
Broad, Samuel. 1936. "Comments." In AIA, *Minutes*, pp. 79–86.
————. 1939. "Extensions of Auditing Procedure to Meet New Demands." In AIA, *PAP*, pp. 41–47.
————. 1941. "Auditing Standards." In AIA, *ATT*, pp. 3–10.
Broaker, Frank, and Chapman, Richard. 1897. *The American Accountants' Manual*. New York: Broaker.

Brown, Isadore. 1955. "The Historical Development of the Use of Ratios in Financial Statement Analysis to 1933." Ph.D. dissertation, Catholic University of America.

Bruchey, Stuart. 1958. "Success and Failure Factors: American Merchants in Foreign Trade in the Eighteenth and Nineteenth Centuries." *Business History Review*, 32: 272–292.

———. 1965. *The Roots of American Economic Growth 1607–1861: An Essay in Social Causation.* New York: Harper & Row.

———. 1976. *Robert Oliver and Mercantile Bookkeeping in the Early Nineteenth Century.* New York: Arno Press.

Brundage, Percival F. 1926. "Treatment of No Par Stock in New York, New Jersey and Massachusetts." *Journal of Accountancy*, April, pp. 241–256.

———. 1950. "Influence of Government Regulation on Development of Today's Accounting Practices." *Journal of Accountancy*, November, pp. 384–391.

Bryant, H. S.; Stratton, H. D.; and Packard, S. S. 1863. *Bryant & Stratton's Counting House Bookkeeping.* New York: Ivison, Blakeman, Taylor & Co.

Burns, Thomas J., and Coffman, Edward N. 1976. *The Accounting Hall of Fame: Profiles of Thirty-Six Members.* Columbus: Ohio State University.

Burton, John C. 1971. "Criticism With Love: An Educator Views the Public Accounting Profession." *Arthur Young Journal*, Winter-Spring, pp. 77–82.

———. 1973. "Some General and Specific Thoughts on the Accounting Environment." *Journal of Accounting*, October, pp. 40–46.

———. 1974. "The SEC and the Accounting Profession: Responsibility, Authority and Progress." In *Institutional Issues in Public Accounting*, edited by Robert Sterling.

———. 1975. "The Auditor of Record." Published lecture, October, University of Massachusetts, Amherst.

Byrne, Gilbert R. 1939. "Accounting for Depreciation on Appreciation." *CAP Correspondence File.* New York: AICPA.

Cadwalader, Mary H. 1975. "Charles Carroll of Carrollton: A Signer's Story." *Smithsonian*, December, pp. 64–70.

Callender, G. S. 1902. "The Early Transportation and Banking Enterprises of the State in Relation to the Growth of Corporations." *Quarterly Journal of Economics*, November, pp. 112–162.

Campbell, E. G. 1941. *Journal of Economic History.* Review of: *The Vanderbilt Legend; The Story of the Vanderbilt Family, 1794–1940.* by Wayne Andrews. New York: Harcourt Brace. May, pp. 111–112.

Canning, John. 1929. *Economics of Accountancy.* New York: Ronald Press.

Canning, R. J. 1958. "Training for an Accounting Career." *Accounting Review*, July, pp. 359–367.

Cannon, Arthur M. 1956. "Challenges to Education in the Report of the Commission on Standards of Education and Experience for CPAs." Manuscript file, AICPA, New York.

Cannon, James G. 1908. "Relation of the Banker to the Public Accountant." In AAPA, *Year-Book, 1908,* 120–126. See also, *Journal of Accountancy*, November, pp. 1–6.

Carey, John C. 1969. *The Rise of the Accounting Profession,* 2 vols. New York: AICPA.

———. 1975A. "The CPAs Professional Heritage," Working Paper No. 1, Academy of Accounting Historians.

——. 1975B. "The CPAs Professional Heritage, Part II," Working Paper No. 5, Academy of Accounting Historians.

Carnegie, Andrew. 1962 ed. *The Gospel of Wealth and Other Essays.* Edited by Edward C. Kirkland. Cambridge, Mass.: Harvard University Press.

Carter, Arthur. 1937. "Correspondence with Committee on Accounting Procedure." CAP Correspondence File, AICPA, New York.

Casler, Darwin J. 1964. "The Evolution of CPA Ethics: A Profile of Professionalization." Occasional Paper No. 12, Michigan State University, Bureau of Business and Economic Research.

Castenholtz, William B. 1931. "The Accountant and Changing Monetary Values." *Accounting Review,* December, pp. 282–288.

Cauley, W. W. 1949. "A Study of the Accounting Records of the Shelby Iron Company." Master's thesis, University of Alabama.

"Certified Public Accountants." 1932. *Fortune,* June, pp. 63, 95–98.

Chamberlin, Henry T. 1940. "Recent Accounting Research." In AIA, *EAP,* pp. 54–59.

Chamberlin, John. 1974. *A Business History of the United States.* New York: Harper & Row.

Chambers, Raymond. 1955. "Blueprint for a Theory of Accounting." *Accounting Research,* January, pp. 17–25.

——. 1956. "Some Observations on Structure of Accounting Theory." *Accounting Review,* October, pp. 584–592.

——. 1963. "Why Bother With Postulates?" *Journal of Accounting Research,* Spring, pp. 3–15.

——. 1966. *Accounting, Evaluation and Economic Behavior.* Englewood Cliffs, N.J.: Prentice-Hall.

Chandler, Alfred. 1954. "The Origins of Progressive Leadership." In *The Letters of Theodore Roosevelt,* edited by E. E. Morrison. Cambridge, Mass.: Harvard University Press.

Charnes, A. C., Cooper, W. W., and Ijiri, Yuji. 1963. "Breakeven Budgeting and Programing to Goals." *Journal of Accounting Research,* Spring, pp. 16–43.

Chase, Harvey. 1914. "Financial Plan or Budget for the National Government." *Journal of Accountancy,* July, pp. 13–29.

Chase, Stuart. 1921. "The Challenge of Waste to Existing Industrial Creeds." *The Nation,* February 28, pp. 284–287.

Chatfield, Michael. 1974. *A History of Accounting Thought.* Hinsdale, Ill.: Dryden Press.

Chatov, Robert. 1975. *Corporate Financial Reporting.* New York: The Free Press.

Clark, John B. 1900. "Trusts." *The Political Science Quarterly,* June, pp. 181–195.

Cleveland, Frederick G. 1905. "The Relation of Auditing to Public Control." *Annals of the American Academy of Political and Social Science,* November, pp. 53–68.

Clews, Henry. 1900. *The Wall Street Point of View.* New York: Silver, Burdett & Co.

——. 1906. "Publicity and Reform in Business." *Annals of the American Academy of Political and Social Science,* July, pp. 143–154.

——. 1908. *Fifty Years in Wall Street.* New York: The Irving Publishing Co.

Cochran, Thomas. 1961. "Did the Civil War Retard Industrialization?" *Mississippi Valley Historical Review,* September, pp. 197–210.

——. 1967. "The History of a Business Society." *Journal of American History,* June, pp. 5–18.

Cochran, Thomas and Miller, William. 1942. *The Age of Enterprise*. New York: MacMillan.

"The Cochran Thesis: A Critique in Statistical Analysis." 1964. *Journal of American History*, June, pp. 77–89.

Cohen, Manuel. 1964. "Current Developments at the SEC—Address at the AAA Annual Meeting." September 1. New York: AICPA.

Cohen, Sol. 1968. "The Industrial Education Movement 1906–1917." *American Quarterly*, Spring, pp. 95–110.

Cole, William M. 1908. *Accounts: Their Construction and Interpretation*. Boston: Houghton-Mifflin.

———. 1909. "The Rise of Accountancy." *Journal of Accountancy*, February, pp. 295–296.

———. 1936. "Theories of Cost." *Accounting Review*, March, pp. 4–9.

Coleman, A. R.; Shenkir, W. G.; and Stone, W. E. 1974. "Accounting in Colonial Virginia: A Case Study." *Journal of Accountancy*, July, pp. 32–43.

Collier, William M. 1900. *The Trusts: What Can We Do With Them? What Can They Do For Us?* New York: Baker and Taylor.

Collins, Clem. 1938. "Address to the Mountain States Accounting Conference, May 31," Manuscript file, AICPA, New York.

———. 1939. "Accounting in the Public Interest," May 1. Manuscript file, AICPA, New York.

Comanger, Henry S. 1950. *The American Mind*. New Haven: Yale University.

Commission on Auditors' Responsibilities (CAR). 1978. *Final Report of the Commission on Auditors' Responsibilities*. New York: AICPA.

Committee on Accounting Procedure (CAP). 1939. "CAP Correspondence File," AICPA, New York.

Committee on History. 1949A. "Early Development of Accounting in New York State." *New York Certified Public Accountant*, March, pp. 157–162.

———. 1949B. "The New York State Society of Certified Public Accountants." *New York Certified Public Accountant*, May, pp. 327–329.

———. 1953A. "The Incorporators of the New York State Society of Certified Public Accountants." *New York Certified Public Accountant*, March, pp. 217–221, 232.

———. 1953B. "The School of Commerce, Accounts and Finance of New York University." *New York Certified Public Accountant*, April, pp. 260–262.

———. 1954. "Is Accounting History Important?" *New York Certified Public Accountant*, August, pp. 511–513, 518.

———. 1956. "The City College of New York, A History of Its Beginnings." *New York Certified Public Accountant*, November, pp. 663–670.

Commons, J. R. 1924. *Legal Foundations of Capitalism*. New York: Macmillan.

———. 1959. *Institutional Economics*. Madison: The University of Wisconsin Press.

———. 1963. *Myself*. Madison: The University of Wisconsin Press.

"Competition Comes to Accounting." 1978. *Fortune*, July 17, pp. 88–94, 96.

Condon, Thomas J. 1968. *New York Beginnings: The Commercial Origins of New Netherlands*. New York: New York University Press.

Cooke, Alistair. 1973. *America*. New York: Alfred A. Knopf, Inc.

Cooper, John A. 1907A. "Draft of a Model CPA Act to Create a State Board of Accountancy and to Prescribe Its Powers and Duties to Provide for the Examination of and Issuance of Certificates to Qualified Accountants and to

Provide a Penalty for Violation of This Act." In *AAPA Year-Book, 1907*, pp. 218–220.

———. 1907B. "Draft of a Model CPA Law to Regulate the Profession." In *AAPA Year-Book, 1907*, pp. 215–218.

———. 1907C. "Professional Ethics." *Journal of Accountancy*, December, pp. 81–94; See also *AAPA Year-Book, 1907*, pp. 133–145.

———. 1913. "Federal Relations: Advancement and Regulation of the Profession." *Journal of Accountancy*, January, pp. 1–9.

———. 1914. "Should Accountants Advertise?" *Journal of Accountancy*, August, pp. 85–94.

Corfias, John. 1973. *125 Years of Education for Business, The History of Dyke College 1848–1973*. Cleveland: Privately Printed.

Couchman, Charles B. 1921. "Classification of Surplus." *Journal of Accountancy*, October, pp. 265–278.

———. 1924. "Principles Governing the Amounts Available for Distribution of Dividends." *Journal of Accountancy*, August, pp. 81–97.

———. 1939A. "The Haunted Balance Sheet—Address at the Third Annual Accounting Conference of the Edison Electric Institute," November 15, Manuscript file, AICPA, New York.

———. 1939B. "Memorandum Depreciation on Appreciation." *CAP Correspondence file*, AICPA, New York.

Counts, George S. 1922. *The Selective Character of American Secondary Education*. Chicago: The University of Chicago Press.

Crandell, J. Chester. 1938. "Principles Related to Inventory Valuation." In AIA, *APP*, pp. 21–25.

Crittenden, S. W. 1877. *An Elementary Treatise on Book-keeping by Single and Double Entry*. Philadelphia: W. S. Fortescue & Co.

Dahlberg, Jane S. 1966. *The New York Bureau of Municipal Research*. New York: New York University Press.

Daines, H. C. 1929. "The Changing Objectives of Accounting." *Accounting Review*, June, pp. 94–110.

Davidson, Sidney. 1963A. "The Day of Reckoning—Management Analysis and Accounting Theory." *Journal Of Accounting Research*, Autumn, pp. 117–126.

———. 1963B. "Old Wines in New Bottles." *Accounting Review*, April, pp. 278–284.

Davies, W. Sanders. 1898. "Professional Accountants Not Detectives." *Business*, January, pp. 33–34.

———. 1926. "Genesis, Growth and Aims of the Institute." *Journal of Accountancy*, August, pp. 105–111.

Davis, G. C. 1962. "The Transformation of the Federal Trade Commission." *Mississippi Valley Historical Review*, December, pp. 437–455.

Davis, Lance E. 1958. "Stock Ownership in the Early New England Textile Industry." *Business History Review*, Spring, pp. 204–222.

———. 1960. "The New England Textile Mills and the Capital Markets: A Study of Industrial Borrowing 1840–1860." *Journal of Economic History*, March, pp. 1–28.

"Dear Woman." 1857. *Harper's Weekly*, January 3, p. 2.

Degler, Carl N. 1964. "American Political Parties and the Rise of the City: An Interpretation." *Journal of American History*, June, pp. 41–59.

Dein, Raymond C. 1961. "A Glance Backward at Research in Accounting." *Accounting Review*, January, pp. 1–8.

Deinzer, Harvey T. 1965. *Development of Accounting Thought.* New York: Holt, Rinehart and Winston.

Demond, C. W. 1951. *Price Waterhouse and Company in America.* New York: Price Waterhouse.

"Depreciation and the Price Level." 1948. *Accounting Review,* April, pp. 115–136. Remarks of J. Dohr, H. C. Greer, E. L. Kohler, W. A. Paton, and M. Peloubet.

Devine, Carl. 1960. "Research Methodology and Accounting Theory Formation." *Accounting Review,* July, pp. 387–399.

Dewey, John. 1900. *The School and Society.* Chicago: The University of Chicago Press.

———. 1910. *How We Think.* New York: D. C. Heath & Co.

———. 1929. "Philosophy." In *Research in the Social Sciences,* edited by W. Gee. New York: MacMillan.

———. 1939. *Intelligence in the Modern World: John Dewey's Philosophy.* Edited by Joseph Ratner. New York: The Modern Press.

Dickinson, Arthur L. 1902. "The Duties and Responsibilities of the Public Accountant." *Commerce, Finance and Accounts,* April, pp. 23–27.

———. 1904. "Profits of a Corporation." *The Financial Record, Lawyers' and Accountants' Manual,* November 2, pp. 38–43.

———, ed. 1904. *Official Record of the Congress of Accountants at St. Louis.* New York: Federation of Societies of Public Accountants.

———. 1905. "Some Special Points in Accounting Practice." *Business World,* April, pp. 157–161 and May, pp. 233–236.

———. 1914. *Accounting Practice and Procedure.* New York: Ronald Press.

"Dispraise of Appreciation." 1932. *Accounting Review,* December, pp. 307–309.

Dixon, Arthur J. 1977. "Commentary on the Metcalf Committee Report." *CPA Journal,* June, pp. 11–18.

Dodd, Donald, and Dodd, W. S. 1976. *Historical Statistics of the United States, 1790–1970.* University, Ala.: University of Alabama Press. Vol. 2, Midwest.

Dohr, James L. 1941. "The Use of Accounting Data By Economists." In AIA, *AAT,* pp. 88–95.

Dorfman, Joseph. 1945. *The Economic Mind in American Civilization, 1865–1918.* New York: The Viking Press.

———. 1959. *The Economic Mind in American Civilization, 1918–1933.* New York: The Viking Press.

Douglas, William. 1974. *Go East Young Man.* New York: Random House.

Dreiser, H. n.d. *A Brief History of the University of Chicago Graduate School of Business.* Chicago: University of Chicago.

Duncan, John C. 1914. "Some Scientific and Educational Problems of the Accountancy Profession." In AAPA, *Year-Book, 1913–14,* pp. 134–149. See also *Journal of Accountancy,* October, pp. 260–275.

Dunlop, Anna B. 1968. "New Old Books." *The Accountant's Magazine,* July, pp. 358–361.

Dunn, Homer A. 1923. "Reorganizing the Institute." *Certified Public Accountant,* October, pp. 261–280.

Durkee, Rodney S. 1939. "What Management Expects of the Auditor." In AIA, *PAP,* pp. 31–34.

Dykema, Frank E. 1976. "American Business and Businessmen's Problems in 1776." Western Economic and Business Historians Meeting, April 30, Tempe, Arizona.

"Economists and Costs." 1934. *Accounting Review,* September, pp. 258–261.

Edwards, Edgar, and Bell, Philip. 1961. *The Theory and Measurement of Business Income.* Berkeley: University of California Press.

Edwards, George W. 1939. *The Evolution of Finance Capitalism.* New York: Macmillan. Reprint. New York: Augustus M. Kelley, 1967.

Edwards, James Don. 1960. *History of Public Accounting in the United States.* East Lansing: Bureau of Business and Economic Research, Michigan State University.

Ernst & Ernst. 1976. *Accounting Under Inflationary Conditions.* Cleveland: Ernst & Ernst.

———. 1977A. *FASB Conceptual Framework: Issues and Implications.* Cleveland: Ernst & Ernst.

———. 1977B. *Social Responsibility Disclosure: 1977 Survey of Fortune Five Hundred Annual Reports.* Cleveland: Ernst & Ernst.

Esquerre, Paul J. 1920. *Applied Theory of Accounts,* 2nd ed., New York: Ronald Press.

———. 1921. "Some Aspects of Professional Accounting." *Administration,* July, pp. 102–107.

———. 1925. "Resources and Their Application." *Journal of Accountancy,* May, pp. 424–430.

———. 1928. "Philosopher-Accountant Takes Inventory of Soul of the Profession." *American Accountant,* July, pp. 19–22.

Etor, J. R. 1973. "Some Problems in Accounting History, 1830–1900." *Business Archives,* June, pp. 38–46.

Eversole, H. B. 1942. "Concerning the Perpetuation of Accounting Fallacies in the Classroom." *Journal of Accountancy,* February, pp. 143–145.

Faulkner, Harold U. 1951. *The Economic History of the United States–The Decline of Laissez Faire.* New York: Rinehart & Co.

Federal Reserve Board. 1917. *Uniform Accounting.* Washington, D.C.: Government Printing Office. Reprinted from *Federal Reserve Bulletin,* April. See also, *Approved Methods for the Preparation of Balance Sheet Statements.* 1918. Washington, D.C.: Government Printing Office, Reprinted from *Federal Reserve Bulletin,* April.

———. 1929. *Verification of Financial Statements.* Washington, D.C.: Government Printing Office.

Federal Trade Commission. 1916. *Fundamentals of a Cost System for Manufacturers.* Washington D.C.: Government Printing Office.

———. 1933. *Federal Securities Act Registration–Statement Form.* Washington D.C.: Government Printing Office.

"Federation of Associations of Public Accountants." 1903. *Commerce, Accounts and Finance,* January, p. 8.

Fels, Rendig. 1951. "American Business Cycles, 1865–79." *American Economic Review,* June, pp. 325–349.

Fertig, Paul E. 1960. "Organization of an Accounting Program." *Accounting Review,* April, pp. 190–196.

Financial Accounting Foundation. 1977. "The Structure of Establishing Financial Accounting Standards: Report of the Structure Committee," Russell E. Palmer, Chairman.

Financial Accounting Standards Board. 1976. "FASB Discussion Memorandum—An Analysis of Income Related to the Conceptual Framework for Financial Accounting and Reporting: Elements of Financial Statements and Their Measurement." Stamford, Conn.: FASB.

Firmin, Peter A. 1957. "Educating Tomorrow's Accountant Today." *Accounting Review*, October, pp. 569–575.

Fisher, F. S. 1933. "Legal Regulation of Accounting." *Journal of Accountancy*, January, pp. 9–29.

Fisher, Irving. 1906. *The Nature of Capital and Income.* New York: Macmillan.

Fleming, John. 1854. Bookkeeping by Double Entry. Pittsburgh: W. S. Haven.

Fleming, Thomas. 1974. "The Cable That Crossed the Atlantic," *Readers Digest*, October, pp. 200–204.

Folsom, E. G. 1873. *The Logic of Accounts.* New York: A. S. Barnes & Co.

Frank, Jerome H. 1939. "Accounting for Investors: The Fundamental Importance of Earning Power." *Journal of Accountancy*; November, pp. 295–304.

———. 1940. "The Sin of Perfectionism." In AIA, *EAP*, pp. 97–113.

Frantz, Joe B. 1950. "The Annual Report as a Public Relations Tool in Three Industries." *Bulletin of the Business Historical Society*, March, pp. 23–42.

Freeman, Herbert C. 1914. "Review of *Auditing Theory and Practice* by Robert H. Montgomery." *Journal of Accountancy*, October, pp. 341–342.

———. 1939. "Unamortized Discount and Premium on Bonds Refunded." *Journal of Accountancy*, December, pp. 397–399.

Fuller, Edmund. 1977. "Our Least Affluent Treasury Secretary." *Wall Street Journal* January 13, p. 14.

Funk, Roland. 1950. "Recent Developments in Accounting Practice and Theory." *Accounting Review*, July, pp. 292–301.

F. W. Lafrentz & Co. 1949. *A Half Century of Accounting.* New York: F. W. Lafrentz & Co.

Gabriel, Ralph. 1956. *The Course of American Democratic Thought.* New York: Ronald Press.

Galbraith, John. 1956. *American Capitalism: The Concept of Countervailing Power.* Boston: Houghton Mifflin.

Gallatin, Albert. 1796. *A Sketch of the Finances of the United States.* New York: William A. Davis.

Gambino, Anthony, and Palmer, John R. 1976. *Management Accounting in Colonial America.* New York: National Association of Accountants.

Garcke, Emile, and Fells, J. M. 1893. *Factory Accounts–Their Principles and Practice.* London: Crosby Lockwood & Son.

Garner, S. Paul. 1954. *Evolution of Cost Accounting to 1925.* Tuscaloosa, Ala.: University of Alabama Press.

Gee, Walter. 1977. "President's Perspective." *Management Accounting*, March, pp. 1, 61.

Gilman, Stephen. 1937. "Is College the Only Way?" *Accounting Review*, June, pp. 105–111.

———. 1939. *Accounting Concepts of Profit.* New York: Ronald Press.

Glad, Paul W. 1966. "Progressives and the Business Culture." *Journal of American History*, June, pp. 75–89.

Glover, P. W. R. 1926. "Regulation of Accountancy by Law." *Journal of Accountancy*, October, pp. 244–253.

———. 1939A. "Basic Questions of Auditing Procedure." *Journal of Accountancy*, August, pp. 92–100.

———. 1939B. Introduction, to AIA, *PAP*, pp. 1–4.

Goldberg, Louis. 1965. *The Commander Theory: An Inquiry Into the Nature of Accounting.* Sarasota, Fla.: AAA.

Golob, Eugene O. 1968. *The "Isms": A History and Evaluation.* Freeport, N.Y.: Books for Libraries Press.

Goodloe, J. S. M. 1920. "Accountant's Report from the Standpoint of the Several Parties at Interest." *Journal of Accountancy,* August, pp. 91–103.

Gordon, R. A., and Howell, J. E. 1959. *Higher Education for Business.* New York: Columbia University Press.

Gordon, Spencer. 1933. "Accountants and the Securities Act." *Journal of Accountancy,* December, pp. 438–451.

———. 1939. "Liability Arising from Accountant's Reports." In AIA, *PAP,* pp. 48–53.

Gore, E. E. 1901. "The Duties of an Auditor." *Commerce, Accounts and Finance,* January 12, pp. 6–8.

Grady, Paul. 1938. "Principles of Depreciation." In AIA, *APP,* pp. 13–16.

———. 1962. "The Quest for Accounting Principles." *Journal of Accountancy,* May, pp. 45–50.

———. 1965. *Inventory of Generally Accepted Accounting Principles for Business Enterprises.* ARS No. 7. New York: AICPA.

Grantham, Jr., Dewey W. 1964. "The Progressive Era and the Reform Tradition." *Mid-America,* October, pp. 227–251.

Green, David. 1966. "Evaluating Accounting Literature." *Accounting Review,* January, pp. 52–64.

Green, Fletcher. 1959. "Origins of the Credit Mobilier of America." *Mississippi Valley Historical Review,* September, pp. 238–251.

Green, Leon. 1937. "One Hundred Years of Torts." In *Law: A Century of Progress,* Vol. 3.

Greendlinger, Leo. 1923. *Financial and Business Statements.* New York: Alexander Hamilton Institute.

Greene, Thomas. 1897. *Corporation Finance.* New York: G. P. Putnam & Son.

Greer, Howard C. 1928. "Where Teaching Lags Behind Practice." *Accounting Review,* September, pp. 289–296.

———. 1932. "A Council on Accounting Research." *Accounting Review,* September, pp. 176–181.

———. 1938. "To What Extent Can the Practice of Accounting Be Reduced to Rules and Standards?" *Journal of Accountancy,* March, pp. 213–223.

———. 1964. "The Corporations Stockholder—Accountants' Forgotten Man." *Accounting Review,* January, pp. 22–31.

Greidinger, B. Bernard. 1942. "SEC Administrative Policy on Financial Statements." *Journal of Accountancy,* March, pp. 219–224.

Gressley, Gene M. 1971. *Bankers and Cattlemen.* Lincoln: University of Nebraska Press.

Groesbeck, John. 1884. *Practical Book-keeping.* Philadelphia: Eldredge & Brother.

Gundelfinger, S. 1924. "Principles Which Should Govern the Determination of Capital and Amounts Available for Distribution of Dividends in the Case of Corporations With Special Reference to the System of Capital Stock Without a Par Value." *Journal of Accountancy,* May, pp. 321–348; June, pp. 420–431; July, pp. 31–41.

Gynther, Reginal S. 1967. "Accounting Concepts and Behavioral Hypothesis." *Accounting Review,* April, pp. 274–290.

Hacker, Louis M. 1961. *Major Documents in American History.* Princeton, N.J.: D. VanNostrand Co.

Hain, H. P. 1965. "History Tells . . ." *The Australian Accountant*, April. Monthly feature April 1964–October 1973.

———. 1972. "History Tells . . ." *Australian Accountant*, September, p. 355.

Hancock, M. Donald, and Sjoberg, Gideon, eds. 1972. *Politics in the Post Welfare State.* New York: Columbia University Press.

Hanson, Walter E. 1977. "Big Brother and the Big Eight." *Management Accountant*, April, pp. 15–19.

Harding, Warren G. 1920. "Less Government in Business and More Business in Government." *World's Work*, November, pp. 25–27.

Harris, Jonathan. 1936. *What Did You Earn Last Month?* New York: National Association of Cost Accountants.

Haskell, John. 1939. "What Does the Investor Expect of the Independent Auditor?" In AIA, *PAP*, pp. 12–16.

Haskins, Charles Waldo. 1901A. "Accountancy and the Economic Association." *Commerce, Accounts and Finance*, January 5, p. 10.

———. 1901B. "Accountancy as a Profession." *Commerce, Accounts and Finance*, January 19, p. 17.

———. 1901C. "The Growing Need of Higher Accountancy." *Commerce, Accounts and Finance*, April 20, pp. 5–7.

———. 1901D. "Higher Commercial Education." *Commerce, Accounts and Finance*, October, pp. 7–9.

Haskins and Sells. 1901. *Report on the Methods of Accounting of the City of Chicago.* New York: Haskins and Sells.

Hasson, C. J. 1932. "The South Sea Bubble and Mr. Snell." *Journal of Accountancy*, August, pp. 128–137.

Hatfield, Henry Rand. 1909. *Modern Accounting: Its Principles and Some of Its Problems.* New York: Appleton.

———. 1913. "Review of *Auditing Theory and Practice* by R. H. Montgomery." *Journal of Political Economy*, November, p. 781.

———. 1915. "Some Neglected Phases of Accounting." *Electric Railway Journal*, October 16, pp. 799–802.

———. 1924. "Historical Defense of Bookkeeping." *Journal of Accountancy*, April, pp. 241–253.

———. 1927. "What Is the Matter With Accounting?" *Journal of Accountancy*, October, pp. 267–279.

———. 1928. "Review of *How to Understand Accounting* by H. C. Greer." *Accounting Review*, June, pp. 210–212.

———. 1934. "Accounting Principles and the Statutes." *Journal of Accountancy*, August, pp. 90–97.

———. 1939. "A Survey of Developments in Accounting." In AIA, *PAP*, pp. 5–11.

Hawkins, David F. 1963. "The Development of Modern Financial Reporting Practices Among American Manufacturing Corporations." *Business History Review*, Autumn, pp. 135–168.

Haynes, Benjamin R., and Jackson, Harry P. 1935. *A History of Business Education in the United States.* Cincinnati: South-Western Publishers.

Hays, Samuel P. 1957. *The Response to Industrialism: 1885–1914.* Chicago: University of Chicago Press.

Heakel, Mohamed. 1968. "A Classification of the Schools of Accounting Thought." Ph.D. dissertation, University of Illinois.

Healy, Robert. 1938. "Next Step in Accounting." *Accounting Review*, March, pp. 1–9.

———. 1939. "Responsibility for Adequate Reports." *Controller*, June, pp. 196–199.

Heilbroner, Robert, ed. 1961. *The Worldly Philosophers.* New York: Simon & Schuster.

Henry, Robert S. 1945. "The Railroad Land Grant Legend in American History." *Mississippi Valley Historical Review*, September, pp. 171–194.

Herrick, Anson. 1969. "I Remember When . . ." *California CPA*, October, pp. 27–29, 72.

Higgins, Thomas G. 1965. *Thomas G. Higgins, CPA, An Autobiography.* New York: Comet Press.

———. 1969. "Arthur Young: 1863–1948." *Arthur Young Journal*, Summer, pp. 20–23.

Hill, Henry P. 1956. "The Necessity for the Experience Requirement for Certified Public Accountants." *New York Certified Public Accountant*, March, pp. 196–199.

Himmelblau, David. 1928. "Some Problems in Property Accounting." *Accounting Review*, June, pp. 149–160.

Historical Highlights . . . John Deere's Contribution to Farm Mechanization. Moline, Ill.: John Deere Co., 1976.

Hockett, Homer C. 1936. *Political and Social Growth of the United States 1492–1852.* New York: Macmillan.

Hoffman, Charles. 1956. "The Depression of the Nineties." *Journal of Economic History*, June, pp. 137–164.

Hofstadter, Richard. 1944. *Social Darwinism in American Thought.* Philadelphia: University of Pennsylvania Press.

Holmes, William. 1974. "Wit and Wisdom from Some Early American Accountants." *World*, Summer, pp. 8–13.

———. 1975A. "Accounting and Accountants in Massachusetts." *Massachusetts CPA Review*, January-February, pp. 15–21; March-April, pp. 16–22; May-June, pp. 12–23.

———. 1975B. "CPAs Owe Much to Puritan 'Wrightings.'" *Boston Globe*, 8 June.

———. 1976. "Digging in Boston's Accounting Dumps." *Accounting Historian*, Summer, pp. 1, 5.

———; Kistler, Linda; and Corsini, Lou. 1978. *Three Centuries of Accounting in Massachusetts.* New York: Arno Press.

Horne, Henry A. 1940. "Accounting Procedure and Research." In AIA, *EAP*, pp. 46–53.

Horngren, Charles. 1959. "Increasing the Utility of Financial Statements." *Journal of Accountancy*, July, pp. 39–46.

———. 1971. "Accounting Discipline in 1999." *Accounting Review*, January, pp. 1–11.

Howard, Stanley E. 1931. "Charge and Discharge." *Accounting Review*, March, pp. 51–56.

Hoxsey, J. M. B. 1930. "Accounting for Investors." *Journal of Accountancy*, October, pp. 251–284.

Hughes, Hugh P. 1976. "The Contributions of Thomas Jones and Benjamin Franklin Foster." Collected Papers, American Accounting Association, Southeast Regional Group, pp. 93–98.

Hurdman, Frederick H. 1919. "Capital Stock with No Par Value." *Journal of Accountancy*, October, pp. 246–257.

———. 1940. "Proposed Revision of Rules of Professional Conduct." In AIA, *EAP*, pp. 76–77.

Hurley, Edward N. 1916. *Awakening of Business*. New York: Doubleday, Page & Co.

Husband, George. 1938. "The Corporate Entity Fiction and Accounting Theory." *Accounting Review*, September, pp. 241–253.

———. 1946. "That Thing Which the Accountant Calls Income." *Accounting Review*, July, pp. 247–254.

Hylton, Delmar P. 1962. "Current Trends in Accounting Theory." *Accounting Review*, January, pp. 22–27.

Institute of Accounts. 1896. "By-Laws." Reprinted by the American Antiquarian Society, New York, 1948,

Institute of Accountants in the United States of America. 1916. *1916 Year-Book of the Institute of Accountants in the United States*. New York: AIA.

Jackson, J. Hugh. 1928. "Teaching Auditing by the Case Method." *Accounting Review*, September, pp. 297–310.

Jenks, Leland H. 1944. "Railroads as an Economic Force in American Development." *Journal of Economic History*, May, pp. 1–20.

Jennings, Alvin R. 1948. "Staff Training—Present and Future." *Accounting Review*, October, pp. 401–407.

———. 1957. "Speech at Annual Meeting of AICPA, October 28." Manuscript file, AICPA, New York.

———. 1958A. "Present Day Challenges in Financial Reporting." *Journal of Accountancy*, January, pp. 28–34.

———. 1958B. "Accounting Research." *Accounting Review*, October, pp. 547–554.

———. 1964. "Opinions of the APB." *Journal of Accountancy*, August, pp. 27–33.

Jennings, R. M. 1962. "Selection from a Pre-Revolutionary Accounting Record." *Accounting Review*, January, pp. 73–75.

Johnson, Hans V. 1976. "Merchant Accountants." *Management Accounting*, October, pp. 57–61.

Johnson, H. Thomas. 1972. "Lyman Mills: Early Cost Accounting for Internal Management Control in the 1850's." *Business History Review*, Winter, pp. 466–474.

Johnson, H. Thomas. 1975. "The Role of Accounting History in the Study of Modern Business Enterprise." *Accounting Review*, July, pp. 444–450.

Johnson, Joseph French. 1902. "The Relationship of Economic to Higher Accounting." *Commerce, Accounts and Finance*, February, pp. 6–9.

Jones, Ralph C. 1956. *Effects of Price Level Changes on Business Income, Capital and Taxes*. Columbus, Ohio: AAA.

Jones, Thomas. 1842. "Analysis of Bookkeeping as a Branch of General Education." *Hunts Merchants Magazine*, December, pp. 513–526.

———. 1859. *Bookkeeping and Accountantship*. New York: John Wiley.

Jones, Thomas F. 1933. *New York University 1832–1932*. New York: New York University Press.

Joplin, J. Porter. 1914A. "Ethics of Accountancy." *Journal of Accountancy*, March, pp. 187–196.

———. 1914B. "Secret Reserves." *Journal of Accountancy*, December, pp. 407–417.

Käfer, Karl. 1966. *Theory of Accounts in Double-Entry Bookkeeping.* Urbana, Ill.: Center for International Education and Research in Accounting, University of Illinois.

Kasyan, Lorraine. 1975. "The Philosopher's Accounts." *Arthur Young Journal,* Spring, pp. 32–37.

Keister, D. A. 1896. "The Public Accountant." *The Book-keeper,* July, pp. 21–22.

Kelley, Arthur. 1958. "Comments on the 1957 Revision of Corporate Accounting and Reporting Standards." *Accounting Review,* April, pp. 214–216.

Kent, E. J. 1975. "The Firm of S. D. Leidesdorf and Company, Certified Public Accountants." Typed memorandum, S. D. Leidesdorf & Co., New York.

Kennedy, John T. 1921. "Federal Tax Laws and the Practice of Accountancy." *Pace Student,* October, pp. 161–163, 172–173.

Kessler, Louis M. 1956. "Let's Build the Profession Through Education." Address at the Annual Meeting of the AIA, September. Manuscript file, AICPA, New York.

Kester, Roy B. 1918. *Accounting Theory and Practice.* New York: Ronald Press.

———. 1936. "Education for Professional Accountancy." *Accounting Review,* June, pp. 99–108.

Kistler, L. H. and Jennings, R. M. 1969. "An Accounting Primer Circa 1831," *Accounting Review,* January, pp. 168–173.

King, Earle. 1948. "Need for a Definite Statement of Accounting Principles." *Journal of Accountancy,* November, p. 369.

Kirchner, Paul. 1961. "Theory and Research in Management Accounting." *Accounting Review,* January, pp. 43–49.

Kirkland, Edward C. 1946. "Comments on the Railroad Land Grant Legent in American History Texts." *Mississippi Valley Historical Review,* March, pp. 557–576.

———. 1967. *Industry Comes of Age.* Chicago: Quadrangle Books, Inc.

Kitman, Marvin. 1970. *George Washington's Expense Account.* New York: Simon & Schuster. (Reviewed in *Management Accounting,* December 1970, p. 60.)

Kittredge, Anson. 1901. "Balance Sheet." *Commerce, Accounts and Finance,* December, pp. 3–7.

Klein, Joseph J. 1969. "Interviews by Thomas Hogan." Typed transcripts, held by authors.

Knauth, Oswald. 1957. "An Executive Looks at Accountancy." *Journal of Accountancy,* January, pp. 29–32.

Knebel, Fletcher. 1974. *The Bottom Line.* Garden City, N.Y.: Doubleday & Co.

Knortz, Herbert C. 1976. "Salute to the Bicentennial." Paper delivered at the NAA International Conference, June 21.

Kohler, Eric. 1934. "A Nervous Profession." *Accounting Review,* December, pp. 334–336.

———. 1939. "Some Old Rules Revised." *Accounting Review,* December, pp. 453–457.

———. 1940. "The Goal of Accounting Education." In AIA, *EAP,* pp. 84–88.

———. 1953. "The Development of Accounting Principles by Accounting Societies." *Accounting Research IV.*

———. 1963. "Why Not Retain Historical Cost?" *Journal of Accountancy,* October, pp. 35–41.

———. 1975. "In All My Years. . . ." *Accounting Historian,* Spring, pp. 4, 6.

Kohler, Eric, and Morrison, Paul. 1926. *Principles of Accounting.* Chicago: A. W. Shaw Co.

Kolko, Gabriel. 1963. *The Triumph of Conservatism: A Reinterpretation of American History, 1900–1916.* New York: The Free Press.

Kottke, Frank. 1959. "Mergers and Acquisitions of Large Manufacturing Companies 1951–9." *Review of Economics and Statistics,* November, pp. 430–433.

Krebs, William S. 1930. "Asset Appreciation, Its Economic and Accounting Significance." *Accounting Review,* March, pp. 60–69.

Krekstein, I. H. 1972. "A Founding Partner's Story." *The Accountant* no. 3, pp. 25–33.

Kreps, Juanita. 1978. "Why We Need a Regulatory Budget." *Business Week,* July 31, p. 14.

Kristol, Irving. 1976. "The Republican Future." *Wall Street Journal,* May 14, p. 18.

Laeri, J. Howard. 1966. "Statement in Quotes." *Journal of Accountancy,* March, pp. 57–58.

Landis, James M. 1933. "Federal Securities Act and Regulations Relating to the Work and Responsibility of the CPA." In *Addresses and Discussion Relating to the Federal Securities Acts . . . ,* New York: New York State Society of Certified Public Accountants.

———. 1935. Address before American Management Associates, October 9. Mimeographed. AICPA library, New York.

Langenderfer, Harold Q. 1954. "The Federal Income Tax, 1861–1872." Ph.D. dissertation, Indiana University.

Lauss, Arthur M. 1970. "A Fat Maverik Stirs Up the Accounting Profession." *Fortune,* December, pp. 96–99, 122–125.

Law: A Century of Progress. 1937. 3 vols., New York: New York University Press.

Lawler, John. 1969. "The Current State of the Accounting Profession." Mimeographed. AICPA, New York.

Lawson, Thomas. 1904. "Frenzied Finance." *Everybody's Magazine.*

Leder, L. H., and Carosso, V. P. 1956. "Robert Livingston (1654–1728): Businessman of Colonial New York." *Business History Review,* March, pp. 18–45.

Lee, Geoffrey A. 1975. "The Concept of Profit in British Accounting, 1760–1900." *Business History Review,* Spring, pp. 6–36.

"The Legal Liability of Auditors." 1910. *Journal of Accountancy,* March, pp. 380–381.

Lindbloom, Charles E. 1977. *Politics & Markets.* New York: Basic Books.

Lindsay, C. H. Forbes. 1908. "New Business Standards in Washington: Work of the Keep Commission." *American Review of Reviews,* February, pp. 190–195.

Link, Arthur S., with Catton, W. B. 1967. *The American Epoch.* New York: Alfred Knopf, Inc.

Linowes, David. 1968. "Development of Socio-Economic Accounting." *Journal of Accountancy,* November, pp. 37–42.

Littleton, A. C. 1924. "Discussion of Principles of Valuation Related to the Balance Sheet." *Papers and Proceedings of the Eighth Annual Meeting of the AAUIA.* American Association of University Instructors in Accounting, pp. 14–15.

———. 1927. "Thomas Jones—Pioneer." *Certified Public Accountant,* June, pp. 183–186.

———. 1928. "What Is Profit?" *Accounting Review,* September, pp. 278–288.

———. 1929. "Value and Price in Accounting." *Accounting Review,* September, pp. 147–154.

———. 1932. "Capital and Surplus." *Accounting Review,* December, pp. 290–293.

———. 1933A. *Accounting Evolution to 1900.* New York: AIA.

————. 1933B. "Social Origins of Modern Accountancy." *Journal of Accountancy*, October, pp. 261–270.

————. 1935. "Value or Cost?" *Accounting Review*, September, pp. 269–273.

————. 1936A. "Contrasting Theories of Profit." *Accounting Review*, March, pp. 10–18.

————. 1936B. "The Professional College." *Accounting Review*, June, pp. 109–116.

————. 1939. "Memorandum—Unamortized Discount and Redemption Premium on Bonds Refunded," May. *CAP Correspondence File*, AICPA, New York.

————. 1941. "A Geneology for 'Cost or Market.' " *Accounting Review*, June, pp. 161–167.

————. 1942. *Directory of Early American Public Accountants.* Bureau of Economic and Business Research Bulletin no. 62, Urbana, Ill.

————. 1946. "Accounting Exchange." *Accounting Review*, December, pp. 459–463.

————. 1953. *Structure of Accounting Theory.* Urbana, Ill.: AAA.

Littleton, A. C. and V. K. Zimmerman. 1962. *Accounting Theory: Continuity and Change.* Englewood Cliffs, N.J.: Prentice Hall.

Lively, Robert A. 1955. "The American System." *Business History Review* 29: 81–95.

Lockwood, Jeremiah. 1938. "Early University Education in Accountancy." *Accounting Review*, June, pp. 131–144.

Loeb, Stephen E., and May, Gordon S. 1976. *A History of Public Accounting in Maryland.* Baltimore: Maryland Association of CPAs.

Loomis, Noel M. 1968. *Wells Fargo.* New York: Crown Publishers.

Lowi, Theodore J. 1969. *The End of Liberalism.* New York: W. W. Norton & Co.

Lybrand, William. 1908. "The Accounting for Industrial Enterprises." In AAPA, *Year-Book, 1908,* pp. 255–290.

Lyon, Leverett S. 1924. "Accounting Courses in Universities." *Journal of Accountancy*, December, pp. 422–429.

MacMillan, William R. 1939. "Sources and Extent of the Liability of a Public Accountant." Reprinted from *Chicago Kent Review*, December. New York: American Surety Co.

Madden, J. T.; Stevenson, R. A.; and Gray, W. R. 1928. "The Place of Accounting in the Commerce Curriculum." *Accounting Review*, June, pp. 189–207.

Magee, Henry C. 1913. "The Accountant's Relation to Inventory." *Journal of Accountancy*, December, pp. 443–456.

Main, Frank W. 1923. "President's Message." *Certified Public Accountant*, January, pp. 3–5.

Main, Lafrentz & Co. circa 1974. *When the World Was Still Young.* New York: Main, Lafrentz & Co.

Mair, John. 1763. *Book-keeping Methodiz'd.* Edinburgh: Sands, Murray and Cochran.

Marple, Raymond P. 1963. "Value-Itis." *Accounting Review*, July, pp. 478–482.

Marshall, Alfred. 1964. *Principles of Economics.* 8th ed. London: MacMillan & Co.

Marshall, Leon Carroll. 1926. "The Collegiate School of Business at Erehwon." *Journal of Political Economy*, June, pp. 289–326.

Mason, Perry. 1961. *Cash Flow Analysis and the Funds Statement.* ARS no. 2. New York: AICPA.

Mather, Charles E. 1948. "The Development of the Accounting Profession." In *New Jersey, Fifty Years*, pp. 7–9.

Mattessich, Richard. 1956. "The Constellation of Accountancy and Economics." *Accounting Review*, October, pp. 551–564.

———. 1957. "Toward a General and Axiomatic Foundation of Accounting." *Accounting Research*, October, pp. 328–355.

———. 1972. "Methodological Preconditions and Problems of a General Theory of Accounts." *Accounting Review*, July, pp. 469–487.

Mautz, Robert K., and Sharaf, Hussein. 1961. *The Philosophy of Auditing*. Sarasota, Fla.: AAA.

———, and Previts, Gary J. 1977. "Eric Kohler." *Accounting Review*, March, pp. 301–307.

May, George O. 1915. "Qualifications in Certificates." *Journal of Accountancy*, October, pp. 248–259.

———. 1927. Letter to the Editor. *New York Times*, 27 August.

———. 1933. Transcript of speech before the Illinois Society of CPAs, December 6. AICPA, New York.

———. 1934. "Position of Accountants Under the Securities Acts." *Journal of Accountancy*, January, pp. 9–23.

———. 1936A. "The Influence of Accounting on Economic Development." *Journal of Accountancy*, January, pp. 11–22; February, pp. 92–105; March, pp. 171–184.

———. 1936B. *Twenty Five Years of Accounting Responsibility*. Edited by Carleton Hunt. 2 vols. New York: AIA.

———. 1938. "Uniformity in Accounting." *Harvard Business Review*, Autumn, pp. 1–8.

———. 1939. "General Purpose of Financial Statements." Memorandum. *CAP Correspondence File*. AICPA, New York.

———. 1943. *Financial Accounting: A Distillation of Experience*. New York: Macmillan.

———. 1957A. "Business Combinations: An Alternate View." *Journal of Accountancy*, April, pp. 33–39.

———. 1957B. "Income Accounting and Social Revolution." *Journal of Accountancy*, June, pp. 36–42.

Mayhew, Ira. 1875. *Mayhew's Practical Book-keeping*. Boston: Nichols and Hall.

Mayer, Caroline E. 1977. "Accountants—Cleaning Up America's Mystery Profession." *U. S. News and World Report*, December 19, pp. 39–42.

McCrea, Roswell C., and Kester, Roy B. 1936. "School of Professional Accountancy." *Journal of Accountancy*, February, pp. 106–117.

McCraw, Thomas K. 1975. "Regulation in America." *Business History Review*, Summer, pp. 159–183.

McFarland, Walter B. 1961. "Research in Management Accounting by the National Association of Accountants." *Accounting Review*, January, pp. 21–25.

McKendrick, Neil M. 1970. "Josiah Wedgewood and Cost Accounting in the Industrial Revolution." *Economic History Review*, 22: 45–67.

McKenzie, Robert H. 1971. "A History of the Shelby Iron Company, 1865–1881." Ph.D. dissertation, University of Alabama.

McNaught, Kenneth. 1966. "The American Progressives and the Great Society." *Journal of American History*, December, pp. 504–520.

Mellon, Andrew. 1924. *Taxation: The People's Business*. New York: Macmillan.

Mepham, M. J., and Stone, W. E. 1977. "John Mair, M.A.: Author of the First Classic Book-keeping Series." *Accounting and Business Research*, Spring, pp. 128–134.

Merino, Barbara D. 1975. "The Professionalization of Accountancy in America: A Comparative Analysis of Selected Accounting Practitioners, 1900–1925." Ph.D. dissertation, University of Alabama.

———. 1976. "Development of American Accountancy from 1876–1976." *CPA Journal*, June, pp. 31–36.

———. 1977. "The CPA Experience Requirement in Historic Perspective." *The Accounting Journal*, Spring, pp. 51–60.

Merino B., and Coe T. 1978. "Uniformity in Accounting: A Historical Perspective." *Journal of Accountancy*. August, pp. 62–69.

Merritt, Rita Perine. 1925. *The Accountants' Directory and Who's Who*. New York: Prentice-Hall.

Middleditch, Livingston. Jr. 1918. "Should Accounts Reflect the Changing Value of the Dollar?" *Journal of Accountancy*, February, pp. 114–120.

Miller, Hermann C. 1937. "A Suggested Program of Education for the Accountant." *Accounting Review*, June, pp. 191–198.

Mills, C. Wright. 1959. *The Power Elite*. New York: Oxford University Press.

Minton, R. W. 1976. "John Law's Bubble: bigger . . . bigger and then BUST!" *Smithsonian*, January, pp. 93–98.

Montgomery, Robert H. 1904. "The Importance of Uniform Practice in Determining Profits of Public Service Corporations Where Municipalities Have the Power to Regulate Rates." *Financial Record*, November 2, pp. 34–38.

———. 1905. "Value and Recent Development of Theoretical Training for the Public Accountant." *Business Man's Magazine*, September, pp. 417–419.

———. 1907. "Professional Ethics." *Journal of Accountancy*, December, pp. 94–96.

———. 1912A. *Auditing Theory and Practice*. New York: Ronald Press.

———. 1912B. "Federal Control of Corporations." In AAPA, *Year-Book, 1912*, pp. 193–211. See also, *Journal of Accountancy*, October, pp. 272–290.

———. 1914. "Accountancy Laboratory—the Connecting Link Between Theory and Practice." *Journal of Accountancy*, June, pp. 405–411.

———. 1927. "Accountants' Limitations." *Journal of Accountancy*, October, pp. 245–249.

———. 1937. "Curse of Balancing or Theory vs. Practice." *Journal of Accountancy*, April, pp. 279–281.

Montgomery, Robert H., and Staub, Walter. 1924. *Auditing Principles*. New York: Ronald Press.

Moody, John. 1916. *How to Analyze Railroad Reports*. 4th ed. New York: Moody's Investor Service.

Moody, Paul. 1845. *A Practical Plan of Bookkeeping by Double Entry*. Philadelphia: J. B. Lippincott & Co.

Moonitz, Maurice, and Nelson, Carl. 1960. "Recent Developments in Accounting Theory." *Accounting Review*, April, pp. 206–217.

———. 1973. "The Beamer Committee—A Golden Opportunity for Accounting Education." *Journal of Accountancy*, August, pp. 64–67.

———. 1974. *Obtaining Agreement on Standards in the Accounting Profession*. Studies in Accounting Research no. 8. Sarasota, Fla.: AAA.

———, and Nelson, Carl. 1960. "Recent Developments in Accounting Theory." *Accounting Review*, April, pp. 206–217.

Moore, R. H. 1899. "Ethics of the Bookkeeper." *The Bookkeeper*, May, pp. 34–37.

Morris, Richard B. 1975. "Financial Wizards of the Revolution." *Ford Times*, August, pp. 32–37.

Mott, Frank L. 1954. "The Magazine Revolution and Popular Ideas in the Nineties." *Proceedings of the American Antiquarian Society*, 64: 195–214.

Mowry, George. 1965. *The Urban Nation 1920–1960*. New York: Hill and Wang.

Moyer, C. A. 1951. "Early Developments in American Auditing." *Accounting Review*, January, pp. 1–8.

Myer, John C. 1931. "Teaching the Accountant the History and Ethics of His Profession." *Accounting Review*, March, pp. 47–50.

Myers, John H. 1959. "The Critical Event and Recognition of Net Profit." *Accounting Review*, October, pp. 528–532.

National Association of Cost Accountants. 1924. *Industrial and Financial Investigations*. New York: NACA.

National Association of State Boards of Accountancy (NASBA). 1955. "Education and Uniformity." *Proceedings of the 1955 Annual Meeting*, October, pp. 22–24.

————. 1973. *NASBA–A Review of the History, Organization, Accomplishments, Policies and Other Activities of the National Association of State Boards of Accountancy*. New York: NASBA.

————. 1976. "Combination of Education and Experience Required for CPAs: Summary of State Laws and Regulations." New York: NASBA.

"National Federation of Accountants." 1902. *Commerce, Accounts and Finance*, December, pp. 17–18.

Nelson, Carl. 1967. "An Accountant's View of Profit Measurement." In *Profits in the Modern Economy*, edited by J. R. Nelson and H. W. Stevenson. Minneapolis: University of Minnesota Press.

————. 1976. "Statements to Make an Accountant See Red." *Business Week*, March 8, pp. 12–15.

Nelson, Charles A. 1976A. "Is There A Past in Our Future?" *World*, Spring, pp. 2–3.

New Jersey Society of CPAs (NJSCPA). 1948. *Fifty Years of Service 1898–1948*. Trenton, N.J.: NJSCPA.

Newman, Maurice. 1967. "Historical Development of Early Accounting Concepts and Their Relation to Certain Economic Concepts." Master's thesis, New York University.

New York State Society of Certified Public Accountants (NYSSCPA). 1897–1912. *Minute Books*. Handwritten in binders, NYSSCPA, New York.

————. 1907. *Ten-Year Book*. New York: NYSSCPA.

————. 1927. *Thirty-Year Book*. New York: NYSSCPA.

New York Stock Exchange. 1978. *Fact Book*, New York: NYSE.

Nichols, Herman. 1927. "Letter on Inventory Valuations." *Journal of Accountancy*, June, pp. 448–449.

Nissley, Warren. 1935. "Education for the Profession of Accountancy." *Journal of Accountancy*, August, pp. 90–103.

————. 1937. "The Future of Professional Accountancy." *Journal of Accountancy*, February, pp. 99–114.

————. 1940. "Charges Against Surplus." In AIA, *EAP*, pp. 38–42.

"No Last Trumpet: Abe Briloff Still Leads the Crusade for Honest Accounting." 1976. *Barron's*, April 12, April 26.

Noble, Edward J. 1939. "Accountancy and the Nation's Business." In AIA, *PAP*, pp. 279–286.

Noble, H. S. 1927. "The Relation of Business Organization to Accountancy." *Journal of Accountancy*, September, pp. 232–236.

Noble, Paul L. 1950. "A Quantitative Analysis of Accounting Curricula." *Accounting Review*, April, pp. 163–169.

North, Douglass C. 1956. "International Capital Flows and the Development of the American West." *Journal of Economic History*, December, pp. 493–505.

Noyes, Alexander D. 1909. *Forty Years of American Finance*. New York: G. P. Putnam's Sons.

———. 1926. *The War Period of American Finance, 1908–1925*. New York: G. P. Putnam's Sons.

Nuawmalee, Prakong. 1957. "The Historical Development of Financial Statements in the United States Between 1900–1933." Master's thesis, University of Pennsylvania.

Oakey, Francis. 1915. "Standardization of Financial Statements." *Journal of Accountancy*, September, pp. 179–185.

Oddy, D. J. 1974. "Ealing Business History Seminar: Accounting in the Nineteenth Century." *Business History*, July, pp. 175–182.

Olds, Leland. 1940. "Responsibility of Accountants in a Changing Order." In AIA, *EAP*, pp. 116–123.

Organization for European Economic Cooperation (OEEC). 1952. *Cost Accounting and Productivity: The Use and Practice of Cost Accounting in the U.S.A.* Geneva: OEEC.

Pace, Homer. 1924. "Relation of the Accountancy Instructor to the Development of Professional Standards in the Practice of Accountancy." *Journal of Accountancy*, May, pp. 349–356.

Packard, S. S. 1868. *Manual of Theoretical Training in the Science of Accounts*. New York: by the author.

———. 1896. "Testimonial Banquet to S. S. Packard." Monograph, privately printed.

Packard, S. S., and Bryant, H. B. 1878. *The New Bryant and Stratton Common School Book-Keeping*. New York: American Book Company.

Palen, Jennie. 1955. "The First Women CPA." *New York Certified Public Accountant*, August, pp. 475–477, 496.

Palmer, John R. 1976. "The Revolution Was Not in Accounting." *Tempo* 22: 19–23.

Parker, R. H. 1965. "Lower of Cost or Market in Great Britain and the United States: An Historical Survey." *Abacus*, December, pp. 156–172.

Paton, William A. 1917. "Theory of the Double Entry System." *Journal of Accountancy*, January, pp. 7–26.

———. 1920. "Depreciation, Appreciation and Productive Capacity." *Journal of Accountancy*, July, pp. 1–11.

———. 1921. "Assumptions of the Accountant." *Administration*, June, pp. 788–802.

———. 1922. *Accounting Theory*. New York: Ronald Press.

———. 1931. "Economic Theory in Relation to Accounting Valuations." *Accounting Review*, June, pp. 89–96.

———. 1932. "Accounting Problems of the Depression." *Accounting Review*, December, pp. 258–267.

———. 1934. "Shortcomings of Present Day Financial Statements." *Journal of Accountancy*, February, pp. 108–132.

————. 1938. "Comments on 'A Statement of Accounting Principles.' " *Journal of Accountancy*, March, pp. 196–207. See also, "Correspondence." *Idem*. April, p. 328.

————. 1939A. "Objectives of Accounting Research." In AIA, *PAP*, pp. 229–233.

————. 1939B. "Plant Write-Ups and Write Downs and the Resulting Treatment of Depreciation." Typed memorandum, *CAP Correspondence File*, AICPA, New York.

————. 1972. Foreward to the reissue of *The Philosophy of Accounts*, by Charles E. Sprague. Houston, Texas: Scholars Book Co.

Paton, William A. and Littleton, A. C. 1940. *An Introduction to Corporate Accounting Standards*. Columbus, Ohio: AAA.

Paton, William A., and Stevenson, Russell. 1918. *Principles of Accounting*, 3rd ed. New York: MacMillan.

Patten, Simon. 1907. *The New Basis of Civilization*. New York: Macmillan.

Peat, Marwick & Mitchell. 1977. "ARS 173—Review Committee Report." Peat, Marwick & Mitchell, New York.

Pedelahore, J. Earl. 1956. "Case for the Dissent—Report of the Commission on Standards of Education and Experience for CPAs." Typed. AICPA, New York.

Peloubet, Maurice E. 1928. "Current Assets and the Going Concern." *Journal of Accountancy*, July, pp. 18–22.

————. 1955. "The Historical Background of Accounting." In *Handbook of Modern Accounting*, edited by Morton Backer, pp. 7–39.

Pemberton, Jackson. 1976. "A New Message—On the Constitution." *Freeman*, July, pp. 408–418.

Pennsylvania Institute of CPAs (PICPA). 1905. *Fifth Annual Banquet*. Philadelphia: George H. Buchanan Co.

————. 1922. *Records of the Twenty Fifth Anniversary Proceedings*. Philadelphia: PICPA.

Penrose, Edith. 1959. *The Theory of the Firm*. New York: Wiley.

Perry, Donald P. 1955. *Public Accounting Practice and Accounting Education*. Cambridge, Mass.: Harvard University Press.

Persons, Stow. 1958. *American Minds*. New York: Henry Holt & Co.

Phillippe, Gerald. 1963. "Corporate Management's Stake in the Development of Sound Accounting Principles." In Collected Papers of the Annual Meeting, AICPA, New York.

Pierson, Franklin, et al. 1959. *The Education of American Businessmen*. New York: McGraw-Hill.

Pixley, Francis W. 1904. "The Duties of Professional Accountants." *Financial Record*, 2 November, pp. 28–34.

Potts, James. 1976. "An Analysis of the Evolution of Municipal Accounting to 1835 with Primary Emphasis on Developments in the United States." Ph.D. dissertation, University of Alabama.

Powell, Weldon. 1959. "Report on the APB." In AICPA, *Minutes, 1959*, pp. 50–57.

————. 1960. "Challenge to Research." *Journal of Accountancy*, February, pp. 34–41.

————. 1961. "Report on the Accounting Research Activities of the American Institute of Certified Public Accountants." *Accounting Review*, January, pp. 26–31.

Previts, Gary J. 1972. "A Critical Evaluation of Comparative Financial Accounting Thought in America, 1900–1920." Ph.D. dissertation, University of Florida.

————. 1975A. "American Accountancy: An Overview 1900–1925." *Business and Economic History* 5: 109–119.

————. 1975B. "Pathways to a New Vista of Accountancy's Past." *Accounting Historian*, Winter, p. 2.

————. 1976A. "The Accountant in Our History: A Bicentennial Overview." *Journal of Accountancy*, July, pp. 45–51.

————. 1976B. "Origins of American Accounting." *CPA Journal*, May, pp. 13–17.

Previts, Gary J. and Sheldahl, Terry K. 1977. "Accounting and 'Countinghouses': An Analysis and Commentary." *Abacus*, June, pp. 52–59.

Price Waterhouse. 1976. *Cost Accounting Standards Board: A Guide to the Background, Objectives, Operations and Pronouncements of the Cost Accounting Standards Board.* New York: Price Waterhouse.

Pryce-Jones, J. E., and Parker, R. H. 1976. *Accounting in Scotland: A Historical Bibliography.* Glasgow: Institute of Chartered Accountants of Scotland.

Queenan, John W. 1962. "Current Problems and Opportunities of the CPA." Speech delivered at Omaha, Nebraska, June 18. AICPA, New York.

————. 1966. "The Development of Accounting Principles." In Haskins and Sells, *Selected Papers 1966.* New York: Haskins and Sells.

————. 1977. "Interview with John Queenan by Barbara Merino." March 1977.

"A Radical Goal for Financial Statements." *Business Week*, October 6, 1973, pp. 46–48.

Rappaport, Louis H. 1963. "Forces Influencing Accounting: The Stock Exchanges." *Lybrand Journal* 44: 43–57.

Reckitt, Ernest. 1953. *Reminisences of Early Days of the Accounting Profession.* Chicago: Illinois Society of CPAs.

Reighard, John J. 1932. "Earning Statements in Periods of Prosperity and Depression." *Accounting Review*, June, pp. 108–114.

Remond, J. L. 1900. "Needs in Municipal Accounting." *Business*, October, pp. 464–465.

"Reorganization of the Accountants Examining Board." 1897. *Accountics*, November, p. 38.

"Report of the AIA Special Committee on Cooperation with the SEC." 1937. *Journal of Accountancy*, June, pp. 434–443.

"Report of the Committee on Behavioral Science Content of the Accounting Curriculum." 1971. *Accounting Review.* Supplement, pp. 260–284.

"Report of the Committee on Management Accounting." 1959. *Accounting Review*, April, pp. 207–214.

"Report of the Sub-Committee on Independent Audits and Audit Procedure of the Committee on Stock List." 1939. New York Stock Exchange, April 15.

"Reports on 'Introduction to Corporate Accounting Standards' and 'A Statement of Accounting Principles'." 1940. *Journal of Accountancy*, October, pp. 48–57.

"Review and Outlook: Accounting's New Horizons." 1973. *Wall Street Journal*, October 30, p. 18.

Richardson, A. P. ed. 1913. *The Influence of Accountants' Certificates on Commercial Credit.* New York: AAPA.

Ripley, William Z. 1927. *Main Street and Wall Street.* Boston: Little Brown & Co.

Roberts, Alfred R. 1975. "American Accountancy: An Overview 1875–1900." *Business and Economic History* 4: 98–108.

Ronen, Joshua, Simcha Sadan, and Charles Snow. 1976. "Income Smoothing: A Review." *The Accounting Journal*, Winter, pp. 11–22.

Rorem, C. Rufus. 1928A. "Social Control Through Accounts." *Accounting Review*, September, pp. 261–268.
———. 1928B. *Accounting Method*. Chicago: University of Chicago Press.
———. 1929. "Replacement Cost in Accounting Valuation." *Accounting Review*, September, pp. 167–174.
Rosen, L. S., and DeCoster, D. T. 1969. "Funds Statement: An Historical Perspective." *Accounting Review*, January, pp. 124–136.
Ross, Edward A. 1916. "The Making of a Profession." *The International Journal of Ethics*, October, pp. 67–79.
Ross, Frances E. 1974. "John Caldwell Colt." *Dividend*, Spring, pp. 17–19.
Ross, T. Edward. 1937. "Random Recollection of an Eventful Half Century." *LRB&M Journal*, January, pp. 7–25.
———. 1940A. *Pioneers of Public Accountancy in the United States*. Philadelphia: E. Stern Co.
———. 1940B. "What the Practitioner Looks for in the College Trained Accountant." In AIA, *EAP*, pp. 89–90.
Rostow, W. W. 1971. *The Stages of Economic Growth*. Cambridge: Cambridge University Press.
———. 1975. *How It All Began*. New York: McGraw-Hill.
Roy, Robert A. 1964. "The Common Body Study—Evidence and Opinions." *Journal of Accountancy*, August, pp. 78–82.
Roy, Robert A., and MacNeill, James. 1967. *Horizons for a Profession*. New York: AICPA.
Rublee, George. 1926. "The Original Plan and Early History of the Federal Trade Commission." *Annals of the American Academy of Political and Social Science*, January, pp. 115–117.
Rudd, George H. 1939. "Bases for Accounting Research." In AIA, *PAP*, pp. 245–252.
Sakolski, A. M. 1909. "The Federal Corporation Law and Modern Accounting." *Yale Review*, February, pp. 372–389.
Sampson, Roy J. 1960. "American Accounting Education, Textbooks and Public Practice Prior to 1900." *Business History Review*, Winter, pp. 459–466.
Samuelson, Paul A. 1962. "Economists and the History of Ideas." *American Economic Review*, March, pp. 1–18.
———. 1975. "U. S. Still the Richest?" *Newsweek*, August 18, p. 66.
Sanders, Thomas. 1939. "Introduction—Progress in Accounting Research." In AIA, *PAP*, pp. 227–229.
———. 1944. "Accounting as a Means of Social and Economic Control." *NACA Bulletin*, December, pp. 319–334.
Sanders, Thomas; Hatfield, Henry R.; and Moore, Underhill. 1938. *A Statement of Accounting Principles*. New York: AIA.
Schein, Edgar H. 1972. *Professional Education: Some New Directions*. New York: McGraw-Hill.
Schlesinger, Sr., Arthur M. 1939. *Political and Social Growth of the United States, 1852–1933*. New York: Macmillan.
Schlesinger, Jr., Arthur M. 1959. *The Coming of the New Deal*. Boston: Houghton Mifflin.
Schluter, William. 1933. "Accountancy Under Economic Self Government." *Accounting Review*, December, pp. 278–284.
Schmidt, Fritz. 1930. "The Importance of Replacement Value." *Accounting Review*, September, pp. 235–242.

―――. 1931. "Is Appreciation Profit?" *Accounting Review*, December, pp. 289–293.

Schmidt, L. B. 1939. "Internal Commerce and the Development of the National Economy Before 1860." *Journal of Political Economy*, December, pp. 798–822.

Schumpeter, Joseph A. 1946. "The American Economy in the Interwar Period." *American Economic Review*, May, pp. 1–10.

Schur, Ira. 1976. "Interview with Ira Schur by B. Merino," December.

Scott, DR. 1931A. *The Cultural Significance of Accounts*. Lawrence, Kan.: Scholars Book Club, 1976.

―――. 1931B. "Unity in Accounting Theory." *Accounting Review*, June, pp. 106–112.

―――. 1933. "Veblen Not an Institutional Economist." *American Economic Review*, June, pp. 274–277.

―――. 1937. "The Tentative Statement of Principles." *Accounting Review*, September, pp. 296–303.

―――. 1939. "Responsibilities of Accountants in a Changing Economy." *Accounting Review*, December, pp. 396–401.

―――. 1941. "The Basis for Accounting Principles." *Accounting Review*, December, pp. 341–349.

"Scrapbook—Elijah Watt Sells." Haskins and Sell Archival Collection, New York.

"Secret Reserves." 1915. *The Accountant*, March 13, pp. 335–336.

Seidler, Lee J. 1972. "The Chaos in Financial Accounting: Will It Continue?" *Financial Analysts Journal*, March–April, pp. 88–91.

―――. 1973. "The Financial Accounting Standards Board: Goldfish in a Pool of Sharks." October *The Accountants Magazine*, pp. 558–566.

―――. 1975. "No Accounting for Conspirators." *Business Week*, June 23, p. 10.

Seidler, Lee J., and Seidler, Lynn L. 1975. *Social Accounting: Theory, Issues and Cases*. Los Angelos: Melville Publishing.

Sells, Elijah Watt. 1906. "Inaugural Address." *Journal of Accountancy*, November, pp. 39–41.

―――. 1908. *Corporate Management Compared With Government Control*. New York: Press of Safety Systems.

―――. 1922. "Causes of Examination Failure." *Journal of Accountancy*, March, pp. 232–233.

Shenkir, William. 1974. "Efforts by Authoritative Bodies to Establish a Conceptual Framework for Financial Reporting," Typed memorandum. FASB.

Shenkir, William; Welsch, G. A.; and Baer, Jr., J. A. 1972. "Thomas Jefferson: Management Accountant." *Journal of Accountancy*, April, pp. 33–47.

Simpson, Kemper. 1916. "Prospectuses of the New Industrials." *Journal of Accountancy*, October, pp. 265–269.

―――. 1921. *Economics for the Accountant*. New York: Appleton.

Smith, Alexander. 1912. "The Abuse of Audits in Selling Securities." In AAPA, *Year-Book, 1912*, pp. 169–180. See also, *Journal of Accountancy*, October, pp. 243–253.

Smith, E. H. 1971. *Charles Carroll of Carrollton*. Reprint. 1942 ed. New York: Barnes & Noble.

Smith, Frank P. 1955. "Progress Report of Commission on Standards of Education and Experience for Certified Public Accountants." In *NASBA 1955 Proceedings*, pp. 28–29.

Sobel, Robert I. 1965. *The Big Board*. New York: The Free Press.

————. 1968. *The Great Bull Market.* New York: W. W. Norton & Co., Inc.

"Some General Thoughts on the Accounting Environment." 1973. *Journal of Accountancy*, October, pp. 46–49.

Sorter, George. 1969. "An Events Approach to Basic Accounting Theory." *Accounting Review*, January, pp. 12–19.

Sorter, George, and Horngren, Charles. 1962. "Asset Recognition and Economic Attributes The Relevant Costing Approach." *Accounting Review*, July, pp. 391–399.

Soulé, Gerorge. 1911. *Soulé's New Science and Practice of Accounts.* 9th ed. New Orleans: Published by the author.

Spacek, Leonard. 1958A. "Can We Define Generally Accepted Accounting Principles?" *Journal of Accountancy*, December, pp. 40–47.

————. 1958B. "The Need for an Accounting Court." *Accounting Review*, July, pp. 368–379.

————. 1964A. "Are Double Standards Good Enough for Investors but Unacceptable to the Securities Industry." *Journal of Accountancy*, November, pp. 67–72.

————. 1964B. "A Suggested Solution to the Principles Dilemma." *Accounting Review*, April, pp. 275–284.

Sprouse, Robert T. 1963. "Historical Costs and Current Assets—Traditional and Treacherous." *Accounting Review*, October, pp. 687–695.

————. 1964. "The 'Radically Different' Principles of Accounting Research Study No. 3." *Journal of Accountancy*, May, pp. 63–69.

Sprase, Robert T., and Moonitz, Maurice. 1963. *A Tentative Set of Broad Accounting Principles for Business Enterprises.* ARS no. 3. New York: AICPA.

Sprague, Charles E. 1880. "The Algebra of Accounts." *The Book-Keeper*, July 20, pp. 2–4.

————. "Income and Outlay," *The Accounting Historians Journal*, Fall, 1978, pp. 79–84.

————. 1906. "Premiums and Discounts." *Journal of Accountancy*, August, pp. 294–296.

————. 1908. *The Philosophy of Accounts.* New York: published by the author.

Staub, Walter A. 1904. "Mode of Conducting an Audit." *Financial Record*, 2 November, pp. 40–43.

————. 1939. "Uniformity in Accounting." In AIA, *PAP*, pp. 3–7.

————. 1942. *Auditing Developments During the Present Century.* Cambridge, Mass.: Harvard University Press.

Staubus, George J. 1958. "Comments on 'Accounting and Reporting Standards for Corporate Financial Statements—1957 Revision.'" *Accounting Review*, January, pp. 11–24.

————. 1959. "The Residual Equity Point of View in Accounting." *Accounting Review*, January, pp. 3–13.

Stempf, Victor H. 1944A. "Some Problems of Professional Advancement." *Canadian Chartered Accountant*, April, pp. 204–214.

————. 1944B. "The Post War Challenge." In AIA, *Accounting Problems*, pp. 1–8.

Sterling, Robert, ed. 1974. *Institutional Issues in Public Accounting.* Lawrence, Kan.: Scholars Book Co.

————. 1976. "Accounting at the Crossroads." *World*, Spring, pp. 51–56.

Sterrett, Joseph E. 1904. "Chairman's Address." In the *Official Record of the Congress of Accountants, 1904*, pp. 23–33.

————. 1905. "Education and Training of a Certified Public Accountant." *Journal of Accountancy*, November, pp. 1–15.

————. 1906. "The Profession of Accountancy." *Annals of the American Academy of Political and Social Science*, July, pp. 16–27.

————. 1907. "Professional Ethics." In AAPA, *Year-Book, 1907*, pp. 108–133. See also, *Journal of Accountancy*, October, pp. 407–431.

————. 1908. "Present Position and Probable Development of Accountancy as a Profession." *Proceedings of the Annual Meeting of the American Economic Association*, pp. 85–96.

Stevenson, H. W., and Nelson, J. R. eds. 1967. *Profits in the Modern Economy.* Minneapolis: University of Minnesota Press.

Stevenson, W. C. 1900. "Development of Principles of Debit and Credit." *Business*, June, pp. 305–307.

Stone, Williard E. 1960. "Can Accounting Meet the Challenge of Liberalized Business Education?" *Accounting Review*, July, pp. 515–520.

————. 1973. "An Early English Cotton Mill Cost Accounting System: Charlton Mills, 1810–1889." *Accounting and Business Research*, Winter, pp. 71–78.

————. 1975. "Accounting Woes, Pilgrim Style." *Massachusetts CPA Review*, November-December, pp. 7–8, 36.

Storey, Reed K. 1959. "Revenue Realization, Going Concern and Measurement of Income." *Accounting Review*, April, pp. 232–238.

————. 1964. *The Search for Accounting Principles.* New York: AICPA.

Suffern, Edward L. 1910. "Accountant as a Financial Advisor." *Moody's Magazine*, June, pp. 437–444.

————. 1911. "Safety First." In AAPA, *Minutes*, 164–170.

————. 1912. "Accountant: What He Is, What He Does and the Place He Occupies in the New Economics of Business." *Canadian Chartered Accountant*, October, pp. 112–117.

————. 1922. "Twenty-Five Years of Accountancy." *Journal of Accountancy*, September, pp. 174–181.

Suffern, E. S. 1909. "Are CPA Examinations Always Fair?" *Journal of Accountancy*, March, pp. 384–389.

Swanson, Theodore. 1972. "Touche-Ross: A Biography." *Tempo*, special anniversary issue.

Sweeney, Henry W. 1930. "Maintenance of Capital." *Accounting Review*, December, pp. 277–287.

————. 1931. "Stabilized Depreciation." *Accounting Review*, September, pp. 165–178.

————. 1932. "Stabilized Appreciation." *Accounting Review*, June, pp. 115–121.

————. 1933A. "Capital." *Accounting Review*, September, pp. 185–199.

————. 1933B. "Income." *Accounting Review*, December, pp. 323–335.

————. 1934. "How Inflation Affects Balance Sheets." *Accounting Review*, December, pp. 275–299.

"A Symposium on Appreciation Prepared by Graduate Students at the University of Illinois with Comments by Andrew Barr, C. C. Carpenter, E. R. Dillavou, Irving Fisher, Louis O. Foster, Henry Rand Hatfield, and John R. Wildman," 1930. *Accounting Review*, March, pp. 1–59.

Taggart, Herbert. 1949. "1948 Revision of the American Accounting Association's Statement of Principles and Comparison with the 1941 Statement." *Accounting Review*. January, pp. 54–60.

Tawney, R. H. 1926. *Religion and the Rise of Capitalism*. New York: Harcourt, Brace and Co. Chap. 10, Sec. III.

Taylor, Jacob B. 1938. "Valuation of Fixed Assets and Principles Related to Write Ups and Write Ins." In AIA, *APP*, pp. 17–20.

Teichmann, M. M. 1901. "National Accountancy Legislation." *Business*, June, pp. 205–210.

Testimonial Banquet to S.S. Packard. 1896. Program of Speeches by his friends on the occasion of Packard's Seventieth Birthday, April 28. New York: privately printed.

"Testimony of Expert Witnesses at SEC Hearings," 1939. *Journal of Accountancy*, April, pp. 199–220; May, pp. 279–297; June, pp. 350–363.

Thelan, David P. 1969. "Social Tensions and the Origins of Progressivism." *Journal of American History*, September, pp. 323–341.

Thomas, Arthur L. 1964. "Value-itis: An Impractical Theorist's Reply." *Accounting Review*, July, pp. 574–581.

Thorton, Frank W. 1928. "Teaching Them How To Think." *Journal of Accountancy*, August, pp. 81–85.

Tinsley, James A. 1962. *Texas Society of Certified Public Accountants: A History*. Houston: Texas Society of CPAs.

Tipson, F. S. 1901. "The Profit and Loss Account." *Business*, November, p. 434.

Towns, Charles H. 1940. "Internal Check and Control." In AIA, *EAP*, pp. 10–15.

Trueblood, Robert. 1969. "Ten Years of APB: One Practitioner's Appraisal." Speech at AAA, privately printed.

Tuckerman, John R. 1970. "Some Aspects of the Development of Accounting Prior to 1900." Master's thesis, University of Sydney.

U.S., Congress. 1898. House. *Public Act 141*.

———. 1900. House. *Preliminary Report on Trusts and Industrial Combinations*. H. Doc. 476. 56th Cong., 1st sess.

———. 1901A. House. *Report of the Industrial Commission on Transportation*. H. Doc. 178. 57th Cong., 1st sess.

———. 1901B. House. *Report of the Industrial Commission on Trusts*. H. Doc. 182. 57th Cong., 1st sess.

———. 1902. House. *Final Report of the Industrial Commission*. H. Doc. 380. 57th Cong., 2nd sess.

———. 1913. House. *Economy and Efficiency Reports*. H. Doc. 104. 62nd Cong., 3rd sess.

———. 1976. House. *Federal Regulation and Reform, Report by the Subcommittee on Oversight and Investigation of the Committee on Interstate and Foreign Commerce*. 94th Cong., 2nd sess. Washington D.C.: Government Printing Office.

———. 1933. Senate Committee on Banking and Currency, *Hearings on the Federal Securities Acts*. 73rd Congress, 1st session.

———. 1976. Senate. *The Accounting Establishment: A Staff Study, Prepared by the Subcommittee on Reports, Accounting and Management of the Committee on Governmental Operations*. 94th Cong., 2nd sess. Washington D.C.: GPO.

U.S. Executive. 1912–1914. "Reports of the President's Commission on Economy and Efficiency—Correspondence with Public Accountants." National Archives Manuscript Division, RG 51, Sec. 311, Washington D.C.

U.S. Treasury. 1794. *An Account of the Receipts and Expenditures of the United States for 1793*. Philadelphia: John Fenno.

————. 1911. *Constructive Recommendations with Respect to Forms of Expenditures to be Used by Several Departments.* Circular no. 35, May 6. Washington D.C.: Government Printing Office.

Vatter, Harold G. 1963. *The U.S. Economy in the Fifties.* New York: W. W. Norton Co.

Vatter, William. 1947. *The Fund Theory of Accounting and Its Implications for Financial Reporting.* Chicago: University of Chicago.

————. 1962A. "Another Look at the 1957 Statement." *Accounting Review,* October, pp. 660–669.

————. 1962B. "Fund Theory View of Price Level Adjustments." *Accounting Review,* April, pp. 189–207.

————. 1963. "Postulates and Principles." *Journal of Accounting Research,* Autumn, pp. 188–197.

Veblen, Thorstein. 1950. *The Portable Veblen.* New York: Victory Press.

Ver Steeg, Clarence L. 1959. "The American Revolution Considered as an Economic Movement." *Huntington Library Quarterly,* August, pp. 371–371.

Voke, Albert F. 1926. "Accounting Methods of Colonial Merchants in Virginia." *Journal of Accountancy,* July, pp. 1–11.

Walsh, Lawrence M. 1960. "Accounting Education in Review." *Accounting Review,* April, pp. 183–189.

"The Way It Was on the Eve of the Revolution." 1976. *U.S. News and World Report,* June 21, pp. 54–56.

Walton, Seymour. 1909. "Earnings and Income." *Journal of Accountancy,* April, pp. 452–469.

————. 1915. "Fixed Assets at Cost or Market." *Journal of Accountancy,* November, pp. 482–483.

————. 1917. "Practical Application of Theoretical Knowledge." *Journal of Accountancy,* October, pp. 276–288.

————, and Finney, H. A. 1918. "Increased Values of Fixed Assets." *Journal of Accountancy,* November, pp. 392–393.

Wasserman, Max J. 1931. "The Regulation of Public Accounting in France." *Accounting Review,* December, pp. 249–260.

Watson, Max. 1921. "Interview with Joseph E. Sterrett." *New York Post,* January 18.

Webster, Norman E. 1944. "Some Early Accounting Examiners." *Accounting Review,* April, pp. 142–150.

————. 1954. *The American Association of Public Accountants: Its First Twenty Years, 1886–1906.* New York: AIA.

Weidenhammer, Robert. 1933. "The Accountant and the Securities Act." *Accounting Review,* December, pp. 272–278.

Wells, M. C. 1970. "A Pulseless, Inanimate and Boneless Thing." *Abacus,* September, pp. 88–90.

Werntz, William A. 1939A. "Subjects for Accounting Research." In AIA, *PAP,* pp. 234–244.

————. 1939B. "What Does the Securities and Exchange Commission Expect of Independent Auditors?" In AIA, *PAP,* pp. 17–26.

————. 1958. "Accounting in Transition." *Journal of Accountancy,* February, pp. 33–36.

————. 1959. "History of the Accounting Procedure Committee—From the Final Report." *Journal of Accountancy,* November, pp. 70–71.

————. 1961. "Accounting Education and the Ford and Carnegie Reports." *Accounting Review,* April, pp. 186–190.

"What are Earnings? The Growing Credibility Gap," 1967. *Forbes*, May 15, pp. 28–39.

"The Wheat Commission Report." 1972. *Journal of Accountancy*, May, pp. 35–36.

Wheeler, J. R. 1907. "The Idea of College and University." *Columbia University Quarterly*, December, pp. 1–13.

"Why Accountants Need to Tell a Fuller Story," 1971. *Business Week*, 6 February, pp. 36–37.

"Why Foreign Investors Turn Their Eyes Toward America," 1977. *U.S. News and World Report*, April 18, pp. 92–93.

Wickersham, George W. 1909. "Correspondence With Public Accountants," Haskins and Sells Archival Collection, New York.

Wiebe, Robert. 1958. "Business Disunity and the Progressive Movement." *Mississippi Valley Historical Review*, March, pp. 664–685.

Wiesen, Jeremy. 1978. *The Securities Acts and Independent Auditors: What Did Congress Intend?* New York: AICPA, 1978.

Wildman, John R. 1914. "Depreciation from a Certified Accountant's Point of View." *Electric Railway Journal*, April, pp. 332–333.

———. 1925. "Favorite Methods of Business Crookdom." *Papers and Proceedings of the American Association of University Instructors in Accounting*, pp. 127–129.

———. 1927. "Significant Developments Relating to No Par Stock." *Haskins and Sells Bulletin*, June, pp. 42–44.

———. 1928A. "Appreciation from the Point of View of the Certified Public Accountant." *Accounting Review*, December, pp. 396–406.

———. 1928B. "Diversity of No Par Stock Statutes Create Problems for the Accountant." *American Accountant*, February, pp. 19–21.

———, and Powell, Weldon. 1928. *Capital Stock Without Par Value*. Chicago: A. W. Shaw Co.

Wilkinson, George. 1903. *The CPA Movement*. New York: Wilkinson, Reckitt & Williams & Co.

———. 1904. "The CPA Movement and the Future of the Profession of the Public Accountant in the United States of America." *The Accountant*, October 22, pp. 464–471.

———. 1928. "The Genesis of the CPA Movement." *The Certified Public Accountant*, September, pp. 261–266, 279.

Williamson, H. F. 1952. *Winchester: The Gun That Won the West*. New York: A. S. Barnes & Co.

Winjum, James O. 1970. "Accounting in its Age of Stagnation," *Accounting Review*, October, pp. 743–761.

———. 1971. "The Journal of Thomas Gresham." *Accounting Review*, January, pp. 149–155.

Winter, S. G. 1928. "The Next Decade in Accounting." *Accounting Review*, September, pp. 311–322.

Woodruff, William. 1966. *Impact of Weatern Man: A Study of Europe's Role in the World Economy, 1750–1960*. London: Macmillan.

———. 1971. *The Emergence of an International Economy, 1700–1914*. London: Fontana Press.

———. 1975. *America's Impact on the World: A Study of the Role of the United States in the World Economy, 1750–1970*. London: Macmillan.

Woodside, Byron. 1964. "Government-Accountants Relations." *Journal of Accountancy*, September, pp. 67–68.

Woodward, P. D. 1956. "Depreciation—the Development of an Accounting Concept." *Accounting Review*, January, pp. 71–76.

Wormser, I. Maurice. 1931. *Frankenstein Incorporated.* New York: Whittesey House.

Wyllie, Irvin G. 1959. "Social Darwinism and the Businessman." *Proceedings of the American Philosophical Society*, October, pp. 629–635.

Yamey, Basil S. 1940. *Functional Development of Double Entry Bookkeeping.* London: Gee & Co.

Zeff, Stephen A. 1972. *Forging Accounting Principles in Five Countries: A History and Analysis of Trends.* Champaign, Ill.: Stipes Publishing Co.

———, ed. 1976. *Asset Appreciation, Business Income and Price Level Accounting.* New York: Arno Press.

INDEX

369

Models, practical, 47-49, 67. *See also*
  Accounting principles *and* Theory,
  accounting and auditing
Monetary system, national, 31-33, 74. *See
  also* "Barter accounting"
Montgomery, Robert, 146, 158, 159, 174,
  182-183, 184, 185, 209-210, 216,
  231-232, 244, 260
Moody, John, 80-81, 84, 85
Moonitz, Maurice, 270, 279, 288
Moore, R. H., 261, 266, 268, 290
Morgan, J. P., 75, 76, 129
Morris, Robert, 21
Moss, John, 318, 320
Multiple valuation models, 229-230
Muncipal accounts, in Gilded Age, 120-122,
  123
  in the 1970's, 313
  in post-Revolutionary period, 38
  in pre-Civil War period, 64, 65
  uniform systems for, 185-187
Municipal Finance Officers Association
  (MFOA), 312

National Association of Accountants (NAA),
  274, 278
National Association of Certified Public
  Accountants (NACPA), 205, 206,
  207
National Bureau of Economic Research,
  273
National Council on Governmental Account-
  ing, 312
National Institution for the Promotion of
  Industry, 31
Nelson, Carl, 294, 298
Neoclassical economics, 136, 169
New Amsterdam, 4-5
New Deal, 249-251
New Jersey, 100
Newton v. *Birmingham,* 180
New York City, capital markets in, 22-24,
  44, 77. *See also* New York Stock
  Exchange
New York State, 100, 214
  CPA law, 91, 96-98, 100, 103, 112, 124,
  138, 139
  professional exclusion in, 147-148
New York State Society of Certified Public
  Accountants (NYSSCPA), 139-140,

142-143, 144, 240, 259
New York Stock Exchange, 89, 129, 205,
  236, 238, 241, 255-256
New York University, School of Commerce,
  Accounts and Finance, 105, 139-140,
  215
Nissley, Walter, 266
Noble, Edward, 250
No-par stock, 231-234
Norris George, 199
Northern Securities anti-trust case, 199
Northwestern University, 142
Norton, Charles, 132-133
Not-for-profit accounting, 311-313

Origin and Progress of Bookkeeping, The
  (Foster), 51

Pacioli, Luca, 6, 14
Packard, S. S., 46, 49, 94, 97, 104, 105-106,
  111
Packard Business College, 106
Palmer Committee, 323
Paton, William, 168, 172, 174, 176, 177,
  181, 183, 185, 216, 220-223, 227,
  230, 231, 261, 266, 293, 294
  accounting principles and, 261-262, 264,
  267-268, 269, 274-275
Patten, Simon, 136
Pecora investigation, 240
Peele, James, 1, 2, 6
Pennsylvania Institute of Public Account-
  ants, 141
Penrose, Edith, 294-295
Periodicals, accounting, nineteenth century,
  93, 95, 114
  twentieth century, 142, 216
  see also specific titles
Perry report, 282
Philadelphia, Pennsylvania, capital markets
  in, 23, 44
Philosophy of Accounts (Sprague), 107
Pierson report, 283
Pilgrims, 2, 3-6, 13
Pixley, Francis, 180
Plymouth Colony, 3, 6, 13-14
Political environment, from 1825 to 1865,
  41-44
  from 1866 to 1896, 71-75
  of the 1970's, 306